Morocco Bound

New Americanists

A SERIES EDITED BY DONALD E. PEASE

Morocco Bound

DISORIENTING AMERICA'S

MAGHREB, FROM CASABLANCA

TO THE MARRAKECH

EXPRESS

Brian T. Edwards

Duke University Press   Durham and London

2005

Printed in the United States of America

on acid-free paper ∞

Typeset in Adobe Jenson Pro

by Keystone Typesetting, Inc.

Library of Congress Cataloging-in-Publication

Data appear on the last printed page of

this book.

The Northwestern University Research Grants
Committee has provided partial support for the
publication of this book. We gratefully
acknowledge this assistance.

FOR KATE, OLIVER, PIA

CONTENTS

List of Illustrations   ix
Acknowledgments   xi
Introduction: Morocco Bound, 1942–1973   1

I   *Taking Casablanca*

1. American Orientalism: Taking Casablanca   29
2. Sheltering Screens: Paul Bowles and Foreign Relations   78

II   *Queer Tangier*

3. Tangier(s): The Multiple Cold War Contexts of the
International Zone   121
4. Disorienting the National Subject: Burroughs's Tangier,
Hitchcock's Marrakech   158
5. ~~Three Serious Writers~~ Two Serious Authors: Jane Bowles,
Mohammed Mrabet, and the ~~Erotics of Collaboration~~
Politics of Translation   198

III   *Marrakech Express*

6. Hippie Orientalism: The Interpretation of
Countercultures   247

Notes   303
Works Cited   335
Index   351

LIST OF ILLUSTRATIONS

17 Still from *Road to Morocco* (1942)

27 Gen. George S. Patton near Maknassy, Tunisia, March 1943

31 Gen. Patton with Moroccan sultan Mohammed V and young Moulay Hassan, 1942

38 Editorial cartoon from *Chicago Defender* (1942): "Man Who Came Back"

38 Editorial cartoon from *Chicago Defender* (1942): "White Christmas"

49 Ernie Pyle in North Africa, 1943

52 Ernie Pyle talking to GIs in the field, Anzio, 1944

68 Still from *Casablanca* (1942)

83 Paul Bowles with Moroccan musicians, Tangier, 1996

89 Paul Bowles at work, early 1950s

103 Paul Bowles with Mohammed Ouild Oajdi in Morocco, 1951

119 Tangier, Petit Socco in 1957

128 Members of the U.S. diplomatic mission in Tangier restaurant, 1950s

132 American School of Tangier, 1950

139 Moroccans and Americans socializing in Asilah, Morocco, mid-1950s

153 Money changer on the Rue es Siaghine, Tangier, about 1950

163 William Burroughs with Peter Orlovsky and Paul Lund at "Dutch Tony's," Tangier, 1957

167 William Burroughs in the Grand Socco, Tangier, 1957

194 Still from *The Man Who Knew Too Much* (1955)

206 Jane Bowles at the Café de Paris, Tangier, 1963

218 Jane Bowles in Tangier market, 1954

234 Mohammed Mrabet with Paul Bowles, 1960s

243 Mohammed Mrabet, Fez, 2004, surrounded by Moroccan students

245 Hippies outside walls of Fez medina, 1970

251 Vagabonds in Marrakech near the Koutoubia mosque, 1970

253 Haircut in preparation for entering Morocco, Algeciras, 1973

277 A young vagabond walks through the Tetouan medina, 1973

ACKNOWLEDGMENTS

For me perhaps the greatest joy of academic work is the collaborative aspect of it. In a project that has been in the works for this long, debts accrue quickly. The friendships, collegiality, and conversations that accompanied the assistance and comments on drafts and presentations of portions of what is included here have been happy by-products. It is with nearly tactile pleasure that I acknowledge some of the many people who helped me as I made this book.

This project had its origins in the American Studies Program at Yale, where in an early and quite different incarnation it benefited from the direction of Alan Trachtenberg, and the expert advice of Jean-Christophe Agnew and Christopher L. Miller. All three mentors have been exceptionally generous. In New Haven, I also learned valuable lessons about culture and history from Bryan J. Wolf, Michael Denning, Richard Brodhead, Ann Fabian, David Marshall, and Candace Waid in the seminar room, and colleagues and friends David Waldstreicher, Matt Jacobson, Charles Musser, Tim Marr, Cathy Gudis, Emily Bernard, Mitch Lasser, Jeff Harwick, and Richard Selzer outside of it.

Since 1993, I have spent extensive time in Morocco, in stretches from a week to a year at a time, doing research, studying Arabic, giving lectures, talks, and hanging out with friends and colleagues in Fez, Tangier, and Rabat. Those conversations have been an important part of my education and have influenced this book. Sadik Rddad, Khalid Bekkaoui, Abdellatif Khayati, Bahanou Akabouch, Moustafa Ouajjani, Driss Mansouri, and Taieb Belghazi are dear friends and valued interlocutors. I have enjoyed intellectual exchanges with Hasna Lebaddy, the chair of the English department at Mohammed V University in Rabat, and her colleagues, including Said Graouid. I thank Lahcen Haddad and Mohamed Dahbi for their critical engagements at various moments. Audiences at Mohammed V (Rabat), Sidi Mohammed Ben Abdallah (Fez), Abdelmalek Essaadi (Tetouan), and Ibn Tofail (Kenitra) Universities, and in Tangier and in

Sousse, Tunisia, helped me rethink and develop my work. Many exceptional students in Morocco have asked good and tough questions of me that have consistently kept the immediacy of much of this material close at hand. And the hospitality of Driss Rhanbou and his family in Fez and the Sahara, of Brahim Temli Soussi in Tangier, and Sadik Rddad and Ouafae Bekkouni and their boys Ahmed, Alae, and Marouan in Fez helps define for me the meaning of *karim*.

Daoud Casewit, Mohammed Chrayah, and Saadia Meski of the Moroccan-American Commission for Educational and Cultural Exchange in Rabat (the Fulbright Commission) all have given good advice and help. Thor Kuniholm, director of the Tangier American Legation Museum, has been supportive for years; his and Elizabeth Kuniholm's welcome has always been sustaining. A series of librarians at TALM, including Elliot Caldwell, were accommodating. Thanks too to Joseph McPhillips III, a headmaster of the American School of Tangier, and Karim Benzakour and Blanca Hamri, for their assistance. My appreciation also goes to my Arabic teachers in Fez at ALIF and in Tangier at the AIMS Summer Language Program.

From 1994, when he replied to a letter inviting me to visit, until 1999 just before his death, Paul Bowles was consistently generous with his time and welcoming. The time spent after the tape recorders were off at the Inmeuble Itesa was most cherished. He is missed. I thank Abdelouahid Boulaich for his patience and forbearance. Mohammed Mrabet, whom I met first in 1994, but whom I did not begin to know until 1999, has been inspiring. The late Mohamed Choukri gave freely of his time and opinions in 1999. And Rodrigo Rey Rosa, the executor of the Bowleses' literary estates and a writer in his own regard, has been generous with permissions and conversation. I thank Millicent Dillon for her elegant responses to queries about Jane and Paul Bowles, and for granting permission to quote from them. Thanks too to Allen Hibbard, Tourya Haji Temsamani, Irene Hermann, Jeffrey Miller, Hammond Guthrie, and Lawrence Stewart for various favors and advice.

Northwestern University has been an ideal setting to develop this project. My colleagues are unfailingly liberal with time, support, and conversation, especially Kevin Bell, Scott Durham, Betsy Erkkila, Reg Gibbons, Bob Gooding-Williams, Jay Grossman, Katherine Hoffman, Chris Lane, Susan Manning, Jeff Masten, Nasrin Qader, Mireille Rosello, Carl Smith, and Dorothy Wang. I have been especially inspired and sustained by collaborations with Dilip Gaonkar and Andrew Wachtel. Dan Linzer and before him Eric Sundquist have been very supportive and generous deans. And the brilliant staff of the English department, especially Natasha Dennison, Nathan Mead, Latonia Trimuel, and Kathleen Daniels, is extraordinary, as is Jeanne Laseman in comp lit. A generous grant from the University Research Grants Committee at Northwestern supported the gathering and reproduction of the images herein. Thanks to Mary Pat Doyle and Dean Andrew Wachtel of the graduate school.

I would like to thank colleagues elsewhere for invitations to speak and intellectual engagements that have sustained me: thanks to David Wald-streicher, Ewa Ziarek, Krzysztof Ziarek, Kathy Psomiades, Steve Toma-sula, Glenn Hendler, Jim Collins, Stephanie Bevacqua, Valerie Sayers, Chris Jara, Hilary Radner, Mark McGurl, Jessica Chalmers, Rebecca Saunders, Doug Chalmers, Zakia Salim, Anouar Majid, Harsha Ram, Tim Marr, Allen Hibbard, Julian Dibbell, Eric Naiman, Michael David-son, David Damrosch, Jonathan Arac, Gayatri Spivak, Beth Povinelli, Benjamin Lee, Michael Warner, Brent H. Edwards, Brian Larkin, Meg McLagen, Kariann Yokota, Moustafa Bayoumi, Dina al-Kassim, Rachel Buff, Suman Gupta, Ronald Judy, and Donald Pease.

Ronald Judy, Gayatri Spivak, Alan Nadel, Allen Hibbard, Donald Pease, Sadik Rddad, Dilip Gaonkar, Thor Kuniholm, Gordon Hutner, Taieb Belghazi, and three anonymous reviewers read portions of this manuscript at various times and in various states; all gave excellent advice for which I am deeply appreciative.

I have benefited from excellent research assistance, always in a rush and at the last minute, from Anne-Marie McManus, Hakim Abderrezak, and Katy Chiles in the United States, and Sadik Rddad and Fayysal Khairoun in Morocco. I thank my students for the privilege of teaching some of this material as it was developing and for their engagement with it and me. I am privileged to work with graduate students at Northwestern such as Hakim Abderrezak, Jyoti Argade, Katy Chiles, Deana Greenfeld, Cole-man Hutchison, Peter Jaros, Bishupal Limbu, and Gayle Rogers.

I would like to acknowledge my appreciation to Rebecca Johnson Melvin and Francis Poole at the University of Delaware Library, Special Collections; Tara Wenger at the Harry Ransom Humanities Center, Uni-versity of Texas, Austin; Candace Fuller at the Patton Museum of Cavalry and Armor; Charity Pollard of the Ernie Pyle State Historic Site; John M. Bennett of the Rare Books and Manuscripts Library, Ohio State; Sean

Quimby, Stanford University Special Collections; Peter Hale of the Allen Ginsberg Trust; Ken Kinslow at the University of Notre Dame Library; Russell Maylone, curator, McCormick Library of Special Collections at Northwestern; and Roman Stansberry, curator of Northwestern's slide library.

My research on this book has been supported by a Fulbright research grant to Morocco (USIA) in 1995–96; an intermediate Arabic fellowship (1996) and a short-term travel research grant (1999), both to Morocco, from the American Institute for Maghrib Studies; a travel grant to Tunisia from the University of Notre Dame (2000); and since then by various travel and research grants and subsidies from Northwestern.

Ken Wissoker of Duke University Press has been a generous editor, a good coach, and just fun to talk to. I value his advice, his patience with me, and his friendship. At the press, I would also like to thank Katie Courtland, Courtney Berger, and Anitra Sumaya Grisales for their editorial acumen and expertise. Justin Faerber guided the book through the production process adroitly. Nancy Zibman compiled the index with creativity and professionalism.

Something as public as a book may not be the apposite place to thank family and friends, whose generosity is inherently private and clannish. So I will gesture only to my longtime friends Cameron Khosrowshahi, James Ketterer, Adam Pincus, Thom Campbell, Peter Robles, and John Kim. I would like to express my deep gratitude to Dr. Ginette Albouze for her hospitality, generosity, and friendship over the years in Paris and Chateauroux.

My parents Ken and Ann Edwards provided a bedrock upon which to build much more than this book, and for that I am grateful. I am pleased to acknowledge my brothers, Cliff and Scott, who have taught me important lessons and who are dear to me, and my family San Edwards, Fran and Ralph Undreiner, Joseph Baldwin, Mary Burt Blume, Barbara Baldwin, Henry Blume, Pam Baldwin, and Elizabeth Baldwin. My late grandparents Rose and Frank Digilio witnessed the first part of the work on this book and were a constant inspiration to travel, to communicate, and to narrate.

And finally, the three to whom this book is dedicated know how deeply inscribed they are in it. The book has separated me from them too often and too far, but they are at the heart of all that is the book. Kate Baldwin has been teaching me about critical engagement and comparative work for as long as this book has been brewing. Oliver and Pia, later arrivals, have each and individually reminded me what language has the potential to do. I look forward every day to their words.

Rodrigo Rey Rosa has given kind permission to reproduce the previously unpublished text by Jane Bowles in chapter 5. A significantly shorter version of chapter 2 appeared as "Sheltering Screens: Paul Bowles and Foreign Relations," *American Literary History* 17.2 (2005): 307–34. Permission to reprint that material here is granted by Oxford University Press. An early version of a portion of chapter 1 appeared as part of "Preposterous Encounters: Interrupting American Studies with the (Post)colonial, or *Casablanca* in the American Century," *Comparative Studies of South Asia, Africa and the Middle East* 23.1–2 (2003): 70–86. It is reprinted with permission. Part of the final two sections of chapter 5 appeared as "What Happened in Tangier?"the introduction to Mohammed Mrabet's *Love with a Few Hairs*, translated by Paul Bowles (Fez, Morocco: Moroccan Cultural Studies Center, 2004), i–xiv.

INTRODUCTION

Morocco Bound, 1942–1973

What are the stakes and conditions of literature in the "American century"? In what ways do American texts translate the world, and how do these translations circulate abroad? (Where do they do so, and why does it matter?) With the ascension of the United States as global superpower, how did Americans negotiate the presence and vestiges of European colonialism? What is the relationship between literary and cinematic representations of the foreign and foreign relations? What is the recent history of American thinking about "the Arab"?

These are some of the organizing questions of this book. In the chapters that follow, I take a focused look at three decades of American representations of the Maghreb—Morocco, Algeria, and Tunisia, plus much of the Sahara—and follow the afterlives of those representations in the Maghreb itself. The last question is the one that originally motivated the study, as a point of entry into thinking about American attitudes toward peoples of the Arab world and its diaspora. Why, then, the Maghreb, the westernmost edge of the Arab world, at the periphery of the Middle East? The answer is partially dictated by the archive. Since the late nineteenth century, the Maghreb has been one of the most familiar locations of the American exotic and one of the places to which filmmakers and novelists turned often for tales of "Oriental" splendor and decadence. If those representations have partially framed American ideas about the Arab world, it was of course an Arab world reduced of its diversity and internal antagonisms by the generalizing logics of Orientalism. Before 1973, when American popular attention turned more decidedly toward the Middle East coincident with the OPEC price hike and Arab oil embargo (which struck close to home because of its effect on domestic fuel prices), representations of the Maghreb played a leading role in the formation of popular American ideas about the Arab. Taking a longer view, the

Maghreb was already familiar to many Americans via a rich tradition of European Orientalism, from Delacroix and Ingres to Matisse in painting, from Flaubert and Fromentin to Pierre Loti, Gide and Camus in litera-ture, and from Louis Philippe, Napoléon III and General Bugeaud to Lyautey and Giraud in political history. Indeed, the region was not gener-ally known in the United States as the Maghreb at all, but as French North Africa until the independence movements of the mid-1950s.

As the distinction between *the Maghreb* and *French North Africa* sug-gests, for Americans the region has been represented almost never as an unmediated exotic location, but in relationship to the presence of the French. So the attempt to identify and analyze an American Orientalism here encounters a complicating factor. From as early as 1830 to as late as 1962, the French were in direct colonial control (Algeria 1830–1962, Tunisia 1881–1956, Morocco 1912–1956), and they remained central in the postcolonial period. In addressing American representations of the Ma-ghreb, I trace what might be called the global flow of Orientalist dis-course. Americans who traveled to the Maghreb—whether physically or via books or visual representations—traveled through French frames: in literature, painting, maps, ethnography, histories and travel accounts, as well as the urban design and theories of the exercise of power. American portraits did not merely extend the constructions and presumptions of European Orientalism, however, nor did they discard them. They shift the frame itself. In literary and popular representations of the Maghreb, American authors pay nearly as much attention to the French Empire as they do to those Berber and Arab cultures and North African landscapes. The complicated presence of the French in such texts encourages us to see these examples of American Orientalism comparatively, not merely as unmediated Orientalist or Africanist discourse, but as texts that engage the complex geopolitical order of the post-1941 period.[1] What gets lost is the particularity with which the French understood and ruled over the Maghreb. If European Orientalism revolved around an exhaustive sense of the history, religion, languages, and cultures of the Maghreb, American representations more frequently detach themselves from the sense that such precision is needed to "understand" and represent the world.

What is common and central to most American representations of the Maghreb during the twentieth century is not, then, the engagement with a tradition of self-referential meaning making about "the Orient," as Ed-ward Said had described the British and French cases, but the encounter with worldliness itself. To observe colonialism in action was itself a part of the interest. Writing about early-twentieth-century French travel writing set in Morocco, Emily Apter has identified what she calls the "protectorate style," within which the presence of the French colonial administration was normalized as a part of the background that did not disrupt the picture of Oriental difference.[2] For Americans, however, the background presence of the French was an integral part of the foreignness of the picture, that which validated it, internationalism in action. Of course, opinions about how to understand French internationalism varied: for Edith Wharton, visiting in 1917, France's engagement with Morocco was an example from which isolationist America could learn; for the African American press during World War II, it was an example of racist domination from which the United States should distance itself.

When Henry Luce declared that the twentieth century should be understood as "the American century," in a *Life* magazine editorial in early 1941, he did more than make an argument for U.S. entry into World War II. He also established a powerful rhetorical device by which Americans of differing political persuasions and racial and ethnic allegiances might understand the role of the United States in organizing the global order. Luce did not by himself originate the idea of an exceptional role for the United States within world history, and his argument for the United States to take its place in a historical sequence of global empires was buttressed by his own institutional location at the head of a media empire. But Luce initiated a logic by which Americans might see foreign spaces newly under the dominion or imagined reach of the United States in a particular temporality—an American time—that would in turn undergird a conservative model for imagining the globe. Like Luce's phrase itself, that model implicitly authorized those who applied it to rely on domestic referents in order to understand foreign spaces, which may be its most influential and debilitating outgrowth. In the period I consider, domestic crises, especially the reconfiguration of racial relations, underlay the impulse to turn away from the difference that was visible abroad. Luce's American temporality could be thus translated as a "global racial time," by which Arabs, Africans, and their descendants in the United States were seen on a different place in the evolutionary scale and understood as not ready for rights and responsibilities. Luce's model was not universally accepted, of course, and I pay attention to several writers and artists who implicitly rejected it. But it was mightily persuasive.

My presumption is that in the wake of Luce's essay, which I examine in chapter 1, and, more importantly, after U.S. entry into a geopolitical space of ascendancy, representations of the world or the foreign played a special role in rethinking the meaning of American national identity. The Maghreb was a particularly interesting place for both the elaboration of American national identity and expressions of dissent. The former builds on a cinematic tradition of seeing in desert sands a tabula rasa for the projection of Western desires and inscriptions (as figured famously in the 1920 film *The Sheik*, where the Algerian Sahara becomes a sandbox for leaving messages—"I Love Ahmed"), along with the American habit of seeing new frontiers in nearly all foreign or sparsely populated places.[3] For those who looked past the sand, however, the dual interest in the Maghreb as scene of colonialism *and* as exotic space of difference could provoke critiques or alternatives to the ur-American impulse to pioneer at the expense of native populations. As both African and Arab, the Maghreb provoked many Americans to see a complex series of possibilities—neither simply "Oriental" antithesis to the West, nor African "blankness" and limitless possibility—that sometimes opened up to radical and disruptive potentialities. Part of my goal will be to recover some of those disruptive expressions that have been overlooked because of reading practices that emerged from the "American century" logic itself in order to separate out the Lucean hypernationalist perspective on the world from other options. More generally, my intention is to show how Americans found ways to understand the succession of the United States as global superpower during and after World War II and carved out an American relationship to the world—particularly the Arab world—that built on but detached itself from British and French empire.

If there is a general change that may be identified during the period covered by this book, it is the shifting political relationship of France to the Maghreb, and of the United States to the region and the world at large. During World War II, American journalists covering the U.S. Army in North Africa and the soldiers themselves struggled to get a foothold in a place long familiar to Europeans. "World travelers had told me that Oran had an Oriental atmosphere, but I couldn't detect it," wrote Ernie Pyle, embedded with the GIs in Algeria (27). Pyle's dispatches, which took what his handlers called the "worm's-eye view," make clear how popular thinking about the region was organized by Orientalist literature and films that preceded the U.S. military incursion: "We seldom saw one of those beautiful Arab steeds that we read about in 'sheik' books," Pyle writes somewhere (44); and elsewhere: "What we saw of the Sahara didn't look exactly the way it does in the movies" (191). For Pyle, the negation of that which preceded the GIs was the first step in rewriting the Maghreb in terms of the American West. In the immediate postwar period, U.S. diplomats still looked at the Maghreb through French lenses, despite the U.S. ascent in global economic and military power, both because France's political stability was of great import to the United States and because the State Department was not yet configured to have fully independent expert analysis of its own. By the later 1960s, as Americans increasingly forged their own relationship to the independent North African states, the French presence was more distant but still important as vestige, as in Clifford Geertz's attempt to rethink the premises of French colonial anthropology about Morocco even while indebted to its extensive archive. For the hippies taking the so-called Marrakech Express, the infrastructure built by the French organized the ascription of a visible and essentialized Moroccan otherness on which the hippie experience depended.

The Maghreb itself as a self-organized region is more than merely a French invention, of course, but France's historical role has left deep traces on postindependence Morocco, Algeria, and Tunisia: the French language, architectural forms, and urban design that define the cities of all three countries, and economic interests that still run deep. France is also the home of much of the Maghrebi diaspora. The allegiances formed during the struggle for independence created political alliances that consolidated Maghrebi regionalism. Still, the Maghreb was a distinct geopolitical entity before modern France emerged, with ethnic, linguistic, and cultural affiliations and a similar relationship to the rest of Africa and the greater Arab world. Separated from the Mashriq (the Middle East) by the sparsely populated deserts of modern Libya to the east and from the rest of Africa by the Sahara to the south, the major populations of the Maghreb (today around 32 million in Morocco, 32 million in Algeria, and 10 million in Tunisia, together roughly one-third the population of the Arab world) live mostly in the fertile areas between the Atlantic and Mediterranean and the mountains that keep the Sahara at bay. The indigenous peoples of the region—known as the Berbers, or Imazighen ("the free men") in Tamazight (Berber language)—are related. The major tribes are the Kabyles in northern Algeria, the Chaouia near the Algerian-

Tunisian border, the Riffians in northern Morocco, and Shleuh throughout southern Morocco. Because the first Arab invasion of the Maghreb
dates to the mid–seventh century, many scholars argue that the overwhelming majority of Maghrebis are of Berber origin. There are historical
connections across the region. When the daughter of a refugee from
Kairouan founded a mosque in Fez, in 857, named the Kairaouine in her
honor and often cited as the oldest university in the world, a crucial link
was made between Tunisia and Morocco and their religious capitals.
During the period of Ottoman rule, from the early sixteenth century until
the French conquest, Morocco was not under Turkish control, as were
Tunisia and Algeria (and Libya), which left vestiges on the architecture,
arts, crafts, and language of the Maghrebi countries to the east.

After the Ottomans, the similarities between the countries of the Maghreb remained greater than their differences. All are deeply affected by
their joint affiliations with the Arab world and the rest of Africa. They
have participated in organizations and alliances such as the Arab League
and the Organization of African States (OAU). Algeria and Morocco were
founding members of the OAU, but Morocco later resigned in protest of
African recognition of Western Sahara. With upward of 99 percent of
their populations Sunni Muslims, all three have formal and informal
affiliations with the larger Islamic world. Their geography also places
them in the Mediterranean region. King Hassan's famous statement likening Morocco to "a tree with its roots in Africa and its branches in Europe"
might apply generally across the Maghreb (as might the Moroccan joke
that illegal émigrés try to drop in on Europe from those branches). Centuries of trade across the Sahara and the deep influence of the Berbers have
produced ethnic, architectural, and cultural forms familiar from Saharan
and sub-Saharan Africa across the Maghreb. During the struggle for
independence in the 1950s, therefore, the peoples of the Maghreb had
more than a shared history of French domination to unite them.

In maintaining that the Maghreb be seen as a distinct entity, I am
neither being controversial nor am I minimizing regional antagonisms or
the movements across the Sahara (and the Mediterranean) that have long
marked the region. As David Seddon argues: "The idea of a 'greater'
unified Maghrib has always been a dream, but the reality has proved more
of a disappointment."[4] Morocco and Algeria have distrusted each other
deeply at times: the conservative monarchy of Hassan II and Algeria's
socialist regime were at odds and in direct conflict in the 1960s.[5] Not long

after the intensification of internal conflict in Algeria in 1991, the border between Morocco and Algeria was closed and heavily patrolled, due to Moroccan distrust of Algerian Islamists and Moroccan management of political resistance at home. But antagonisms and political systems notwithstanding (Morocco is a constitutional monarchy, Tunisia and Algeria are presidential republics, all three with elected parliaments), both the geopolitical and ethnic similarities and the shared cultural experience of French colonialism distinguish the Maghreb as an important organizing force. That said, I must address portions of the greater Maghreb to which I give less attention. Though Libya and Mauritania are sometimes included in the Maghreb and some Moroccan nationalists make claim to a "greater" Morocco that would stretch to Senegal, and while conflict between the Moroccan kingdom and the native Sahrawis continues over the Western Sahara, I limit my scope to Morocco, Algeria, and Tunisia and the contiguous portions of the Sahara. This is less a political argument than it is a choice to focus on those places that have been of major American interest (in chapter 1, I do look at a Hollywood representation of the war in Libya).

In addressing U.S. fiction, journalism, cinema, anthropology, and political discourse that represents the Maghreb (plus some music and a cookbook) from World War II's North African campaign through the first wave of hippie fascination with Morocco, there is a great deal of primary material for a relatively short period. The Maghreb, and Morocco in particular, is a place that during these three decades was vital to American literary history, to Hollywood cinema, and after 1965 to U.S. cultural anthropology, as well as a key route on the global itinerary of a variety of communities. Dating back to the early American republic, North Africa had been a place of fascination and fantasy. The Barbary pirates and white slavery garnered much attention in late-eighteenth-century media and political discourse and found their way into literature: Royall Tyler's 1797 work *The Algerine Captive* is numbered among the first American novels, and the first excursion of the U.S. Marines "to the shores of Tripoli," sent there by Thomas Jefferson, is immortalized in a familiar anthem. After 1900 the mass popularity in the United States of British novels by Robert Hichens—and later P. C. Wren and Edith Hull— brought the region back into focus. With the advent of feature-length films, improved travel technologies, and a greater interest in European affairs after World War I, U.S. audiences were presented with an abundance of texts and films set (if not filmed) in sand-swept terrain, French colonial outposts, and labyrinthine casbahs. In the 1920s and 1930s American travelers followed in the footsteps of characters from Hichens's *Garden of Allah*, Wren's *Beau Geste*, Hull's *The Sheik*, or the film versions with Rudolf Valentino, Agnes Ayres, Adolphe Menjou, Marlene Dietrich, Gary Cooper, Charles Boyer, Hedy Lamarr, Douglas Fairbanks, and others. Paul Bowles once remarked in conversation that in 1933 he visited Biskra, Algeria, explicitly drawn there by *The Garden of Allah*, where he encountered an entire industry grown to cater to travelers' demands for scenes that Hichens had described: "In the book it sounded like an authentic village, but when I was there it wasn't at all. It was completely touristic. Hoked-up. . . . Hichens could have been made the mayor of Biskra."[6] A 1929 *Guide Michelin* bears out Bowles's memory. It lists two four-star hotels with 230 rooms, plus another 200 rooms at the two- and three-star level, a large casino, and a list of points of interest. A travel guide from 1992, in contrast, makes the briefest mention of Biskra, with no comment about its former place in literary and tourism history: "There is really no reason to stop here."[7]

The U.S. military landings at Casablanca, Algiers, and Oran in November 1942, and the large deployment of ground forces, ushered in a new wave of attention that both drew on earlier portraits from Euro-American Orientalism and rewrote the region in terms of the new American interests there. After World War II, Morocco was the most often represented of the three countries, in direct correlation to the frequency with which Americans found themselves drawn there. Algeria and Tunisia exhibit more of a presence before and during the war than they do later. The long and violent Algerian Revolution (1954–62) was a disincentive to travel, especially so since relations between colonized Algerians and French settlers were fraught and since the nationalists had embraced socialism, further removing them from U.S. sympathies (Senator John F. Kennedy did announce support of the Algerian cause in 1957, however, breaking with the Eisenhower administration). The relative stability and calm of Morocco and its more developed tourism industry made it the more common choice, whether for anthropologists, tourists, expatriates, or hippies. Surely a related factor was the approach that the French had taken in colonizing Morocco, in contradistinction to that which they had practiced earlier in Algeria. In Morocco, the logic of the protectorate system, perfected under Hubert Lyautey, the first resident-general, was to preserve Moroccan cultural distinctiveness, enframing it within European infrastructure and administration.[8] Such an arrangement—based on an urban design that placed European administrative quarters outside traditionally organized Moroccan medinas—idealized the viewing of difference for both tourists and expatriates. As if in appreciation of this arrangement, Edith Wharton dedicated her 1920 book *In Morocco* to Lyautey, who had invited the author to Morocco with the explicit hope that she would publicize his work there.[9] Paul Bowles's 1955 novel *The Spider's House* contains a critique, on both philosophical and topographical grounds, of the urban design initiated on Lyautey's watch.

Notwithstanding the density of American attention to the region and in spite of the relatively short time frame covered in this book, I do not attempt to write cultural history, trace quasi-Foucauldian genealogies, or look comprehensively at American representations of the Maghreb, except perhaps in snapshots. As a methodological principle, I do not assume an easy or transparent relationship between representations of the foreign in cultural production and the world of foreign relations. A cultural history approach to representations must argue that representations effect change, and this it seems to me is an especially knotted question in the case of the United States, whose foreign service apparatus does not privilege regional expertise, reassigns foreign service officers to different regions to keep them fresh (i.e., not overly entrenched in a single region), and distrusts the loyalties of career "Arabists."[10] Edward Said's point, made in *Culture and Imperialism*, that American popular attention to regions of the world works in "spurts"—"great masses of rhetoric and huge resources ... followed by virtual silence"[11]—also informs my reluctance to embrace cultural history; there is simply not a continuity of attention to the Maghreb, the Arab world, or any other region save the USSR during the twentieth century. The place is frequently redefined, reimagined, and relocated as if from new. Nonetheless, I do examine some of the most important bursts of attention in three snapshot chapters: on the North African campaign of late 1942 and 1943, on the fascination with Tangier from the late 1940s through mid-1950s, and on young American interest in Morocco in the late 1960s through mid 1970s. Within those snapshots, something like the texture of Orientalism starts to appear and a logic that collapses domestic frames of reference and representations of the foreign is operative. In the first case, this implicates what I called earlier "global racial time" and domestic thinking about race both as representational logic and as a way of conceiving of North African rights. In the second, hypernationalist American anxieties about productivity, internationalism, and sexuality converge in McCarthy-era responses to Tangier. And in the third, a racialist turn away from seeing Moroccan youth politics as connected to American youth politics unwittingly reinscribes the global racial time of the 1940s.

While there are points of overlap, the spheres of cultural production and foreign policy are, however, generally separated by an institutional chasm. In the absence of institutions that would force them into contact (such as London's School of Oriental and African Studies or the French Institut des Hautes Etudes Marocaines), that chasm is rarely bridged in the United States. Simply put, some representations have more impact on political history than others (those by diplomats and policy planners over those by novelists and cineastes). The question of how to put the two spheres together haunts Americanist work, which has tended lately to avoid the ghost by collapsing representations of the foreign and foreign policy under the guise of "discourse," defined rather broadly and left uninterrogated. It is relatively easy to elaborate "cultural logics" operative in mainstream, middlebrow texts, and to imagine and imply that those logics somehow explain or influence or carve out an epistemological space within which foreign policy might operate. It is, further, enticing to do so, for it reassures the Americanist critic, who is generally motivated by the best intentions of constructive anti-imperial critique, that his or her work is productive in rethinking the political arrangements of things (albeit in some trickle-down way). But the fact that such work rarely if ever has any tangible political effect, or even casts a shadow on the realm of foreign affairs, is due precisely to the reason that such work befuddles itself: the institutional chasm between the State Department and the humanities prevents it from doing so. What we should attend to instead is that institutional chasm itself, how it is constructed, how it operates, how it organizes reading practices, and how current reading practices leave it undisturbed. When I do so, I most often expose the construction of that gulf or space and how it's made invisible by criticism, history, and media. Some of the same institutional causes for the dissociation of realms of academic Orientalism and foreign service training are echoed in the reading practices that emerged—and did not emerge—in the early cold war.

This book argues that grappling with the American encounter with the Maghreb matters to our understanding of public thinking about the role of the United States in the world after 1941 and the contested meanings of American national identity in the wake of that encounter. It also argues that several of the texts where this encounter was most richly figured have been overlooked or misunderstood because the critical mechanisms in place in the United States were caught in a hypernationalist scheme that did not know how to read them. At heart, then, this book is interested in the question of circulation—how textual representations circulate through the world—and it summons up a methodological/disciplinary critique that I attempt to practice throughout. I am as interested in these texts as I am in what we do with them, how they circulate, and how we might reread them so as to rethink the role of American culture in the world and imagine alternative possibilities for an American encounter with the world. What I attempt to put in play is a critical practice that interrupts the nationalist interpretive practices that have looked away from such possibilities. This is pursued variously: via the introduction of Maghrebi archives, by following American representations of the Maghreb into Maghrebi cultural production, and in examining moments of actual collaboration between Americans and Maghrebis. In some cases I attend to moments of conversation that failed, such as the foreclosure of Arabic language in Hitchcock's Marrakech-set film *The Man Who Knew Too Much*, or the distancing of communities of young Moroccans and young Americans during the hippie era. In such cases, the interruption is of a different sort than when I attend to productive collaborations, such as the prolonged collaboration of Paul Bowles and Mohammed Mrabet, or the brief one of Ornette Coleman and the Master Musicians of Jajouka. But in both cases, the intent is to redirect Americanist accounts of the authors and artists I consider, as well as accounts of periods (World War II, the early cold war, the 1960s) that have not yet taken seriously enough the importance of the American encounter with the Maghreb.

These are not separate projects. Many of the reading practices that emerged for Americanists did so in the midst of the emerging cold war consensus, when the interdisciplinary field of American studies was consolidated. Having long repressed the question of empire that lies at the foundation of American studies approaches to reading literature, the danger now is that institutional arrangements—by which I mean the language and field requirements for Americanists, which tend to discourage multilingual work, and the resulting dissociation of Americanist work from the fields of comparative literature and postcolonial and diaspora studies—are entrenched. As the British scholar Paul Giles puts it, American studies thereby may find itself unable to "break the magic circle between text and context, to hold in suspension those conditions whereby the progressivist formulas of American studies would—naturally, as it were—underwrite a rhetoric of emancipation."[12] That magic circle is operative in most criticism of the major authors and texts I examine: Paul and Jane Bowles, William Burroughs, and Clifford Geertz, among others, and films such as *Casablanca* and *The Man Who Knew Too Much*. The failure to engage the textually rich and potentially disruptive presence of the Arab and Arabic language is a failure encouraged and authorized by reading practices that emerged from the cold war consensus.

Robert Young's recent reminder that the transition from colonialism to postcolonial forms of domination is "at the heart of the struggle for global mastery in the Cold War" is consonant with my claim. Young links the U.S.-Soviet contest with the political struggle for and within Europe's former colonial holdings and the cultural formations that emerged from those struggles.[13] Considering the cold war inseparable from the postcolonial period encourages studies of post-1941 U.S. culture to consider the frequent representation of the foreign in a different, more nuanced light. The pervasive trope of foreignness in 1940s and 1950s culture—in everything from science fiction films about alien invasion to Biblical epics set in the Middle East to Orientalist costume dramas and musicals to noir's obsession with contagion—should be seen not only as reflections of fears of the Soviet threat, third terms of a cold war binarism, but also as ways of figuring the diverse theaters in which the cold war was played out. Crossing disciplinary borders, we must recall that all those "third terms" had real histories and were affected by real engagements and interventions by the United States, which through its own apparati (the station chiefs and diplomatic corps of the State Department and the cultural arms of the United States Information Agency (USIA) and the United States Information Service (USIS) and the scholars and programs they funded) was simultaneously figuring and judging the foreign and basing policy on those judgments. The Maghreb was of particular interest to the U.S. State Department from 1946 through 1962, during which the struggles for independence were seen as thickly intertwined with the political swings in France, the largest recipient of Marshall Plan aid.

Questions of language and legibility are central to the American encounter with the Maghreb. Ernie Pyle, the most widely syndicated reporter during World War II, suggested that it was impossible for Americans to make the sounds of Arabic—the fricatives and the glottal stops. Pyle turns frustration into humor as he resolves the epistemological "noise" of a system not conforming to a perceived monolingual anglophone Americanness by translating a string of sounds. Here he is discussing a manual distributed to GIs by the Army:

> The book said, "Talk Arabic if you can to the people. No matter how badly you do it, they like it." That was good advice but how any American was to go about trying to talk Arabic was more than I knew. Most of us couldn't even learn enough French to get by, and Arabic is an almost impossible language to learn. . . . The book ended by saying that some Arabic sounds were almost impossible for Americans to learn. For example, it said that 'kh' resembled the sound made when clearing the throat, and that 'gh' was a deep gurgling noise. If we were to sneeze, cough, whistle, choke and hiccup all at once, that would mean "I love you, baby, meet me in front of Walgreen's right after supper, and leave your veil at home."[14]

For Pyle, the difficulty in pronouncing the Arabic letter serves to remind him of the ridiculousness of the place itself. The sounds that cannot be produced by American mouths stand out. Pyle's impulse to "translate" Arabic by rendering it in terms of domestic consumer culture is not unique, neither during World War II nor later when a "second American invasion" established American business enterprises in the region. When Pyle advocates making oneself "at home," he means editing out that which prevents North Africa from seeming like the American West and containing (or omitting) the Arabs who ruin the picture, as we'll see in chapter 1. That Pyle ridicules Arabic and veiled North African women is ultimately beside the point. More to the point is that he jokingly imagines a Walgreen's in Algiers. He and his readers knew that the comforts of home were not to be found in wartime North Africa, but it made what was an often incomprehensible experience much more tolerable to translate the experience into a familiar idiom.

Several of the texts that I consider do not, however, take this turn toward the resolution of incomprehensible speech and do not domesticate Arabic by imagining it to be reducible to a familiar American commodity. Instead, they represent the limits of the cold war American subject as it encounters the foreign and challenge the powerful impulse toward purging the domestic of foreignness generally speaking. There are, to be sure, texts treated in *Morocco Bound* that emerge from a variety of locations, and while in chapters 1, 3, and 6 I examine a wide cross-section of American texts, in the other three chapters I pay extended attention to particular texts and authors that disrupt the larger discursive impulses. Throughout, I am interested in responses to American projects emerging from a variety of locations—scholarly, media, and literary and cultural production—by Maghrebis who have interacted with, read, or responded to and in various ways recoded American representations. Following the global flow of Orientalist discourse reveals new and sometimes surprising meanings as that discourse moves into new contexts.

I take as a point of critical departure a series of statements made regarding American Orientalism in Edward Said's work, namely that with global ascendancy in World War II, the United States assumed the European mantle of thinking about the world. If I attempt to add nuance to that point as I look at a particular region, I do not reject Said's larger argument, which I think has been misinterpreted in some recent Americanist engagements.[15] In retrospect, of course, the representations I examine might be said to have relevance to contemporary meanings of the Arab. This is, however, justifiable without recourse to the vagaries of discourse as organizing principle. As Said argued in his early and powerful methodological statement, beginnings are distinct from origins.[16] In his work leading up to *Orientalism*, Said was much moved by Giambattista Vico's eighteenth-century elaboration of the concept of beginnings: "Doctrines must take their beginning from that of the matters of which they treat" (347). As Said elaborates Vico's method, he makes clear that his own project is the study of institutional history, not "logical, sequential continuity" or origins (351). There are at least two crucial points to bring forward: first, as Timothy Brennan has demonstrated, Said's greater interest in questions of institutions than Foucauldian "discourse"; and second, Said's elaboration of Vico's method: "everywhere to amass evidence by correlation, complementarity, and adjacency" (352). My own interruptive practice is inspired by this Said, the same Said who late in life critiqued the United States imperial state on institutional grounds, allied with the corrupt scholarship on the Middle East that he had elsewhere critiqued. My attention to circulation, as methodological principle, is allied as well with Said's interest in adjacency. *Circulation* describes the movement of many of the representations I address and is further a principle by which to comprehend meaning itself. Dilip Gaonkar and Elizabeth Povinelli's recent claim that "meaning" operates within a circulatory matrix is a compelling way of bringing together thinking about globalization as the transnational movement of peoples, financial instruments, technologies, and ideologies (as Arjun Appadurai describes it) and a careful attention to the global circulation of various and particular representations themselves. Gaonkar and Povinelli's point is intensified when paired with Michael Warner's theorization of the formation of publics and counterpublics based on forms of address. These concepts are elaborated in chapter 5, where I use them to elaborate interruptive practice in terms of the relationship of individual texts and "authors" to circulation, and the ancillary concepts of translation and collaboration. For now, we may say that if meaning making operates within a circulatory matrix, so should academic critique itself. As texts such as Warner Brothers' *Casablanca* circulate within and without different publics across time and space, different "meanings" adhere to the texts. Some of those meanings operative in parallel publics that do not register in the United States (e.g., Moroccan print culture, Maghrebi cinema) may offer compelling disorientation of the hegemonic meanings we as critics may have felt saddled by. Bringing together some of these meanings will, it's hoped, disorient the Americanist conversation about U.S. culture and imperialism.

I take the title for this book from the 1942 film *Road to Morocco*. Produced by Paramount, *Road to Morocco* was shot in Imperial County, California, not far from Yuma, Arizona, a desert landscape that stands in for Morocco in so many Hollywood films. "This must be the place where they empty all the hourglasses in the world," Bob Hope says to Bing Crosby as they ride a camel through endless dunes, neatly capturing and reinscribing the sense of timelessness with which Americans associated North Africa. Despite the sense that Morocco stood outside of an American temporality, on November 8, 1942, three days before the film was released in New York, U.S. troops had made surprise landings in Morocco and Algeria. This launched the North African campaign, the first major ground offensive of the U.S. Army in World War II. *Road to Morocco* was produced several months earlier, of course, but coincidentally released just at the moment of massive American attention to the region.[17] Although "geography means nothing in a Crosby-Hope film," as Bosley Crowther put it in the *New York Times*, the film's ability to offer a "delightful 'escape'" was seen in context of political reality: "[Escape] may sound a bit ambiguous, considering Morocco's current significance in the news."[18] Henceforth, North African space, already familiar to Americans via all those other films shot in Imperial County, would have a more immediate meaning to Americans. And the ways in which North Africa was subsequently represented would play a part in developing the national narrative of America's involvement in "the world."

In the magnificent theme song to the film, Bob Hope and Bing Crosby make a complex pun. The refrain, "we're Morocco bound," puns on the two dictionary meanings of the word "Morocco": the name of the country in northwest Africa and, with a small m, a fine leather used primarily in bookbinding. "Like Webster's dictionary, we're Morocco bound," Hope and Crosby sing. "Like a set of Shakespeare, we're Morocco bound." To be "Morocco bound," that is, to be on one's way to Morocco as an American, suggests that Morocco itself is bound in webs of representations. Thus the song can invoke the familiar Orientalist tropes of violent, misogynous men and seductive, cloistered women to conjure up a set of familiar scenarios and create comedic expectation: our duo is going *there*. The camera pans across a ludicrous bilingual road sign perched in the sand. The sign is marked "Road to Morocco," in English, with Arabic script below it. The camera scans from left to right, the direction of reading in English. To attempt to read the Arabic script—which is read from right to left, and which may be transliterated *tariq al-Marraksh*—is to work against the grain of Paramount's camera and highlights the additional cultural work of Hope and Crosby's pun on "Morocco bound." The Arabic text translates as "Road to Marrakech," removing the Arabic name of the country—*al-Maghrib*—or, we may say, re-Orienting it.

The words *Morocco* in English, *Marruecos* in Spanish, and *Maroc* in French are all indeed derived from the name of the city Marrakech, pronounced *mar-raksh* in Moroccan Arabic (accent on the second syllable), a trading city founded in the eleventh century and the former capital of a kingdom that stretched from present-day Spain to Senegal. Within French colonial discourse, *Maroc* pertains to the so-called Orient, although Fez lies to the west of Paris. In English, *Morocco* orients itself around the French word, and more importantly around the idea that Morocco is as much the land of French colonialism as it is the land of Moroccans. Following Hope and Crosby's lead, then, I'd like to suggest that the English word *Morocco* is itself morocco bound. The name for the country in Arabic, *al-Maghrib*, means "the west," or in its fuller form, *al-Maghrib al-aksa*, the farthest west, the land of the setting sun. In Arabic,

Road to Morocco: Bing Crosby, Dorothy Lamour, and Bob Hope as Yankee pashas. *Courtesy of the Wisconsin Center for Film and Theater Research.*

the country's name implies a different movement of culture, a different global orientation, than Hope and Crosby's Morocco-bound. *Al-Maghrib* is a country to the west of the rest of the Arab world, to the west of Mecca, the name of the prayer one says at sunset. Due to associations with both "the west" and "sunset," the word yields multiple associations in Arabic. Its trilateral root, *gha-ra-ba*, produces a series of intimately related words—to set, as the sun; to be strange, or odd; to be a stranger; to go west; to exile; to go far from one's homeland; and even to become Westernized, or Europeanized.[19] These are meanings necessarily lost in the English word *Morocco*. Remembering and reinscribing *al-Maghrib* as *Marrakech* unwittingly maintains the Orientalist frame of the Reconquista, the epic battle between Spain and the Moors.[20] In the arabophone world, however, *al-Maghrib* is oriented to the East, toward Mecca and Cairo, the political and religious centers of Islam and the Arab League, respectively. In other words, *al-Maghrib* is the "land of the furthest west" with respect to the Arab and Islamic worlds. Only as *Maroc* or *Morocco* can the region be thought to belong to "the Orient." By attempting to elicit the tension in that road sign in *Road to Morocco,* between the left-to-

right Morocco-boundedness and the right-to-left *tariq al-Marraksh*, and
the disruptive potential of Arabic within American texts, my effort is to
reorient the critical direction from which we examine American representations of the Maghreb and disorient the national(ist) subject undergirding that Orientalism.

Morocco Bound is organized in three parts. Part 1, "Taking Casablanca,"
examines the possibilities and limits of the idea of an American Orientalism. By focusing on the rhetoric that emerged from and described the
U.S. military invasion of North Africa in 1942, chapter 1 looks at the con-
vergence of Orientalist discourse, the American mythology of the frontier, Hollywood and journalistic formulas, and military power. More than
in any other period, the representations of the Maghreb that emerge from
the North African campaign (November 1942–May 1943) suggest the
overlap of cultural and political discourse, where one seems to influence
the other. I explore moments (such as General Patton's own understanding of his role in the Maghreb and Warner Brothers' marketing of *Casablanca*) when this is the case. What emerges from this conjuncture is an
understanding of North Africa within a particular American temporality,
one that builds on Luce's concept of the American century as a logic for
global dominion. This temporality was a powerful delimiting framework
within which to understand North African political legitimacy, imagined
as immature, and it coincided with the racialized thinking that was prevalent in American hegemonic institutional locations (the State Department, Hollywood, etc.). The global racial time that emerged collapsed
African American and North African rights and restrictions while rendering them separate. Such a temporality informs the single most influential American representation of the Maghreb, the film *Casablanca*, which
was screened for GIs and was popular in the United States and which
figured influentially the dissociation of African Americans from an affiliation with colonized North Africans.

Chapter 1 is what I earlier called a snapshot chapter, and the descriptive
texture that was achieved during World War II would be abandoned soon
after U.S. troops were withdrawn. So thickly was the Maghreb described,
however, that journalists writing about North Africa and Hollywood
filmmakers making desert war films in the postwar 1940s could count on
residual familiarity. Thus, during the period during which Paul Bowles
was traveling in Algeria and Morocco and writing his novel *The Sheltering
Sky*, journalists who described the "second U.S. invasion" of North Africa

referred to a familiar place. Still, Bowles's novel, which enjoyed a good deal of popularity upon its publication, operated in a different institutional space than had some of the most influential cultural production of the North African campaign. Chapter 2 takes the case of Paul Bowles's writing to interrogate more carefully the relationship between cultural representations of the foreign and foreign relations. I redraw the deep geopolitical context of Bowles's bestselling first novel. By layering a reading of postwar U.S. diplomatic engagement with the Maghreb with a close reading of *The Sheltering Sky*, I intend to do two things: first to demonstrate the necessity for a comparative and interdisciplinary approach to American Orientalism, and second to make a methodological argument for how to read post–World War II literature representing the (post)colonial space within a geopolitical, cold war context.

Part 2, "Queer Tangier," elaborates this critical practice, uses it to relocate and reread several familiar texts from the period, and thereby expands upon the interrelationality of the cold war, the postcolonial period, and U.S. cultural production. The section focuses on the International Zone of Tangier during what I consider its cultural and political renaissance: from 1946 through the 1950s. Tangier played a crucial and underappreciated role in postwar U.S. literature and a small but important part in cold war American thinking about the international realm. First, in chapter 3, I examine the variety of ways in which Tangier was figured and how it signified during this period, what I call the various "Tangiers" in simultaneous circulation. I do so for a number of reasons: to push forward my analysis of the institutional space or gap between cultural production and foreign relations; to look at the ways in which Tangier posed a challenge to middlebrow/mainstream American journalism, which regularly represented and often disparaged Tangier; and to set the stage for the close readings of the works by William Burroughs, Jane Bowles, and Mohammed Mrabet that I take up in subsequent chapters. Here I make a case for the challenges posed by the international experiment of the International Zone, especially from 1946 till 1952, after which a new protocol removed the most promising internationalist possibilities from the Zone's statute. The potential for supranational community and international coordination was, despite limitations in practice that comparatively disadvantaged the Moroccan population, a significant challenge to the opposing hypernationalist atmosphere in the United States. Journalists working for the major publications in the United States responded to this challenge by representing Tangier through a logic of excess and queerness, conflating the city's tolerance of homosexuality and the financial particularity of the source of its wealth: as a free port and tax haven, profiting off exchange and speculation rather than traditional production. Tangier was thus an early formation of that which would become the norm after 1973 with global financial markets.

Having reestablished the fraught status of Tangier, I argue in chapter 4 for a reconsideration of William Burroughs's masterpiece *Naked Lunch*, written in Tangier during this period. Though Burroughs's work is celebrated within American(ist) criticism, I argue that the full contribution of the author's thinking about his geopolitical moment has been largely discounted because of an inability to see the novel as deeply engaged in its Tangier context. My reading of *Naked Lunch* forwards Burroughs's sense of larval potentiality in the international formations of Tangier during the revolution. Living and working in this generative environment, Burroughs sees the interchangeability of the structural violences of race in the domestic United States and in the American expression of global imperial power. His experimental form emerges from a departure from national(ist) thinking that is intimately related to and helps to explain Burroughs's Tangier discoveries.

Before pursuing two other major Tangierian works, I take a detour through a film from the same period set in Marrakech, Alfred Hitchcock's *The Man Who Knew Too Much*. Hitchcock's film, a remake of his own earlier film and mediated through Hollywood films such as *Casablanca*, is in a decidedly different relationship to the Morocco of the 1950s than Burroughs's work. Hitchcock and his writers spent only a brief time in Marrakech. When the film was shot on location, however, Morocco was in the midst of its revolutionary "troubles." Morocco provided Hitchcock with the opportunity to think through a series of questions that are foregrounded in the film: race, domesticity, and the tensions between the United States and Europe as Americans take their place on the world stage. The celebrated film that emerged is a more complex response to the interplay of the domestic and the international than critics have acknowledged. My reading attempts to elicit the possibilities the film raises for thinking through this encounter in its representation of Arabic language and the racialized Arab other. In a pivotal scene of the film, the encounter with a "native informant" is foreclosed, but it suggests again that representation of the Maghreb offered the space for the expression of dissenting thought.

In chapter 5, I take a careful look at two projects that most fully interrupt the cold war episteme. I read Jane Bowles's later fiction, written after her encounter with Moroccan language and the community of Moroccan women with whom she was deeply engaged, and Paul Bowles's collaboration with the illiterate Moroccan artist Mohammed Mrabet. Neither Jane Bowles nor Mohammed Mrabet has registered fully in American literary criticism, a fact that I reconsider in terms of the topic of circulation. Both authors rethink circulation as a concept and as a literary practice, and their work expresses the perils and possibilities of living in translation. Jane Bowles produces a difficult and brilliant form of writing in a minor English, one that is as challenging to the hypernationalist presumption of a global American voice as it is hard to describe critically. In order to attempt to do so, I venture into Sufi philosophy and the concept of *al-barzakh*, a spatio-temporal location between locations. I also rethink usual accounts of Jane Bowles's literary career by arguing that her eventual self-removal from circulation was not (merely) career failure, but a logical and coherent outgrowth of her thinking about circulation itself. Mohammed Mrabet lives as an author "in translation" in a different sense: his work appears first in Paul Bowles's translations from colloquial Moroccan Arabic. Mrabet's work rethinks the circulation of meaning in another, equally compelling way. Caught within a collaboration that was both enormously generative and potentially constricting, Mrabet originated a sequence of creative techniques and modes that rethink the collaborative encounter and the translator-translated relationship. In so doing, Mrabet's work resists the labels that Moroccan nationalists and postcolonial critics initially applied to the works (by which they denigrated and dismissed Mrabet) and puts pressure on the categories that literary study in the United States uses to organize itself. The extended Mrabet-Bowles collaboration emerges from the "Queer Tangier" I elaborated earlier. Even in the face of unequal relationships of its actors to the global economy, it offers the promise of transnational or supranational communication and shows what such literary work might look like.

Part 3, "Marrakech Express," takes the study into the 1960s and a later formation, one that recedes from the potentialities that emerged from Tangier in the 1950s (even though Paul Bowles's and William S. Burroughs's writing had influenced hippie counterculture). Chapter 6 examines the overlapping interest in Morocco among two communities of young Americans: the hippies who went to Marrakech (and elsewhere in the country) and the young anthropologists doing research nearby, who produced work that would have a major influence on the field of cultural anthropology. In both cases, the Maghreb offered a more feasible space for the encounter with third world "otherness" than could Vietnam, the latter being the location that defined the generation and itself connected to the Maghreb via logics of Orientalism. (Indochina and the Maghreb had long been allied in U.S. State Department thinking because of the importance of France's colonial empire.) By reading a variety of texts from the hippie encounter with Morocco (including travel guides, song lyrics, poems, journalism, cookbooks, and fiction by figures such as Clifford Geertz, Paul Rabinow, Jane Kramer, Vincent Crapanzano, Paula Wolfert, James Michener, and others), I argue that a conservative recoil from difference pervades the hippie encounter. Moroccan youth were major actors in a fraught period in postcolonial Moroccan history, and the 1965 Casablanca riots, violently repressed by the government, are but one vivid example of a global wave of youth protests that swept Europe and the United States. Yet this population barely registers in the hippie archive and helps reveal the traveling hippies' turn away from both Vietnam and contemporary, urban Morocco in relation to Orientalism. The interest of anthropologists such as Geertz and Rabinow in rural forms and questions of tradition and textuality is related, and in its own way theorized the hippies' turn away. Though such anthropologists thought deeply about the complexity of their encounter with Moroccans and provided a series of theoretical statements that would themselves be influential on academic fields such as literature and American studies, I argue that their work helped to extend the institutional chasm between representation and foreign relations. What ultimately was at stake for the Johnson administration was the Moroccan king's authority and stability. By theorizing a gap between the representation/comprehension of the Maghreb and the advancement of "significant social progress," Geertz unwittingly justified the hippies' turn away from contemporary Morocco as irrelevant.[21] There are potential moments of interruption in this era too, especially Ornette Coleman's project with the Master Musicians of Jajouka. But there is also a sense that emerges from Geertz's seductive prose that the American encounter with Morocco has reached an impasse. Geertz's

Moroccan work, however, is seen not as a final discovery about this encounter, but as the fullest expression of that which could issue from the national episteme. In Geertz's work we see the denouement of that episteme. The lines of connection into the subsequent moment, globalization, are to be found in the preceding chapters, particularly in the work of Mrabet and Jane Bowles.

As originally conceived, this book would have gone to "the present," which when I began meant the Clinton administration and the post–Gulf War (I) response to the Arab world that both extended cold war presumptions and started to crack at the edges. But the events of September 11, 2001, which I watched on my television at home in the Midwest, wondering for most of a late-summer Tuesday about the fate of my father, who worked on the seventy-first floor of Tower 1 of the World Trade Center, forced me to reorganize that plan and indeed to write a different book than I had conceived. Jacques Derrida notes that the promise is also a threat, and the threat then to the work I was doing was also the promise that it might open itself up differently than in the way I had prior imagined, though its ostensible subject had not changed. Since then, I have added four of these six chapters and completely reimagined and rewritten the other two. It is no accident then that this book treats moments of textual rupture and of possibility. If American ideas about the Maghreb were bound to a certain extent by the success of films like *Casablanca* to frame them, several of the figures I discuss here were actively working outside those limiting frameworks. And while some of the texts I discuss were appreciated—a couple even lionized—they were frequently read within practices that themselves were bound by exceptionalist methods of misreading. I here attempt to interrupt those reading practices and reread some of these same texts from which exciting new possibilities emerge.

There are specific referents and also an episteme that I identify with the moment 1942–1973, the more precise period to which the subtitle of this book gestures. The opening referent is two events in November 1942: the Operation Torch landings that inaugurated the North African campaign, and the premiere of *Casablanca*. The close of the period refers to the end of what I call hippie Orientalism and has a number of referents, both in relation to the end of a wave of American interest in Morocco and more broadly. The year 1973 also refers to the beginning of an episteme that might be associated with globalization. As Benjamin Lee and Ed LiPuma suggest in their work on cultures of circulation, 1973 saw a number of events that ushered in a notably different era, including the Middle East oil crisis that "signaled the declining influence of Fordist production on the U.S. economy; the creation of the Chicago options exchange, the first institutional market in the U.S. specializing in options trading; and the discovery, or invention, of the Black-Scholes equations governing price options and other derivatives."[22] Roughly corresponding with these developments in world financial markets is the end of the Vietnam War and the collapse of the Nixon administration, as well as major unrest in Morocco. A couple of years later, the Green March into Western Sahara had a major effect on quelling Moroccan dissent by redirecting it. In addition, 1973 is the publication date for Geertz's *Interpretation of Cultures*, a landmark book that represents the limit of a certain type of encounter between American and Moroccan. Anthropologist George Marcus calls the moment after the mid-1970s the "changing mise-en-scène of anthropological fieldwork." Marcus sees, in Geertz's work, a limit reached in understanding within the traditional fieldwork encounter; for Marcus, Geertz is the "apogee" of that encounter. This is further justification for seeing 1973 as a turning point. Globalization as episteme would suggest an end to the period referred to as "postcolonial," as Ronald Judy has suggested in his powerful work on global Englishes. Following Judy and Marcus, I do not here move into the changed mise-en-scène of globalization but instead try to understand and describe thickly that which immediately precedes it. At the same time, I reach from the later episteme back to the earlier one in order to try to elicit strands of otherwise foreclosed possibilities and bring them into present and future critical work. And if the key figures are Americans who worked between 1942 and 1973, I also spend time looking at work by Maghrebi writers, artists, and scholars who worked later and take comparative glances at earlier American texts on the Maghreb by Mark Twain, Gertrude Stein, Edith Wharton, and Claude McKay. Thus if there is a carefully considered periodization that organizes this book, I reach across it in order to unseat or disorient America's Maghreb and locate counterdiscursive accounts. In this sense I follow Said's lead by looking throughout at the institutional arrangements—that corporate aspect of Orientalism—that have framed America's Maghreb.

This book was conceived and researched and lived during the later episteme, of course, both in the United States and with extensive time in Morocco and Tunisia. What Marcus calls the changed mise-en-scène has been vivid to my own lived experience in the Maghreb. Much of this book has been thought through in engagement with Moroccan colleagues over the past decade, with whom I have been engaged in a variety of projects and conversations. These projects are ongoing. My own extended affiliation with the Moroccan Cultural Studies Center at Fez, and elsewhere in Moroccan universities, is both a part of the research for this book and another aspect of the expression of its larger project. Conversation and more broadly opening lines of communication is where *Morocco Bound* ends and what it sets as its goal.

I

Taking Casablanca

1

AMERICAN ORIENTALISM

Taking Casablanca

Taking Casablanca

Shortly after his arrival in Casablanca on November 8, 1942, General George S. Patton Jr. had a chance to notice his surroundings. Unlike many American travelers to Morocco, Patton had arrived on Moroccan shores amid gunfire. He was the leader of the Moroccan portion of Operation Torch, simultaneous surprise landings at Casablanca, Oran, and Algiers that marked U.S. entry in the North African campaign, which extended until the liberation of Tunis in May 1943, a turning point in World War II. After the relatively quick victory over Vichy-loyal forces at Casablanca, Patton wrote his wife, "This town (Casa) is a cross between the ultra modern and the Arabian nights but is quite clean."[1] A couple of days later, he revised his initial impression, describing Casablanca as "a city which combines Hollywood and the Bible."[2] Since the French were under conflicting orders and there were no German or Italian troops in Morocco—Allied forces were engaged with them further to the east in Libya and Tunisia—Patton remained based in Morocco until early February, when he was finally summoned to Tunisia. In the meantime, often frustrated that his talents were being wasted, he read, worked on his French, wrote a short story about a soldier in combat, and recorded his observations.[3] A self-professed "profound student of history," Patton paid careful attention to detail in his elaborate descriptions of Moroccan palaces and interiors. On November 17, Patton described his first meeting with the Moroccan sultan at Rabat in another letter to Beatrice: "I certainly wish you could have been along yesterday. . . . It was the most colorful thing I have ever seen and would be worth a million in Hollywood . . . What I saw inside the palace and what Marco Polo saw did not differ except that the guards had rifles in the court[;] but inside, the twelve apostles had long curved simaters in red leather scabbords which stuck out like tales [*sic*] when they moved."[4] In his diary, describing the same scene, Patton changed the referent: "Having passed through this second gate, we came into the Old Testament, a large court which was completely encircled by men dressed in white Biblical costumes."[5]

Patton's sense of being at once within the Arabian Nights, the Bible, on the Silk Road with Marco Polo, and on a Hollywood soundstage echo and conflate the impressions earlier Westerners visiting Morocco had expressed. Edith Wharton, who visited in 1917, kept seeing the Bible when she wasn't evoking "Haroun-al-Rachid land"; Claude McKay felt in Fez as if he were "walking all the time on a magic carpet"; Wyndham Lewis tracked down American film director Rex Ingram "faking a sheik" in Morocco in 1931.[6] Indeed, despite his key role in the Operation Torch landings—which relied on their very timeliness to surprise German forces in Africa—Patton's unselfconscious time travel places his diaries and correspondence in the company of accounts that confused North Africa with the romantic Orient of the Arabian Nights.

Patton's profession, however, and the political and military importance of U.S. presence in North Africa distinguish his writings and place them in proximity to foreign relations of the most immediate sort. Patton did not choose to travel to North Africa, but while there he was intrigued by the spectacle of religious festivals, "ornate" pashas' palaces, the pomp of the Moroccan court, as well as banquets and belly dancers and boar hunts. At the same time, as official representative of the United States he spoke frequently with the Moroccan sultan and his representatives about the war and U.S.-Moroccan relations in the future. In his letters, Patton remarked on the importance of maintaining the respect of the Moroccan people and government, while stepping cautiously around the French protectorate's relationship to its colony. Patton's analysis was that "the prestige of the French Army is the only thing holding the Arabs in check." Since he saw his primary role as "to maintain Morocco as a gateway for the Americans entering the continent of Africa," Patton felt he needed to reject a preexisting plan to have the French surrender to the United States. "Morocco could not be used as a gateway if it were in the throes of an Arab uprising," he wrote, and he estimated the number of troops needed to occupy the country.[7] Taking a markedly different tone in his diaries, he wrote an ethnographic essay called "Notes on the Arab," which

Gen. George S. Patton (second from right) with Moroccan sultan
Mohammed V and young Moulay Hassan, then about fourteen years old,
late 1942. *Courtesy of the Patton Museum of Cavalry and Armor.*

speculates on the cultural meaning of turbans, burial rites, agricultural "habits," and "the similarity between the Arab and the Mexican" (35–38).

The interest of Patton's writing is not the complexity of its analyses of Moroccan culture, or the literary quality of his descriptions of festivals and interiors, but rather the ease with which Patton moves between such writing and diplomatic dealings with the Moroccans and the French. Or, put another way, that Patton took time at all to describe the cultural forms of the land that he briefly administered and saw himself as the American heir to Marco Polo helps us to identify the intertwined nature of representations of Maghrebi people and culture and the military and diplomatic objectives of the North African campaign. Patton's way of understanding North Africa is symptomatic of the wave of attention given to the region by American writers, journalists, filmmakers, and regular GIs during the North African campaign. Seeing the Maghreb as Oriental, as Patton did, was a common first impulse. It was frequently followed for American observers, however, by the sense of disillusion that the Maghreb wasn't Oriental enough, which often led to the identification of a frontier aspect to the desert landscape and sometimes elaborate comparisons of the Maghreb to the American Southwest (as in Patton's thoughts about Mexicans). By invoking the popular imaginary of the American West, journalists and filmmakers explained U.S. actions in North Africa by further distancing the campaign from the actual North Africa. The most sophisticated of the journalists who did so were aware of the trick—the *New Yorker's* A. J. Liebling later attempted to theorize it—yet the success with which the North African campaign was imagined as a Western allowed the United States to make sense of an otherwise foreign setting and confusing military action. The foreignness of North Africa and the complexity of the political landscape—with Free French and Fighting French, the ambiguous position of the French colonial administration, and Italian, German, Spanish, and British colonial holdings and ambitions in the region—could be made understandable if reduced to a frontier tale. Indeed, the images that were arguably the most successful in depicting the campaign—and have lasted the longest in the popular imagination—were those in a spate of Hollywood combat films and melodramas that adopted the Western motif to a desert terrain.

Reference to the frontier is, of course, a common and long-standing American response to foreignness. In the case of the war in North Africa, however, it produced a peculiar relationship to an important theater of war that encouraged American observers to project domestic concerns—particularly regarding race—onto their understanding of North Africa. The representations that issued provided a way to bracket the deep paradoxes of World War II and of the North African campaign in particular: the segregation of African American troops and the concentration camps for Japanese and Japanese Americans on the home front in the former case, and the alliance with the French colonial regime in the latter. To be sure, these paradoxes were frequently and eloquently noted by members of the Negro press and by left-leaning journalists. The *Chicago Defender*, for example, had a notably different perspective on the North African campaign that did not fall victim to the impulse to write off the native population of colonized Africa—though some pieces in the *Defender* did draw firm lines between North Africa and African America and implicitly differentiated sub-Saharan Africa from the Maghreb. The *Negro Quarterly* too noted that the war to end Hitlerism and the colonial domination threatened by the German Führer should attend to similar forms of domination in Africa exercised by the Allies. In the fall 1942 issue of *Negro Quarterly*, John Pittman, an editor for *People's World*, wrote that he hoped that the "coming influence of the United States in determining the future of Africa" would bode well for both African peoples and African Americans.[8] In the following issue, Kweku Attah Gardiner chastised the mainstream press: "We hear of troop movements and the capture of towns, but nothing is ever said of North Africans. What has happened to the Arab national 'fanatics' who were being imprisoned by the French even before the outbreak of the war?" For Gardiner, identified as a recent immigrant from West Africa, American journalists refused to discuss European colonialism in Africa or to poll African opinion: "African leaders . . . are not the ignorant, care-free, child-like peoples globe-trotters say they are. They alone know the yearnings and demands of their people for freedom."[9] And Kenneth Crawford argued that the U.S. government's collusion with French colonial bureaucracy was "disillusioning and distressing," part of "a series of fatal moral compromises." In August 1943, in a foreword to a collection of his war correspondence, Crawford lamented: "Some [liberals] argued that, in winning the battle for North Africa, we had lost the moral values for which the war was being fought."

But such accounts circulated far less widely than the syndicated columns of embedded journalists working for the major papers, or Hollywood's fantasies of the war in North Africa, and did not determine the prevailing narrative of the campaign. While W. E. B. DuBois noted, in early 1943, that the Negro press was finally gaining the attention of white America, the dominant narratives about North Africa as a theater for war were written elsewhere.[10] Those representations in turn provided a means by which to manage, by narrativizing, the potentially disturbing implications of the allegiance with the French in Africa. Portraying modern Moroccans and Algerians and Tunisians as Biblical characters—and later as American Indians—not only rendered them in a different temporal register from Americans in general, but it also dissociated them from a more immediate fraternity with African Americans who were deeply interested in the global dimensions of the war. Patton's writing is therefore a cipher for a strategy that recurred multiply and that worked to turn American attention—whether the Americans were African American or not—away from the association of African Americans with colonized North Africans.

Recently historians have drawn extensive parallels between the philosophy and practice of racism in the domestic United States and American foreign relations.[11] World War II is a key turning point in this complex matrix, because of the deep racial crises that marked the war years on the home front, the racial aspect of the war with Japan, the rhetoric and practice of the Nazi regime under Hitler, and the ascension of the United States as a global power concomitant with victory during the war—an ascension that would leave the United States in a particularly influential position after World War II as Europe's colonies struggled for their independence. Drawing on historian John Dower's work, which documented the racial character of the Pacific War, Thomas Borstelmann comments: "World War II was not racial in its origins, but in the Pacific it became for most American soldiers a racially coded conflict" (30). Borstelmann himself describes gracefully the complexity of American racism and the European war: the United States was fighting "the most murderous racists in modern history" but itself expanding the reach of Jim Crow overseas via a policy of segregating troops (31–37). The war years led African American intellectuals such as W. E. B. Du Bois to call publicly for recognition of the international linkages between oppressed peoples, including both African Americans and peoples in European colonies. Such discussions entered and framed the debate over the new United Nations charter in 1945. The charter, under the pressure of the divided U.S. delegation, supported the principle of nondiscrimination—"a significant symbolic step"—but "refused to take a strong stand against colonialism."[12]

The North African campaign posed a special challenge to thinking about the role of the United States in the war, since race and European colonialism were central. Because the Maghreb was already imbricated in generations of narratives that had sought to define it—from European Orientalism to more recent American films and travelogues—it is not surprising that it would fuel such representational energies. In the Negro press, there was ambivalence and hesitation about how to respond to North Africa. The Maghreb—and greater North Africa—has a complicated relationship to the conceptualization of Africa both outside and within the continent. For geopolitical reasons—the expanse of Sahara that separates North Africa from the rest of the continent, the history of Arab slave trading, and the political strength of Arab regimes—North Africa has a troubled relationship to sub-Saharan Africa, to which most African Americans trace their ancestry. Historians and theorists of Africa such as John Hunwick and Achille Mbembe have, however, encouraged us not to see the Sahara as an unbridgeable divide. Mbembe has recently urged outsiders to recognize a different and multiple set of borders operative within the continent.

Before the North African campaign, the idea of a North Africa connected to sub-Saharan Africa was available in African American letters. Claude McKay, a key figure of the Harlem Renaissance, had spent extensive time in Morocco and published a widely read account of his time there in his 1937 autobiography *A Long Way from Home*. McKay's self-portrait of his time in Morocco, "When a Negro Goes Native," made affiliations between North Africa and African America imaginable. In 1930, while living in Tangier, McKay completed a short story titled "Little Sheik," which he published in his 1932 collection *Gingertown*. "Little Sheik" responds to the craze occasioned by Rudolf Valentino's *Sheik* films, a phenomenon that fused racialized desire and anxiety about immigration to the United States in the 1920s.[13] McKay's story depicts a "rose-ivory tint[ed]" American woman, "one of those independent U.S.A. girls a little difficult of placing, socially or financially," who travels alone in a "Moorish" country. There she encounters a "slender youth" with a complexion McKay describes as the color of "blood under brown."[14] McKay reverses Edith Hull's story by having the white woman, filled with desire, "kidnap her brown idol," at least in metaphor. The "little sheik" guides her around the city, a world McKay describes as "Afroriental." But when he leaves her briefly at an Islamic *medersa*, she is greeted by the unwelcome advances of an Arab student, whose complexion is likened to "a full-ripe lemon." McKay's Maghreb contains both the brown African sheik and the lemon-yellow Arab student, an Afroriental world that Miss U.S.A. describes in terms that mix the Islamic and the African: "Her delight in the striking diversity of that life and its whole cohesive unity. Color, devotion, music, form, all welded in one authentic rhythm" (270). McKay's Maghreb thus privileges the African but sees a native harmony between North African Arab and sub-Saharan. In other work McKay began in Morocco, a story called "Miss Allah" that he apparently did not complete, he imagined what he called the "Afra-Arab mind."[15] There McKay provided a sense of the racial diversity of Morocco, distinguishing "Albino-type Riffian[s]," Moors, and those living in the Moroccan south, "where the sun was gorgeously warm and the native population sympathetically Negroid" (37).

The image of the Maghreb's racial diversity could be found elsewhere in 1930s culture, such as in Leland Hall's 1931 novel *Salah and His American*, published in Knopf's influential series "The Negro" alongside titles by Melville Herskovits, Langston Hughes, James W. Johnson, Carl Van Vechten, and Walter White. Hall's novel portrays a white American man who returns to Marrakech, where he has lived before, and hires a darker-skinned African as his servant. Though Hall portrays Morocco as a place where "the Negro" has a lower social status and not one of "their own parts of Africa" (8), he also shows Morocco to be a multicultural place of racial tolerance. Josephine Baker had contributed to the idea that African Americans had a special claim to the Maghreb. In 1935 Baker starred in *Princesse Tam-Tam*, a film shot in Tunisia, in which she played a Tunisian goatherd. In late 1942, Baker was rumored to have died. (The *Defender* ran tributes, including one by Langston Hughes.) But in 1943 she turned up in North Africa. Happy to announce their error, the *Defender* published a photograph of Baker entertaining troops in a Red Cross theater "somewhere in North Africa." The headline over the photograph, "First Picture of Jo Baker in Africa," compounded the *Defender*'s apparent joy in publishing the photograph of the previously lamented star. That Baker and the five uniformed African American servicemen behind her were in North Africa was an occasion for pride.[16]

The coverage of the North African campaign in the *Chicago Defender* demonstrates the possibilities and limits of the affiliations that McKay and Baker had depicted. The *Defender* responded to the North African campaign in a number of ways, particularly when it became apparent that African American troops had participated in the landings. Most immediately, the paper's editors saw the landing of African American troops in North Africa as a heroic return to the continent. One editorial cartoon published in November 1942 was titled "The Man Who Came Back," with two panels: the first, labeled "America 1619," depicted white slavers leading chained Africans off a ship; the second, labeled "Africa 1942," renders muscular American GIS storming the African coast. In December, after the *Defender* had confirmed that African American troops were in North Africa, the paper ran a cartoon of Hitler in flight across a desert, chased by three soldiers representing a diversity of African peoples: a Negro soldier in U.S. uniform, a bare-chested and barefooted African soldier in a Fez cap, and a bare-chested man wearing a turban and holding a scimitar. The caption makes the racial alliance between African Americans, North Africans, and sub-Saharan Africans clear. Hitler says: "I'm dreaming of a white Christmas." In the background an angry Sphinx looks on; the Sphinx recalls the masthead image used by the *Defender* itself and suggests the paper's own racial solidarity with the triumvirate of soldiers.

The *Defender*'s writers and columnists were less sure. Though columnists openly worried about Hitlerism as a racializing strategy for domination, they generally stepped gingerly around the question of France's own domination of North Africans. Nonetheless, columnists drew direct connections between Africans colonized by Axis and Allied powers and African Americans. When Tripoli fell in late January 1943, columnist John Robert Badger commented: "Many an African Arab and Negro smiled with satisfaction." Badger considered the victory in Libya as a blow to the Axis and a step in the "destruction of Hitlerism." He also drew the parallel to the home front:

> Well may Negro Americans rejoice at this ignoble end of the Italian colonial empire. Every blow struck at empire in any corner of the world cannot but reverberate in Darkest Dixie, where yet the bulk of Negro American people live in conditions of colonial subjection. The unequal status of Negro Americans is but part and parcel of a world system in which empire and imperialism is still the dominant aspect. But we who live today can observe this world system disintegrating before our very eyes.[17]

"The Man Who
Came Back," edito-
rial cartoon by Jay
Jackson, *Chicago
Defender*, Novem-
ber 28, 1942.

"I'm Dreaming of a
White Christmas,"
editorial cartoon
by Jay Jackson,
Chicago Defender,
December 19, 1942.

Badger went on to give a capsule history of Italian imperial history in Libya and its part in the world system. He suggested that the "ouster of the Axis" from Libya made the "complete expulsion of Axis armies from African soil" that much closer. But he also suggested, more vaguely, that the Allies—namely France—posed a "danger to Allied aims." The danger was less immediate and lay "on the horizon." He closed his column not by pursuing the "confusion in French Africa," but by worrying that the United States might later offer the restoration of Italian control of Libya as "bait for disaffected elements in Italy." While the cynicism was biting, the retreat from a critique of French empire in North Africa is notable. The following week, Badger commented on the recently concluded Casablanca conference, but instead of pursuing the line regarding empire and the world system and extending his critique to French colonialism in Morocco, Badger focused on symbolism—"the conference marked the first time in modern world history that the fate of Europe and Asia has been decided on the Continent of Africa"—and applauded Roosevelt's subsequent trip to Liberia, where he and the Liberian president inspected African American troops.[18] While FDR's trip to Liberia was surely cause for pride, and much celebrated in the *Defender*, the paper's hesitance to critique French colonialism in North Africa suggests both a patriotic internalization of the war effort and the paper's reluctance to make too close an alliance with North Africans. The *Defender*'s unsigned editorial on the Casablanca conference suggested an opening: "The locale of the Roosevelt-Churchill meeting is very interesting." Commenting that Hitler "had proclaimed Negroes as 'half apes,'" the writers appreciate the irony that it will be from Africa that Hitler's doom is sealed. The editorial argues that Africans now must be armed and colonials freed. North Africans, however, are not specified, in favor of Liberia, "a semi-colony" and "Firestone plantation." Still the call, albeit vague, to "Free the colonies. Put life into the Atlantic Charter," emphasized that the status of all colonies was one that African Americans should share.[19]

Perhaps ironically, representations of the North African campaign in the mainstream press and Hollywood films were less hesitant about imagining the potential fraternity of North Africans and African Americans and turned those imagined relations to conservative use. These representations were in much wider circulation than those in the Negro press. Their definition of the Maghreb during and immediately following the campaign established an idea of North Africa that took hold in the American imagination. During the war, the region was made known by embedded journalists such as Ernie Pyle, John Steinbeck, and A. J. Liebling, Hollywood studio pictures such as *Sahara*, *Five Graves to Cairo*, *Casablanca*, and to a lesser extent by comedies such as *Cairo*, *Road to Morocco*, and *Lost in a Harem*, combined with advertising, newsreels, and letters home. It is not incidental that the attention given to the Maghreb—even by the Hollywood fantasies—was inseparable from the war that led the United States across the region, establishing military bases and diplomatic relationships along the way. Orientalism, as Edward Said taught us a generation ago, is after all not merely the confusion of reality and romance in the lands of North Africa and the Middle East. Rather, according to Said, Orientalism names a long Western tradition of literary and scholarly representations of a region named (by the West) "the Orient" that corresponds with Western political domination of the lands to the South and East of the Mediterranean. "To be a European or an American [writing about the Orient]," Said writes, "means being aware, however dimly, that one belongs to a power with definite interests in the Orient, and more important, that one belongs to a part of the earth with a definite history of involvement in the Orient almost since the time of Homer."[20] But the extended moment of the North African campaign, which Churchill would famously call "the end of the beginning" of the war, was also the beginning of the end of European models of colonialism and empire. There is an intertwined relationship of American Orientalism, if we may call it that, to French Orientalism. That film—with its own generic patterns and working within the constraints and structuring conditions of the studio system—plays such a large part will not be incidental. The association of American empire with a world placed in the temporal lag of racial time was, as I'll argue, central to the cultural work of Luce's essay "The American Century" and was the paradigmatic American expression of "benevolent" global hegemony.

For U.S. journalists and filmmakers, and the audiences they addressed, involvement with North Africa came quickly after November 8, 1942. Patton's sense of his own place on the historical continuum is apparent in his juxtaposition of Marco Polo's journeys to his own. So, too, is Patton's sense of the American inheritance of the Orientalist mantle, an antique land ever exotic (evoking *Arabian Nights* and the Bible) visible now American-style ("would be worth a million in Hollywood"). For all his romanticization of his own role, Patton's writing accurately predicts the confusion of American military presence with popular culture interest. "Taking" North Africa in a military sense seemed to authorize taking it for narrative purposes as well; the desert quickly became a tabula rasa on which to project and resolve anxieties about American identity during a period of crisis.

Said's work in *Orientalism* and *Culture and Imperialism* focuses on British and French Orientalist discourse, long-standing traditions that derive their richness from "a particular closeness experienced between Britain and France and the Orient."[21] According to Said, American participation in "Orientalism" can be dated "roughly from the period immediately following World War II, when the United States found itself in the position recently vacated by Britain and France" (290). World War II itself, which Said neglects, was the crucial period during which Americans attained that particular "closeness" to North Africa. Before the arrival of U.S. troops, the region was indeed "distant"—the wave of sheik and Foreign Legion films in the 1920s and 1930s portrayed an almost unmarked Sahara, far removed from geography and history. With the attention of the American public focused on U.S. troops in North Africa, however, journalists brought the region "closer" through narrative. Never before had so many Americans traveled through North Africa nor so many homebound Americans read about it. If World War II marks the ascension of the United States as a global power, and the relative decline of Britain and France, then the study of American Orientalism must address the North African campaign.

In military history, the North African campaign is considered a turning point in the war, the crucial testing period of U.S. ground forces, which engaged German troops for the first time, and a strategic stroke of brilliance. During those months, the focus of the war shifted from the Pacific, where initial U.S. engagement with the Japanese at Guadalcanal, Bataan, and elsewhere had been demoralizing, to North Africa, where British General Montgomery had been struggling with the German military genius Erwin Rommel since 1940. With the support of the first major commitments of the U.S. Army, the Allies pushed back and defeated the Germans at Tunis and moved from there into Sicily.[22] Diplomatically, the January 1943 Casablanca Conference saw Churchill and Franklin Roosevelt bring Free French leader Charles de Gaulle into an uncomfortable proximity with his political rival General Henri Giraud, commander-in-chief of French forces in North Africa.[23] The Allied leadership (minus

Stalin and Chiang Kai-shek) decided there to fight for complete victory
along the North African coast and to prepare for the invasion of Sicily.
The most famous outcome of the conference was the announcement of
the policy of unconditional surrender, issued somewhat spontaneously by
Roosevelt in Casablanca on January 24.[24]

World War II marks also a turning point in the history of colonialism,
as North African independence movements began to gain ground. While
Roosevelt was in Morocco he met with Sultan Mohammed V, who represented a people still and throughout the war under a French-administered
protectorate. That meeting, according to the sultan's son, King Hassan II,
who would himself rule Morocco from 1961 until his death in 1999, was
particular inspiration for the independence movement. A Moroccan organization calling itself the Roosevelt Club was founded in 1943 to help
Moroccan political elite meet senior members of the U.S. military and
was active after World War II in the independence struggle.[25] According
to Hassan, then a fourteen-year-old *prince heritier*, Roosevelt as much as
promised his father that collaboration with the Allied effort would have
dividends. "Sire," FDR reportedly told Mohammed V in 1943, "given the
effort which Morocco—in so far as it is a protectorate—has agreed to give
to defend the cause of peace, I can assure you that ten years from now
your country will be independent."[26] The meeting and the statement are
famous in Morocco. What seems apparent now are the ways in which
Roosevelt's implicit deal set the stage for the postcolonial relations between Morocco and the United States, shifting the paradigm of global
power from the colonial model generally accepted in 1943 to something
different. Roosevelt does so by the invocation of "racial time"—the injunction by the dominant group for the subordinate group *to wait* for rights,
where FDR's grandiloquent promise of independence in a decade is also a
deferral of the immediacy of the Moroccan claim. This suggests both the
continuity of the colonial address of the African as "immature" and the
postcolonial shift to global racial time. Before the November landings,
U.S. intelligence services had predicted in classified reports that after the
war the Moroccan sultan would be ready "to throw himself in the arms of
Mr. Roosevelt. Provided Mr. Roosevelt will accept him and his country."[27] What's important here is not only that the Office of Strategic
Services was investigating American global hegemony, but also that it
understood national protection to be the stakes of global domination.
FDR himself was already imagining postcolonial forms of patronage.

Meanwhile, the French worried that U.S. ambitions in North Africa were for more than a foothold from which to fight the Germans. As William Hoisington has demonstrated, Resident-General Charles Noguès was concerned that anti-French sentiment among Moroccans left the field open for the establishment of an American protectorate. Roosevelt rejected the establishment of an American colony, however, and concentrated on maintaining French supremacy even while the United States established economic interests in Morocco.

If inspiration for North African struggles against colonialism came from the United States precisely at the moment when U.S. troops were moving across French-held colonies, at the same moment American audiences were presented with conservative ideas regarding the proper "place" of the North African population. Even if American attention turned to North Africa only briefly, the intensity of coverage served to bring the region into the rapidly expanding American empire, or as Luce had it, "the American century." The burst of attention is perhaps due to the qualitative difference of the American empire after World War II from European colonial empires that precede them. As Said suggests, "the [U.S.] foreign-policy elite has no long-standing tradition of direct rule overseas, as was the case with the British or the French, so American attention works in spurts; great masses of rhetoric and huge resources are lavished somewhere (Vietnam, Libya, Iraq, Panama), followed by virtual silence."[28] The ways in which North Africa was and was not represented, then, in 1940s American culture are of importance because there was little chance that they would be immediately revised. Indeed, those representations so often include images of windblown sand dunes and barren desert landscapes, as if to suggest the irrelevance of confirming anything in such a place.

Patton's incidental comment that what he saw in Casablanca "would be worth a million in Hollywood" was quickly proven accurate. Shortly before U.S. forces landed at Casablanca, Warner Brothers put the finishing touches to a film that had, quite by chance, been named Casablanca. An adaptation of an unproduced stage play called *Everybody Comes to Rick's*, the film had been renamed to evoke the atmosphere of the successful 1938 film *Algiers* (a remake of the French masterpiece *Pépé le Moko*).[29] When the surprise landing at Casablanca brought the city into the news, however, Warner Brothers rushed to get the film in the theaters. The premiere in New York on Thanksgiving was preceded by a Fifth Avenue parade of Free French supporters and the singing of the "Marseillaise" to the Free French flag in the theater, provoking the *Hollywood Reporter* to comment: "The occasion took the tone of a patriotic rally rather than the premiere of a timely motion picture." The general release was timed to coincide with the Casablanca Conference in January. The ad campaign celebrated Warner's "split-second timing," again conflating geographic space and temporal break. The ad boasted "the Army's Got Casablanca— and *So Have Warner Bros!*" under a photograph of a stopwatch.[30] From the start, Patton's association of the North African military "theater" with Hollywood, and Hollywood's confusion of the theater with North Africa, are wrapped up in each other. Posters proclaimed: "A story as exciting as the landing at Casablanca!" If *Casablanca* the film stood in for Casablanca the city, Warner Brothers' sense of their right to "Casablanca" came close to Patton's. When the Marx Brothers were making their 1946 send-up *A Night in Casablanca*, Warner Brothers tried briefly to claim a copyright on the word *Casablanca*, in an extreme version of representation-as-ownership. (With characteristic brilliance, Groucho Marx suggested his entity's control of the word *brothers* and ended the standoff.)[31] And if Hollywood could make use of the war, the war could also make use of a Hollywood film. De Gaulle requested a copy to inspire his London staff. American soldiers might have seen the film too, but the U.S. Office of War Information prevented the copy Warner Brothers sent to North Africa from being shown—the symbolism of Claude Rains tossing a bottle of Vichy water into the trash was not convenient while the United States maintained relations with the Vichy government.[32]

Casablanca names the peculiar collusion of U.S. cultural production and post-1941, postcolonial foreign relations, a major and precise moment when U.S. texts become worldly in a new way. *Casablanca*, the film, renders invisible the way in which the strategic alliance of the United States and the French regime that controlled the colonies in North Africa—criticized by left-leaning journalists during the war, justified by historian William Langer in 1947 as "Our Vichy Gamble," yet named within *Casablanca* itself as "the beginning of a beautiful friendship"—was not only expeditious for war goals but also redefined the meaning of the war and the postwar settlement itself. Post–World War II articles in the U.S. popular press that reported on the return of ex-GIs to North Africa establishing businesses that would sell the products introduced to the local population during the North African campaign of 1942–43 furnished such a redefinition explicitly. Under titles such as "Young Man, Go to Casablanca" and "We're Invading North Africa Again," the popular press redefined the earlier military campaign in corporate terms, now mobilized within cold war interests: the development of "underdeveloped regions" under Truman's Point Four program.

Warner Brothers' proprietary sensibility overlapped with a military understanding of "taking" a city. Beatrice Patton wrote her husband a birthday letter three days after the landing: "This afternoon I took an African violet to Mrs. Stimson [wife of the Secretary of War] with a message from you that you had captured it at Casablanca."[33] That an African violet might be growing wild in Casablanca is as detached from reality as Warner Brothers' depiction of the city. Mrs. Patton goes on: "As soon as [the Secretary of War] saw me, he called out, 'Well, George had the toughest job of them all and he has got Casablanca for his birthday.'" To "get" Casablanca is of course to have taken it, which generals, major-publication journalists and Hollywood filmmakers decided permits one to portray it as they wished.

Confusion Is Normal in Combat

In November we came to a continent with a Blue Book
Telling us what to do, what to say, how to say it,
But when we hit the beaches we forgot the Blue Book
and we did it our own way,
said it our own way and in our own voice,
And the people were glad to see us and we made ourselves at home.
—Sgt. Milton Lehman, *Stars and Stripes*, June 12, 1943

War was confusing, as many journalists who attempted to depict it in words pointed out. U.S. state censorship, combined with a tendency of American journalists toward self-censorship, only compounded the challenges inherent in reporting from the battlefields. "Truth" became a relative term, as historian John Blum has pointed out, particularly during the first years of U.S. involvement in the war. Government organizations such as the Office of Facts and Figures (established October 1941), the Office of Censorship (December 1941), and the Office of War Information (June 1942), disseminated, controlled, and suggested the flow of images and words that Americans at home received about the war.[34] While material was frequently censored—Margaret Bourke-White, for example, would routinely send the negatives of her photos of the 1943 Italian campaign directly to the Pentagon, where they were developed and approved before being sent to her publisher[35]—journalists responded to the usually unwritten rules of the government propaganda and censorship machine by internalizing its presumed goals. As John Steinbeck later recalled about the details that he left out of his war correspondence: "That they were not reported was partly a matter of orders, partly traditional, and largely because there was a huge and gassy thing called the War Effort. . . . Gradually it became a part of all of us that the truth about anything was automatically secret and that to trifle with it was to interfere with the War Effort."[36] Assumptions about the requirements of the war effort authorized a style of reporting that implicitly acknowledged its divergence from the complete "truth."[37] Passing the facts of the North African campaign through the screens of Orientalist films and of Western frontier tales allowed the truth of the campaign to correspond to a believable and useful fiction. This last statement applies less rigorously to the Negro press, which as I've suggested engaged in a vigorous conversation—played out in columns, editorials, and readers' letters—about the racial character of the war and the urgency of freeing colonized populations from Western domination. Yet readers of such publications had to rely on mainstream papers' reportorial coverage for detailed coverage of the war on the front. The news pages of the *Chicago Defender*, for example, during the North African campaign focused much more extensively on domestic questions—including the poor treatment and segregation of Negro troops on the home front—than on the details of the military campaign or the experience of GIs abroad. The first time the North African campaign received a front-page headline in the weekly edition of the *Defender*, for example, did not come until November 28, nearly three weeks after the Operation Torch landings, when the paper was able to confirm "Negro Troops in Africa." That the source for the lead was none other than Eleanor Roosevelt herself, and that the story could go no further than Mrs. Roosevelt's vague assertion, demonstrates the limitations on the Negro press as far as international war coverage.

The gap between the truth, whatever that might be, and what got re-

ported in the major papers was most obvious to those soldiers and reporters at the front. Early U.S. defeats in the Pacific against the Japanese in
1942 were rendered as accounts of American heroism against great odds,
frustrating and angering embattled soldiers who knew better. Descriptions of U.S. soldiers began to conform to "all-American" types (athletic,
team-oriented, and unintellectual, in John Blum's analysis), homogeniz-
ing both the soldiers and their stories. As Blum points out, "Correspondents at the front used what data they had to endow the soldiers they
knew with recognizable qualities of person and purpose. In the process,
truth became selective. Whether consciously or inadvertently, the reporters tended to find in the young men they described the traits that
Americans generally esteemed."[38] The various state apparatuses of information control combined with journalists' impulse to organize their stories as tales of American heroism created a split between truth and fiction
that paralleled the gap between front and home. Truth, in this formulation, became equated with the war, a truth that necessarily became fiction
as it was relayed home.[39]

For GIs, the disorientation of war was compounded by a lack of familiarity with the lands in which they found themselves. But the Army's
attempt to help was met with suspicion. In North Africa, the Army
distributed a short booklet—known as the Blue Book—to provide background information. For soldiers like the poet quoted in the section
epigraph, however, official facts quickly receded to the background once
American soldiers arrived: "We forgot the Blue Book and we did it our
own way."[40] Official truths were associated with a suspicious and anonymous authority that could be abandoned. Journalists such as Ernie Pyle,
the popular journalist who wrote for the Scripps-Howard chain of papers,
adopted the necessarily partial view accessible to the GIs as an antidote to
the inability to locate a larger truth. Pyle and other American writers
covering the North African campaign embraced the popular mythology of
the American West as a means to translate the strange land and people
they found there. In doing so, they followed the lead of many of the GIs. In
the popular soldier song "Deep in the Heart of Tunis," soldiers imagined a
Tunis they had not yet reached to the tune of a popular song about Texas.

The Tommies and Yanks are using bombers and tanks,
Deep in the heart of Tunis.

> They're giving Jerry the feel of the Allied heel,
> Deep in the heart of Tunis.
> From Chicago and Trent, from Seattle and Kent,
> They're marching down through Tunis.
> From Dakar to Algiers they're getting millions of cheers,
> They'll hear them too in Tunis.
> They got blistered feet trailing Rommel's retreat,
> Not so far from Tunis.[41]

Ernie Pyle wove Wild West imagery into his articles, taking on a spare narrative voice and producing what sometimes sounded like cowboy tales: "The sun came up slowly over the bare mountain ridges. The country was flat and desertlike. There was not a tree as far as we could see. It looked like West Texas. We passed Arabs blue with cold, shepherding their flocks or walking the roads. There was hoarfrost on the ground, and sometimes we saw thin ice in the ditches."[42] If North Africa looked like West Texas (for other journalists, the varied desert terrain recalled other parts of the American Southwest), the native population could be made to fit the topography, blips on the sparse terrain. Just as General Patton had reimagined the Arabs as Mexicans, American journalists turned Maghrebis into American Indians, when they didn't write them out entirely from their narratives.

The frontier narrative was frequently put into play during the war irrespective of terrain, as Richard Slotkin has shown, and provided some of the overarching narratives with which Americans commented on the war. For Slotkin, such a familiar narrative was required by the various crises of the war years, the cultural confusion of a mobilized America, and concomitant changes in the domestic economy; the frontier story was necessary to make sense of an enemy that threatened to end "civilization as we know it." The repetition of the iconography and mythology of the frontier thus had both local and global referents for Americans, as it instructed them how to make sense of the changes on the home front and how to grapple with military defeats and the insecurities of a drawn-out war abroad. In the face of the prevalence of newsreels, Slotkin argues that Hollywood's depiction of the war as a Western made narrative films seem "more real" than the newsreels' putatively neutral depiction of events. Narrative journalism such as Pyle's, A. J. Liebling's, and Steinbeck's worked similarly. Americans' understanding of the "real war" was filtered

Ernie Pyle talking
on a field phone in
North Africa, 1943.
*Courtesy of the Ernie
Pyle State Historic
Site, copyright Indi-
ana State Museum
and Historic Sites.*

through the frontier myth, but since truth was not infinitely flexible, the myth itself was altered and enlarged by the course of the war.

Henry Luce's influential essay of 1941, "The American Century," did much of the ground clearing that would allow Americans to see North Africa as an extension of the American West. When Luce called the twentieth century the "American century," ten months before the bombings at Pearl Harbor, the immediate context of his pronouncement was an argument for why the average citizen should support U.S. entry into the war. Yet his *Life* magazine editorial moved boldly beyond a local perspective, as he looked both forward and backward in the century, both within the boundaries of the United States and across the oceans, finding everything in that range "American." "We are *not* in a war to defend American territory," Luce wrote. "We are in a war to defend and even to promote, encourage and incite so-called democratic principles throughout the world."[43] For Luce, the promulgation of American "principles" was an imperative America could not refuse: "America is responsible to herself as well as to history, for the world environment in which she lives. Nothing can so vitally affect America's environment as America's own influence upon it" (24). If such an "environment" confused moral with economic goals, what is intriguing about Luce's argument is his nomenclature. For Luce, U.S. isolationism was not possible in the twentieth century; yet internationalism for Luce means that the world becomes "our" world, an "American" world, an "American century." I will come back to the time lag of this phrase in my discussion of *Casablanca*, but I want to note that for Luce American cultural production—and more largely what he calls "imagination"—has a key role to play. For Luce American cultural production already was international before Americans (as represented by the readers of *Life*) were ready to engage the foreign and is summoned to justify the logic of his argument. Luce's examples—American slang, jazz, Hollywood film, and U.S. technology—reveal that by "internationalism" Luce means the export of U.S. cultural products rather than a mingling of cultural forms; these examples suggest the linguistic manipulation central to his project (that language, like temporality, must be Anglo-American). The logic of "The American Century" sounds a bit like General Patton's comments about the "taking" of Casablanca and its potential worth to Hollywood: if the readers agreed that Hollywood's influence was international, they might see that U.S. troops should follow.

Luce places high value on the role of creativity: "We need most of all . . . to bring forth a vision of America as a world power which is authentically American and which can inspire us" (35). Whether they were directly inspired by Luce's essay or not, the cultural work done by journalists and filmmakers who saw the American West in the Maghreb helped create that "authentically American" version of the North African campaign.

If Luce had cleared the theoretical space, the landscape needed to be cleared of its markers if it was to be an American frontier. Other than the resident Arabs and Berbers, the greatest obstacle was the constellation of Orientalist images already in place. North Africa may have been distant, but there were ideas in the popular American imaginary about the area, and they all involved the presence of European colonials. The *Sheik* films depicted British colonials, while the *Beau Geste* films treated the French foreign legion. Claude McKay had described his interactions with French authorities, while Jesse Fauset's Algiers pieces revolved around the French community. Americans arriving during the war frequently expressed disappointment that North Africa did not look as Oriental as they had been led to expect. Here is Ernie Pyle:

World travelers had told me that Oran had an Oriental atmosphere, but I couldn't detect it. It seemed much more like a Latin city than an Oriental one. And it could be compared in many ways with El Paso, discounting the harbor. The climate is roughly the same. Both cities are in semiarid country. Both are dusty in the spring and very hot in summer. Both are surrounded by fertile, irrigated land that produces fruit and vegetables and grain. . . . The native crafts are largely silverwork, rugs, and leather. Some of the Algerian rugs resembled our Navajo Indian ones. They were beautiful and the prices were about the same. (27–29)

Rather than accepting inherited tales, Pyle proffers El Paso as a model for Oran, familiar and free of Europeans. Such a move is typical of Pyle's anticosmopolitanism. Pyle was widely championed as the "regular GI's" journalist, free of the pretensions associated with experts and Europeans. "Out of the foxholes he shared with them, and from his own heart straight to the folks back home," announced the flap copy of Pyle's 1943 collection *Here Is Your War*. Pyle was marketed as much like the GIs themselves: "Living, gallant, unpretentiously heroic Americans who are writing one of the great chapters of our history." Pyle's writing was claimed to record the history being written by the soldiers themselves, allowing his publishers to make a claim for the greater "reality" of his approach: "He just sat down without pretending to know any more than his observing eye could see. He just wrote about folks," claimed a tribute reprinted on the inside back flap of the 1943 first edition. "And that is why he was able to give the American people the only real news out of Africa since the American invasion." The wartime paperback edition called his perspective "a foxhole view," written with an eye "for the detail that counts—the 'worm's-eye' view."[44]

Pyle settled on a depiction of Maghrebis as American Indians. "The Arabs seemed a strange people, hard to know. They were poor, and they looked as tight-lipped and unfriendly as the Indians in some of the South American countries, yet they were friendly and happy when we got close to them" (44). Instead of trying to understand the Arabs' "strangeness," Pyle substitutes a more familiar image to explain them (here South American Indians, elsewhere Navajo). Of course, in doing so, Pyle is offering another "strange" and "hard to know" people in place of the Arab (his depiction of South American Indians is less sympathetic than his portrait of Arabs), a substitution that paradoxically writes out the threat of the Arab. If North Africa was like the American Southwest of popular

Ernie Pyle talking to GIs in the field, Anzio, 1944. *Courtesy of the Ernie Pyle State Historic Site, copyright Indiana State Museum and Historic Sites.*

mythology, and the Arabs like Indians (with the GIs cowboys), the enemy here was clearly not the Indians but the evasive Desert Fox, Rommell. So we see the shifting of the frontier myth. When used in the Western Pacific, the frontier narrative made use of the role of the Indians as savages for its explanatory power.[45] In the North African campaign, the Indians recede and the desert landscape is foregrounded. The Arabs must be distinguished from the enemy. Thus, they are "friendly and happy when we got close to them"; they resemble Indians with their crafts, their architecture, and their farming—Indians after the Trail of Tears, Indians already on reservations. There were exceptions, of course. In some suspenseful B movies of the war years, such as *Adventure in Iraq*, directed by D. Ross Lederman (1943) and the serial *Secret Service in Darkest Africa* (1943), Arabs were portrayed as malignant Nazi collaborators (an image that would become much more common decades later, after the OPEC crisis, in films such as *Raiders of the Lost Ark*). The representation of the Arab in these films of the 1940s, however, is outside the norm of mainstream U.S. cinema of the war years and owes as much to genre as to filmmakers' desire to create horror by reversing the usual interpretation of Arabs as friendly.

The relationship of film to the representation of reality was a topic of considerable concern for wartime journalists and became an occasion for speculating about the problems of representation. "What we saw of the Sahara didn't look exactly the way it does in the movies," Ernie Pyle wrote after taking "a sortie far into the Sahara, just to find out what it would be like." Pyle was generally disappointed by what he found, save once, when he went "where the yellow sand was drifted movielike in great rippled dunes" (191–92). For Pyle, the desert was a disappointment because it could offer "nothing more spectacular than the country in the more remote parts of our own Southwest." Pyle cannot be blamed for seeing American landscapes when he looked at the Sahara. His imagination was framed by American culture more than he knew (or let on). Those popular Hollywood films of the 1920s and 1930s had been filmed in the California desert, most often in the "sand hills" of Imperial County.[46] When an audience watched *The Sheik* or *Morocco* or *The Garden of Allah*, they looked at depictions of actors strolling through the dunes of Imperial County's Buttercup Valley. When we consider that the same patches of California desert had been used in the filming of Westerns, the portrait becomes completely self-referential, bound within a Hollywood version of "West" and "East" where each can stand in for the other. Feeling at home in the desert leads only at first blush to a feeling of comfort. Ultimately, the "similarity" of the Sahara and the American landscape reminds Pyle of just how far he and the GIs have traveled from home. But he imagines that distance through precisely the matrix that Luce had described. For Pyle and his huge audience, the Maghreb was "bound" in frames of American imagination.

A. J. Liebling, who covered the North African campaign for the *New Yorker*, noticed his own impulse to explain North Africa by reference to locations in the American Southwest. Liebling decided that the urge to compare North Africa to landscapes in the United States was a response to the "normal confusion" of combat. In trying to theorize the confusion, Liebling approached his subject differently from Pyle. If Pyle took an anticosmopolitan worm's-eye view, Liebling made references to opera, literature, and architecture, dropped French phrases into his prose, and did not hide his Francophilia: "It never occurred to me that [Hitler] might destroy France, because it would have been as hard for me to prefigure a world without France as survival with one lobe of my brain gone. France represented for me the historical continuity of intelligence and reasonable living. . . . nothing anywhere can have meaning until it is re-established."[47] The Francophilia may have led him to turn away from a vigorous investigation of French colonialism in North Africa, but he did not otherwise fail to discuss history comparatively. In any case, if Liebling's references suited the readership of the *New Yorker* under editor Harold Ross, and Pyle's syndicated Scripps-Howard columns targeted a more middlebrow audience, they agreed that North Africa looked like the American Southwest. Writing about Tunisia, in the company of AP correspondent "Boots" Norgaard, Liebling comments:

> Norgaard often said that southern Tunisia reminded him of New Mexico, and with plenty of reason. Both are desert countries of mountains and mesas, and in both there are sunsets that owe their beauty to the dust in the air. The white, rectangular Arab houses, with their blue doors, are like the houses certain Indians build in New Mexico, and the Arabs' saddle blankets and pottery and even the women's silver bracelets are like Navajo things. The horses, which look like famished mustangs, have the same lope and are similarly bridlewise; burros are all over the place, and so is cactus. These resemblances are something less than a coincidence, because the Moors carried their ways of house-building and their handicraft patterns and even their breed of horses and method of breaking them to Spain, and the Spaniards carried them to New Mexico eight hundred years later. All these things go to make up a culture that belongs to a high plateau country where there are sheep to furnish wool for blankets and where people have too little cash to buy dishes in a store, where the soil is so poor that people have no use for heavy plow horses but want a breed that they can ride for long distances and that will live on nearly nothing. (260)

Liebling's elaborate parallel asserts a relationship between "Moor" and "Indian." Without going so far as to claim a North African ancestry for the Navajos, Liebling as surely traces a cultural genealogy for "Navajo things." The logic is compelling: "Moors" carry cultural artifacts to Spain, and the Spanish carry these things to New Mexico. What Liebling leaves out, of course, is that such artifacts were the carry-on baggage of imperialism, the engine that launched these migrations. His is a sophisticated portrayal of global circulation that nonetheless leaves out global politics. To be critical of Spanish occupation of the Southwest in the past would be to wonder about French and U.S. occupation of North Africa in the present. Liebling instead suggests environmental causation for similarities in architecture, decoration, and landscape (both are "high plateau country" with poor soil).

Despite this account of the Maghrebi ancestry of American Indian culture, Liebling frequently found himself imagining that he was in the less specific space of the movies: "I strolled around the post to see what it was like. As the sun rose higher, the air grew warm and the great, reddish mountains looked friendly. Some of them had table tops, and the landscape reminded me of Western movies in Technicolor" (243). Liebling, himself, was curious about the mental slippage that could move from Moorish Spain to the latest Hollywood technologies. After the war, as Liebling gathered his war correspondence for republication, he added a footnote to this passage: "This use of the familiar false as touchstone of the unfamiliar real recurred often both in writing and conversation during World War II. 'Just like a movie!' was a standard reaction. It assured the speaker of the authenticity of what he had just experienced."[48] "Authenticity" here names something outside the realm of the real or the false; it is Liebling's own attempt to deliver a journalistic truth in a place and time where truth was difficult to find. If Liebling and Pyle and the GIs they were writing about knew that they were not in a Western movie, to imagine that they were made their own confusing experience more comprehensible. To comprehend, in Liebling's construction, is to make one's experience authentic. To be confused during war suggested not knowing where one was, and, by extension, what one was doing in North Africa. Liebling spent time after the war footnoting such incidences in his war correspondence. Confusion was normal in combat, Liebling argued, and so was the desire to authenticate one's position by offering a "familiar false." To embrace the "unfamiliar real" would mean to admit that this land had no place in an American epistemology. That would be impossible if long months were to be endured.

Still, Liebling needs to be reassured that Hollywood is the right referent. He goes out asking: "I got talking to a soldier named Bill Phelps, who came from the town of Twenty-nine Palms, California. He was working on a bomber that had something the matter with its insides. He confirmed my notion that the country looked like the American West. 'This is exactly the way it is around home,' he said, 'only we got no Ayrabs.'"[49] For Liebling, *West* and *Western* are interchangeable. Phelps's comment both confirms Liebling's point and suggests that which doesn't fit. The identification of the "Ayrabs" as the crucial difference—as both exception and embellishment—is key to the various manipulations I have been discussing and where we now turn. "Ayrab" represents a possibility of disruption that had the potential to upset the entire picture. In what follows, I show how that potentiality was managed and disempowered in mainstream journalism and film and then try to summon some of the suppressed energies of the "Ayrab" to disrupt American century accounts of the North African campaign.

The End of the Beginning of a Beautiful Friendship

As the war moved from North Africa into Italy, some journalists tried to account for the role the native population had played. A July 1943 piece in the Algiers edition of the Army newspaper *Stars and Stripes* gave them their moment: "The ubiquitous Arab made the North African campaign different from any the American Army has ever undertaken in the past or is likely to undertake in the future. The Arab gave the operations their only truly African flavor. Without him to clutter up the landscape North Africa might well have been mistaken for a dozen other coast lines." The Arab provided the Americans with the flavor of difference, the exception to the rule that all coastlines are the same when under military occupation. The native population could be made to disappear when having an uncluttered landscape suited narrative goals. But, when the patina of difference could contribute, they were always available to come back and "clutter up the landscape" again:

> If the Arab was often a pest and pretty generally a nuisance, he nevertheless was indispensable. He shined our shoes, sold us oranges, delivered eggs to our front lines right through enemy fire, and continually reminded us what blessings we had in the form of chewing gum, chocolate, and cigarettes. Above all he provided the American soldier with plenty of jokes. . . . Actually the Arab was a spectator rather than a participant in last winter's grim business. You can chalk that spectator attitude up to history, of which he has seen quite a lot. He used to be a fighting man himself, but that was a long while ago, when the zeal of the Prophet Mohammed's followers expressed itself in a continuous brandishing of the sword. Since that time he has learned to wage his campaigns with oranges, eggs, dates, almonds, and shoeshine boxes rather than with hand grenades and howitzers. The North

African Arab hasn't been intimately mixed up in a first-class war for centuries now, having been by and large content to let the other men of other
races do the squabbling. . . . it's a fair assumption that he has developed by
this time what could be called a neutral attitude.[50]

For the official Army newspaper, the native population was at once
peripheral and ubiquitous, a bit role perhaps but one that held the drama
together. In order to make the claim that the native was spectator rather
than participant, the Army's writer cancels any larger historical significance for North Africa. The "Arab" can be a backdrop to the war only by
being understood as "neutral," like a tolerant house slave. Thus the gross
historical error—that Maghrebis had not fought for "centuries"—obliter-
ates recent resistance to French colonialism (such as the Rif War in
Morocco in the 1920s, or the clashes between Moroccans and French in
1936–37).[51] The struggle against colonialism is forgotten in order to make
World War II a "first-class" war. In so doing, the challenge North Africans embodied—particularly the alliance with French colonialism and
racial crises at home—were marginalized. Pushed to the side, North Africans wouldn't remind anyone that the campaign itself reinscribed the
imperialism and racism that it nominally opposed.

Frequent references to Arabs as "nuisances" suggest an awareness of the
problem of too much Arab visibility. "To most American soldiers the
native is a tricky, thieving 'gook'—a nuisance best brushed off with an
'allez, scram!' and a gesture of menace," wrote Kenneth Crawford. "Many
soldiers told me that Uncle Sam was making a patsy of himself by reim-
bursing the natives for property damage and safeguarding their food sup-
ply."[52] Exploring the hotels of Casablanca, Crawford, like so many other
Americans, imagined that he was in America: "Except for the *bidet* in the
corner of every room it might have been the leading hotel of Ashtabula,
Ohio, temporarily occupied by men in uniform. The only false note was a
grinning, jet black elevator operator and handy man in pantaloons and
fez. His name being Abdul, he was inevitably called Eight Ball." This
Casablanca Abdul, like the Abdul in the film *Casablanca* we will encounter shortly, is a "false note," an eight ball whom no one wants to get
behind. He is the exceptional difference that marks the picture.

The racial undertone of these passages is striking. Whether it's references to shoeshine boys, or Crawford's imagery, the Maghrebis here are
not passive Indians, as they were in the work of Pyle and Liebling, but

servile Africans, temporally retarded, with little claim to historical immediacy. Thus the moment of regard, of attention to the native population
outside the sheltering screen of the frontier myth, is precisely the moment
when North African and African American claims to immediate freedom
and equality are implicitly disavowed. This is achieved both rhetorically
and by perpetrating historical error. To say that Maghrebis were specta-
tors and not participants ignored the participation of the Moroccan
Goumiers who fought during the campaign and then alongside American
GIs in Italy. The Goums, as they were known, did play a part in the
imaginary of many soldiers during the war. According to Edward Bimberg, who fought alongside them in Corsica in 1943, the Goumiers had a
reputation for savagery. The Goums were a "paramilitary police" formed
by the French "to maintain order among the fiercely independent tribes of
their own regions."[53] Their uniform was what struck most American
observers: distinguished by a striped djellaba, turban, sandals, and outfit-
ted with both French bayoneted rifles and the native *koumia* (a long
knife). As the Americans approached Casablanca for Operation Torch,
rumors circulated that the Goums (who fought on behalf of the French)
were fierce warriors waiting for the Americans. (They were in fact not
involved in the November 1942 conflict.) During World War II, several
Groupes de Supplétifs Marocains—each of about 1,500 men—were as-
sembled for the Allied cause. Many thousands of Maghrebis were indeed
active participants in the war.

Other Maghrebis did not stand by silently as the Americans occupied
their lands, though their testimony did not register in American accounts
at the time. Fatima Mernissi, in a recent memoir, notes the comments of
Moroccan women in Fez about the Americans during the early 1940s:
"The other intriguing thing about the Americans was that they had
blacks among them, and this surprised everyone." Mernissi, then a child,
had been told that blacks come from Sudan. She is told that these Americans are the descendants of slaves. But then a further mystery presents
itself, the retelling of which she offers as a potent critique:

> We could not figure out why, unlike the Arabs, white and black Americans
> did not mix and become just brown skinned, which was what usually hap-
> pened when a population of whites and blacks lived together. "Why are the
> American whites still so white," asked Mina, "and the blacks so black? Do
> they not intermarry?" . . . it turned out that indeed, Americans did not

intermarry. Instead, they kept the races separate. Their cities were divided into two medinas, one for the blacks and one for the whites, like we had in Fez for the Muslims and the Jews. We had a good laugh about that on the terrace, because anyone who wanted to separate people according to their skin color in Morocco was going to run into severe difficulties.[54]

Mernissi suggests that racial segregation in America is, after all, like the segregation of the sexes in her family's harem, and like the separation of Muslims and Jews in greater Fez. She makes the comparison fully aware that American observers of the Arab world use Muslim claustration of women and attitudes toward Jews as touchstones for civilizational critique. (Her own work offers a feminist, Muslim critique of her own society that resists Western models for that critique and often turns those models on their heads.)[55] The ways in which Mernissi plays on American self-mythology, so powerfully imported to the Maghreb in 1942, will be played out below in the variety of Moroccan responses to *Casablanca*.

Mernissi's comments were circulated decades later, but Maghrebis responded to the American occupation immediately, some publicly. In the wake of the American landings, Houcine Slaoui (1918–51), a Moroccan folksinger, sang mordantly "zin u l'ain az-zarqa jana bkul khir," or "The beautiful blue-eyed one brought us all good things." Slaoui's song "Al Mirikan" (The Americans), written and performed shortly after the 1942 landings, is an anthem of the era, with lyrics known to Moroccans born long after the war. With references to "shwing" (i.e., chewing gum) and cosmetics polluting Moroccan culture, the song stands as a rejoinder to accounts of the seamlessness of the entry of American soldiers. Slaoui incorporates American language into his lyrics—"OK, OK, come on, bye-bye" is the song's refrain—highlighting the interruption of American words within the Moroccan cultural landscape. But he also remakes those American words into Moroccan ones by his pronunciation (the refrain is not immediately understandable to a non–Arabic speaking listener) and by having them repeated by a high-pitched chorus of Berber women, familiar within music of the Middle Atlas. Despite his fame, Slaoui's voice goes unheard within American accounts of the North African campaign.[56] If Maghrebi texts such as these might have offered points of affiliation for African Americans at the time, they were out of American circulation. Journalistic and Hollywood representations of the war sidestepped the possibility of alliances between two populations struggling for equality.

Positionless Positions: *Sahara*

Hollywood films that based their moral rightness on the depiction of Nazis as racist Aryan supremacists confronted a problem: how to screen out the audience's awareness of American racial discrimination at home. During 1943, it was difficult to ignore the signs that the United States was hardly the land of the free for members of minority groups. In that year, protests against racist housing laws sparked riots in Detroit, while in Harlem, black residents clashed with police over persistent discrimination. On the West Coast, Americans of Japanese origins and ancestry began to be relocated to internment camps before the dust had cleared over Pearl Harbor, a shocking decision that was nonetheless supported widely in California. In Los Angeles, police arrested Mexican American youths indiscriminately based on an unapologetic policy of racial profiling, leading to the "zoot suit" riots. Meanwhile, Hollywood turned out films that perpetuated racist thinking. The *Daily Worker* and the Negro press campaigned against MGM's 1943 film *Tennessee Johnson*, a film biography of Andrew Johnson that was compared to *The Birth of a Nation* for its pro–Jim Crow message.[57] And combat films such as *Bataan* (1943) regularly represented the Japanese enemy as monkeylike, borrowing slurs used to denigrate African Americans, thereby simultaneously dehumanizing the Japanese and reinscribing the dehumanization of American blacks.[58]

Such was the climate at the time of release of the most famous of Hollywood wartime films set in North Africa—*Casablanca* and *Sahara*—two films that took the desert as a template on which to remap American identity. *Sahara* and *Casablanca* explored what we might call the problem of national location. Both anchored their fictions in recent military events, while fictionalizing the desert campaign. These films addressed the difficulty journalists expressed of making a confusing war comprehensible by attempting to make sense of Americanness in the desert. At the same time, as films set in Africa, their vision of Americanness (as white, masculine, and symbolized by Humphrey Bogart) played itself off of Hollywood's conception of Africans, highlighting tensions in the definition of American identity as based in whiteness. Further, by confusing Africa with African Americans, Hollywood filmmakers shifted their attention away from the native population of North Africa and contributed

mightily to the failure for Americans to recognize that the war to free
the world from fascism and imperialist aggression was fought while the
United States allied itself with French colonialism. This structured the
turn away from an alliance, or point of commonality, that mattered to
the Negro and leftist press.

If North Africa was the setting and inspiration for these films, they
were of course detached from the specificity of the North African landscape. Filmed in California with little attention to the geography and
architecture of Casablanca or Libya, both confidently remap North Africa as they plot their vision of Americanness onto the cleared space.
Indeed, the fact that both films revolve around actual maps—*Casablanca*
begins with one, and the characters of *Sahara* are betrayed by one—
suggests the filmmakers' anxiety about the substitution of their invented
North Africa for the "real" one. The films invoke literal maps only to
discard them, in turn reinscribing America on what become imagined as
arbitrary desert positions.

In both films, the protagonist played by Humphrey Bogart is placed in
a triangular relationship with a European military officer and an African
scout or African American sidekick. These triangles (which are mirrored
in both films by secondary triangles involving a character or object identified as female—Ilsa, played by Ingrid Bergman, in *Casablanca*, and in
Sahara the tank named "Lulubelle," referred to as a "dame"—and tertiary
triangles of the representative American, the Allied soldier, and the enemy) are plotted over and against the unplottable and shifting desert in
which the dramas occur. The geometry of the various triangles in these
films places a patina of certainty over the uncertainty of war and American war aims. Thus, the strategies of representing both the confusion of
combat and the unmappable desert sands *overlap* the representation of
Americanness. In these films, mapping Americanness cannot exist without mapping the desert: the desert is made comprehensible by being made
American. But if the desert is understood as a tabula rasa, a Cartesian
plane, Americanness is located on a point—or in the vocabulary of war, a
"position"—revealed as arbitrary.

In both films, Humphrey Bogart's character learns to take a stand. Yet
he positions himself and his politics of commitment in a necessarily unstable location: the shifting sands of the desert. These aggressively patriotic films base their vision of Americanness on that loose foundation.
Casablanca employs an exaggerated depiction of unpredictable French-

ness (emblematized by Captain Renault, played by Claude Rains) as a counterpoint against which to assert a portrait of reliable Americanness. While Renault shifts with the political winds (supporting the Germans while patronizing Rick's Café Américain, then switching his allegiances to the Allied side), Rick is more stable. Rick's steady progress toward political commitment is contrasted to Renault's vacillation between extremes. Yet in proffering this contrast, the film distracts attention from the instability of its depiction of Americanness. Rick's Café Américain is, after all, a casino, a place where the roulette wheel has been fixed to allow Captain Renault to win, and a place where hypocrisy is acknowledged to be part of the game—Renault shuts Rick down stating that he's "shocked, *shocked* to find that gambling is going on in here," then collects his winnings from a smirking Rick. And in *Sahara*, Sergeant Joe Gunn's lost battalion fights the Nazis for and from a desert position that is both arbitrary and without value (a dried-up well). Both places are "oases," at least in metaphor, and both oases define America's role in the war. The arbitrariness of the "positions" must be pushed to the background for these films to have their power in the struggle for the elusive "war effort."

Zoltan Korda's *Sahara*, released in November 1943, depicts the history of a fictional survivor of the devastating Battle of Tobruk. Sergeant Joe Gunn (Bogart) has been cast away from his battalion. Surrounded on all sides by German forces, Gunn is ordered by radio to retreat south into the desert. On their way south, Gunn and two other American survivors encounter a group of three British soldiers, a white South African, and an Irishman, all led by a Captain Halliday (Richard Nugent), plus a Frenchman. The group is stranded and decides to join the Americans, all now under Gunn's command. With no map and little sense of direction, the battalion resembles the "lost patrol" of the 1934 film by the same name, its uncredited source.[59] With the same morbid cynicism of John Ford's film, the members of the detachment worry that they will die in the desert: "Supposing we get stuck in this graveyard without any water?" Gunn's map shows a series of wells, which they head off to find.

Further south, they encounter a soldier in the uniform of the British Sudanese battalion named Sergeant Tambul (Rex Ingram), accompanied by an Italian prisoner. A brief interview reveals that Tambul will be a valuable resource—a scout. Although the inclusion of Tambul was considered a boon for race relations, the assumptions made about the African character (played by an African American actor) are revealing. Tambul is assumed to "know" the desert, although he is purportedly from Sudan, a thousand miles south of Tobruk. Although Tambul's prisoner hails from a country closer to the action of the film, both geographically and politically (Libya was an Italian colony), Tambul's dark skin makes him the likely candidate for a knowledge of this place. By mapping Tambul as African (and thereby representative of *all* of Africa, with access to the entire continent), the blank desert is made less blank for the soldiers and for the film's audience. By including Tambul, *Sahara* breaks from *The Lost Patrol*, in which a group of soldiers wanders aimlessly through the desert with no maps or "native" guides.[60] *Sahara* thereby adopts the formula of a Hollywood Western. The soldiers become a group of cowboys to Tambul's Indian scout, trading tales of women left at home while allowing Tambul to do an unfair share of the manual labor. Gunn's tank "Lulu-belle" is the trusted and doted-on horse of a cowboy tale; indeed, we are told that Gunn named his tank after a horse he had when in the cavalry.

When the detachment shoots down a Nazi pilot, Tambul's dual role as African character and African American actor becomes still more complicated. Gunn orders Tambul to search the Nazi (played by Kurt Kreuger, whose blond hair and tall stature make him appear the paradigmatic Aryan *Übermensch*). The Nazi balks, complaining that he does not want to be "touched by an inferior race." Gunn snaps back: "Tell him not to worry about it being black. It won't come off on his pretty uniform." But Gunn's rebuke sounds like reassurance: Tambul can safely be admitted to this multinational platoon without the fear that his blackness will come off. Tambul is both a member of the detachment and detached from it. The choice to cast an African American actor in the role of an African conflates the portrayal of Tambul as "natural" with the person of Ingram himself. In the context of the segregation of African American troops during the war, the film reveals related suppositions about African Americans—that they are closer to the native Africa and should thus be kept further from white Americans so that their blackness doesn't come off on the uniform.

Still, the inclusion of Tambul was lauded by liberal voices in America. Walter White, a syndicated columnist and ranking member of the NAACP, praised the film for its "progress" in representing black characters. Contemporary film studies have agreed. In *Making Movies Black*, Thomas Cripps states: "It is *his* desert and only he knows how to find water, abandoned forts, and old caravan trails—the lore that Europeans cannot know."[61] Such comments reify the film's portrait of Tambul as closer to nature, which in the film itself justifies the delegation of menial tasks to him. For Clayton Koppes, Tambul's role is "heroic" and demonstrates that combat films offered more possibilities than films set in the United States: "African-American figures' best chance to bend the bars of the cage of unity occurred in combat pictures, where Hollywood gave blacks more equality than the war or navy departments were prepared to consider."[62] *Sahara*'s screenwriter, John Howard Lawson, a member of the Communist Party of the United States of America is credited with the progressive portrayal. Without disputing the progressive step, the portrayal of Tambul should not be whitewashed. When *Sahara* was released, Rex Ingram was known primarily for his portrayal of Jim in the 1939 film version of *The Adventures of Huckleberry Finn*. Ingram had then played the genie in the successful 1940 remake of *The Thief of Baghdad*, on which Zoltan Korda had collaborated. His role in *Sahara* neatly combined the two: half genie in a bottle, half plantation slave. Thus, when the detachment finally comes across a nearly dry well, it is Tambul who is lowered into the pit to rescue the remaining drops of water for the group—if there is water, he can work to collect it; if there is none, he can conjure it up. As a series of tin cans is dropped to Tambul, he fills them, lapping up his own share from the moisture left on his hands while the other men drink out of cups.[63] Now he resembles Jim more than the genie, taking on another plantation role: that of a wet nurse, the "mammy" figure, to the white men. If Tambul nourishes the other soldiers with a moisture associated with his own body, he is kept at a remove from them down in the well. The uniqueness of Tambul's position is reflected in Gunn's exclusion of him from the detachment's democratic values. Gunn orders the men to each take "three swallows" of water. After the Allies get their share, Gunn orders first the Italian, then the Nazi, to be given water. The others object. Gunn responds, "Everybody gets three swallows." Gunn is a democratic hero, following military rules of fair play even when the Nazi is deceitful. Yet Tambul is excluded from the ritual, getting his water from the residue on his own hands. He abides by different rules.

Later, a moment of friendship transpires between Tambul and a soldier from Texas named Waco (Bruce Bennett). Waco lowers himself into the well and offers to relieve Tambul. Tambul refuses, and Waco offers him a cigarette. Waco soon reveals a prurient curiosity about Islam. He mentions that he's married: "The boys up top were telling me you Mohammedans have as many as 300 wives." Tambul sets him straight: "No. The Prophet tells that four wives are sufficient for a true believer."

> Tambul: The Prophet says one wife makes a miserable life, for she always get boring. And two wives make a mess of your life also, for they always quarrel and you never know which one is right. And three wives are bad too, for two always take sides against the third. But four wives makes real happiness.
>
> Waco: How?
>
> Tambul: Two and two are company for each other, and the man, he has rest.
>
> Waco: That sounds all right. You got four, huh?
>
> Tambul: No, I have only one.
>
> Waco: What's holding you back?
>
> Tambul: Well, if you had this law in your Texas, would you have four wives?
>
> Waco: No. My wife wouldn't like that.
>
> Tambul: It is the same with me. My wife, she would not like it.
>
> Waco: You sure learn things in the Army.
>
> Tambul: Yes, we both have much to learn from each other.

Waco's questions cannot help but refer to his sense of gender relations in America. He describes a desire to return to his new wife "when this is finished." The association of the war abroad and the maintenance of domestic arrangements was paradigmatic among GIs, as Robert Westbrook has argued.[64] Waco's comment "you sure learn things in the Army," then, is a hint that American ideas about race and gender could fill in the blanks when imagining North African reality. What Waco "learns" and what the film teaches is that the tyranny of women is universal: both men's wives "wouldn't like that" and keep their husbands from what they would otherwise desire. Waco learns that American law is based on what *Sahara* suggests is a universal truth: that women are jealous of other women and want to have unique access to their husbands. Thus, American law and the "natural" law of monogamy are one, and by extension Islamic law is unnatural.[65] The film suggests that it is Tambul—the natural African at one with the desert—who can learn from America.

The Café Américain: *Casablanca*

Henry Luce's essay "The American Century" is built around an imagined temporal lag. Central to the rhetorical power of the essay is the way the spatial remove of other parts of the globe is figured as temporal—the *century* has a nationality placed on it. In context, this is productive for Luce's argument against those who would avoid entry into the war. That time lag is repeated in Luce's naming of the entire century some four decades in, an act that reaches backward temporally, just as his adjective reaches outward geographically. The temporal and special manipulation of Luce's gesture—linking the power of Luce's institutional and economic base and his rhetoric—is the tactic by which he succeeds in promulgating his terminology and its logic. The time lag is Luce's space-clearing gesture.[66] And as a critical tactic, the interruption of the logic of "The American Century" as it permeates outward through so much U.S. rhetoric about and cultural representations of the international space requires unhinging the easy assumption of American temporality as perquisite of global supremacy. As I discussed above, Luce understands the manipulation of space via an American time to be effected in part by American "imagination." For Luce, this is the work of American cultural production.

The time lag of geographic manipulation is central to *Casablanca*, a major text of "the American century," one that might be said to enact it. When Rick asks, "Sam, if it's December 1941 in Casablanca, what time is it in New York?" the time lag of the question, like that in Luce's "American century," is mobilized as an argument for American engagement and internationalism. The explicit point of Rick's rhetorical question is that in retreating to Casablanca—a place imagined here as existing in a different temporal register—he had meant to leave behind the world ("Of all the gin joints in all the towns in all the world, she walks into mine," he will say a couple of lines later). And yet in naming a specific and charged moment (December 1941, the month of the Pearl Harbor bombings, roughly a year before the film's release) and given the widely noted political parable of the film, the implicit point of Rick's loaded question is that Americans abroad, such as Rick, know already before the Pearl Harbor bombings that the United States can no longer afford to be on a different time zone from the rest of the world—"I bet they're asleep in New York. I bet they're asleep all over America," Rick answers his own question—and must engage immediately in the global conflict. But Rick's question also suggests that Pearl Harbor will reorganize U.S. participation in the war and the world and reorient the center of both to an American time frame. It will be an American century, in Luce's sense.

Sam's response to Rick's question, "My watch stopped," suggests the conservative racial politics of this hypercanonical film, a film that mas-

querades as liberal.[67] In this context, Sam's line provides a vivid representation of what Michael Hanchard has called "racial time," namely "the
inequalities of temporality that result from power relations between racially dominant and subordinate groups." Hanchard argues that racial
time has operated as a "structural effect upon the politics of racial difference" and is one of the ways that racial difference, which has an elusive
materiality, neither reified and static nor mere social construct, has material effects on individual and group interaction.[68] Sam's trademark song
"As Time Goes By" invokes the "fundamental things" against the "speed
and new invention" of the present; as Sam repeats the song on demand
"again" and again, both the lyrics and the repetition further identify him
with temporal stagnation.[69] Here, performing at the center of Rick's Café
Américain, the expression of racial time silently places Sam in the imagined temporal register of those Moroccans who live in Casablanca, invisible within the film. This is the very same register Rick was seeking in his
flight to Casablanca from a France associated with Ilsa—the subsequent
scene will be a Paris flashback sequence ending with Rick (and Sam)
abandoned by Ilsa at the train station under a big clock. If Rick expected
or hoped that Casablanca would remain on a different temporal register,
however, both the "world" and Ilsa have found him. But the script of
Casablanca will not permit Sam to move temporally, and he remains on
the old Casablanca time.[70]

The complex yet readily apparent ways in which *Casablanca* brackets or
suppresses concerns of gender and race—Ilsa's infamous willingness to
allow Rick to think for the two of them and Sam's participation in what
can only be called the film's slave economy via the subplot of whether or
not he'll consent to work at the Blue Parrot for Signor Ferrari (Sydney
Greenstreet) for double the pay—are a way of distracting viewers from a
more potent possibility repressed by the film: that Sam, as a racialized
subject of U.S. colonialism, might enter into a conversation with the
colonized Moroccan subjects who are relegated to the film's background.
The potential for such a diasporic confederation of African American and
North African haunts *Casablanca* and emerges even while it is apparently
suppressed by the time lag of Rick's question and the racial time of Sam's
response. As Hollywood historian Robert Ray suggests, "The genuine
threats posed by World War II to traditional American ideologies surface
only in the cracks of films consciously intended to minimize them" (31).
Casablanca barely acknowledges the presence of Moroccans in its own

Casablanca: playing it again and again at the center of the Café Américain.
Courtesy of the Wisconsin Center for Film and Theater Research

depiction of Morocco. To do so would have challenged the French phrase
"Liberté, Egalité, Fraternité," one of the movie's opening images. Seeing
the invisible Moroccans in *Casablanca* opens a crack in the film.

Like *Sahara*, *Casablanca* plays on the importance of memory in the
desert and replots Americanness. When Claude Rains hears Bogart's
Rick say he came to Casablanca "for the waters," he blurts out, "What
waters? We're in the desert." "I was misinformed," says Rick. But the
misinformation is itself misinformation. Casablanca isn't in the middle of
a desert; it's a coastal city bracketed by beaches and farmland. Who knew?
After all, *Casablanca* figures the United States as both the end and center
of the world, the place of which refugees dream and the nationality of the
neutral Rick's Café Américain where they while away their time. Inserting
a new memory of a Casablanca that never was, Warner Brothers' *Casablanca* participated in the interpretation of the North African campaign
as a frontier tale. As Robert Ray has argued in one of the most extensive
critical discussions of the film, "*Casablanca* reincarnated in Rick and

Laszlo the outlaw hero-official hero opposition, and in doing so, summoned the entire frontier mythology to support its contemporary story of refugees fleeing the Nazis."[71] For Ray, *Casablanca*'s success is due to its ability to acknowledge the challenge to the "American ideal of separateness" that the war posed and to find a way to overcome this challenge through narrative. *Casablanca* summons the frontier mythos (outlaw hero versus official hero) and then moves from an "abstract issue" (U.S. intervention) to a "particular melodrama" (the Rick-Ilsa-Laszlo triangle). Ray shows how the film foregrounds Rick as an outlaw hero and relegates Laszlo to the periphery in its very framing. He notes the crowding of Laszlo to the edge of frames, the lack of close-ups of Laszlo, and that Laszlo shares most shots with others (89–104).

But we should not be distracted from the portrayal of Sam, the African American pianist played by Dooley Wilson who is so central to Rick's story. In an important critique, Robert Gooding-Williams has taken earlier critics to task for emphasizing the Rick-Ilsa-Laszlo triangle over the others he identifies and participating in the conservative recoding of racial difference enacted by the film. Contesting those who champion *Casablanca*'s liberalism, he argues that the " 'liberal' turn away from racial stereotypes involves a complicated reassertion of racial subordination."[72] Gooding-Williams writes that Sam occupies the role of cupid in the relationship between Rick and Ilsa, wherein he is both the "producer of erotic value" and the "tie to a sexuality that belongs to others." While Ray sees Rick created as charismatic hero through the camera's framing, Gooding-Williams argues that through Sam Rick is shown to be more charismatic than Laszlo. This importance comes at the expense of a replication of stereotypes equating blackness with sexuality and refuses Sam his own sexual relationship.

Sam is central to two more important triangles. First, he is at the center of a business relationship between Rick and Ferrari. As in *Sahara*, Bogart plays an uncomfortable race hero: "I don't buy or sell human beings," Rick tells Ferrari, while keeping him as "a black servant who devotedly sings his master's love song," as Gooding-Williams describes it (206). Finally, there is an erotically charged political triangle involving Rick, Renault, and the Nazi Strasser, in which Renault moves from Vichy loyalties to an allegiance with Rick. The homoerotics of Renault's relationship to Rick—"If I were a woman . . . I should be in love with Rick"—are key to their pairing off. By the film's end, these four triangles have been resolved into three couples (Ilsa-Laszlo, Sam-Ferrari, and Rick-Renault), reinscribing a conservative set of values. Ilsa and Laszlo are reunited; Ferrari does get to "buy" Sam; and Rick walks off with a French collaborator.[73]

At the center of every triangle is Rick, whose Café Américain is the focal point. Like the dry well in *Sahara*, it is an ambiguous center, just as Rick is an ambiguous character with a mysterious past. But Rick is nonetheless established *as* the center. As American audiences are taught to identify with him, *Casablanca* also teaches them to see North Africa as Rick sees it: to relegate the native colonized population to the background. To wonder where the Moroccans are in *Casablanca* might seem beside the point to an American audience (though not to a Moroccan one). But that is precisely the question we must ask of the film.

In *Casablanca*, the writing, casting, and the camera itself teach audiences not to pay attention to the Moroccan population. The first point is that there are so few Moroccan characters. But even when they are there, the camera's manipulation of point-of-view perspective makes certain that the audience never takes the Moroccan's side. The famous opening sequence at Rick's café offers a wonderful case in point. The scene, which introduces the audience to Rick, allows the camera itself to wander the room of the Café Américain, establishing Rick's point of view as central, and subtly constructs a relationship between American and Moroccan. Robert Ray has examined the film language of this opening scene in detail and does a frame analysis of the sequence within which the audience sees through Rick's eyes. Within this sequence, Rick is called to the doorway of the café by his Moroccan doorman (played by Dan Seymour). Abdul, the name given to the doorman, wears a Fez cap, vest, and poofy pantaloons. The scene establishes Rick as center and also establishes the dynamic of the Café Américain during the war. Abdul summons Rick to enforce his refusal of entry to a German. There is a brief visual triangulation of the relationship between Rick, Abdul, and the German, symbolically suggestive of the desert war itself. In reinscribing the American as center while refusing to take Abdul's point of view, the camera structures the lack of attention to North African issues at the center of U.S. policy. Ray shows how "the point-of-view manipulations encourage identification with the protagonist Rick, but not with the inconsequential doorman." Abdul is inconsequential to the story, as the screenplay leaves him at the doorway. And the camera reinscribes that insignificance. Indeed, Abdul is paradigmatic of the American representation of Maghrebis throughout the North African campaign. Abdul opens the door for Americans to make Casablanca a playground or a battlefield, as the case may be; his loyalty to the Allied cause is assumed.

The marginalization of Abdul, then, is similar to the racial recoding of Sam. Neither the African American character nor the North African character is granted a perspective of his own. Each is isolated from the other. Although both are subservient to Rick, *Casablanca* never suggests any similarities between Sam and Abdul, placing them both in the temporal lag of racial time, a temporality within which they cannot join in an alliance. The film itself teaches us not to pay attention to such trivialities. Indeed, Warner Brothers justified *Casablanca* to the Office of War Information by arguing that it promoted "international understanding" by representing characters of different European nationalities. Warner Brothers also pointed to the inclusion of Moroccan characters who "appear in the background in numerous scenes."[74] In keeping the Moroccans in the background, Warner Brothers made certain that the types of critiques published in the *Negro Quarterly* and *Chicago Defender* in 1942 and 1943 remained peripheral to the wider understanding of the situation in colonial North Africa.

Casablanca is the paradigmatic example of "American Orientalism." As a fiction, it diverts its audience's attention away from a critique of its politics. As a product of 1942, presented just days after the U.S. Army had landed at Casablanca, it borrows its authority from the political and military authority gained via Operation Torch. As such, the release of the film—which depicts the transfer of narrative authority from France to America—is a key turning point in the cultural history of Western representations of the Maghreb. As Rick and Renault walk into the distance, they utter the line that everyone knows, the new ending to a film that could not previously find its ending. "I think this is the beginning of a beautiful friendship," the American says to the Frenchman. Sam has been sold to Ferrari, and Abdul has long ago been left behind. General Patton has taken the city. At the dawn of decolonization, it is left to the representatives of two imperial powers to stroll into the sunset, secure in their knowledge of the fundamental things.

Following Casablanca

What would it mean to follow *Casablanca* to Casablanca? Before moving on in chapter 2 to a later moment in the 1940s, I want to interrupt my narrative with a postdisciplinary tactic. Though anyone who has been to Casablanca would recognize the 1942 film's ignorance of specificities of the place, reproductions of the film's poster grace cinemas and cafés across Morocco.[75] In the large hall of the Cinéma Renaissance, on the Avenue Mohammed V in the capital Rabat, one watches projected films through the parentheses of two giant wall paintings: a towering reproduction of the *Casablanca* poster on one wall and, on the facing wall, an image of the poster from von Sternberg's *Morocco*, another film shot entirely in California. Whatever the origin of the film being projected, the location of the cinema theater itself is marked as Moroccan, and Moroccan cinema might in turn seem to originate with these Hollywood inventions.[76] But rather than see the frequent reminders of *Casablanca* in Morocco as a culturally insecure search for external validation of a place in (cinema) history, further evidence of Hollywood's hegemony, we might see Moroccan representations of *Casablanca* as critical interruptions. References to *Casablanca* and *Morocco* allow Moroccan cultural producers to refer to the classic period of cinema—which corresponds to the height of French colonial control of Morocco (1912–56)—without reference to the French and their own representations of Morocco.[77] Hollywood representations of those years are obvious and distant fantasies and offer a less threatening site than the more elaborate and proximal French representations of Moroccan reality. Postcolonial Moroccan cultural production— francophone or arabophone—from the start is operating in a global context in which the United States is deeply present as a liberating alternative and, simultaneously, as a new form of domination. If after leaving the Cinéma Renaissance, you travel south on Mohammed V, passing Rue Patrice Lumumba, you'll eventually come to Avenue Franklin Roosevelt. America as liberator and America as cold war betrayer are both near at hand.[78]

Attending to Moroccan representations of *Casablanca* disrupts the operating liberal assumption within much of American cultural studies work that the export of U.S. cultural production, especially popular culture, is unidirectional, unchallenged, and fully legible. I will confine the remainder of this chapter to this particular critical interruption. I will not be suggesting that Moroccan recodings of *Casablanca* are acts of cultural resistance. Attention to the ways in which cultural forms circulate transnationally productively upsets a dichotomous and dichotomizing understanding of the relationship of culture to politics. Following *Casablanca* to Casablanca, *Casablanca* takes on and sheds a variety of meanings, sometimes standing as alternative to French representations of Morocco, thereby triangulating the references of postcolonial cultural production; sometimes as a synecdoche for American fantasies of the Maghreb (or Western fantasies in general); then again recoded as canonical film text in order to buttress a new vision of Moroccan contemporary society.

Those who live in Morocco and have any contact with the tourism industry—the largest or second-largest source of foreign income in the 1980s and 1990s—are well aware of the Western-created fantasies that most international tourists (at least those from Europe, the United States, Australia, New Zealand, and Japan) bring with them.[79] Rather than resist these stereotypes, the Moroccan tourism industry has generally adopted the strategy of performing the stereotypes and profiting off the performance.[80] By countless accounts in U.S. and European newspapers, business travelers and tourists from around the world come to Casablanca looking for *Casablanca*, only to be frustrated. Sometime in the mid-1980s, the Casablanca Hyatt Regency decided to profit from that frustration, opening "Bar Casablanca," a piano bar that loosely recreates the ambiance of the film and is decorated with film stills and poster reproductions from *Casablanca* and staffed by Moroccans wearing Bogartesque trenchcoats and fedoras or 1940s French colonial uniforms.[81] A piano player plays the obvious song on request. Not only does the bar profit from the foreign business travelers who come looking for Rick's Café Américain from the film, satisfying the need they have—and will satisfy nowhere else in the city—to find "the real" behind the fiction, but the staffing of the bar also interrupts, retroactively, and recodes the film itself. This is partially done by satirizing Warner Brothers' casting; here Moroccans play *all* the roles. If Moroccans play Bogart, they also play the roles of Renault and the French police; the pianist has been Lebanese, Egyptian, and African American, at various times and for various tenures. Bar Casablanca, in which the piano player is the focal point, doesn't let us forget the alliance of African American and North African. Here in Bar Casablanca the frequent repetition of the song "As Time Goes By," rather than serving as an example of postmodern timelessness and placelessness, is the Moroccan site's continual interruption of the song's meaning in the film, where it signified Sam's inability to dispense with racial time. It is made here newly dynamic.

Bar Casablanca relocates the site represented by *Casablanca* from a U.S. narrative imagined from afar to the geographically located, postcolonial Casablanca. This happens daily when tourists and visitors enter the bar and is further propagated by occasional travel articles in the foreign press and by foreign travel guidebooks. Occasionally, Bar Casablanca reaches out itself: in November 1992, fifty years after the film and Operation Torch landings, the Casablanca Hyatt held a large party, flying from London the winner of a trivia contest and further identifying itself as the "real" location of the film. The Moroccan tourism industry, which after the 1991 Gulf War dropped off precipitously and remained low for several years despite the fact that Moroccan troops joined the U.S.-led alliance against Iraq, itself knows that such identification is important. As Abderrahim Daoudi, Casablanca's then–director of tourism, said in 1992: "There's no similarity; the movie was filmed entirely in a studio. But it had an enormous impact. Every day, somewhere in the world, it's shown. . . . It's an excellent publicity ad."[82] A decade later, a Moroccan beer company latched onto the mystique with Casablanca Beer; its motto: "The legendary beer from the legendary city." Casa itself was not legendary before 1942; it is an elaborate French construction of the early twentieth century, as Gwendolyn Wright has shown, made "legendary" by the American film.[83] The Moroccan beer company invents a tradition by piggybacking on an American one.

If the bar at the Hyatt relocates *Casablanca* to Casablanca, the Moroccan interruption is yet more complex when 'Abd al-Qader Laqt'a brings Bar Casablanca into his feature-length film, *Al-Hubb fi al-Dar al-Baida* (*Love in Casablanca*). In an important scene, Laqt'a invokes the 1942 film and reorients it for his own purposes. His critical interruption of *Casablanca* reveals the ways in which a Moroccan director can disorient an American understanding of *Casablanca*. It is a major creative recoding of a major work of American culture, yet a film virtually unknown in the United States, including scholarly discussions of *Casablanca*. Yet Laqt'a is

ultimately not (primarily) interested in interrupting American understandings of the film. I'm not suggesting that Laqt'a doesn't have extra-
Moroccan aspirations. But in *Al-Hubb fi al-Dar al-Baida*, his first feature
length film, Laqt'a incorporates *Casablanca* within a film directed at a
Moroccan audience. His recoding is in the creative service of an argument
about contemporary Moroccan culture.

In the film, Seloua (Mouna Fettou) is a young woman caught between
two men. Trying to extricate herself from an affair with an older lover,
Jalil, she becomes involved with a young photographer, Najib. In a key
scene, Seloua and Najib enter the Bar Casablanca to have a drink. The
camera focuses on a poster from *Casablanca* on the wall, then pans down
to the couple. Najib asks Seloua if she's seen the film; Seloua says no.
Najib recounts the plot, but in a way that serves both Najib's purposes
and *Al-Hubb fi al-Dar al-Baida*'s concerns. "It's a bit old, from about the
fifties," Najib says, speaking in colloquial Moroccan Arabic, clearing space
for his own version of the American film via a temporal displacement,
relocating the film by a decade.[84] He's seen it in a ciné-club, he says, a
comment that naturalizes the fact of viewing the American film as something typically Moroccan. "It's the story of a woman who loves two men,"
Najib says. Seloua looks down, feeling the relevance of the plot to her own
situation. "She finds herself in a dilemma," Najib goes on, "whether to go
back to her husband or with her lover." Seloua, embarrassed and intrigued, suggests taking a closer look at the film stills mounted on the wall.
The camera lingers over the stills, then cuts back to a shot of the couple
approaching the stills, thus distinguishing its own relationship to *Casablanca* from that of the characters. *Casablanca* is being used doubly. That
Najib's synopsis of the film is idiosyncratic and revolves around his own
interests is confirmed by the stills, which include portraits of Humphrey
Bogart and Ingrid Bergman as Rick and Ilsa and representations of a
couple of other scenes, but not Paul Henreid as Victor Laszlo, Ilsa's
husband. "A shame," Najib says, turning the lack of a still of Laszlo to his
advantage, "that the husband isn't here." Seloua asks how the woman's
problem is resolved. "In the American cinema," Najib explains by way of
an answer, "the woman goes back to her husband, rather than follow her
lover. The cinema has to preserve traditions in order to avoid problems
with the censor." He steps away to ask the piano player to perform music
from the film, and Seloua regards the stills alone. As she focuses on a

headshot of Bogart, she hallucinates and sees an image of Jalil peering between the photos, as if reflected in the glass from behind her. Visually, Jalil's face overlaps Rick's, and the viewer is presented with a palimpsest wherein *Casablanca* is the background upon which the Moroccan film lies. This visual palimpsest figures and orders the narrative palimpsest that Laqt'a's dialogue stages.

If the story told about *Casablanca* seems a misreading, it is a productive one for Laqt'a. In this, the director's first feature-length film, the older film is summoned up as support for the director's plot and his daring representation of a sexually liberated young Moroccan woman. Laqt'a's recoding of *Casablanca* is a creative act that recasts the American film as pertaining to an older and moribund tradition and poses *Al-Hubb fi al-Dar al-Baida* as pertaining to a dynamic and modern Moroccan culture. Moroccan audiences who view *Casablanca* after *Al-Hubb al-Dar al-Baida*, or who visit Bar Casablanca for that matter, cannot help but view the earlier text(s) through the lens of the later film. This itself is a key interruption of both Moroccan and American national narratives, rewriting contemporary Morocco as young, vibrant, and modern and the United States as antiquated and outmoded.

Laqt'a's films have been controversial within Morocco because of their frank treatment of sexuality and their uncompromising look at the less appealing side of Casablanca life. *Casablanca*—his version of *Casablanca*— lends Laqt'a narrative authority to make his controversial films, both because of the American film's international cultural capital and Laqt'a's ability to manipulate its plot and meaning.[85] The American film provides him with a defense for refusing to conform to Moroccan cultural traditions. When Najib explains that American cinema must stick within "traditions" or be censored, he both recounts a truth about U.S. cinema from its classic period and interrupts American accounts of the United States as liberal and modern. Najib employs the word *taqalid*, a word that translates as "mores" or "traditions," and one that implies "blind adoption, unquestioning following."[86] It is of course well known in the United States that Hollywood has always operated under various production codes, particularly during World War II. But here American cinema is presented as an institution bound blindly to "tradition," and the United States as a state that censors that which errs from conservative morality. America here is imagined as more conservative than contemporary Morocco, a place where Laqt'a's film might be made. American self-presentation in the international scene, particularly in comparison to a Muslim Arab nation, is bucked by this marvelous scene. Incorporating Laqt'a's text into American accounts of *Casablanca* and of cultural production that represents the Maghreb, Laqt'a's work becomes an interruption of American exceptionalism, both as national narrative and as academic practice. It is a tactic that will recur in *Morocco Bound*.

2

SHELTERING SCREENS

Paul Bowles and Foreign Relations

Interrupting the American Archive

When Paul Bowles died in Tangier on November 18, 1999, the story was covered widely in the U.S. press. U.S. obituaries portrayed Bowles, with remarkable consistency, as an American expatriate connected in spite of self-imposed exile in North Africa to many of the most intriguing writers and artists of Euro-American modernism. The omissions in the portrait—especially the importance of Bowles's Maghrebi context—are endemic to a narrow conceptualization of the author's career. They are also more generally indicative of the logic that limits American thinking about U.S. literary and cultural production since 1942, after which through a more immediate and massive engagement in global affairs, Americans reorganized their thinking about the foreign. From the late 1940s through the 1970s, Paul Bowles played a significant part in imagining the relationship of Americans to the foreign, in general, and to Europe's former colonies in particular. But by the time of his death that part and the challenges Bowles made to "American century" visions of the world had apparently been buried in cold war paradigms of American literature and its limits. Bowles's career challenged the circumscribed sense of what counts as American literature as well as the perceived chasm separating cultural production from international politics. His residence in Tangier, beginning in 1947, corresponds with a deep involvement in Moroccan affairs by the U.S. government during which Bowles wrote frequently about North African politics and culture. After independence in 1956, Bowles was the most prominent U.S. citizen living in Morocco, someone whose statements were widely circulated and frequently disparaged by Moroccans. His work was not free of its own limitations, nor were his politics liberating. But his writing emerged from a crucial moment before U.S. supremacist attitudes were consolidated. Yet most U.S. accounts of Bowles have perpetuated the cold war tendency to translate the foreign within the logic of exceptionalism. Bowles himself had long since taken a path that diverges from such a nationalist or even nation-based logic.

After September 11, 2001, Bowles's name reemerged in U.S. media as a prescient and missed American writer.[1] With the posthumous publication of a major collection in late 2001 and a two-volume Library of America edition of his works in 2002, Bowles's place in the American canon seemed yet more assured because of an implicit connection of recent history with his alleged "prediction" of a world gone terribly wrong in the encounter of Americans and Arabs.[2] Despite a shelf of biographies and studies, however, the scholarly record reflects little more than a smattering of information on his longtime Moroccan artistic collaborators, friends, and lovers.[3] The absence of such material may encourage critics merely to spin the established version of Bowles's career—a writer separated by a modernist scrim from engagement with his geopolitical context—and discourage others from seeing Bowles as deeply involved in the complex interplay of cultural and geopolitical concerns that animated the U.S. presence in the region.[4] In order to recuperate and reimagine alternative potential trajectories of the engagement of Americans with "the world"—in particular the Arab world—that might be distinct from U.S. foreign policy ambitions, this chapter reexamines Bowles's North African writings and collaborations.

If there is to be a twenty-first-century rediscovery of Bowles, the pedagogical and critical danger is that readers will continue to view Bowles through the cold war lenses that focused his earlier reception. When Americanist readers reread Bowles in the context of U.S. empire, it may prove difficult to step outside what Paul Giles has derided as "the magic circle" suspending an interrogation of the relationship between text and context; what emerges from that circle limiting American Studies, according to Giles, is merely an empty "rhetoric of emancipation" (263). Criticism that names Bowles's texts "Orientalist" based on purely textual concerns is caught within a similar circle. This chapter is interested in *interrupting* those frames by offering a Moroccan archive on Bowles's Moroccan context and attending to the various forms of disruption that Bowles's work includes and produces. One strand emerging from the Moroccan archive seems to affirm—and extend—what's been called a postnational approach, namely one that sees the nation form and the related question of national literature as elaborate and influential but also historically delimited constructions. In the United States those constructions reemerge with new ferocity in the early cold war, the same period during which Bowles was writing narratives of Americans who depart from the various "cages" that have held them in the United States. As Bowles's case demonstrates, there are American authors of the 1940s– 1970s whose work sits uneasily within the hypernational framework of the period. Not only does this work require a comparative, multisited approach to be read properly, but its departure from the national episteme helps rethink the relationship between cultural production and foreign relations. Bowles's relationship to Tangier is to a place with a historically fraught relationship to the nation form, a space at once extranational and international, and a place of diasporic convergences. Bowles's early work refuses the neocolonialist/anti-imperialist polarity that has emerged as the choice critics must make about his writing and exhibits a potentiality for an alternative engagement across national boundaries, literatures, and subjectivities. This potentiality, emerging from his early work and developed later, offers an important counterpoint to the forms of containment being consolidated on the home front while he wrote.

In what follows, I take two steps. First I examine U.S. and Moroccan portrayals of Bowles, in media and scholarship. American accounts rely on a cold war tendency to translate the foreign space within the exceptionalist logic of the "American century," a logic from which Bowles himself had departed (in part through expatriation at a moment prior to the consolidation of U.S. global supremacy). Reading through Moroccan critical responses to Bowles, I derive a manner of reading his work through an inter- or extranational formation I call Tangerian lit. Then I use this category to reread Bowles's best-known novel, *The Sheltering Sky*, in order to pursue the novel's relation to its geopolitical context and the potentiality Bowles explores and figures within the novel for identifications that exceed national classification. By doing so, and by contrasting diplomatic representations by the U.S. state department apparatus, I reconsider the space between literary representations of the foreign and foreign relations. Bowles's attitude toward that space is complex and forces Americanists to reconsider easy invocations of the international, or the political, in discussions of post-1941 American literature.

Thirty-six years old when he set sail for Casablanca in 1947 with a contract for an as yet unwritten novel he called *The Sheltering Sky* (he had lived in Morocco in the early 1930s, and in Mexico for a year during World War II), Bowles made a departure that was a definitive rupture and that at times bothered reviewers of his novels and has constrained the parameters for interpretations of his work ever since. Nearly all of his writing was set either in North Africa or Central America and took as its recurring subject the encounter of Anglo-Americans with these places and the people, both foreign and native, who live there. During the 1940s and 1950s, when Bowles first made a name for himself as a writer—having achieved a degree of fame earlier as a composer—his dedication to representing life outside of the United States alternatively worried cold warriors and titillated the counterculture. In 1950, for example, Charles Jackson reviewed Bowles's second book negatively in the *New York Times Book Review* and suggested that Bowles would do better to return to "his native scene" and take up "everyday" American concerns; Jackson recommended American adolescence, a subject he claimed to be "universal."[5] But in resisting such suggestions and via controversial and daring work, Bowles himself became attractive to generations of Western beatniks, hippies, and their successors. He exerted influence on U.S. literary culture and the counterculture through a variety of activities, each of which paid dividends: he popularized French existentialism through his early fiction and translations (as the translator of *Huis clos* for its Broadway premiere, it was Bowles who named Sartre's play *No Exit*); he unwittingly attracted William S. Burroughs to Tangier in the 1950s, introduced Berber and Arab musical forms to the West through field recordings, published a collection of cannabis-fueled fiction in 1962 (and his recipe for hashish jam in *Rolling Stone* a dozen years later), and collaborated with illiterate Moroccan authors in the postcolonial period. This collaboration would have pronounced and still developing ramifications on Moroccan literary culture.

On his death, journalists couldn't help but express judgment on his decision to have stayed "away" till the end. In Mel Gussow's account in the *New York Times*, Bowles's choice to spend his life abroad demonstrated something approaching a moral failing. "In many ways his career was one of avoidance," Gussow put it. "[He] retreated to Tangier . . . and moved farther away from the worlds of publishing and society toward an unknown destination."[6] The tone of Adam Bernstein's obituary for the *Washington Post* recalls Charles Jackson's comments half a century earlier:

"Since the late 1940s, he had all but *renounced* the United States, embracing *what he considered* the sexually, socially and culturally liberating environment of Morocco."[7] Writers from the major papers efface Bowles's oft-repeated critique of the decadence of U.S. consumer and political culture. The invention of an attitude that Bowles did not express about Morocco (that it was liberating) emerges from the journalists' fabrication of his renunciation of the United States. The decision to remain outside leads to extreme and polarized responses from those whose careers have relied on remaining within.

Despite the interpretative weight of Bowles's choice of residence on the meaning of his life, however, not one of the U.S. obituaries and tributes considered his half-century in Tangier in the context of the major political and social transformations in the city, in Morocco, or in the greater Maghreb, which moved from colonialism to independence through various intense struggles in the postcolonial period. In his full-page obituary, Gussow writes off all of Moroccan history in a sentence: "Eventually his dream city of Tangier was invaded by tourists and became something of a nightmare."[8] The excuse for the omission would seem to be the U.S. media's firm distinction between realms of cultural production and political history. Yet Bowles's career challenges that binarism throughout: he published a novel about the Moroccan independence movement; wrote articles about politics in Kenya, India, Sri Lanka, Algeria, Morocco and Portugal for the *Nation* and other publications during the 1950s; feared returning to the United States because of prior membership in the Communist Party; composed the score for a Belgian documentary about the Congo on the verge of decolonization; and saw his own extensive recording of Moroccan music in the postcolonial period as a response to the cultural program of Moroccan nationalists.

Critics must reexamine the relationship of post-1941 U.S. literature and foreign relations. By "foreign relations" I mean both U.S. international politics and the ways in which through cultural production Americans are taught to imagine the foreign; the interplay between these two meanings of the term must not be collapsed, as has become routine. In Bowles criticism published in the United States, for example, Bowles's relations with foreigners are either a point of prurient interest (what sorts of "relations" did he have with Moroccans?) or ignored. Bowles's intriguing life was made familiar via many interviews, profiles and accounts of visits to the errant author himself in situ. In themselves these accounts of Bowles

Paul Bowles listening to Moroccan musicians, Tangier, 1996. In the foreground is a boy dancer. *Photo by Brian T. Edwards, copyright 2005.*

among the Arabs (to paraphrase a recent one) along with the obituaries constitute an archive, stocked with frequent repetitions, stereotypes, and regurgitation of colonial banalities about the Maghreb. Its predictability, however, does not diminish the power of this archive to frame readings of Bowles's work and American understandings of the Maghreb. The un-checked interpretation of Morocco that emerges implied and constructed a contrasting setting from which readers read the articles. They repeat-edly constructed the binarism, then, that Edward Said has argued marks Orientalism and challenge the recent argument that American represen-tations of the Arab world since World War II move us beyond Said's formulation. Bowles is distanced from what is imagined as "normal" back in the United States: he is suspect insofar as his relationship to Morocco is seen not as an engagement with the foreign, but as a prolonged lost weekend, as Charles Jackson implied, an irresponsible bender. As a result, he became not only the conduit to the purportedly "liberating environ-ment," its translator, but also a tourist site himself. By the 1990s, Bowles entered the travel guidebooks as something like required reading and as a part of the scenery.[9]

If American obituaries told one story about Bowles's life in Morocco, a different story about Paul Bowles was being told in Morocco. In both French- and Arabic-language newspapers, Bowles's death was front-page news. A couple of papers ran multiple articles on the same day. There is more proximity in the Moroccan accounts and a greater sense that the death of Paul Bowles *matters* somehow, immediately. If American accounts had Bowles fleeing to a curious and marginal place, Moroccan accounts invariably ask about the effects of his writing on the postcolonial nation. There is a greater diversity of opinion regarding Bowles in the vibrant Moroccan media than one finds in U.S. criticism. Such a disparity reminds us that Arab interruptions to American accounts of the world extend to the realm of literary criticism.[10] Yet the Moroccan archive is "silenced" in criticism at large: Nexis search engines won't locate, Internet searches won't reach, MLA bibliographies don't list, and U.S. libraries don't collect the Moroccan sources that discussed and debated the significance of Bowles's passing. As Michel-Rolph Trouillot has taught, the hegemonic archive regularly silences the past.

It is safe to say that the Paul Bowles who lived in Tangier and Fez in 1931 and 1932, and who found himself dreaming of return after World War II, did not imagine that Moroccans would eventually be reading his books.[11] But on his return in 1947, and especially after the fall of that year when he met Ahmed Yacoubi in Fez, the earlier Bowles quickly ceded to a Paul Bowles who became involved (artistically, intellectually, professionally, socially, and sometimes romantically and/or sexually) with Maghrebi nationalists, intellectuals, artists, and later academics and students. He did not always approve of their positions (most notably on what he thought was the tendency of Arab nationalism to squelch Berber culture and to embrace the West's worst aspects) but he could not and did not ignore the changing tide in the Maghreb. The public discussion of Bowles's work by Moroccans did not register for a couple of decades—Abdallah Laroui critiqued him in 1967 and Tahar Ben Jelloun denounced him in *Le Monde* five years later—but as early as the 1950s it was clear that Bowles's work had a Moroccan audience. The nationalist hero 'Allal al-Fassi reportedly appreciated Bowles's 1955 novel about the anticolonial uprising in Fez, *The Spider's House*.[12] With the rise of postcolonial theory in Morocco, extended in Morocco by the work of Abdelkebir Khatibi, and popularized by Moroccans returning home from the United States with literature PhDs, Bowles's work gained an academic audience. His earlier writings made their way onto Moroccan syllabi in the early 1990s as Moroccan academics looked for ways to respond to the Gulf War, which had been controversial because of Moroccan participation in the U.S.-led alliance. Moroccan students wrote theses on Bowles's work and occasionally confronted him directly in interviews.[13]

A couple of years before Bowles's death, Mohamed Choukri started a firestorm with the publication of a book—*Paul Bowles wa 'uzla Tanja*—that criticized Bowles harshly as a homosexual, as someone whose Arabic wasn't as good as he claimed, as someone who, in Choukri's construction, loved Morocco but hated Moroccans. For Choukri, who had collaborated with Bowles in the 1960s and 1970s, such retrograde attitudes demonstrated that Bowles had worn out his welcome. A Tangier weekly gave Bowles the opportunity to respond; Bowles accused Choukri of insanity and referred obliquely to Choukri's well-known and much-frowned-upon alcoholism while asserting his own right to stay "as long as the government permits me."[14] In 1997, Muhammad Abu Talib suggested in a Rabat-based cultural journal that Moroccans stop giving an "unnecessary, excessive interest" in Bowles or his work, which he claimed denigrated the nationalist movement.[15] Though Abu Talib admitted some respect for Bowles's literary abilities, he was yet another foreign writer afflicted with what the Moroccan poet and scholar archly called, using English, "Moroccanitis." Abu Talib implicitly criticized Choukri for his involvement with Bowles and noted a "disturbing influence by English" on Choukri's Arabic prose. Softer versions of this opinion appeared on Bowles's death in the Moroccan daily *Libération*, which called the writer's passing the completion of a circle of Tangier's colonialist ghosts; in these accounts, Bowles's death—which followed by a couple of months the death of King Hassan II, who had ruled Morocco for nearly four decades (1961–99)— was further confirmation of the arrival of a new more hopeful era.[16]

A different tack was taken by Tariq as-Saidi, who remapped Bowles's career in terms of its relationship to Moroccan culture: "the center of the world for him shifted from Paris to Tangier."[17] Writing for the daily *Al-Ahdath al-Maghribiya*, as-Saidi makes a compelling case for Bowles's embrace of the Moroccan imaginary as an escape from a more limited and limiting American understanding of daily life (one of the subheadings of the article translates "Ordinary Moroccans saved Bowles from American stupidity"). The official obituary, which ran on the Maghreb Arabe Presse (MAP) wire service, similarly emphasized Bowles's embrace of Moroccan culture. MAP foregrounded Bowles's translations of works by Moroccans

and his recordings of an "inventory" of popular Moroccan music of the
Atlas and Rif to the exclusion of most other facets of his career.[18] The
account by the national news agency thus offered a major interruption to
U.S. treatment of Bowles's career, on the other pole of where, say, the
Library of America Bowles edition stands. This is the Moroccan Bowles;
Bowles, the archivist of Moroccan national culture; Bowles, the anglo-
phone African author.

The accounts I've mentioned thus far interject aspects of Bowles's life
that are omitted from most U.S. accounts. But in their projection of
Moroccan desires and cultural concerns they do not fully reorganize a
reading of Bowles's literary career. Such a possibility, however, does
emerge from writing by Zubir Bin Bushta, who published two articles in
the days following Bowles's death, one in the influential *Al-Ittihad al-
Ishtiraki* and the other in *Al-Mithaq al-Watani*. Bin Bushta knew Bowles
personally and writes movingly of conversations about him with the Moroccan concierge at Bowles's building and with a Moroccan nurse at the
hospital.[19] Well aware of Bowles's international reputation, Bin Bushta
points to his influence on Moroccan letters and calls him the leader or
scout (*ra'id*) of *al-adab at-Tanji*, a phrase I translate "Tangerian literature."
(*Tanji* is an unusual Arabic form; *Tanjawi* is the usual term that desig-
nates Arab residents of the city. *Tangerino* denotes expatriates.) Bin
Bushta emphasizes that he is departing from national categories: "Paul
Bowles is a writer categorized in the column of foreign literature in America. And he is esteemed as a foreign writer in Morocco. I firmly believe
that he created a new literary movement/trend [*tayyar*] that can be called
al-adab at-Tanji."[20] The phrase *al-adab at-Tanji* is also used by Abdarrahim Huzal, who calls Bowles "one of its founders and one of its major
representatives."[21] Writing in *Al-'Alam ath-Thaqafi*, Huzal responds to
what he calls "naive" accusations about Bowles's feelings for Morocco (he
names Choukri) by arguing that writers have imaginary relations to nations and therefore may have multiple, apparently contradictory relationships to a nation. Bin Bushta's and Huzal's articles move beyond the
nationalist framework of Abu Talib or MAP and organize their referent
around extranational affiliations. That both connect their understanding
of Bowles's relationship to the nation form to his residence in Tangier is
important. A city with a long history of international coexistence, Tangier
is understood both in and outside of Morocco as exceptional. Legally an
International Zone from 1925 to 1956 and multilingual and "multicul-

tural" throughout the twentieth century, Tangier challenges the primacy of national identifications and resists any experience of monolingualism or unidirectional affiliation. An understanding of Bowles's writing as "Tanji" as opposed to Tanjawi or Tangerino emphasizes this aspect of the city and disrupts the national framework organizing most understandings of his work. As I'll suggest in the final section of this chapter, the categorization helps us to rethink Bowles's important translations of the narratives of illiterate Moroccans and allows us to see them not in terms of bringing fame to otherwise underappreciated "writers" (MAP's term) but rather as extranational collaborations with those marginalized by the Moroccan nation.

Rereading *The Sheltering Sky*

These analyses by Moroccan critics are a wedge with which we can pry open Bowles's early writing. While his work matures and alters in response to his life in Morocco—never a home, always a tentative stop—and while the later work has been neglected, I want here to go back to Bowles's earliest major representation of the Maghreb: *The Sheltering Sky*. A rereading of this novel is called for not only because of the ways in which it stands as the pillar in Bowles's writing career, determining everything else that follows for readers, the first (and often only) book that Americans read by Bowles. But another reason: written in 1947 and 1948, published in late 1949 and a best seller in early 1950, the novel is intricately a part of that moment when the United States is coming to terms with itself as a global power, a reckoning that was being played out in popular media as well as in classified State Department documents. As I've argued elsewhere, the cold war must not be seen separately from the postcolonial period, the shifting of geopolitical and racial relations on a global scale.[22] *The Sheltering Sky* imagines—and stages—an American relationship to the foreign. As such it engages deeply, by which I mean creatively and not programmatically, the problems and limits of the new world order that was emerging simultaneous to Bowles's travels in Morocco and Algeria, as he wrote his novel. The novel's ability to imagine and figure interruptions to its own narrative of "pioneering" opposes it to American narratives of a complete and transparent translation of the globe that were increasingly common. Bowles was writing in the wake of one of the most influential

American narratives about the foreign, Henry Luce's "The American Century," discussed in chapter 1, in which what we might call an easy translation of the world was seen to be a prerogative of U.S. global supremacy: the power to recreate the world environment "by imagination."[23] Luce's conservative vision of a circular or tautological American understanding of the world—where U.S. global positioning is imagined as supreme within an "imaginative" American recreation of global power relations—is something from which Bowles clearly excepted himself. We must thus be careful not to apply reading practices that unwittingly follow from Luce's logic to our understanding of Bowles. To say that we must learn to reread *The Sheltering Sky* outside an American-century framework means also that we must learn to reread Bowles outside an Americanist framework.[24]

In a 1946 short story, "A Distant Episode," Bowles established a set of terms that informs the disruption he will figure in *The Sheltering Sky*. "A Distant Episode" describes the dangers—and potentialities—of venturing too far from an American frame of reference.[25] In the story, a Western linguist (apparently American), referred to only as "the Professor," returns to a desert village in southern Morocco where ten years prior he had spent three days. The purpose of his current trip is to "mak[e] a survey of variations on Moghrebi" (291).[26] The professor pays a visit to a café owner with whom he had earlier established a friendship. On arrival, however, he learns that the owner has since died. "But I don't understand," he says. The professor attempts to have a conversation with the new *qahaouaji*, whom he wants to hire to guide him to a place where he can buy rare boxes made of camel udders. The qahaouaji is angered by the request since such boxes are produced by Reguibat, a tribe feared and disdained by local residents, but he reluctantly agrees. Despite his vague distrust of the man, the professor follows him out of the village. The qahaouaji points the professor in the direction of the Reguibat, accepts his payment, and departs. The professor goes on alone and is met by some Reguibat men who immediately take him prisoner and cut out his tongue. The linguist is in turn "trained" to perform for the Reguibat, who fasten belts made of the bottoms of tin cans to him and teach him to dance, perform acrobatics, and make obscene gestures. Finally, a year later, the linguist is sold to a wealthy man from another tribe (the Touareg), a "venerable gentleman" who himself shows off in front of other Touaregs by reciting the Koran in classical Arabic. After so many months of hearing only the

Paul Bowles at work, early 1950s. *Courtesy of the Tourya Haji Temsamani and Tangier American Legation Museum.*

linguistic "gibberish" of the Reguibat (the linguist apparently knows no Berber dialects), when the linguist hears classical Arabic being spoken, "pain began to stir again in his being." He is unable to perform for the Touareg gentleman. The Touareg, embarrassed by "his property," beats the professor and goes off to murder the Reguibat who sold him soiled goods. When the Touareg is consequently arrested by the French military police, the professor is left alone. The next day, hungry and confused, he goes into a rage, escapes from his prison, and wanders into the desert. A French soldier sees the professor, recognizes him only as a "holy maniac," and takes a few shots at the professor as he staggers off into the "great silence."

What to make of such a tale? Set up as a "distant episode" in a nearly anonymous place, Bowles's story would seem to be an abstract parable for American readers of the late 1940s. Indeed, many were confused. As Charles Jackson described the story in the *New York Times*, it "is one of such unspeakable horror and brutality that there is no sense in trying to describe it; one's emotion, as one reads the tale, is far less that of repulsion than active anger for having to put up with it at all."[27] Though the tale of a mute linguist left Jackson nearly speechless, Bowles's choice of punishment was clearly not arbitrary. The retribution for the insensitive scholar of tongues is that his own tongue is removed. The Westerner who would collect exotic objects is himself made into an object. The suggestions of the crime for which the linguist will be punished are introduced like clues in a detective story, a metaphor Bowles himself used in describing his narrative technique.[28] And so the professor's inability to recognize the immediate danger he has placed himself in by visiting the Reguibat is evidenced by his rehearsal of the "maxims" "uttered" by Moroccans about the feared tribe: "'An opportunity,' he thought quickly, 'of testing the accuracy of such statements'" (299–300). When the professor is closest to a realization of his "crime," it is too late: "'What are you thinking about?'" he asks the inscrutable qahaouaji. Getting no response and hearing a Reguibat flute in the distance, the professor says to himself, "'These people are not primitives'" (297).

If "A Distant Episode" raises probing questions about anthropological projects undertaken in Morocco and suggests a prescient critique of non-reflexive anthropology, the annihilation of an American who travels south into the desert connects the tale to *The Sheltering Sky*. Bowles named the professor a model for Port in *The Sheltering Sky*. Bowles's sense in "A

Distant Episode" is that the problems of cultural misunderstanding revolve around problems with tongues.[29] His interest in inhabiting a space
outside American understanding leads him to imagine a commerce with
nomadic Berber tribesmen—people who operate in a linguistic register
outside the Moroccan nation and apart from the political structures of
French Morocco. The comment that the Reguibat are "not primitives,"
realized too late by the character, suggests an alter-native to the otherwise
reductive role of "native informant" to which they are otherwise subjected
by both cultural anthropology and the epistemology of the "American
century." With this established, let us return to *The Sheltering Sky.*

Set just after World War II in Algeria, *The Sheltering Sky* depicts three
Americans in their thirties—Port and Kit Moresby and their friend Tunner. Like *Casablanca*, it is a love triangle set in the desert, and as in
Casablanca the secondary triangles are more interesting than the primary
one: Port, Kit, and the Sahara; errant Americans, stir-crazy French colonials, colonized Algerians. Port and Kit are fleeing the decadence of the
West, attempting to escape the incursion of what the novel calls the
mechanistic age. They are also attempting to bridge a gap in their marriage. To do both, they travel further and further "in" to the Sahara,
ditching Tunner. (With his "Paramount" good looks, Tunner stands in
for the America they have left behind; he also has seduced Kit.) Before
Port and Kit reconcile or come to a decision about their feelings about life
in Algeria, Port becomes ill and dies of typhoid in a remote French
outpost, leaving Kit alone. Kit, plagued through the first half of the novel
by omens and fears, hitches a ride with a passing caravan, leaving Tunner
to bury Port. She becomes attached to a Touareg trader named Belqassim, who brings her across the desert to his home, has sex with her and
stands by while his older companion does the same, disguises her as a boy,
smuggles her past his three wives, then confines her. Kit doesn't object;
rather she craves his sexual visits. When she decides to escape, she does
so rather easily. Kit makes it back to the U.S. consulate in Oran, but
the novel suggests she has strayed too far. Though she is located, she
"cannot get back" to some place familiar to the Americans and is lost in
full view.

Despite its explicit rejection of what it calls American "civilization," the
novel quickly became popular in the United States. Later a cult novel, it
has been continuously in print. Bernardo Bertolucci's 1990 film adaptation of the novel, while receiving mixed reviews and modest box office

success, occasioned enough media attention to bring yet another generation of readers to the novel. Bertolucci's is what we might call a strong
misreading of Bowles's novel; "strong" both because it misreads Bowles's
novel for its own creative uses and because its interpretation has itself
been influential, initiating a second Bowles renaissance. Though Bertolucci pays careful attention to the text and his scenes seem to be faithful
to it (at least through Port's death), his failure to render the novel's deep
concern with French colonialism, his decision to film the novel as an epic,
and the nostalgic tone of the film for imperialism are significant errors of
interpretation that recast the novel differently—more conservatively—
than the reading I highlight here.[30]

The novel is continually read within a framework it rejects: namely that
Americans have an innocent relationship to "the world." Bowles is com-
plicit with this misreading, not only because he places American concerns
at the center. He also structures this misreading because he is apparently
ambivalent within the novel about the individual's relationship to the
nation. The characters set out to reorganize their relationship not only to
each other, but also to their national culture itself through comparison:
"another important difference between tourist and traveler is that the
former accepts his own civilization without question; not so the traveler,
who compares it with the others, and rejects those elements he finds not to
his liking. And the war was one facet of the mechanized age [Port] wanted
to forget."[31] By proposing that an individual might "forget" aspects of his
or her "civilization" and select others from contrasting formations in their
place, Bowles initially demonstrates an understanding of national identity
as one of selective memory, as some had theorized the concept of the
"nation" in the nineteenth century. Yet the terms with which the project is
expressed are decidedly American. The novel will later compare Port's and
Kit's travel to the familiar American act of pioneering: Port thinks of his
great-grandparents' encounter with the American landscape (108); the
Sahara is called a wilderness (166). Through such metaphors Bowles
imagines the translatability of the American frontier—the place where,
according to Frederick Jackson Turner's 1893 thesis, the American national character had been formed—to a new location and places his novel
in the company of other postwar accounts of Americanness that engaged
the frontier thesis.[32] Simultaneously, Henry Nash Smith was writing
Virgin Land, which critiqued Turner's thesis but maintained its basic
premise: that American national identity was formed in relation to (myths

of) open spaces. Smith's analysis of the expansion of U.S. empire in the nineteenth century emerges in the context of post–World War II U.S. global expansion, but it does not address that coincidence.[33] Burying the problems of the present in accounts of the American past is common in the early cold war.[34] During an "age of doubt," with domestic morale low after the September 1949 news that the U S S R had exploded its first atomic bomb and the "fall" of China to the communists in October, a climate that fed the imminent crisis of McCarthyism, the attractions to the American book-reading public of fleeing to a new frontier were tangible.[35]

As it proceeds, however, *The Sheltering Sky* exhibits a sense of the discontinuities of the world, the awkwardness of translating the foreign in American terms, and the inability of Algerians to experiment with national identity. The last highlights the contingency of national identity, which throws the American characters' project into crisis. Bowles recognizes that the project of reordering one's identity is authorized by a U.S. passport. Port's losing his removes more shelter than the novel's existentialist framework might have led readers to expect. "It's strange," Port reports to a French colonial administrator, "how, ever since I discovered that my passport was gone, I've felt only half alive. But it's a very depressing thing in a place like this to have no proof of who you are" (164). Port's experience of the Algerian landscape previously viewed from dominating vistas is now made "senseless." After falsely accusing an Algerian hotelier of the theft—a racialized assumption the novel deconstructs in Poe-like fashion in a scene that elaborates and distinguishes French attitudes toward Algerians from American ones (the scene is left out of Bertolucci's film)[36]—Port loses the anchor that drove the first portion of the novel. He thereby discovers that the American project in the desert can work only while the travelers block out the Algerian population. Doing so would mean also to block out the visibility of the French colonials and the relationship of American projects (whether political or epistemological) to French ones. This becomes impossible. Port's experiment in cultural comparison must now end in failure; his death is represented as a breakdown of meaning and language. From the shards of that shattered relationship to U.S. national identity, the potentiality of the novel emerges.

Before looking more carefully at the way the novel figures this breakdown, I want to recover the geopolitical context of Bowles's writing in order to show how his departure from a "national" framework matters. Despite the later implication that he was eccentric in his travel, Bowles was in fact one of many Americans who returned to the Maghreb after the war. A few months before *The Sheltering Sky* was published, the *Saturday Evening Post* ran an article by Demaree Bess titled "We're Invading North Africa Again." The reference was to U.S. businessmen who, urged by Truman's Point Four program (the so-called Marshall Plan for the third world), were returning to the places that GIs had been during the war and doing their bit to stave off the spread of Soviet influence.[37] That there could be a second invasion emphasizes the cultural importance of the first one. If the North African Campaign was successful in military terms—Churchill called it the "end of the beginning"—it had different ramifications within the Maghreb itself. From the point of view of most postwar "invaders," World War II represented the introduction of Americans and their products to the Maghrebi market and of the Maghrebi market to Americans. "Our GIS . . . demonstrat[ed] a new way of life to the local people," wrote Edward Toledano in 1948.[38] The title of his *Harper's* essay, "Young Man, Go to Casablanca," made reference to Horace Greeley's injunction to "go west" in the previous century; it thus echoed Bowles's association of the post–World War II Maghreb with the nineteenth-century American frontier. Toledano, however, embraced the metaphor: "By their relish for the small-big things of culture—Camel cigarettes, Hershey bars, Coca Cola—[the GIS] were unconscious but very effective salesmen for American products. Morocco didn't realize it, but the Fuller brush man had been taken to the bosom of its family. Eventually it was bound to cherish and buy his line" (111).

Morocco was "bound" indeed. Toledano's understanding of the richness of the Maghreb is built upon the erasure of the incomprehensible aspects, especially Arabic language, occluded as "noise" or gibberish. The only illustration in Toledano's article is a line of magnified Arabic, the visual presence of which starkly interrupts the column of text: "The hieroglyphics stare at you," Toledano writes forbodingly, "from buses, stores, and even from the walls of Le Roi de la Bière [a café-bar]" (112). But no sooner is this threatening mark of difference quoted than it is translated, à la Luce, into a *market* of difference: "It means Coca Cola in Arabic. An American who had formerly been in the diplomatic service obtained this franchise for Morocco." The interruption of Arabic for Toledano, then, and of Arab difference for U.S. corporations is no interruption at all, but the decorative space of another market. This contrasts sharply with what Bowles will do with untranslated Arabic. For Bowles, the mark of difference opens the potentiality for a different relationship to the Maghreb, and thereby to Americanness itself.

Despite Toledano's suggestion, Moroccans *did* note the arrival of American consumer culture with the GIs, and some spoke about it. In chapter 1, I mentioned Houcine Slaoui's song "Al Mirikan" about the arrival of American soldiers in Morocco in 1942 and noted that Slaoui's challenge to American presence was not audible to American ears or visible within the record of the North African campaign. Bowles, however, would later invoke Slaoui's song as a key text and moment in Maghrebi history, including it in *Points in Time*, his 1982 lyrical history of Morocco. Though he offers no comment, his suggestion is that U.S. arrival marks a rupture in Moroccan history. Bowles thereby refuses to follow a seamless American translation of the Maghreb.[39] A related suggestion emerges from *The Sheltering Sky*: that the encounter of Americans with the Maghreb is disruptive to U.S. thinking about North Africa, an interruption to the reapplication of the frontier myth. This will be signaled by two Bowlesian tactics: his incorporation of untranslated Arabic to figure that disruption and produce it within the text, and the narrative turn toward Kit's relationship with Belqassim, a nomadic Touareg. Because global and domestic politics were deeply intertwined in the early cold war, the latter turn is complicated. Kit's relationship with Belqassim might for the novel's first readers have evoked the threat of sexual congress between white women and African Americans. Her embrace of Belqassim also permits the novel to explore the escape from national identification: the Touareg are antagonists of the nation form; they are identified with no nation-state and in retreat from Moroccan and Algerian national culture. These possibilities suggest both a part of the reason for the novel's success in the marketplace—its ability to be recast as lurid exoticism—and Bowles's disruption of dominant cold war understandings of North Africa and the North African. Understanding this disruption helps explain more than Bowles's novel: it helps approach the ways in which literary and diplomatic representations of the foreign setting confront, build their cases off of, and in Bowles's case evade or rewrite the same set of categories.

In order to argue that Bowles's representation of the Maghreb in *The Sheltering Sky* interrupts its moment deeply, I must account for other representations of the Maghreb—particularly those by American diplomats. So I will take a brief detour through official U.S. relations with the Maghreb. While U.S. corporate interests were publicly attending to

Maghrebis and their alleged embrace of the American "way of life," the U.S. Department of State was paying careful attention to Maghrebi political attitudes. To students of cold war politics it comes as no surprise that the State Department would be concerned about political change in the Maghreb, as it was with many economically less developed regions; still, the intensity of the discussion is impressive. Bowles's textual accounts were in a different institutional relationship to power than were those emerging from the U.S. consulates in the Maghreb, but they respond to a similar set of circumstances in their attempts to represent postwar North Africa.

In July 1946, the department asked its arms in the region to begin producing fortnightly aerograms on communist activities in the region. The principal worry was that North African nationalists might seek a temporary alliance with French communists, who threatened to gain control of the government in upcoming French elections. As the Acting Secretary of State put in a secret communiqué: "The dangers to the Nationalists of attempting such an alliance cannot be overemphasized as such alliances almost invariably result in advantages for the communists at the expense of the other party."[40] To read the resulting communications between the embassies and consulates in Tangier, Rabat, Algiers, Casablanca, Tunis, Cairo, and Paris, and the Office of Near Eastern and African Affairs (NEA) in Washington, from 1946–1950, now declassified and published in the late 1970s in *Foreign Relations of the United States* (*FRUS*), is to witness intense analysis of and speculation about such issues as France's future in the Maghreb, the compatibility of Islam and Marxism, the influence of the French Communist Party (PCF) on Maghrebi nationalists, the role of the United States in the region, how to push France to liberalize or decolonize, and the activities of various Maghrebi groups and individuals. Despite the range of topics and opinions, what is immediately clear is that official U.S. thinking about the Maghreb after 1946 was inseparable from U.S. thinking about France.

The period during which Paul Bowles was writing *The Sheltering Sky* and the immediate context of its publication (1947–50) constituted a key transitional moment in U.S. relations with France. France, the largest recipient of Marshall Plan aid, was vital to U.S. interests, and to cold warriors it seemed fragile. There were domestic referents for this fragility—the continual fall of governments under the French constitution of 1946, which established the Fourth Republic—and international ones, particularly France's increasingly tense relations with its colonies in Indochina and North Africa. In *The United States and the Making of Postwar France, 1945–1954,* Irwin Wall argues that in the early cold war the United States was "drawn into a network of western institutions and alliances of the postwar era rather than, as is more commonly depicted, [establishing] its role as creator or innovator."[41] If we are to examine U.S. Orientalism, whether in literary and cultural production or in political history, it follows then that we must do so comparatively and extend Wall's thesis, to posit that U.S. thinking about North Africa was framed by French thinking about the Maghreb. This will not mean that domestic American concerns—particularly regarding race—would not play a powerful role in U.S. foreign relations. But as I suggested in the introduction, when American writers, journalists, filmmakers, anthropologists, and diplomats looked at the Maghreb, they attended to European colonials as much as they did to Maghrebis; their attitudes about the one were impossible to separate fully from their observations about the other. For the State Department, that dual attention was now of strategic importance.

The same war that the characters of *The Sheltering Sky* are attempting to escape was being replayed by U.S. business interests (the second "invasion") and the State Department, the latter haunted by strategic decisions made during World War II. Most important of those wartime decisions was the U.S. decision to leave French colonial structures in place in the Maghreb—what historian William Langer justified in 1947 as "Our Vichy Gamble"[42]—despite U.S. propaganda circulated in Morocco and Algeria at the time of the November 1942 Operation Torch landings publicizing the Four Freedoms and the Atlantic Charter (which declared U.S. "respect [for] the right of all peoples to choose the form of government under which they live"). In the context of that propaganda, conversations between Franklin Roosevelt and the Sultan of Morocco, Sidi Mohammed, in January 1943 were interpreted to promise U.S. support for Moroccan independence.[43] Yet the United States declined Sidi Mohammed's offer to declare war on Germany and Italy, not willing to imply a commitment to the Sultan over De Gaulle, with the announcement that European colonies would be independent only when their leaders could govern themselves properly, a formula familiar within late colonial rhetoric and one that lurked at the heart of postwar U.S. thinking.[44]

It was also a formulation familiar within domestic conversations about race, namely the invocation of "racial time." The U.S. deferral of Maghrebi independence is a powerful example of racial time and is linked to the description of a time lag in *Casablanca*, as discussed in chapter 1. The connection between the U.S. deferral of Maghrebi independence and racialist thinking in the domestic United States is more than metaphor. Thomas Borstelmann and Penny Von Eschen have both shown the deep interplay of foreign relations and domestic racial politics after World War II, which Borstelmann calls "central to the American experience of the early Cold War."[45] Borstelmann sees the escalation of such connections after the war as part of a global reconfiguration: "The swelling tide of racial tension and violence that rolled through the American South in 1946 and 1947 was part of a global phenomenon of race relations being reconfigured in the aftermath of the defeat of history's most murderous racists, the Nazis" (53). In official American thinking about the Maghreb, then, there was an interplay of racialized thinking (the domestic referent in response to the global reconfiguration) and the tendency to see the region as the French framed it. Bowles's writing, starting with *The Sheltering Sky*, reflected this interplay. It also refigured it.

From his arrival at Casablanca in the summer of 1947, Bowles was writing his novel in a climate in which Maghrebi nationalist claims against the French were unmistakable; his letters make this clear. It was a tense period in the Maghreb. Several years of drought exacerbated complaints against French treatment.[46] The French had responded to an uprising at Setif, Algeria, in May 1945 by slaughtering thousands of Algerians, as they had killed thousands of Tunisians who rose up to protest the deposing of Moncef Bey two years earlier. In April 1947, the French killed hundreds at Casablanca.[47] In February 1947, at the Conference of the Arab Maghreb in Cairo, Maghrebi participants—representatives of the Moroccan Istiqlal (Independence) movement, the Tunisian Destour party and the Parti Populaire Algérienne—declared the protectorate treaties over Morocco and Tunisia terminated and stated their "non-recognition of the rights of France over Algeria," demanding evacuation of their territories occupied by "foreign forces."[48] The conference was noted by the United States. Though the United States had given aid to Moroccans during the famine, it maintained a delicate line: urging French reforms, worrying about the allegiance of nationalists and French communists, and continued belief in political "evolution" of Maghrebi leaders and a gradual "time table" for independence. If there was a theoretical inclination toward an anticolonial position, U.S. interests in France kept it in check. As journalist Demaree Bess wrote in 1949, "In theory, many Americans may still disapprove of the European colonial system. In practice, the United States is reinforcing it."[49]

After Sidi Mohammed made an influential visit to Tangier in April 1947, a turning point in popularizing the independence movement, Secretary of State George Marshall became anxious about France's "short range conception" in its dealings with North Africa and expressed a sense of urgency regarding the implementation of reforms. In a secret telegram to the U.S. Embassy in Paris, Marshall emphasized that a "solution [to] this problem is a matter of urgency lest [the] situation in North Africa develop into one comparable to that now existing in Indo-China"; additional worries were that the Moroccan or Tunisian case for independence would be brought to the UN General Assembly and complicate France's— and the United States's—position by provoking international publicity.[50] But by mid-1949, despite no improvement and a harsher, more conservative French administration in Morocco, the State Department had shifted course. As the cold war deepened, the United States listened increasingly to French proposals for dealing with the colonies' demands for independence. U.S. diplomats meeting in Tangier could now agree unanimously that "the ultimate objective of Stalinist Communism [was] the separation of these dependent areas for the so-called 'imperialistic exploiting nations' and eventually their integration into the orbit of Moscow."[51] The reference to Stalinism and by extension the Soviets—though there was no visible Soviet presence in the Maghreb and it was clear that communists were limited to French *colons* and trade unions sympathetic with the PCF—signals a retrenchment toward a simpler binarism.

The resulting deemphasis on the timetable toward independence is also explained by renewed U.S. comfort with the new French leadership, Prime Minister Henri Queuille, and the government he formed in late 1948. Queuille had broken a crippling strike movement in the metropole, while creating alliances with the noncommunist left and keeping a distance from de Gaulle. In 1949, as the North Atlantic Treaty was being drawn up, Queuille took advantage of his U.S. backing and successfully insisted on the inclusion of French Algeria as territory protected within the treaty, against the initial resistance of Secretary of State Dean Acheson and President Truman. Queuille's victory had the effect of causing the United States to reaffirm French rights on the colony, though Congress took pains to say that the treaty did not ally the United States with

colonialism.[52] Meanwhile, in Morocco, Resident-General Juin's proset-
tler policies and hard line on the nationalists were accompanied by major
new investment in Morocco, a good deal by the United States.[53] In December 1950, the United States and France agreed that the United States
would rebuild its air base at Port Lyautey (now Kenitra) and build three
new bases. That this was agreed without consultation with Sidi Mohammed underlines the economic, military, political, and symbolic shift toward collaboration with the pro-colon French; according to the agreement, the French flag would fly at Port Lyautey, but the United States
would have unrestricted use of the base.[54] Marshall Plan aid to France had
begun with food and raw materials in 1948; now in 1949 and 1950 military
assistance took center stage (the larger shift toward military buildup was
codified in March 1950 with NSC-68). By 1953–54, the United States
would be bankrolling nearly the entire French war in Indochina.[55] To understand some of the permutations involved in justifying the shift in policy, the 1950 U.S. statement on North Africa policy bears close reading:

> Our policy has been to encourage the French on all appropriate occasions to
> put forward a program of political, economic and social reforms which
> would lessen the resentment of the natives toward France and would assure
> their gradual evolution toward self-government. We believe, however . . .
> that France is the country best suited to have international responsibility for
> Morocco. We have therefore avoided putting pressure on France by giving
> aid and comfort to the natives directly, although we maintain open contact
> with them, and consider their friendship and good will very important.[56]

That dual tone—diplomatic civility and economic patronage for the
French versus paternalism regarding the "gradual evolution" of the "natives" with whom "open contact" is maintained—crystallizes the contradictions of the U.S. attitude toward French colonies. The tension inherent in such a position manifests itself in the last sentence, where "open
contact" with the natives is kept in check by the refusal of direct "comfort,"
a formula of desire and disgust.

Given this context, the energies and impulses of the second American
"invasion," and the network of interests monitored by the U.S. state
department, how do we reread *The Sheltering Sky*, a work that emerges
from this time and place? In locating Bowles's dual disruption—figured in
his representation of Moroccan language and pursued in the narrative

interruption of Port's death and the narrative embrace of the nomadic Touareg—I have begun to sketch an answer, which I'll pursue more closely in a moment. Given my attempt to interrupt the Americanist archive, I want first to ask about the relationship between literature and foreign relations. Because I have foregrounded reading practices, these concerns are intertwined.

I suggested earlier that Edward Said's work provides an adequate model for understanding the institutional constructs that limit American accounts of Paul Bowles. As I move beyond media and academic practice and into the complex network of literature and foreign relations, I want to refine that statement with two contentions. First, I argue that accounts of U.S. Orientalism in the Maghreb—in both cultural production and foreign relations—must consider U.S., French, and Maghrebi representations and counter-representations of each other. That in practice this means triangulating the object of analysis emerges from the texts themselves, which elude both the binarizing logic of the cold war and Americanist reading practices that emerged at the same time. *The Sheltering Sky* is as deeply engaged by the French presence as it is the Algerian. Or to put this another way, the novel cannot divorce the presence of the French from its vision of the Maghreb, which is the problem the novel confronts, and which leads to the breakdown of its initial frame, namely the "pioneering" or revision of American identity on a new "frontier."

My second contention begins with a methodological warning: while literature representing the foreign and foreign relations may emerge out of the same historical context, the disparity between the institutional locations from which the novel and foreign relations operate maintains a gulf between them in terms of material effect. We are mistaken if we read literary and cultural production as somehow engaging political history on equal grounds—grounds made equal by the space of criticism—as has been a common temptation within American studies in the wake of Said's work. Such a temptation, however well intended, is based on a misreading of Said and a failure to attend to his emphasis on questions of institutions rather than on "discourse." Such arguments ultimately rely on the transparency of literary production and its continuity within the land of cultural and political discourse rather than recognizing its own disjuncture from political discourse. Though invocations of the international are now common within American studies, institutional disincentives to multisited, multilingual work contribute to the methodological bind. My insistence on comparative work and the interruption of a Moroccan archive that I have argued for are meant to challenge those formulas.

As an alternative imagination of the relationship of literature to political history, Gayatri Spivak's distinction between philosophy and literature is helpful: "the first concatenates arguments and the second figures the impossible."[57] Such a distinction attends to the institutional locations within which the critic works and provokes Spivak's assertion of the unavoidability of the role of the native informant. Spivak's statement provides the critical space to attend to Bowles's departure from the national episteme as a figuration that matters to foreign relations. His interruption of the American national subject—one with whom he can barely identify and will eventually drop, as we'll see—within a novel allegedly concerned with the pioneering of a new American identity is thus seen not as an irredeemable contradiction, but rather as an impossible figuration in Spivak's sense. That such an interruption is provoked by Bowles's acknowledgment of the "native informant" is crucial, as it is precisely that figure—"these people are not primitives"—that allows Bowles's disruption, his movement outside the logic of the American century's impulse to translate out or "foreclose" the native informant. How does this matter to foreign relations? If the novel departs from a national epistemology, it is the same on which the State Department necessarily rests, and the same that would be trumpeted hysterically in the months following the novel's publication in the domestic red scare. That scare would not only reframe meanings of the foreign, both at home and abroad, but it would also anchor its hysteria on the idea of the reliable testimony of the (native) informant, that is, that the naming of names could contain the spread of communism. The 1950 review I referred to earlier—which suggested that Bowles return to the United States to provide "native . . . reflections or refractions of everyday living"[58]—demonstrates the interplay between literary representation of the foreign and the domestic crisis of McCarthyism, showing its immediate relevance to Bowles's case. Bowles's emerging focus on the Maghrebi informant—concomitant with his exploration of various Americans' departures—moves beyond the limiting frames of national identification.

Bowles's discovery of this departure in a novel that is about the simultaneity of physical and philosophical travel—CANNOT GET BACK is Kit's telegram to the world—does not however provide readers with a

Paul Bowles with Mohammed Ouild Oajdi outside an aban-
doned brothel in Morocco, 1951. *Photograph by Mohammed
Temsamany, courtesy of the Paul Bowles Papers, University of
Delaware Library.*

tangible politics to follow. The second impossible figuration in *The Sheltering Sky* is the dissociation or distancing of American reading subjects
from the developing political relationship to the Arab world that deeply
informed Bowles's novel and was thickly woven into the political and
economic fortunes of the United States. This distancing emerges from
the novel's existentialist frame, within which the novel (influenced by
Poe's Dupin stories and Camus) suggests that what might be called the
"truth of surfaces" offers a lesson about the proper relationship of individuals to existence (sheltered by a two-dimensional sky) and between individuals (who are granted recognition as masks). For Bowles, the "truth of
surfaces" extends to the superficiality of language itself—the mannerisms
of speech, the difference of foreign language, as screen, as printed type—
and will provide a figure for disrupting the national episteme. But the
political effect of erecting this existentialist screen is in fact the inscription

of distance between the (literary) representation of the foreign and foreign relations and unwittingly benefits the imperial state. Stepping back, then, Bowles may echo something like the process Giorgio Agamben has described by which the "state of exception" captures "bare life" within the political order while simultaneously excluding it.[59] Indeed, most readers who followed Bowles to North Africa ended up following the "wrong" message. As early as 1951, Bowles lamented the arrival of young Americans come to Morocco to "explore" and for the hashish; even those American hippies who evaded the U.S. draft by traveling to Morocco more often took a kif-fueled "Marrakech express" than engaged the local population or political climate.[60] Bowles himself had already moved decisively toward engagement with those Moroccans at the margins of national(ist) identification.[61] By attending to the geopolitical context of Bowles's departure, I intend to make visible (and thereby bridge) the accompanying distance between realms of cultural production and foreign relations that is so beneficial to the state. That Bowles's writing unwittingly helps to forge that distance is its limitation, but it still offers a potent figure for disrupting the processes that would discipline it.

The argument I am making need not only apply back to literature. In a work that brings the fields of political science and cognitive psychology into engaged dialogue, Azzedine Layachi has made a compelling argument about the interplay of images of the foreign and foreign policy. Layachi's premise is that images held by the U.S. foreign policy–making elite are *"intervening variables* affecting U.S. policies"; he argues that "mental images—which give meaning to perceived facts and incoming information—serve as bases for deciding which actions to take in order to affect, or respond to, the operational environment."[62] Taking two case studies—a policy reversal on arm sales to Morocco during the Carter administration in 1979 and a 1981 Reagan-administration decision to allow a major natural gas contract between Algeria and the United States to devolve—Layachi goes through extensive cognitive mapping, both of official (collective) images about the Maghreb and of private images held by individual foreign policy makers. What he finds is that less-complex cognitive maps corresponded "with rigid views of Algeria, of U.S. security concerns, and with a shortsighted view of U.S. interests as well as of those of all the parties involved." Highly complex maps, on the other hand, led to "less conflictual and competitive" decisions. The "east-west prism is almost absent, and there seems to be an awareness of a regional character to the issue" (178). Layachi admits the difficulty of certain quantification and is modest about his findings, but he is confident that images play a tangible role in policy making.

Rereading Paul Bowles's work may contribute to such discussions by offering an account of divergence from national thinking at the foundational moment of the post–World War II/United Nations era. That Bowles will take a different route in thinking about the Maghreb than U.S. policy makers emphasizes that they emerge from a shared premise: to think of U.S. presence in North Africa—and the developing world—in terms of American pioneering, with the potential to recreate American nationality implied.[63] Bowles departs from national(ist) thinking in the novel on the same terms that corporatists such as Richard Toledano and State Department officials ultimately embraced such thinking: the proper relationship to France, and a sense of language and the belief in clear translation.

While *The Sheltering Sky* mobilizes some of the tropes and conventions of French colonialist discourse, from the start it distances itself from a French position. Within the context of French Orientalism, Bowles interjects a narrative of American mobility through a French space. Bowles thereby interrupts the French vision of the Maghreb, what Emily Apter has called "the protectorate style" of twentieth-century popular French representations of the Maghreb, in which the colonial administration was naturalized in its location. Reading Bowles's letters from the time, we can see that the geopolitical context was deeply a part of his thinking. In December 1947, Bowles commented on nationalist posters in a small shop in Fez.[64] Algerians in the Sahara would sometimes salute Bowles because he wore clothing that resembled French military garb (his fair complexion and blond hair drew attention to his presence). Bowles conversed regularly with the French Pères, and according to his autobiography he "made it a point" to pay respects to the colonial administrators in whatever region he was traveling in. Such proximity to the French led him neither to reinscribe the difference of his Americanness, nor to embrace his ability to "pass" as colonial master. Rather, in his novel, he considered the limitations of national identification and imagined departure from the national framework itself.

The scene between Port and an officer named Lieutenant d'Armagnac makes this clear. In his description, Bowles plays up the nationally inflected stereotypes the two men have of one another. That Port speaks

French surprises d'Armagnac but also highlights the difference in their attitudes toward Algerians. Port's passport is missing. Port has accused a hotel owner named Abdelkader: "Logic indicates him as the only possible thief. He's absolutely the only native who had access to the passport" (161). D'Armagnac disagrees: "To me it seems just the kind of thing that would *not* have been done by a native" (162). D'Armagnac turns out to be correct, but his loyalty to the Algerian is based on a sympathy that is a by-product of colonialism rather than material evidence. Port's racialized assumption—"[it is] the sort of thing that would *naturally* turn out to have been done by a native—charming as they may be" [my emphasis]—is based on distance from Algerians and is distinguished from d'Armagnac's decadent proximity. D'Armagnac's drawing-room logic, it turns out, is informed by his bedroom colonialism. The scene, reminiscent of Poe's tales of ratiocination, is a turning point in Port's project of redefining himself in relationship to Americanness. D'Armagnac's presence is a reminder that the desert is not merely a frontier for Americans. That a passport is in question is after all the point, for it marks the relationship of the individual to his or her nationality. Its loss provokes a crisis for Port, and the attention to the Maghrebi and to Arabic that the novel uses to figure the resulting detachment emerges from Port's sense of proximity to (the) French.

Bowles's thinking is complex: the link between nationality, colonialism, and detachment revolves around a sense of language's superficiality. From Poe and Camus (whom he was reading at the time), he arrives at what I call the "truth of the surface" as both the proper existential relationship between individuals and a corresponding logic of communication: his basis for disrupting the national episteme. Earlier, Port takes Kit to have tea with an Algerian man named Chaoui. The hoped-for friendship fails to materialize. For Kit, who offends Chaoui by remarking that she is cold, this is because Algerian conversation is superficial. Port disagrees: "You don't say a frieze is superficial just because it has only two dimensions." Kit responds, "You do if you're accustomed to having conversation that's something more than decoration"; Port objects: "It's just another way of living they have, a completely different philosophy" (133). Port's defense of the "superficiality" of their interaction with Chaoui recalls again Poe's Dupin, who in tales such as "Murders in the Rue Morgue" and "The Purloined Letter" had argued for what we might call the meaning of surfaces.[65] For Port, the superficial is the only level on which members of different cultures can hope to understand one another. Thus when Port later imagines a relationship with a blind dancer in Bou Noura, it is a communion that would necessarily exist outside of (or above) national and cultural identifications. Port imagines that they can communicate on an "existential" level—which would emphasize what they have in common, rather than their differences. This level is knowable, in Bowles's vision, via an examination of the "masks" that they both wear.

Port and Kit continue to move away from the places where French presence is visible because they are increasingly unable to separate their own position from that of the colonizers. Bowles runs up against the limits of his sense of the "pioneering" experience precisely when he recognizes that the Algerian characters cannot be elided from his imagined frontier. The attempt to create a meaningful—yet consciously superficial—interaction between Port and the Bou Noura dancer demonstrates to Bowles the problems with a belief in an exceptional American relationship to national identity. His attraction to an Algerian woman bespeaks a desire to learn how to reorder his own identity from Algerians, much as his travel into the Sahara is intended to instruct him in how to forget aspects of the mechanized age. This desire merges the people of North Africa with the landscape, where both offer lessons in how to redefine the "edge" between individuals. In the latter case, Port's desire for the dancer is aroused when he realizes that she is blind: "The knowledge hit him like an electric shock" (142). Yet if the recognition of the young woman's blindness alerts Port to his sexual desire, it is a physical manifestation of something he has already detected in her dance: that she has developed a more existential relationship to existence. Port watches her dance:

The motions, graceful and of an impudence verging on the comic, were a perfect translation into visual terms of the strident and wily sounds of the music. What moved him, however, was not the dance itself so much as the strangely detached, somnambulistic expression of the girl. Her smile was fixed, and, one might have added, her mind as well, as if upon some object so remote that only she knew of its existence. There was a supremely impersonal disdain in the unseeing eyes and the curve of the placid lips. The longer he watched, the more fascinating the face became; it was a mask of perfect proportions, whose beauty accrued less from the configuration of features than from the meaning that was implicit in their expression— meaning, or the withholding of it. For what emotion lay behind the face it was impossible to tell. It was as if she were saying: "A dance is being done. I do not dance because I am not here. But it is my dance." (141–42)

When his companion Mohammed fails to arrange a meeting with the dancer, Port feels "not that a bit of enjoyment had been denied him, but that he had lost love itself" (144). Port fantasizes about the liaison that will not occur and the woman's "imperturbable, faintly questioning face in its masklike symmetry" (145). The secret of the dancer is to be found in her masklike face, and her blindness ensures for Port that his own face will not be seen. What Port sees in the dancer's mask/face is her own achievement of an existential relationship to her body and in turn to her identity. The woman's commitment to her dance—"it is my dance"—is acknowledged, but her dependence on the dance itself is fluid—"I do not dance because I am not here." This is Bowles's version of the Sartrean idea of freedom and authenticity (or freedom in "good faith"), an idea that focuses itself on the individual's "radical freedom," and less on the freedom of colonized Algerians as a nation (in which Sartre himself would become more interested only later in the 1950s). Port's reading of the Algerian woman by her "mask" is a conscious reduction of the woman to a superficiality. The loss of a personal and sexual interaction with the dancer is profound for Port because he imagines that it might have instructed him in locating the type of relationship between the "nowhere" and the "somewhere" in himself that he is unable to find in the disconcerting opening chapter of the novel, which begins with Port waking up confused about where he is in time and space. The dancer's relationship to her body is that which Port too is attempting to find for himself in relationship to his nationality, so that he might say: "There is an American nationality. I am not American because I am not here. But it is my nationality." Unfortunately for Port he will be unable to arrive at this statement. His reverie is interrupted by a deep chill, the harbinger of the typhoid that will kill him.

In choosing a blind dancer as the personification of the ideal balance of the nowhere and the somewhere, Bowles sets up a problematic relationship between American and Algerian. For Port, the woman's face—a "mask of perfect proportions"—is beautiful "less from the configuration of features than from the meaning that was implicit in their expression—meaning or the withholding of it." By positioning Port as the perfect reader of that implicit meaning, Bowles suggests that Port can successfully interpret the dancer by examining her face, which *as superficial* reveals that which they have in common (their existential relationship to "humanity"). But if the woman's face is truly a mask, a two-dimensional covering of something hidden underneath, the implicit meaning of her mask/face would seem to be little more than that it is a mask. In other words, by describing the woman's face as a mask, Bowles implies that there is a reality underneath the mask, being obscured by the mask. The mask would seem to have only an explicit meaning. What is implicit, then, would have to be below the mask, or it would have to be an interpretation of the mask; in reading the implicit meanings of the mask, Port must project his own existentialist concerns onto the woman. Since of course the blind dancer is unable to look back at Port, unable to read the meanings in his own face/mask, it would seem that Port deprives the Algerian character of any agency in the interaction. The only possible agency she is left with is the parenthetical proposition that the face might indeed express the "withholding" of meaning—an option that seems to negate Port's sense that the face reveals meaning. But the fact that for Port the dancer's face expresses meaning and the withholding of meaning simultaneously testifies to Port's sense of his ability, indeed his right, to perform the reading of her face; meaning is placed in his framework. If the woman's face is a screen, it is Port who will determine what will be projected on it.

To consider the woman legible as a mask would seem, on the one hand, to repeat what Frantz Fanon identified as the paradigmatic act of Western whiteness toward the colonized subject. "What is often called the black soul is a white man's artifact," Fanon writes in his 1952 book *Black Skin, White Masks*.[66] Fanon suggests that there is a tyranny of visibility and invisibility in the relations between white and black culture, which leads black individuals to "mask" their own skin in features recognizable to whiteness so as to become visible to white culture (and ultimately to recede back into invisibility). Visibility, for Fanon, thus objectifies the colonized subject—"I found that I was an object in the midst of other objects" (109), Fanon writes—by placing the black subject in the regard of the anonymous white person: "Look, a Negro!" That Bowles's blind dancer cannot look back at Port and say "Look, a white man!" would seem to contain her all the more forcibly in this system of objectification. As David Theo Goldberg writes, in a discussion of visibility in Fanon, "one's visibility is predicated also on the assumption of self-determination. Being recognized—whether as self-conscious or as Other, and thus being visible, requires that one be outside of the Other's imposition, free of the Other's complete determination."[67] From his position as spectator of the blind woman's dance, Port is outside of the Algerian woman's "imposition," while she—as she is known to the readers of the novel—is completely determined by him. Thus if she is visible to Port (in the sense that he can see her and determine her), she would seem to be "invisible," in Fanon's terms, since she is not the one who determines the meaning of her dance; it is imposed upon her.

On the other hand, the dancer's blindness works to make an existential communion between American man and Algerian woman *more* possible than it would be if she could see Port. Port does not imagine he is determining the meaning of the dancer, but rather that she (who cannot see him) determines the proper relationship to identity for him. The dancer's blindness, in this understanding of the interaction, is a measure of her own independence from Port's determination of her. Port's brief moment of ecstasy, the "electric shock" of desire, announces itself when he realizes that she cannot see him; he is freed, momentarily, from his own visibility as an American—a freedom that usually eludes him. When Port worries that the Algerian hotel workers will see Kit's possessions spread out in her hotel room, it is the worry that Port and Kit's comparative wealth will be too visible. If Port believes that his own visibility, the superficial level on which he appears to Algerians, is something to be avoided because it imparts a false meaning to his Algerian audience, he is nonetheless able to believe that the masks of the native population express the limits of the truth he can gather about Algerians.

In reading the dancer's face as a mask, a two-dimensional screen on which her existential relationship to her body has been projected, Port treats the dancer much as he does the North African landscape. The Saharan landscape also is considered to be knowable only by its surfaces. For Bowles, the desert is a pair of surfaces: land and sky. In a travel essay, "Baptism of Solitude," written shortly after *The Sheltering Sky*, Bowles elaborates: "Immediately when you arrive in the Sahara, for the first or the tenth time, you notice the stillness. . . . Then there is the sky, compared to which all other skies seem faint-hearted efforts. Solid and luminous, it is always the focal point of the landscape. At sunset, the precise, curved shadow of the earth rises into it swiftly from the horizon, cutting it into light section and dark section."[68] With a solid sky as the focal point, the Saharan landscape takes on an exaggerated two-dimensionality; sky reflects earth, where both are solid screens. In the scene that clarifies the title of the novel, Port expresses a sense that the desert sky is a "solid thing . . . protecting us from what's behind." When Kit asks Port, "What *is* behind?" he responds: "Nothing, I suppose. Just darkness. Absolute night" (100–101). The Saharan sky is like the dancer's mask, then, in that a surface imagined as two-dimensional (the face, the sky) is a screen that reveals meaning. In both cases, what is behind the mask is unknowable, inaccessible, and ultimately a void, and indeed part of the meaning visible on the surface is that what is underneath is *unknowable*. Thus both dancer and landscape can be properly understood only by plotting their meaning across their two-dimensional aspects: by reading the mask, or by mapping the landscape. Thus it is appropriate that when Port is unable to go further than imagining a relationship with the dancer (which he imagines no less superficially), he turns back to the Sahara itself to find his instruction. For in *The Sheltering Sky*, Algerians and Algeria are barely distinguishable from each other. Both are best understood by examining their surfaces.

If faces are masks, for Port this is an effect of the material age itself. Earlier, Kit has pondered the relationship of the "superficial" and materialism when confronted by the face of a deformed Algerian: "She found herself wondering why it was that a diseased face, which basically means nothing, should be so much more horrible to look at than a face whose tissues are healthy but whose expression reveals an interior corruption. Port would say that in a non-materialistic age it would not be thus" (82–83). In a non-materialistic age, apparently, the deformed face would not be horrifying because materialism prefers the perfect and offers a new object in the place of a defective one.

Since the historical tragedy of *The Sheltering Sky* is that it *is* a materialistic age, Port's response is to reembrace the mask, which means both to leave private that which is below it and to relegate that which is visible on the surface to primary importance. Yet if the mask is a protective device—like the "sheltering sky," "protecting us from what's behind"—then Bowles's choice to embrace the superficial in the interaction of American and Algerian falls apart. In attempting to leave behind the international imperatives of Western capitalism, and the concomitant graying of cultural particularities, Port imagines that by keeping his relations with North Africans on the superficial level, he can escape his participation in the West and reorder the meaning of his Americanness. Having failed to find the dancer, Port goes back to the landscape itself in an attempt to locate the relationship of the somewhere to the nowhere. His conclusions about the meaning of the Sahara substitute his own appreciation of the landscape for the communion that cannot occur with the dancer. In both cases, Port plots his own concerns onto an Algerian surface and rejects the possibility that he can understand anything valid from a deeper interaction. This is a protective device: a deeper intercourse (a penetration of the surface) is avoided via the recourse to the alleged truth of the superficial. The superficial solution reveals itself to be vacant because it reaffirms precisely the wrong aspect of pioneering that Port is engaging in: Port's "stripping down" of identity relies on exploitation. If the Algerian is to remain a mask, Port imagines that the unknowable difference of the Algerian is after all an existential sameness. Thus difference and sameness cancel each other out, and the Algerian ends up as an absolute nothingness.

If Bowles's existentialism shelters him from a deeper commitment to the challenging difference of the Algerian, there are already cracks in the surface. These are presaged by the startling narrative rupture of Port's death. As he dies, Port's project of pioneering a new relationship to national identity breaks down. This is figured in words losing their ability to be centered, which opens the most important potentiality in the novel and distinguishes it from the national episteme of the FRUS papers.[69] The failure of language to protect Port from the nothingness behind language is imagined in *The Sheltering Sky* in spatial terms. If Port's journey—the ceaseless drive away from the markers of his own civilization—leads to a place of "exile from the world," it is because words lose their stability for him. Thus, the name of the town where Port dies, Sbâ, becomes a kind of joke when language fails to function for him; without that anchor, *Sbâ* becomes an arbitrary word marking an equally arbitrary place. With Port's death, Kit also loses her ability to designate her own relationship to the world, and she enters a long period of silence. For Kit, words cease to make sense; again, the word *Sbâ*, the place Sbâ, becomes absurd: "Once she almost laughed, it seemed so ridiculously unlikely. 'Sbâ,' she said, prolonging the vowel so that it sounded like the bleat of a sheep" (218). Kit greets the contingency of language with laughter. The "joy of being" she vows to hold on to once abandoning language's shelter leads to her deterioration. When the "earth's sharp edge" turns back to reveal a terrifying nothingness, which is what the sky shelters us from, it is a warning that language will do the same. Language like the American passport is a sheltering screen, protective because disciplined. The ridiculousness of words, of place names, of markers opens up a potentiality within the work, that which it might have been.

The Sheltering Sky is a novel that is especially open to what Giorgio Agamben has called the work of art's potentialities, the potentiality to be something other than what it is, "the prologue . . . of a work never penned."[70] The novel's emphasis on movement at once connects the novel to a postwar sense of American mobility and permits an opening to the idea that American mobility has a limit. Though Agamben suggests that one is always not writing the work implied by the potentiality of the present work, stepping back critically from *The Sheltering Sky* permits us a sense that Bowles discovers, though ambivalently and in the margins, an interruption to the American project of reordering American national identity in the empty space of frontier. That interruption is figured as the interruption of untranslated Arabic, as the impossible dialogue with the Maghrebi subject, and in the future of Bowles's work, as a collaboration with the Maghrebi.

In *The Sheltering Sky*, Bowles frequently inserts untranslated Maghrebi Arabic in the novel, an inclusion at first disorienting to the reader who does not speak Maghrebi dialects of Arabic. Since language in the novel is considered by Port and Kit a kind of two-dimensional screen, the inclusion of Arabic phrases and sentences might at first seem mere "decoration." Within French texts set in North Africa, such phrases might adorn, provide local color, the familiarity of their foreignness, with a glossary to help.[71] But here, there is no glossary, no French proximity. Arabic does not conform to the Americans' screen—the totalizing, pioneering effort fails to contain it. Port and Kit speak French, but when Algerian characters speak Arabic in their presence, the Americans are uncomfortable: "The language barrier annoyed him, and he was even more irritated by the fact that [they] could converse together in his presence" (29). When Algerian characters address the Americans in Arabic, the phrases are for the most part straightforward ("*Ya sidi, la bess âlik? Eglès, baraka 'laou'fik,*" an Algerian prostitute says to Port—"Sir, are you well? Please sit down"). Because Bowles leaves the phrases untranslated, they become textual interruptions for the American reader, a discontinuity within the American century. And since the phrases that Bowles includes are not necessary to advance the plot, they stand out all the more strongly as marks. The words he gives to Algerians stand for disruption.

This textual interruption challenges the reader—as it challenges Port— to acknowledge the limits in the Lucean proposition of an American century. The difference of Arabic is not erased here (as it was in Toledano's account of Arabic "hieroglyphics"); rather, it is emphasized. This disruption is repeated narratively by the protagonist's early death, which leads to an important shift of focus to Kit and her relationship with Belqassim. Kit's embrace of Belqassim, and the novel's embrace of both, in the context of the intertwined domestic and global referents of the cold war, is an important turn. It allows Bowles to restage radically the American global encounter in terms that more fully disrupt the Lucean model than other contemporary novels. In 1950, that sexual relationship could be read in a domestic context, within which it disturbed a racist culture and also titillated it. But the novel refuses simply to offer American miscegenation as its meaning and insists on an extranational referent. There are more parts to this story—Bowles's critique of American ideas about gender within his masochistic staging of Kit's fate, for example—and there is much more work to be done by other critics. For now, I want to emphasize that the potentiality embedded in these dual disruptions is Bowles's greatest contribution to thinking about the 1946–50 moment, a potentiality rapidly left behind by the cold war and its modes of thinking, but one that we may now recover.

Letters from Morocco: The Refusal

> One is what one is ... that is, until one changes.
> —Paul Bowles, *In Touch*

Bowles himself was not the type of novelist to crusade, to paraphrase Eudora Welty, his exact contemporary. The difference of untranslated Arabic that in 1949 might challenge the transparency of Luce's American century could in later political and economic contexts signify the difference that American-based global capital seeks to incorporate. And that is one more reason why it is necessary to reread the novel in its geopolitical context. Yet the potentiality of this novel and of Bowles's career emerges from these disruptive moments in *The Sheltering Sky*, and they will eventually lead Bowles to a refusal to continue in the mode of his first novel, cast by Bowles in the 1948 letter from the Sahara, quoted here, as a change or in *The Sheltering Sky* as a departure. Such a refusal will be not a lack of engagement with the Maghrebi, but rather an intense collaboration, one that takes Bowles further from the Americanist framework that he has here started to reject.

Bowles's subsequent two novels, *Let It Come Down* (1952) and *The Spider's House* (1955), are set in contemporary Morocco. Both build on the strand I have located in *The Sheltering Sky* and open themselves up further to Maghrebi voices and subjectivities, against which are juxtaposed the various restrictions of American national identity. In *Let It Come Down*, Richard Dyar escapes the "cage" that restricts him in postwar New York City (he works as a bank teller) to plunge into the epistemological and legal uncertainties of the International Zone of Tangier. In *The Spider's House*, an American writer living in Fez debates the meanings of modernity, political commitment, and Americanness with an idealistic woman from the United States while the Moroccan revolution surrounds them. In both cases, the errant Americans are in conversation with Moroccan counterparts: Thami in *Let It Come Down* and a young Moroccan named Amar as well as members of the Istiqlal in *The Spider's House*. Meanwhile, in Bowles's journalism, there is a decisive turn toward listening to Maghrebi voices, whether in travel pieces for *Holiday* magazine or in his more political essays. If some of the essays at first resemble more literate versions of reports by foreign service officers in the "field"—in a 1951 article for the *American Mercury*, Bowles discusses the inhospitality of the idea of communism to Moroccan Muslims and suggests the vulnerability of educated Moroccan elite to propaganda—their turn toward conversation with the Maghrebi coincides with a refusal to maintain the positive frame that underlies such analysis. "I'm heading south," Bowles ends his *Mercury* article.[72] The essay suggests not only that "Morocco" is impossible to judge because of the inherent unreliability of testimony, but that cold war binarisms themselves are impossible to maintain once one moves from the abstraction of the general to an engagement with the particular.

Increased conversation with the Maghrebi leads Bowles, in the postcolonial period, to a new textual politics and to projects that most firmly challenge the categories of national literature (both American and Maghrebi). Bowles's decision to stay on in Morocco after independence in 1956 is reflected in his later work, which opens itself increasingly to Maghrebi voices and the Arabic language and exhibits a deep interest in Moroccan narrative. Bowles's postindependence work is marked by a changed relationship to the Maghrebi subject, both in his later short fiction and in his extended and underappreciated project of gathering and translating the tales of illiterate Moroccan authors. This project, as Allen Hibbard has argued, may be seen to effect Bowles's late prose style, itself an important interruption to Eurocentric ideas about literary influence.[73] Further, the very project disfigures the disciplinary frames by which the U.S. academy has taught us to apprehend American literature. With one Moroccan in particular, Mohammed Mrabet, Bowles engaged in an extended literary project. The analphabetic Mrabet dictated to Bowles, in colloquial Moroccan Arabic, stories, novels, an autobiography; together they published twelve books, with both names on the title page, published first in English. There is no "original" Arabic edition available, or even possible without a further translation of the unwritten Moroccan dialect into Standard Arabic. Such a project, the productive collaboration of two men, has been controversial in Morocco, where it challenged the nationalists' ideas about Standard Arabic, as well as those francophone Maghrebi writers who critiqued the nationalists—the francophone author Tahar Ben Jelloun called it "a bastard literature."[74] But it has been slighted or ignored in the United States, where it has seemed a marginal project that does not conform to our categories of American, African, or Arab literatures. This collaboration, which I will consider further in chapter 5, and Maghrebi literary criticism of Bowles's earlier works, which began to be circulated in the 1980s and 1990s, are yet another archival interruption of Americanist criticism. And if we listen to those Moroccan critics—themselves hardly mainstream—who propose Bowles as the leader of *al-adab at-Tanji*, many of the categories within which Bowles is generally considered are best left behind.

When these projects are written out of Bowles's career—because they are "translations" rather than single authored works of fiction—his earlier works are both elevated and misread. Indeed, if we open up our sense of Bowles's career to include his work in the 1930s and early 1940s, when he was more occupied with musical composition—especially for the theater, a deeply collaborative enterprise—we may trace the impulse for his work with Mrabet back further. In his autobiography, Bowles characterized the writing of fiction as built on shared points of reference with an imagined reader: "Long ago I had decided that the world was too complex for me ever to be able to write fiction; since I failed to understand life, I would not be able to find points of reference which the hypothetical reader might have in common with me."[75] Bowles is discussing his return to fiction in the mid-1940s, but this statement, written in 1972 near the end of his wife

Jane's long illness and well into his collaboration with Mrabet, offers an explanation for the shift in Bowles's own career. The move toward collaboration with Mrabet may be seen as a sort of refusal of the American literary context that was his necessary point of reference in the four books of fiction he published between 1949 and 1955. Though Bowles habitually ascribed secondary importance to the translation projects in interviews, such a position is belied both by the enormity of the project and when we locate the potentiality for such collaboration in his earliest work.

In the twenty-first century, the definitive end of the American century, there is a critical necessity to reflect back on the potentialities suppressed by cold war reading practices. Because *The Sheltering Sky* represents the encounter of Americans with the foreign during a transitional moment in cultural and political history, the novel is especially open to misreadings that mistake its representation of the Maghreb as mere exoticism, as a translation of the foreign for the domestic market. That exoticism is surely present in the novel and contributed to its initial financial success and offered a marketing strategy. But as I have argued, the novel sits uneasily in such a frame and discovers a challenging relationship to the borderless North African Berber, figured as linguistic disruption. In summoning up popular and critical misreadings of Bowles's work, I am attempting to *read through* such misreadings and the conditions that produce them.[76] If a less rigid sense of the nation and of national literature results, it is not my suggestion that such formulations be abandoned or that they have no meaning—the rise in "patriotism" in the United States and the neofascist nationalisms in Western Europe suggest otherwise. Neither is it my contention that cold war binarisms have not left a strong residue in post-9/11 U.S. foreign relations; the fact that they so obviously have means that the work to locate other paradigms for imagining the place of America and Americans in the world is urgent. At the same time as *The Sheltering Sky* quietly challenged the logic of the American century, however, it also figured the engagement of individuals across national borders in a way that underlined—even exacerbated—the disjuncture between the space of cultural production and the realm of foreign relations, a separation familiar to us today. Rereading Bowles's writing may help us make progress on the bridge from cultural production—including critique—back to that otherwise untouchable space.

II

Queer Tangier

Overleaf:
Petit Socco, Tangier, 1957. *Photo by Allen Ginsberg,*
courtesy of the Allen Ginsberg Trust.

3

TANGIER(S)

The Multiple Cold War Contexts

of the International Zone

[Next to Tangier] Sodom was a church picnic and Gomorrah was a
convention of Girl Scouts, Hollywood would never dare to do a movie
about Tangier because it would be accused of hoking up the script even
if the truth about the town were underplayed. . . . [Tangier] also contains more thieves, black marketers, spies, thugs, phonies, beachcomb-
ers, expatriates, degenerates, characters, operators, bandits, bums,
tramps, dipsomaniacs, politicians and charlatans than any other
place I ever saw.—Robert Ruark, 1947

Tanger is the prognostic pulse of the world, like a dream extending
from past into the future, a frontier between dream and reality—
the "reality" of both called into question.—William S. Burroughs,
letter to Allen Ginsberg and Jack Kerouac, 1955

Burroughs is in Tangiers I don't think he'll come back it's sinister.
—Allen Ginsberg, "America"

Tangiers (Plural)

To most Americans in the 1950s, the city of Tangier conjured up
images of excess. From about 1946, when Woolworth heiress Barbara Hutton outbid Generalissimo Franco to purchase a complex of
twenty-eight neighboring houses in the Kasbah (where she lived occa-

sionally, alternatively throwing extravagant parties and distributing munificent amounts of charity), until late 1959, when the former International Zone was finally fully absorbed into Morocco three years after the nation's independence (and what foreign capital remained left overnight, along with many of the expats), Tangier had a special place in the American imagination.[1] "Tangier has won the awe-stricken interest of the outside world," Raoul Simpkins wrote in the *Atlantic* in 1950. "Everybody's no man's land" ... "boom town" ... "anything goes" ... "free-wheeling" ... "an earthly paradise" ... "outlandish" ... "a booby prize" ... "a glorious 'Lost World'" ... "queer megalomania"—the phrases used to describe Tangier mixed easily superfluity and lack, a surplus of dissoluteness.[2] The excesses of Tangier that fascinated were financial, sexual, social, and governmental. That the city and its environs were the possession of no one nation-state but administered by a committee of eight Western powers, including the United States—with the end of the International Settlement in Shanghai, Tangier was the only internationally administered zone left in the world—and that it bordered and in some way pertained to a colonized nation fighting for its independence was the crucial background to the portrait.[3] Americans in Tangier enjoyed extraterritorial rights, meaning that they were immune to municipal laws that the United States didn't assent to, a situation that was the well-known basis on which the American individual and corporate presence rested. Tangier was good copy in 1950s America, a "paper city" in more ways than one. Periodicals as diverse as the *Saturday Evening Post, Fortune, American Mercury*, the *Nation, Wall Street Journal, Travel*, the *New Yorker, Newsweek, Flair, Time*, the *Atlantic, Vogue*, the *New York Times Magazine, Colliers*, and *Holiday* all published substantial articles on the city during the decade. And a number of Hollywood films, such as *That Man from Tangier, Tangier Incident*, and *Flight from Tangier*, to name just those released in 1953, played on the intrigue the name of the city summoned.[4] The city itself didn't hesitate to trade on its image: the Tangier Chamber of Commerce frequently ran an ad in the Paris edition of the *Herald Tribune* with the enticing tag "Tangier knows no restrictions of any kind!" The reference was to the lack of any taxes and the free currency market; the implications extended into the social and sexual.[5]

To those who lived in Tangier—a city that grew from 100,000 in 1946, with a quarter of that number non-Moroccan, to 185,000 by 1956, a boom fueled by the doubling of the foreign population[6]—there was a notable gap between the perception of Tangier back in the States and the "Tangerino" experience of the city. Tangier was tamer in most ways and more provincial than its reputation, as contributors to the local English-language *Tangier Gazette* often remarked. From afar, Tangier seemed more glamorous, its writers' colony denser, its gay scene wilder, its cosmopolitanism more liberating, its opportunities for rapid financial gain more certain, even its weather less changeable. Such assumptions drew the curious to visit or even move to the city, where some were initially disappointed. Still, those who stayed on learned to appreciate Tangier's particular forms of multiplicity. For many Tangier-based Americans (who numbered in the hundreds), Tangier was connected intimately to excess of a different sort: a city of numerous architectural modes and spatial experiences, both compressed and expansive at once; a place of plural legal, financial, governmental, and even postal systems, a space of no-space; a truly multilingual city; a place where experience was multiplied. "Tangier seems to exist on several dimensions," William S. Burroughs wrote in a 1955 essay he intended for the *New Yorker*, describing the experience of walking in the city. "Here fact merges into dream, and dreams erupt into the real world."[7] For Americans who did not make that trip, for whom Tangier existed on the page and in the imagination, Tangier remained a figure within the early cold war, a unique and fascinating place that played a small but important role within the American imaginary during a crucial decade-and-a-half when American self-definition—and America's role in the world—was rapidly changing.

This chapter examines the multiple Tangiers in circulation during this period and attempts to open up our understanding of the way the city signified in a variety of contexts: the public Tangier circulating in American popular discourse; the Tangier of the U.S. State Department; Tangier as haven or staging ground for Maghrebi nationalists; the Tangier experienced by local residents. The local Tangier included both an active population of European and American residents (some of whom had been born in Tangier) and a much larger population of Arabs and Riffian Berbers. As a result, the city is known by several names—three are represented in this chapter's epigraphs—leading to a confusion that I want to harness for its critical energy. Though the standard American name for the city is *Tangier*, many Americans refer to it as *Tangiers*, which is what the British call the place. French and Spanish names for the city are both written *Tanger*, though pronounced differently: in French, as Jean Genet put it, the city rhymes with the French word *danger*. In Arabic, the city is *Tanja* and a Moroccan resident is a *Tanjawi*. (Members of the anglophone community are referred to as Tangerinos.) There were also significant Sephardic Jewish and Indian communities. Though I prefer *Tangier* when referring to the city in English, it seems appropriate to use *Tangiers* as a collective plural to refer to it during its international days (1925–1956, officially, and till 1960 by extension of the royal decree), since it suggests at once multiple populations who made the city their own. *Tangiers* also suggests something about the way the city signified at once excess and lack during the early cold war. All of these Tangiers are important to a fuller appreciation of American literary and cultural history of the 1950s and for what the fascination with Tangier helps illuminate—and illustrate—about the early cold war itself.

Allen Ginsberg's wonderful line in "America" (1956) poses Burroughs's presence in Tangiers as a commentary on the dismal state of America: "America I'm putting my queer shoulder to the wheel," the poem ends.[8] What's "sinister" about Tangier is its turn away, its left-handed (Latin: *sinister*) queerness. Ginsberg would soon visit, when he went to help Burroughs edit *Naked Lunch*. And in his major poem "Howl" (1955), Burroughs's (unnamed) presence in "Tangiers for the boys" (18) is a part of Ginsberg's long catalog of the fate of the "best minds of my generation" (9). Many of the crucial writers of the decade lived in or spent time in Tangier during this period. Paul and Jane Bowles, William Burroughs, Brion Gysin, Truman Capote, Tennessee Williams, Gore Vidal, Ned Rorem, Jack Kerouac, Allen Ginsberg, and others all wrote about their time in Tangier or figured it in their work. In Tangier they socialized or crossed paths with important European and Moroccan writers and artists, including Samuel Beckett,[9] Francis Bacon, Ian Fleming, Josef Kessel, Robin Maugham, Rupert Croft-Cooke, Mohamed Choukri, Moumen Smihi, Mohammed Mrabet, Tahar Ben Jelloun, and Ahmed Yacoubi, and later, in the sixties, Jean Genet, Juan Goytisolo, Joe Orton, and American writers such as Alfred Chester, Timothy Leary, and Ted Joans. Several major works of literature came out of Tangier during the fifties—Burroughs's masterpiece *Naked Lunch* (1959); Paul Bowles's novel *Let It Come Down* (1952); Jane Bowles's 1953 play *In the Summer House* and her novella "Camp Cataract"; and the earliest of Paul Bowles's collaborations with Moroccan storytellers—texts intimately linked to their authors' experiences and understandings of the International Zone. These texts emerged from that local Tangier experienced by residents, even though they were received by audiences for whom the more exaggerated—and flatter—Tangier was known. That split may help to explain the failure in most early criticism to notice what was perhaps most strange and original about the interplay of aesthetic innovation and political vision in these texts, and to focus instead on a more predictable set of excesses or essentially to ignore the work. Recently, these three American authors have gained more critical attention. Yet influenced by earlier criticism of their work—which tended not to question the relationship of literature to geopolitics—the specificity of the Tangier they inhabited has been neglected. Such a position has been justified by separating the authors from their surroundings. The exaggeration of Burroughs's morphine-induced disaffection from Tangier and in turn from the process of writing his own book, for example, has enabled such a critical stance. Counter to such critical assumptions, however, all three authors were deeply engaged with their surroundings, as I'll explore in greater depth in chapters 4 and 5.

Residents of Tangier might have paid varying amounts of attention to the news, and sympathies regarding Moroccan independence ran the gamut for the foreign communities. But with occasional riots in the streets, an active diplomatic community mingling in the cafés and at parties (where rumors of espionage were rampant), and with Moroccan nationalists organizing actively to defeat the French and Spanish protectorates to the south, Tangier in the 1950s was not a place in which complete apathy was possible. The *Tangier Gazette*, a weekly English-language newspaper, covered the political scene avidly, and even those who read the paper for the amusing columns or accounts of social events would come across articles discussing the local political administration, nationalists' activities in Tangier and environs, exposés of poor living conditions for Moroccans, and calls for reform. Further, Tangier's shifting and uncertain status after the 1952 riots—and certainly after 1955, when Moroccan independence seemed finally inevitable—until the end of the decade, when the new Moroccan government rescinded its always tentative offer to extend Tangier's unique conditions, was of concern to all foreign residents. Even those foreigners who eventually stayed on in Tangier after 1960, such as the Bowleses, had worried in the 1950s that they would be ejected by the new Moroccan government. The Tangier of the 1960s, which a different wave of Americans sought out, was in any case qualitatively different. The particular political, economic, and social configurations of International Tangier disappeared when the Moroccan regime removed the last vestiges of its special conditions in 1960.

Tangier and greater Morocco were during this period both in the midst of a political transition that would ultimately bring them together. In 1946, a series of meetings of the Unity Party took place in Tangier; they were covered in the *Tangier Gazette* and open to the public. In April 1947, during a three-day visit to Tangier from the French Zone (a visit that had been anticipated in Tangier and delayed by the French), the sultan, Sidi Mohammed ben Youssef, made a historic speech that popularized the independence movement and solidified his own place at the helm of the future nation, as the figurehead for the nationalist impulses of the people. After he was forcibly exiled to Madagascar by the French in 1953, Sidi Mohammed was the face of the revolution—Moroccans imagined they saw him in the moon. That 1947 Tangier visit also had had a more immediate effect on the French governing regime: it resulted in the recall of liberal resident-general Eric Labonne, and a hard-line crackdown on the nationalists and was a turning point in the revolution. In the subsequent eight-and-a-half years it would take to win independence from the French, Tangier was a haven, albeit a risky one, for nationalists in exile or in hiding from the Spanish and French protectorates to the south. For such figures, Tangier was on an axis with Cairo, the headquarters of the Arab League, and a staging ground for the political organization against both zones; Tangier was where Moroccan nationalists such as 'Allal al-Fassi, Abdelkhalek Torres, Mohammed Laghzaoui, Abdellatif Sbihi, and Abdelkebir al Fassi were based. The city was spared the bulk of rioting and visible political unrest that much of Morocco to the south was undergoing during the 1950s. To be sure, there were political demonstrations, and in 1952 and 1955 some were violent, but it was nonetheless a key location for the independence movement. In 1950, when Habib Bourguiba, the Tunisian nationalist leader, arrived suddenly in Tangier to meet privately with nationalists in exile, the French—in cahoots with the president of the Committee of Control, a Belgian who did not consult the other members of the governing body—had him quickly sent back to Madrid, setting off a wave of international protest at the breach of the Tangier Statute. Tangier was in principle a free zone, but practice could diverge from principle. Al-Fassi also eventually decamped to Cairo after being arrested by the French.[10]

After 1945, Tangier's political status, as well as the political fate of what

Americans called French North Africa, was of increasing interest to the U.S. Department of State. The U.S. maintained a diplomatic mission in Tangier, housed in a forty-five-room complex in the medina. The American Legation had grown around the site of the original residence of the American consul, a gift of Sultan Moulay Slimane to the United States in 1821.[11] The Tangier Legation was a crucial component of the U.S. diplomatic machinery for the Maghreb as a whole, and in June 1949, the annual North African conference on the Maghreb was moved there from Paris (an item on the agenda investigated the "possibility of [U.S.] personnel in Algeria and Tunisia benefiting from the Tangier exchange rate.")[12] Despite their proximity to events, and in spite of some consular officials' warnings, the U.S. political establishment did not recognize how close Maghrebi independence was, nor the extent of popular support the nationalists enjoyed. As I discussed in chapter 2, during the Truman Administration the United States was concerned with the political fortunes of the Maghreb in large part because of the depth of the investment in postwar France and the fear of French instability. The commitment to France would become yet more entrenched in the 1950s, especially after the escalation of the war in Vietnam and the fear that the Maghreb might become "another Indochina." Publicly, the United States backed France until very late in the struggle for independence, much to the dismay of Moroccan and Tunisian nationalists who expressed their sense of betrayal in closed-door meetings with State Department officials. Among themselves, American Foreign Service Officers (FSOs) expressed frustration at the slowness of French reforms. Fearful of offending the French, the United States kept the Moroccan case off the United Nations agenda again in 1951 and subsequently supported France over the nationalists in the UN General Assembly meetings on the Maghreb. A 1953 UN statement affirming the "right of the people of Morocco to free, democratic political institutions" was one vote short of passing, killed by U.S. abstention.[13] After 1950, when agreements were signed with France for the expansion of U.S. military bases without consulting the Sultan, the U.S. investment in French Morocco helped buttress the major new investment in the country and arguably delayed the movement toward independence.

As late as June 1955, just five months before the deposed sultan was back on the throne, the Operations Coordinating Board reviewing U.S. National Security Council policy on French North Africa was still urging a "middle-of-the-road position" even while noting united opposition at the

Members of the U.S. diplomatic mission in a Tangier restaurant, late 1955 or early 1956. Julius Holmes, chief diplomatic agent, is sitting in the back right. Legal officer Edwin Smith is second from the left, talking to FSO Edward Clarke, who wears Moroccan clothing, as does security officer Murray Jackson, at the far right. Members of the orchestra and personal servants sit in the foreground; a waiter stands in the background. *Courtesy of the Tangier American Legation Museum.*

recently concluded Asian-African Conference at Bandung, Indonesia, and North African resentment of U.S. policies.[14] Still, much of the French public criticized the United States for not taking a firmer pro-French stance and decried what was called the Coca-Colanization of their country. When Moroccan independence did come, the United States would have to renegotiate its place in the bases with the kingdom, yet in late 1956, months after independence, President Eisenhower still wanted to include the French in talks with Morocco, though his joint chiefs of staff urged him to deal directly with the Moroccans.[15] (The base negotiations would be the primary political issue between the United States and Morocco for the next couple of years. After spending millions of dollars in payoffs to keep them running, the United States eventually closed the bases in the 1960s.) Even after Moroccan and Tunisian independence, the United States continued to stand by France against Algeria. On July 1, 1957, Senator John F. Kennedy introduced a resolution to push for a negotiated peace that would provide for Algerian independence or autonomy, a break with the long-held U.S. position. Kennedy's speech angered the French, who were in turn reassured by Secretary of State John Foster Dulles that any such resolution would not bind the Eisenhower administration.[16] The slowness of the U.S. political establishment to recognize or acknowledge the sea change in the Maghreb is partially explained by political interest and diplomatic expediency. But it was also the response of an institution to a series of representations of the region by its own members—the staff consular reports, policy analysis, FSO telegrams, and so on—and subject to the limitations of that institution's conceptual framework, here based on a sense that national participation was something that Maghrebis were not quite ready for and not especially interested in.

Within this third context, then, Tangier had a particular meaning that was both distinct from the other meanings of *Tangier* concurrently in circulation and overlapped with them. Much of the official American interest in Tangier was secret, yet it filtered through the literary community and in the collapsed social worlds of Tangier via social crossings that bridged the realms of government, business, and the media. And since foreign policy draws upon representations of particular areas or contexts, these same overlapping worlds of Tangier suggest movement in the other direction as well: from media or literary representations back into the political. Recovering some of those overlaps allows us to make a case for the interplay of political context and aesthetic innovation, so vividly present in Burroughs's work and, in different ways, the Bowleses'. Still, the relationship between foreign relations and literary production needs to be carefully enunciated rather than taken for granted or suggested by juxtaposition, as I argued in chapter 2, and we'll need to continue to derive a method for reading "Tangerian lit."

In Tangier, the density of the population and the social and physical layout of the city meant that there were inevitable crossings of communities; these crossings challenge the assertion of complete separation between spheres. Physically, Tangier's center had been laid out for a population of a few dozen thousand and was unaltered despite the boom in the city's population, producing crowds on the major streets and constant encounters that echoed and produced some of the crossings that occur in the pages of *Naked Lunch*, *Let It Come Down*, State Department reports, and the *Tangier Gazette*. Allow me to sketch the urban center, since it was frequently on the narrow streets and compressed physical space of Tangier that such crossings occurred and since those streets produced the sense of multiplicity I have named earlier. The two major axes of the city—the east-west Boulevard Pasteur and the north-south Rue du Statut—intersected at the Place de France, a bustling roundabout ringed by popular cafés frequented by the diplomatic community and Moroccan nationalists. Boulevard Pasteur was the main artery of the newer part of the city, developed early in the twentieth century and lined by international-style buildings. It lay at the top of a high hill with a magnificent view of the Straits of Gibraltar. From the Place de France, the Rue du Statut ran downhill, north toward the harbor. A few steps down was Madame Porte's tea salon, a social institution among the expat set; further down the hill, the Rue du Statut twisted and emptied into the Grand Socco, a major open-air marketplace (from the Arabic word *suq*, meaning market, and referred to by the Spanish as the Zoco Grande). Across the large square and through a gateway to the medina, the Rue des Siaghines picked up where Rue du Statut left off, running downhill even more steeply, to the northeast, straight through the heart of the medina into the Petit Socco (or Zoco Chico in Spanish), a crowded and compressed plaza filled with open-air cafés; on the other end of the Petit Socco the road continued downhill past the grand mosque and finally, at the bottom of the hill, and with a sharp right, ended at the harbor. Burroughs described "an inexorable process of suction" moving foot traffic downward from the

Place de France into the Zoco Chico.[17] Both ends of that corridor and the space between them drew the full range of people in Tangier. As there are only very few ways to get anywhere in downtown Tangier, walking in the center of town was (and is) more practical than traveling by automobile. Within most of the medina driving cars is generally impossible because of the narrowness of the streets (the American Legation is to this day reached on foot).

The street encounters that were impossible to avoid were echoed in a collapsing of social worlds in the cafés and parties of Tangier—little wonder that language and ideas reappear across these multiple spheres. It was common for journalists to remark—regarding the American School of Tangier or the American Library, for example—that cultural institutions were doing political work for the United States, via propaganda or in providing a model of the "American Way of Life," as the sanguine phrase went. Such a comment also made it into classified State Department reports where it stood as analysis. Did the recurrence of the "fact" occur because it was a shared impression or because FSOs read the papers too?[18] The Bowleses and William Burroughs counted among their friends and dinner partners journalists and experts in Moroccan political affairs, such as Charles Gallagher, a member of the American Universities Field Staff, who, starting in 1955, was writing frequent reports on Morocco and the greater Maghreb and who would publish a political history of the Maghreb, and David Woolman, an amateur anthropologist who wrote columns on Tangier for the Casablanca-based *Moroccan Courier*. Conversations between these friends moved information and even attitudes in both directions. A similar exchange of ideas occurred between Americans who worked at the three major American employers in Tangier—Mackay Radio, RCA, and the Voice of America (Coca-Cola also had a bottling plant)—and others who may have sent their children to the American School of Tangier or borrowed books from the American Library or were members at the American Club in Brooks Park or attended one of Barbara Hutton's spectacular gatherings.

There were significant gaps between these Tangiers too, however, caused as much by structural differences between them and the contrasting impulses that those structures encourage. The journalistic impulse toward exaggeration separated the public Tangier from the Tangerino experience of the city. The diplomatic need for secrecy, the briefer tenure of diplomats stationed at Tangier, and the dominance of a cold war

Outside the gate of the American School of Tangier, October 2, 1950, in the first days after it opened. Left to right: George C. McGee, under secretary for Near Eastern, South Asian, and African Affairs; Ruth C. Sloan, public affairs staff of the State Department; Robert Sheehan, public affairs officer, American Legation, Tangier. *Courtesy of the American School of Tangier.*

geopolitical frame through which FSOs saw the local separated out their Tangier from the others. Questions of language, translation, and a different cultural frame of reference (orientation toward Cairo and Mecca rather than Washington and Moscow) kept the Tanjawi Tangier somewhat isolated from American discourse about it. Ultimately I am most interested in the crossover moments, however, texts that engage multiple publics, and I name these multiple Tangiers a bit schematically in part to produce the sense of disorienting multiplicity in the city to which I think the most astute observers of it—such as Burroughs—responded.

National Jealousies and Supranational Cooperation

Before moving back into the more pubic Tangiers in circulation, I'd like to explore further the meanings of Tangier within the U.S. Department of State apparatus. Though operating secretly, for the most part, the U.S. delegation was a key component of the American presence in Tangier. Read closely, the diplomatic maneuvering and behind-the-scenes political machinations suggest the tensions between national identification and its alternatives at the heart of the double game the United States was playing in Tangier and in French Morocco. Understanding these tensions will also be useful in the third section of this chapter, which looks at Tangier's "queerness" in the American imagination and the relationship of the fascination with International Tangier to the American national narrative.

Diplomatically, the decade after World War II in Tangier was dominated by a series of questions regarding the legal position of the United States in the International Zone and jockeying for positions of influence within the political administration of the zone. In part because of the myopia regarding how close independence throughout the Maghreb truly was, the State Department's interest in Tangier focused more on cold war geopolitics than on Tangier's relationship to Morocco or its local population. Underlying the various episodes was an abiding fear that the Soviets would turn up to assert a presence in Tangier. This extended to the consular staff and those appointed to lead the United States delegation, who after Maxwell Blake's retirement in 1940 after fifteen years in Tangier tended to remain for shorter periods and thus have less opportunity to shed Washington's cold war lenses. According to Graham Stuart in 1955, the shorter tenure of American representatives put the United States at a disadvantage: "[The job] can only be done effectively if the officer is left at the post long enough to be completely familiar with the background of the many problems facing the Zone. He must be able to carry on his negotiations in Spanish and French as well as English. He must be able to defend American interests in competition with top-flight European diplomats, many of whom have spent decades at Tangier."[19] Stuart's advice went unheeded.[20] His prescription might well have been extended to North Africa generally, that it might be understood on its own terms outside the limiting binarism of the U.S.-Soviet struggle. Egypt's Gamal Nasser, for example, exploited the American tendency to see the region within a cold war binary frame.[21]

In 1945, the United States was invited by France and the United Kingdom to participate in a provisional administration being set up after World War II. The first order of business was to eject the Spanish, who during the war had occupied Tangier militarily and abolished the internationally administered Committee of Control, which had ruled the zone since 1925. After the three powers met in Paris, in July 1945, the Soviets announced their interest in participating. Russia had been a signatory to the 1906 Act of Algeciras, which had established the basis for an International Tangier. But with virtually no population in Tangier, the Soviets had shown little interest in the city and had no political presence in the Tangier Zone.[22] The apparent motivation of the Soviets now was to make certain that Franco Spain was kept from the Tangier administration. The Final Act of 1945, agreed to by the United States, United Kingdom, France, and the USSR, and the Anglo-French Agreement of the same year, ejected Spanish troops and reestablished international administration. The reorganized Committee of Control had representatives from Belgium, France, Italy, the Netherlands, Portugal, the United States, and the United Kingdom. Spain was allowed to participate on the committee but forbidden to assume administrative posts.[23] The Soviets, however, protested the presence of the Franco government on the committee at all and never assumed the seats they were entitled to under the 1945 agreement. Nonetheless, the international administration created by this agreement was perhaps the closest Tangier got in fact to international, neutral governance.[24] No wonder that as the new United Nations organization was considering sites for its headquarters, the Tangier Chamber of Commerce—naively or not—proposed their own city as an ideal site.[25] The Tangier government shirked its share of problems, to be sure, but as the British author Rom Landau put it in 1952, "Today more than ever the example of a constructive, co-operative effort on the part of different countries, representing different systems and possibly mutually antagonistic interests, should be of some value to the rest of the world. In a world hungry for security gained through common endeavour, every small crumb of comfort is welcome."[26]

The international balance and the impulse toward neutrality were not, however, to last for long. After riots broke out in Tangier on March 30, 1952—the fortieth anniversary of the Treaty of Fez, which had formally established the French protectorate in Morocco—Spain used the disorder as pretext to press for increased participation in the Tangier administration.[27] Recognizing Spain's large population in the city and the fact that the Tangier Zone was surrounded by Spanish-controlled territory, the United States did not oppose. By this point, however, U.S. interests in Tangier had increased markedly. The U.S. had grown in prestige via the establishment of three radio-transfer stations (Mackay, RCA, and the Voice of America) and of military bases in the French Zone. The State Department considered Mackay and RCA integral to national security and crucial to guard, though they were private companies. By 1956, RCA would move 15 million messages a year through Tangier—one-fourth of all of RCA's message business—and had invested $6 million in its Tangier plant.[28] The geopolitical importance of Tangier's location had rapidly shifted from guardian of the Straits of Gibraltar to a point of easy access to Europe and the Mediterranean by military aircraft and to the rest of the world by radio wave. Despite its investment in Tangier, to the United States Spain's 1952 request was seen less as a power play and more as an opportunity to kick the Soviets off the Committee of Control and out of the Legislative Assembly, even though the Soviets had still not occupied any of the seats provided for it seven years earlier. Cold war fears of the Soviets were stronger for the United States than local experience, and in the end, Spain gained much for the willingness of the Americans to consent to their proposals. As diplomats in Tangier negotiated, a flurry of attention to the manner of ridding Tangier of the Soviets absorbed the U.S. State Department, from extensive analysis by international law experts to secret counsel from George Kennan, then still in Moscow as U.S. ambassador. Kennan's advice—not to "disturb [a] dormant situation" since the Soviets had neglected Tangier for thirty-five years and to avoid provoking them to save face—was influential.[29] But the legal analysis reveals the ways in which Tangier was a cipher for cold war diplomatic concerns, and makes visible underlying assumptions behind the U.S. policy.

In a May 1952 report, Smith Crowe, a legal adviser for Near Eastern, South Asian and African Affairs grappled with the question: would it be better to exclude the Soviets by arranging for a *dahir* (decree) from Sidi Mohammed or to push for the Committee of Control itself to vote the Soviets out? The question was thorny because it dealt not only with competing agreements and protocols for the administration of Tangier, but also with whether the Sultan of Morocco's jurisdiction extended to Tangier, a question related to the legality of the French protectorate itself. Crowe pointed out that even if a Sultan's dahir was preferable (since it ostensibly hid U.S. involvement), it was awkward in terms of dealings with the French, for it would "leave open the possibility of independent action by the Sultan with respect to Tangier affairs which would not only be embarrassing to the French, but inconsistent with their long stated position of control and influence over Moroccan foreign policy."[30] Crowe recommended dealing through the Committee of Control, rather than employing the "use of a legal fiction"—that is, the dahir. Crowe's use of the term *legal fiction* hints at the competing legal fictions in play, fictions that sustained the U.S. presence in the International Zone. If the United States provoked a dahir, the sultan's claimed authority over Tangier politics would implicitly challenge the primacy of one colonizing regime (the French) while maintaining another (the Committee of Control, on which the French sat); better to maintain the larger fiction that the authority of the French Zone was not put into question by the sultan's relationship to the Tangier Zone.[31] The U.S. position in Tangier was based on this uneasy relationship between Tangier and Morocco, which were in a sense structurally opposed—the one based on an agreement that was international in gesture, the other on the supremacy of the nation form (as basis for colonialism). (As we'll see, this opposition is at the heart of Burroughs's and Paul Bowles's sense of Tangier's possibility within the world order.) Lowe's report also demonstrates the ways in which the specter of the Soviets persistently upset more immediate interests in Tangier or longer-range strategy for Morocco. It does not, that is to say, more than pause over the conflicting legal presumptions he exposes: they are instead the opportunity for Crowe's analysis.

The new protocol, signed November 10, 1952, but not effective until August 1, 1953, was a disappointment for those who looked at Tangier as a model for the future.[32] It ultimately benefited Spain and France greatly, and Britain and Italy to a lesser extent, while only indirectly addressing the Soviet presence in the Committee of Control.[33] The United States would continue to worry that the Soviets might build their own radio transfer stations in Tangier, though there was never any evidence of Soviet designs to do so; the establishment of diplomatic relations with Libya and an arms sale to Egypt were as close as they apparently got.[34] The U.S. Diplomatic Agent concluded that the new protocol had, in effect, moved Tangier away from its 1945 conception, which held neutral powers in control and an international balance of power, back to the prewar situation that gave Spain and France increased power. Having second thoughts, the United States attempted to protest that to which it had tacitly assented, setting off a diplomatic flurry that sometimes reached the point of absurdity (such as when the French complained that the United States couldn't express reservations retroactively). As the powers grappled with the American objection, the United States analyzed its own position in Tangier. Recognizing the legal tenuousness of its claims to extraterritorial status, the fragility of which was underlined by a court case at the Hague that had recently gone against the United States, and responding to the new protocol, U.S. representatives shifted their attention toward protecting commercial interests in the Tangier Zone rather than in the experiment in international governance.

Central to this design was maintaining extraterritorial rights for U.S. citizens and businesses in Tangier, which the United States claimed in both Tangier and French Morocco—a point of contention with France and later with the Moroccan state. This legal advantage was the basis on which the entire American presence in Tangier (official and nonofficial) rested. The popular mythology regarding William Burroughs's flight to Tangier to escape legal restrictions at home was true for the entire American population and supported actively by the diplomatic service. Burroughs remarked on it in his letters, and nearly every European in Tangier was well aware of the special legal status of Americans. As Landau commented, "The American in Tangier is as free and as much his own master as he would be in his own country."[35] (In *The Man Who Knew Too Much*, which I discuss in chapter 4, Hitchcock will suggest that extraterritorial rights are unnatural; but of course there the beneficiaries are not Americans.) The rights, claimed on the basis of an 1836 treaty, were upheld by both tradition and political might. Over the next couple of years, the

United States fought and appealed court cases that challenged the rights and used temporary advantages to press for a local ordinance that would bypass the fragile law and protect U.S. radio interests in Tangier.[36]

Despite these manipulations, there is still much to suggest that Tangier gave face to a different political opportunity in the postwar period. Landau characterized it as the opposition of the "national jealousies" that marked the rest of the world and the "supra-national co-operation in the political, economic and social spheres" that he found in Tangier, thus naming a space that exposed the nation form as a fiction (xi). This Tangier is the basis for what I called "Tangerian lit" in the previous chapter. Even if the political machinations of the Committee of Control echoed cold war geo-politics (which dictated them), the ambiguities of the legal codes and over-lapping and conflicting statutes and systems of Tangier repeated the mul-tiplicity of Tangier's spatial and experiential environment. In other words, the diplomatic Tangier is but one of the several Tangiers in simultaneous operation. Even on the political level, Tangier meant one thing to Moroc-can nationalists and apparently quite another to the jockeying Western cold war powers. For residents, aware of the political maneuverings behind the scenes, at least in vague outlines, a more "supra-national" experience might be found in the everyday experience of the city itself. The multiple curren-cies, post offices, school systems, and languages simultaneously in opera-tion in Tangier were tangible elements of daily existence.[37] Even if some claimed that the communities lived in a certain amount of isolation from one another, there was no doubt that Tangier was no one nation's posses-sion at all (even the Moroccans'); individuals did not need to live multi-lingual lives and have friends of multiple nationalities (though many did) to be a part of an experiment in internationalism on the larger scale.[38] The political machinations that moved Tangier from an experiment in interna-tional (or supranational) governance in 1945 toward a return of national supremacist conditions after 1953 were one thing, but the city itself, and the experience of living in it, maintained a supranational feeling. What we might call the "potentiality" of 1945–53 Tangier's political structure—a word that implies that something about Tangier remains available to be reactivated, or activated elsewhere, as in Burroughs's work—survived as vestiges after 1953 and through the decade.[39]

That Tangier did not remain an international zone is not to be la-mented, for the independence of Morocco that would reclaim it was just and appropriate. The independence of Morocco represented the victory

On the rooftop of Dr. Benabad's beach house in Asilah in the mid-
1950s. Left to right: unnamed American newspaper journalist;
Mohammed el Khatib, teacher at the American School of Tangier;
Julia Wittinghill, wife of a political attaché at the legation; Dr.
Ahmed Benabad. Foreground: Stuart Gates, assistant attaché at the
legation. *Courtesy of the Tangier American Legation Museum.*

of the nationalists—the alliance of the Istiqlal (independence) party, the
sultan, and other parties—over the French and the Spanish, two colonial
powers. And if we consider colonialism and imperialism more largely as
expressions of nationalism taking their natural course, then it seems only
appropriate that fights for independence be waged in the same register, as
Frantz Fanon had argued in *Les Damnées de la terre*, even while signaling
his own misgivings. Further, the commitment to Tangier for most of the
powers and corporations present was clearly toward profit and escape
from regulation, rather than a commitment to a principle worthy of
defense—such as to the land or the collectivity as pertaining to something beyond the national form. The Moroccan population, which even
at the peak of the international population still outnumbered the non-
Moroccan, bore the brunt of the free zone's freeness. The lack of an
income tax produced no money for social services, and poverty among the
Moroccan population was at stark contrast to the international community, as many noted.[40] Legally, the Moroccan suffered harsher penalties

than the Europeans. This is not debatable, but neither was it the necessary precondition for a multi- or supranational governance—it was perhaps the fatal flaw. There was in fact a strong tradition of reform within those committed to the International Zone. We may therefore still lament the loss of a supranational potentiality that briefly and imperfectly flourished in Tangier and that was repressed by the 1952 protocol. The latter revision represented not only the return of the Spanish to administrative power and an increase in French power, but more largely the return of the nation-form to dominance over the principle of supranational cooperation. This predicted and made necessary the eventual loss of the International Zone to independent Morocco because it shifted the register back to one foregrounding national identification, within which Moroccan nationalism would necessarily be the just response. In this sense, we may understand Burroughs's antinationalist statements and Paul Bowles's critique of the Moroccan nationalists as displaced laments for what the Europeans did to Tangier rather than anti-Moroccan sentiments, as they have been sometimes taken. Tangier represented—briefly and imperfectly—a possibility outside of the nationally focused movement between European empire and American hegemony. This was true variously for the U.S. political establishment, so slow in recognizing the change coming to North Africa, and for residents who had no connections to government, such as Burroughs. The State Department's sense of Tangier's internationalism was quite different from Burroughs's Interzone, but they emerge from and shared the same environment.

Queer Tangier

Tangier, everybody's no man's land on the western shores of North Africa, has no national anthem other than the sweet melody of hard cash. Those extraordinary 140 square miles, administered jointly by ten powers, have been alternately called the planet's meanest smugglers' den, a noble experiment in international government, paradise for rugged entrepreneurs, a queer hell patronized by the world's lustiest rascals. But anybody lured to Tangier by one of these somewhat contradictory claims is in for sad disappointment.
—*Fortune*, August 1950

[Robert Ruark] attribut[es] most of the known and many of the
unknown vices of humanity to Tangier and its inhabitants. We have
heard the theme so often that it has begun to pall, but doubtless the
backwoods men of Ohio and Texas will lap it up and be amused. . . .
There is the further revelation that in Tangier "murder often does
not even make the papers, because [it] is a business between killer
and killed." Well, well, well!—*Tangier Gazette*, August 1, 1947

In the first section of this chapter, I distinguished between an image of
Tangier in the American imagination and a variety of more locally defined
"Tangiers," where the latter referred variously to the experience of particular communities and of individual resident writers. I want now to look
briefly at the more popular Tangier, that which circulated in the United
States, in order to make an argument about how it functioned in cold war
discourse. Though the American media frequently exaggerated Tangier's
particularities, I don't intend to counter with a positively defined reality of
Tangier in this period (except that laying out a number of "Tangiers" may
give a fuller sense of it). The *Tangier Gazette* columnist quoted above
responds to Robert Ruark's fabulous claim about Tangier—that the city
was so dissolute that even murder was unexceptional—not by offering
statistics to disprove the public exaggeration.[41] Rather, the Tangier columnist's "Well, well, well!" is a response befitting Tangier itself: it suggests differing realms of reality and representation. It is an acknowledgment that *Tangier* had become something of a floating signifier, and that
an image of it as decadent and dissolute was what provincial America
desired—"the backwoods men of Ohio and Texas will lap it up and be
amused"—and did not impinge upon meanings of *Tangier* held locally.
The context within which the writing by Burroughs, the Bowleses, and
others was received in the United States contributed to disciplining out
their important departures from cold war thinking. But more broadly
than these works of literature, the popular representation of "Tangier"
attempted to contain a more challenging potential that the city threatened: its supranational potential and its queerness. Mainstream journalists often used the word *queer* in their descriptions of Tangier, promoting
a logic that would seek to contain Tangier's challenge by rendering it
abject. In summoning a more potent use of the same word, I seek to evoke

the potentiality of "queer Tangier" contra those cold war strategies, or in the gaps of their logic.[42]

First I want to look carefully at the Tangier produced for "the backwoods men of Ohio and Texas," as well as for the readers of *Colliers* and the *Saturday Evening Post*. What in these exaggerated portraits provided the "amusement"? If the State Department's interpretations and representations of Tangier had material effect on Tangier because they influenced policy, representations of Tangier in the American media were at a further remove. Yet they served a function within the national narrative of cold war America, a narrative that critics such as Alan Nadel, Donald Pease, Elaine Tyler May, Robert Corber, and others have analyzed in terms of the rich interplay between global politics and domestic concerns. The *queerness* of Tangier, a term that most commentators employed while describing the city (or suggested or signified) was about more than Tangier's well-known relationship to gay male tourism. (The presence of an openly gay population was only hinted at by some journalists.) More largely, there is buried within the American fascination with Tangier a sense of a potential that might threaten domestic America at its roots. Thus the need within the national narrative to cordon off the city, to repress that potential, so that the route to Tangier did not become a detour. As Etienne Balibar has argued, the nation form is neither natural nor best understood as a linear development, relying on the continual production of outsiders, of foreigners, to help produce the people (a "fictive ethnicity" in Balibar's terms), its primary goal and the basis of the state.[43] Tangier's double threat then was that Americans there were apparently living happily and that a state was apparently productively organized around a formulation different from that in the United States.

If this was a crucial time in the history of the city and of greater Morocco, the period from 1946 to 1959 was also a hinge in American cultural and political history. The domestic and international crises faced by the United States were deeply intertwined, as questions of national identity and America's place in the global order reflected on one another. The so-called Age of Doubt of the postwar 1940s (the anxiety about a return of economic depression and another outbreak of global war), McCarthyism, the escalation of tensions with the USSR and the PRC, the Korean War, growing involvement in the French war in Indochina, the domestic crisis of segregation and the violent struggle for civil rights, the Suez Crisis, decolonization in Africa, and a host of other domestic and international emergencies must be seen as a network in which doubts at home fueled or were fueled by international crises. As historians of cold war race relations have reminded us, domestic problems regarding segregation reverberated internationally, and conflicts located in Ethiopia or South Africa were translated back on the domestic scene, where they helped forge the meaning of African Americanness. The blanching of Tangier, then, is one of the more obvious conservative turns in popular accounts, a turn away from the Tanjawi population itself, except when docile and when "they love us," as one headline went. The Tanjawi population of Tangier was comprised of a complex array of ethnicities, from Riffian Berbers and Arabs to darker-skinned people from southern Morocco and Saharan and sub-Saharan Africa. But this spectrum of ethnicities, which was not segregated and which did intermarry, was rarely if ever the topic of American coverage of Tangier during the 1940s and 1950s. A more immediate concern to American journalists was the Anglo-American community in Tangier as ciphers for something challenging and disturbing about the city itself. The turn away from race was a turn away from Tangier as African.

During the late 1940s and the 1950s, defining the meaning of American national identity was a popular topic. Among mainstream U.S. intellectuals, a turn toward consensus marked public and academic discourse as an enormous amount of ink and paper was dedicated to analyzing the national "character" and reinterpreting U.S. history in the wake of World War II. The question, whether implicit or explicit, was: What about the American character had produced the conditions for U.S. victory in the war and global supremacy? And, by extension, what message did the United States have for the world? As Jackson Lears has shown, such discussions, even those critical of the widely derided conformism of the postwar American population, almost invariably avoided an analysis of contemporary power relations. Early cold war intellectuals instead turned abstract concepts (such as abundance, organization, society) into historical actors, shifting their attention toward an analysis of images—a shift "from Wall Street to Madison Avenue, from the financial power behind advanced capitalism to the cultural values associated with its products."[44] Employing Antonio Gramsci's terminology, Lears argues compellingly that a *hegemonic historical bloc* had come into its own in the postwar period. What marked this bloc or "new class," in the process of formation since early in the century and comprised of "salaried managers, administrators, academics, technicians, and journalists," was that they were people who "manipulated symbols rather than made things, whose stock in trade consisted of their organizational, technical, conceptual, or verbal skills." Subcultures (within or without the United States) that did not conform to the bloc—African Americans or the working class, in his examples—were dismissed or ignored, and thereby "rendered marginal or even invisible to the wider public culture" (50).

Lears's analysis provides a framework within which to understand the importance for Americans of making sense of Tangier on the symbolic level. A scene in Bernard Dryer's bestselling 1958 novel *The Image Makers*, set largely in International Tangier during the mid-1950s (also in Greenwich, Connecticut, and in Paris, a compelling triangle), highlights the way in which members of what Lears called the hegemonic historical bloc might battle over Tangier's meaning as image. As the novel's title suggests, the members of the international class that the novel takes as its subjects—surgeons, financiers, journalists, Maghrebi nationalists—are seen as manipulators of images. Dryer pits one of his protagonists, the cosmopolitan founder of a major Tangier bank, against a reporter for the *Wall Street Journal* who has come to report on the alleged flight of capital from Tangier (the scene, which places recognizable phrases used to describe Tangier by Ruark and other journalists in the mouth of the fictional journalist, seems to be based on an article that in fact appeared in the *Wall Street Journal* in 1956). The stakes of such a meeting have been made clear when Obenpharo, the bank founder, asks his manager whether he should agree to talk to the journalist.

> "What for? He wants a front-page story for his editor, not facts. He never leaves the El Minzah bar. Yet he writes the authoritative standard *merde* about Tangier, city of sinfulness, city of smugglers. With the Moroccan crisis the banks are doomed. All our money is running back to Europe to hide in Switzerland. Et cetera, cetera. He'll cut our veins for his damn story."
>
> "Well, isn't that about frightened money half true?"
>
> "With all our problems? Do we need half truths now, too? This is the country of the straight from the shoulder half truth."[45]

The banker, however, a member of the hegemonic bloc (as is the journalist), knows that the battle over images is not won by ignoring the request for a meeting. Aware of the symbolic power of the gold in his vaults, he instructs his manager to manipulate the journalist via a (false) show of gold reserves. He himself faces off against the journalist in a battle over the "half truth."

In Dryer's popular novel, which spent eleven weeks on *Publishers' Weekly*'s best-seller list in the summer of 1958, the gold bars in Oberpharo's bank's safe symbolize the political and economic stability of the International Zone and the confidence of the international financial establishment in the maintenance of the Tangier administration.[46] But the idea that Tangier-based gold might be transported elsewhere (and that there were no restrictions on its sale or movement) connects the symbol of gold within *The Image Makers* to a larger set of images associated with Tangier. Such images revolved around financial excess and a lack of productivity—a conjunction central to Tangier's "queerness"—and were subtly associated with Tangier's departure from the national form. Following Lears's sense that the cold war corporate cultural hegemony focused on "cultural values associated with [the image]," the ways in which Tangier was represented, the motifs that recurred, were related to the domestic debate over national character. If Tangier was an image to battle over, therefore, what was really at stake were the cultural values associated with the purported meaning of Tangier.

That there was a location during the early cold war in which national identification might be held in check or even suspended as a matter of course posed a problem. That such a location would be tolerant of homosexuality and the open use of cannabis linked individuals and activities deemed threatening to the national security state to Tangier's suspension of national identification. Tangier thus threatened the dominant national narrative of the period, what Alan Nadel has called the "straight story" of early cold war America. Nadel has analyzed cold war narratives and the ways in which motifs of "containment" cross over from U.S. foreign policy to the realm of domestic culture. Containment was in Nadel's formulation a "rhetorical strategy that functioned to foreclose dissent, preempt dialogue, and preclude contradiction."[47] Nadel himself builds on work by the historian Elaine Tyler May, who has argued that containment had a powerful referent in the plight of American women during the cold war, and Robert Corber, whose work on homophobia and the American cold war subject investigates the ways in which intellectuals "limit[ed] the fund of interpretive possibilities available to [Americans] for understanding . . . lived experience."[48] What's at root here is the relationship between history and event, which Nadel argues is broached by narrative: "Narratives are not the opposite of facts, but rather their source and their condition of possibility" (3). Nadel draws on Jean-François Lyotard's concept of meta-narratives and the ways in which political power resides in controlling the surplus between the production of knowledge and the comprehension of it. He sees a threatening duality concealed by the culture of containment. Bringing together Lears's analysis of the hegemonic bloc's manipulation of symbols with Nadel's sense of the national narrative's rhetorical struggle, then, we may understand the need of cold war journalists working for the mainstream press—from liberal to conservative, and from *Fortune* to *Flair*—to accommodate or eliminate the fascination with Tangier. The excess and multiplicity of Tangier represented a surplus that was threatening.

Tangier mattered to 1950s domestic America because it suggested an alternative to the dominant national narrative, indeed to the idea of a *national* narrative at all. Nadel asserts that during this period there was a general acceptance of "a relatively small set of narratives by a relatively large portion of the population" (4). Journalists working within the presumptions of the hegemonic bloc—those for whom the containment narrative seemed to offer a compelling strategy for understanding contradiction—had two choices: ignore Tangier, or represent it in such a way that the challenge of the alternative it posed was diffused and re-presented in such a way as to be of use to the narrative. Based on the evidence, those who responded to challenging Tangier did so by exaggerating Tangier's purported dissoluteness and thereby making it abject.[49]

A Tangier rendered abject allowed the national narrative a way to work through the contradictions and dangers of the early cold war American mythos of abundance. Tangier's excess, recast as "queerness" and thereby linked with the abject, became the container for the surplus that an embrace of American abundance could not manage. Abundance was a key concept in the consensus vision of American exceptionalism. As fears of a return to economic depression ceded to recognition of the widespread economic prosperity, "abundance" was inscribed as pertaining to the American national character itself. In his major 1954 study *People of Plenty*, David Potter argued that the American character was determined by a culture and history of economic abundance. Potter's influential argument revisited Turner's 1893 frontier hypothesis, which had sought to identify the national character for a different generation. According to Potter, the frontier was of primary importance to the creation of American character only while it offered the lowest threshold of access to America's abundance. Since cultural changes had drawn the focal point of abundance away from the western frontier, and since abundance is not only based on natural resources but is also socially created, Potter argued that one should look more generally at the signs and loci of economic abundance in America to understand the American character. For Potter, postwar America did indeed have a "revolutionary message" to offer the world, but the message was not about democracy and its freedoms. For Potter, it was "not democracy revolutionizing the world, but abundance revolutionizing the world."[50]

I have elsewhere examined Hollywood films from the late 1940s and 1950s and traced the ways in which Potter's logic carried over into the U.S. film industry's attempts to win back audiences being lost to television.[51] Based on the evidence of an extraordinary number of lush films set in North Africa and the Middle East, films such as *The Egyptian, Yankee Pasha, Land of the Pharaohs, Kismet,* and many others from this period, Hollywood seemed to agree that abundance held within itself a compelling message.[52] The primary attraction for Hollywood of Arabian Nights pictures, Ancient Egyptian epics, and luxuriant films set in North Africa marketplaces and harems was to locate venues that would best show off Hollywood's ability to replicate abundance on an appropriately colorful and grand scale. In doing so, Hollywood could enact an image of itself and of the United States that placed the industry and the nation in the company of great empires of the past, a message underlined by publicity advertising casts of thousands and productions that replicated or remade Ancient Egypt, as in *Life*'s coverage of the making of *Land of the Pharaohs* in Egypt). As Pauline Kael commented in 1955, "Though it is easy to scoff at the advertising which emphasizes the *size* of a picture—the cast of thousands, the number of millions spent—magnitude in itself represents an achievement to the public."[53] Within the global contest against the Soviets, Technicolor, CinemaScope films such as these offered a more confident argument against the supposed colorlessness and narrowness of the Soviet Union than did anticommunist propaganda films, and they were subtler with that message. A staging of abundance countered the imagined austerity of state-sponsored communism more effectively than any lesson in economic systems. In making such films, Hollywood did not explicitly set out to create subtle and coded anti-Soviet propaganda; it set out to create escapist entertainment. But the logic of the early cold war led filmmakers to make and remake films that emphasized the abundance and lushness of the Orient, with the political and moral shortcomings of the characters conveniently displaced onto the caliphs and the pharaohs of other centuries and continents. These films do not celebrate democracy; that is not their message about American superiority. Rather, they celebrate abundance. These films were allegedly "about" Baghdad or Egypt or Morocco, but they were also "about" Hollywood's unique ability to create ornate and expansive renditions of empire.

The problems these films face is that in traveling to the Orient for their excuse to portray abundance, they are inevitably drawn to depictions of women's sexual excess. In depicting the sexual excesses of imagined Oriental harems, Hollywood filmmakers replicated what Ella Shohat has called "harem structures."[54] And since the straight story of American national identity was based around a heteronormative procreative family unit, these representations of abundance as American motif were troubled. In other words, the logic of containment came up against its surplus in the presentation of abundance. The difficulty was both that familiar American actors were portraying the lascivious harem keepers and desirable women of the super-female space and that the studios themselves had conjured up narratives that resisted being contained. In these films, the solution to these problems most often is to punish the women—often to bury them alive, literally or figuratively, as in the horrifying ending to Howard Hawks's *Land of the Pharaohs*, in which Joan Collins, in her first Hollywood role, is smothered by her husband's collapsing pyramid. And in *Yankee Pasha*, a 1954 Universal picture based on an Edison Marshall novel, the filmmakers respond to the visual pleasure the film takes in presenting its harem—the film featured the reigning Miss Universe and nine runners-up as members of the Moroccan sultan's harem—by condemning the female protagonist (an American woman who has been captured by Barbary pirates and taken as a white slave) to an American marriage depicted as a replication of her enslavement in Morocco.

This is the logic Hollywood films that evoke oriental abundance summoned to deal with the surplus of sexuality they had been drawn to. While they are not directly linked to the ways in which American journalists portrayed Tangier, such films are part of a field of cultural responses to the Arab world by Americans pertaining to that class that Lears called a historical hegemonic bloc (or what Dryer called "image makers"). Frequent media portrayals of the various excesses of Tangier—such as accounts of Barbara Hutton's fabulous wealth and her extravagant lifestyle in the casbah ("Moderation is a bore" was a favorite Hutton saying)—emerged from the same cultural interest in abundance.[55] Nonfiction representations of Tangier were more immediately linked to questions of American national meaning than Hollywood's cold war Orientalism because of U.S. political participation in the zone. That political role opened the door for journalists to comment on the "meaning" of Tangier, appropriately enough, and to put the American community under scrutiny. But rather than comment on the U.S. government's support of a neocolonial regime in the Tangier Zone or on U.S. collaboration with French and Spanish protectorates, the media instead derided and sensationalized the city itself and criticized U.S. support of that exaggerated entity. As the *Saturday Evening Post* put it starkly, for example: "Uncle Sam Sponsors a Smugglers' Paradise."[56] This conforms with and confirms Lears's general assessment that images rather than power relations tended to be analyzed by the hegemonic bloc.

The *Wall Street Journal* article that apparently inspired the scene in *The Image Makers* discussed above provides an example of how even a timely news account of Tangier's political status reflected on the question of American national definition. Appearing on the newspaper's front page under the title "Tangier Turmoil," a number of subtitles set the scene and established a tone: "Tiny, Shadowy Land of Fiscal Freedoms Undergoes the Shakes / Bankers, Smugglers, Radio Hucksters Fretful about Moroccan Independence / Keep Drinking and Smiling."[57] The lead itself suggests that the financial worries experienced by the foreign community in Tangier were deserved because of Tangier's perversion of a more correct order, that is of an order conforming to the American narrative: "This minuscule African haven of four freedoms—freedom from taxes, freedom to exchange the world's currencies, freedom from customs duties on goods in transit, and freedom to incorporate and operate in secrecy—has got a terrible case of the shakes." By employing Franklin Roosevelt's Four Freedoms as the standard from which an immoral (or "shadowy") Tangier has erred, the *Wall Street Journal*'s reporter makes explicit what is often implicit in other articles on Tangier during the late 1940s and 1950s: that mocking, prurient, or sensationalist representations of the city and its foreign (including American) population were directed at domestic narratives of Americanness. Even those who found some bright spots in their reporting on Tangier—such as coverage of the American School of Tangier in *Colliers* and the *New Yorker*—sought to counter positive elements of

Tangier with a larger picture that condemned it.[58] In the case of the *Wall Street Journal's* invocation of Roosevelt, the overwhelming irony is that Roosevelt's own wartime message to the Moroccans—the spreading of the text of the Atlantic Charter as propaganda and meeting with Sidi Mohammed in 1943—had inspired the Moroccan nationalists but was later rejected by the U.S. State Department against those nationalists' appeals. Raoul Simpkins's 1950 *Atlantic* article, "Banking in Tangier," also invokes Roosevelt's famous figure as an anchor against which to measure Tangier's perverse drift. In Tangier, Simpkins writes, there is a "delightful Fifth Freedom": "the Freedom to Own Gold Outside of Fort Knox."[59] Again, Tangier is in excess (five freedoms where four are standard), and again Tangier is ridiculed in terms that buttress the straight story at home.

Within the national narrative, then, Tangier's function was that it allowed for a way to deal with the surplus that a focus on abundance could not otherwise handle. Tangier's excess connects to a key tenet of cold war self-definition (abundance) but becomes abject in the hands of most journalists working within the major press because of its inversion of those tenets. What ultimately was most threatening and titillating about Tangier was the challenge it posed to key tenets of cold war domestic America—the developing dialectic of heteronormative domestic arrangements, namely the concept of the procreative couple as family unit, and the primacy of the nation form within the postwar world order. That this took place on the African continent, albeit at its closest point to Europe, made the challenge yet more necessary to contain; Tangier's proximity to Europe may even have magnified the threat. The deep structural racism of cold war culture allied Tangier's queerness—as excess—and the cold war figure of "blackness." So to bring out their alliance in popular representations of Tangier, now imagined as a queer African city as opposed to a queer expatriate destination, would be to summon too much energy.

There were a number of strategies for making Tangier abject. Of the many types of magazines that published articles on Tangier during the period, each had its own take, but the points of reference recur. Business publications were fascinated by the city as a tax-free zone and with its multiple legal currencies and entrepreneurs yet could not abstain from reference to its social scene as a "queer hell," as William Schlamm did in *Fortune* in 1950. Culture magazines and news media fascinated by the American and international colony of expatriates did not fail to mention the fiscal excesses of the city, fueling what John Taberner called a "phoney gold rush" in a 1952 essay for *American Mercury*. Tangier was queer in this double sense, the parts never separable: its excess and lack were a direct (but implicit) challenge to the dynamics of the home front. So when I call Tangier "queer" it is to signify simultaneously its financial "queerness," its refusal to conform to heteronormative ideas of sexuality, and its destabilizing of the nation paradigm/episteme. Within the national episteme of the 1950s, both sides of what seems like a seismic divide—metropolitan and revolutionary—seemed to tend toward a "straight story." Fanon's account of the domestic family unit as building block of the revolutionary nation, directed to a different public at the same time, played on French representations of its empire as a family with the colonial subjects as children.[60] In the United States, McCarthy and his aides, especially Roy Cohn, represented nonprocreative sexuality as threat to national security.

The financial queerness of Tangier had several referents: the multiple currencies in play, the free currency exchange, the lack of restrictions on gold trade, lack of income tax, ease of incorporation, and the apparent fact that the money being made (and lost) in Tangier was from no real commodity but from money itself. "Tangier grows or produces hardly anything but profits," wrote Schlamm in *Fortune*, in a long essay that both downplays the exaggerated accounts of Tangier's sinfulness and produces a more elaborate condemnation of the city's alleged immorality by criticizing its economic basis in loaded terms. "It's something like a tangible abstraction—the completely uninhibited dream of free money. . . . And like any other dream of wish fulfillment, Tangier is a negation of the rigid workaday world around."[61] Tangier as negation of the "workaday world" is the economic component of the trouble it poses to the straight story, intimately related to queerness through the financial writer's sense that free money is a perversion of straight productivity (no "rigid workaday" undergirding it). Schlamm comes back to this several times in his essay: "Once in Tangier, your career is determined by either the size of your disposable cash or your flair for financial wizardry, whichever is larger. Nothing else counts in Tangier where only money can beget money" (70); "in terms of productivity, this town of 135,000 people cannot begin to compete with a U.S. village of 1,500 inhabitants" (136). For the business writer, an unproductive economy is worse than straying from the sexual straight and narrow. Schlamm ultimately comes back to his own comment on Tangier as "queer hell" in order to undercut it. He mentions "the Arabs' traditional cooperation with homosexuals," and then sidesteps any further discussion of the gay scene. Instead, as evidence that Tangier's "licentiousness" has been "overadvertised," Schlamm reports that visitors to the most expensive of Tangier's forty-two licensed bordellos (where women only were licensed) comment that the experience "isn't worth a penny more" than the low price of "a transaction."

Though John Taberner doesn't use the word *queer* in his article on Tangier's "phoney gold rush," the concept is implicit throughout. Taberner's account of Tangier is marked by rhetorical tension between his representation of the place and assertions of the impossibility of knowing, or counting, or mapping anything in Tangier. Each time Taberner proposes a fact about Tangier (the population, for example), he says it's impossible for him to be sure of his accuracy: "Any figure you take can only be approximate, because the bulk of the population is made up of Arabs, who object to being counted and are adept at dodging the census-taker."[62] Similarly with the physical space, "when it came to the medina the cartographers gave up; it appears on the map as a blank area decorated with a few wispy lines leading nowhere" (84). The motif is a familiar one from what Christopher Miller has called Africanist discourse and repeats the tendency of French nineteenth-century authors to express an inability to know anything for certain regarding Africa. The resulting gaps in his understanding of Tangier, such as in the map of Tangier's medina, are also redolent of what Judith Butler has identified as the queer: "the sudden gap in the surface of language."[63] The twist here is that Taberner resolves the inability to be certain of anything in Tangier with its attitude toward money—one he calls "phoney." The multiple languages used in Tangier are not comprehensible to him, but it doesn't matter because they all speak of one thing: "You don't have to understand the language to know what the topic is: in Tangier there's no time for small talk—money is the only thing that counts." In the sense that Schlamm saw Tangier as unproductive (and thus queer in my account), Taberner too worries about Tangier money's lack of productivity. The wispy lines lead nowhere on that map. The "fantastic boom" he locates in Tangier is not to be located, since "no one has struck oil"; to borrow Schlamm's word, there is nothing "rigid" underneath the phony gold rush. "What does it all mean?" Taberner asks. Taberner attributes the phony gold rush to "the very odd nature of Tangier's government." He has a compelling image for the multinational Tangier administration: "When you get eight hens to sit on a single egg, none of them is likely to prove a particularly fond mother. So

Money changer on the Rue es Siaghine, Tangier, about 1950.
Reprinted from *Portrait of Tangier*. *Photo by Rom Landau*
(*London*, 1952).

what you have is an example of international government with the lid off.
In Tangier anything goes" (81). In the imagination of the article, the
hens are queer: not productive, out of place, and uncomfortable in their
role, and the source of the "phoney"-ness attributed to Tangier. (Robin
Maugham, in *North African Notebook*, published in New York in 1949,
refers to Tangier's government as a "queer sort of international republic
unique in the world.")[64]

The image of queer hens sitting on eggs not only links homosexuality,
homosocial excess, and lack of productivity, it is also an image of sitting
and of anality, the trope that links the excess of free currency in Tangier
to the fascination with male homosexual sex. (The latter was not de-

picted by American writers or journalists representing Tangier during the 1950s, where only references to Tangier's tolerance of homosexuality were made.) Anality is the ultimate locus for excess, for waste and surplus, and thus deeply linked to questions of economy.[65]

Burroughs will turn the motif of anality inside out, as it were, but before pursuing this in the next chapter I should remark that a focus on the economics of anality is not original to him among American writers in Tangier. Mark Twain, who had visited Tangier in 1867, perhaps identified this conjunction of senses of Tangier's queerness. I want to end this chapter somewhat anachronistically with Twain because of the ways in which he powerfully links images that I have been discussing and helps make sense of them. In Twain's account of a day-long trip to Tangier, published in *The Innocents Abroad*, the young author provides an account of the city's ancient history: "Tangier has been mentioned in history for three thousand years. And it was a town, though a queer one, when Hercules, clad in his lion-skin, landed here, four thousand years ago. . . . The people of Tangier (called Tingis, then,) lived in the rudest possible huts, and dressed in skins and carried clubs, and were as savage as the wild beasts they were constantly obliged to war with. But they were a gentlemanly race, and did no work."[66] What is it about Tangier that makes it a "queer" town here? Among the evidence provided: that the people are savages but also gentlemen, that they war with animals, wear them, and above all that they do not work. Queer in this usage seems to accrue the sense of contradiction, multiplicity, and nonproductivity.

But the alleged queerness of Tangier for Twain will carry over into other associations. Twain is initially rhapsodic about Tangier because it was "clear out of the world" (71). Leaving the American cruise ship the Quaker City and its prepackaged itinerary behind, the narrator and a couple of friends ditched their puritanical American cotravelers. "Care can not assail us here. We are out of its jurisdiction." Twain's narrator was exhilarated to enter a city "thoroughly and uncompromisingly foreign— foreign from top to bottom—foreign from centre to circumference— foreign inside and outside and all around—nothing any where about it to dilute its foreignness—nothing to remind us of any other people or any other land under the sun" (61). The sense of escape from the familiar quickly leads to a fear, however, expressed when he lunches with the American consul-general and his family—"Tangier is full of interest for one day, but after that it is a weary prison. . . . It is the completest exile that

I can conceive of" (71). The fear is of being withdrawn from circulation, perilous to an unproven journalist like the young Twain, and is figured in economic terms. Twain's marvelous account of the consul-general's family expresses their boredom in terms of excess value: "His family seize upon their letters and papers when the mail arrives, read them over and over again for two days or three, talk them over and over again for two or three more, till they wear them out, and after that . . . ride out over the same old road, and see the same old tiresome things that even decades of centuries have scarcely changed" (71). Since they are out of circulation in a place that is built around excess—Twain describes the city's religious diversity as excess: "They have three Sundays a week at Tangier" (69)—the family has perverted the economic order, and their repeated readings and ridings contribute nothing; it is the punishment of their exile.

Twain's descriptions of Tangier's currency link this motif to anality. Twain, like Paul Bowles, Bernard Dryer, William Schlamm, and several American journalists of the 1950s after him, is fascinated with Tangier's money changers.[67] Twain writes:

> These coins are not very valuable. Jack went out to get a Napoleon changed, so as to have money suited to the general cheapness of things, and came back and said he had "swamped the bank; had bought eleven quarts of coin, and the head of the firm had gone on the street to negotiate for the balance of the change." I bought nearly half a pint of their money for a shilling myself. I am not proud on account of having so much money, though. I care nothing for wealth. (65)

If Tangier is marked by excess coins that have little value, it also has a small coin with great value:

> They have also a small gold coin worth two dollars. And that reminds me of something. When Morocco is in a state of war, Arab couriers carry letters through the country, and charge a liberal postage. Every now and then they fall into the hands of marauding bands and get robbed. Therefore, warned by experience, as soon as they have collected two dollars' worth of money they exchange it for one of those little gold pieces, and when robbers come upon them, swallow it. The stratagem was good while it was unsuspected, but after that the marauders simply gave the sagacious United States mail an emetic and sat down to wait. (65)

Aside from Twain's slip in referring to the Moroccan mail as the U.S. mail, the passage is compelling because of its association of cash, anality, and shit. Both the Arab marauders and their Arab courier victims are sitting in Twain's final image—or if we take Twain's slip as intentional, perhaps Americans too are sitting. Gold and the anus are deeply connected under capitalism, of course, since the economy relies on waste and nonrecycled refuse in order to keep a profit. Gold remains in circulation and as precious metal is always recyclable, but as Michael Warner comments regarding Freud's discovery of the proximity of gold and shit: "Gold and waste get their respective valences only by virtue of the axiomatic economic condition of scarcity." "Money retains anality's pleasure," Warner writes.[68]

Twain's anecdote allows us then to see how the fascination with Tangier's free gold market, and the lack of restrictions on holding gold, are deeply related to the anxiety over Tangier's queerness, broadly considered. The "terrible case of the shakes" the *Wall Street Journal* reports in Tangier in 1956 refers to the shifting of gold and is an image that plays on travelers' diarrhea (economic incontinence in an African port town). In Dryer's novel gold is moved, removed, melted, and turned into art in the context of a collapsing International Zone, a revolution that in the novel's imagination produces the social conditions for an outbreak of pneumonic plague, a "daytime nightmare" of feverish death and scenes of Brueghelian horror. The sense that Tangier, among its other excesses, was a place where gold was free and unfettered fills out the sense that the city revolved around a queer economy antagonistic to the rest of the world. It was common to remark that Tangier's boom relied on Europe's and America's financial instability, with the obvious implication that once the West straightened itself out and the global economy returned to productivity, Tangier's moment would end.

Eighty years after Twain, William Schlamm ends his *Fortune* essay on Tangier by expressing doubt about Tangier's future: would Tangier's economic boom—its "selfish dream" (140)—continue, or would the (financial) world "recover its senses" and Tangier "shrink to the size of a Moroccan ghost town haunted by memories of a queer megalomania"? In the context of his long essay, Schlamm's final use of *queer* is ambiguous, so collapsed have his terms become; the "queer megalomania" that is the last phrase of the essay is not necessarily the same as the "queer hell" in his lead. Rather it is a reflection on the state of the city's economy, its governance, and the people who have taken advantage of both. When considering the future, however, Schlamm allows for a potentiality to emerge from a Tangier that he has otherwise criticized strongly: Africa may awake, or the rest of the world may remain asleep, among the possibilities he sees, or else Tangier may "mutate into a commercial center of a vivified African continent." In describing and laying out a "queer Tangier" I am attempting to do two things: first, identify the terms and logic by which journalists made Tangier abject and thus subsumed it within the national narrative, and second, to recover a different potentiality from Tangier's queerness that will not be so subsumed.[69] For though I began this chapter with a distinction between different "Tangiers," Tangier's potentiality may be recovered from the crossing of communities that marked the experience of living in the city at this time. The terms for that potential may be drawn out from these disparate yet complementary worlds. I want to summon this sense of Tangier's possibility as I move into a reading of Burroughs and then, in the following chapter, of Jane Bowles's writing and Paul Bowles's collaborations with Mohammed Mrabet, where we shall find some of that potentiality enacted.

4

DISORIENTING

THE NATIONAL SUBJECT

Burroughs's Tangier, Hitchcock's Marrakech

It is no longer the formal or superficial syntax that governs the
equilibriums of language, but a syntax in the process of becoming,
a creation of syntax that gives birth to a foreign language within
language, a grammar of disequilibrium.—Gilles Deleuze,
Essays Critical and Clinical

The Tangerian *Naked Lunch*

A week after his arrival in Tangier, in January 1954, William S.
Burroughs wrote to Allen Ginsberg: "I like Tangiers less all the
time. No writers colony here or they keep theirselves hid some place. . . .
And don't ever fall for this inscrutable oriental shit like Bowles puts down
(that shameless faker)."[1] The Tangier that he had read about in Paul
Bowles's 1952 novel *Let It Come Down*, in which a New York bank clerk
leaves behind postwar America for the decadence and lawlessness of International Tangier, seemed provincial to Burroughs up close. (Bowles
would later claim that the Tangier he described in *Let It Come Down*
disappeared after the 1952 riots.) The informal writers' colony that had
been celebrated in the American press did not seem to exist. Charles
Rolo's 1950 article "The New Bohemia" had placed the city at the center
of a new cultural movement: "In the dining room of the Hotel El Farhar,
perched on a cliff outside Tangiers, a group of American writers are
listening to one Themistocles Hotis, a be-bop man or hipster, celebrating
the virtues of hashish"; the article was illustrated with a photograph of
Paul and Jane Bowles, accompanied by Truman Capote and Paul's parrot

(27).[2] When Burroughs finally met Bowles, however, the latter was cool and distant (Hotis had moved to Marrakech). Burroughs was lonely and lovesick for Ginsberg. He had quickly gotten hooked on Eukodol, a discontinued synthesized morphine substitute still available in Tangier. Tangier in winter, despite what the travel articles say, is damp and cold.

But things did begin to improve, and by the middle of 1955, Burroughs had changed his mind about Tangier rather starkly. A November 1955 letter to Ginsberg and Jack Kerouac began this way: "Tanger is the prognostic pulse of the world, like a dream extending from past into the future, a frontier between dream and reality—the 'reality' of both called into question."[3] He urged his friends to join him. They wouldn't make it for another year and a half, until early spring 1957, by which point Burroughs was not the man they had known in New York and Mexico. After several false starts, he had kicked his junk habit, had befriended Bowles, was rowing in the bay daily, and had made solid progress on the writing project that would become *Naked Lunch*. Burroughs would live in Tangier off and on for four years until January 1958, returning briefly in 1959, then for extended stays in 1961 and from June 1963 to December 1964. Tangier would play a major role in his life and work, and his own influence on Tangier was in turn substantial. By 1961, when he spent the summer in Tangier in the company of Ginsberg and an adventurous Timothy Leary, the hipsters who followed in the wake of *Naked Lunch* had turned the Boulevard Pasteur into a "North African Bleecker Street," in the words of Iain Finlayson.[4]

James Grauerholz, Burroughs's longtime secretary and the editor of much of his work, describes the author's time in Tangier as a hinge in his career: "In these four crucial years, 1954–57, Burroughs had been transformed into a writer."[5] The agent in Grauerholz's sentence is not Burroughs, but something outside of him: a context and an environment. Despite the power of Grauerholz's statement, critics have in one way or another avoided a serious inquiry into the relationship between Burroughs's major text and his response to Tangier, pushing the role of the city into the passive background. Ted Morgan's 1988 biography has been influential in this regard, signaled by Morgan's choice to detach his reading of *Naked Lunch* entirely from his chapter on Burroughs's time in Tangier.[6] For Morgan, it's not that *Naked Lunch* is unconnected to history or the author's movements; in fact, he calls the book "a vision of the post-Bomb society" that Burroughs "dredge[d] up, from his experience as an addict and wanderer" (350). Yet Morgan, who lived in Tangier for a time himself (as Sanche de Gramont, his given name, which he changed when he became an American citizen), does not make the link between Burroughs's vision of Tangier, the postwar world, and *Naked Lunch* and distances Tangier from material reality: "Tangier was as much an imaginative construct as a geographical location, a metaphor for limbo, for a dead-end place, a place where everyone could act out his most extreme fantasies. On one level, Tangier was a reconstruction of the world in a small place" (253). Morgan compares Burroughs to Bowles and finds that "Burroughs made no attempt to learn about the country or to speak the language. . . . made no effort to adapt, and the thought that he was an exile never crossed his mind, for wherever he might be . . . he remained as American as the general store in a one-horse town" (254). According to his spare endnotes, Morgan's source for the statement, which bears much of the weight for his interpretation, was apparently Bowles himself. But Morgan misinterprets Bowles (or Bowles misunderstands Burroughs) by implying that Burroughs's refusal to adapt to Morocco or to learn Arabic translates into a failure to respond to and learn from Tangier itself or that *Naked Lunch* would be the same book—or a book at all—without Tangier. Bowles's own early essay "Burroughs in Tangier" would seem to affirm the immediate political context of *Naked Lunch*. Bowles describes Burroughs reading from the work in progress: "He would suddenly (paper still in hand) go into a bitter conversational attack upon whatever aspect of life had prompted the passage he had just read." The text is loaded with references, every (and any) page with a material referent; Burroughs, Bowles writes, "always makes sense and is always humorous."[7]

Following Morgan's lead, recent critics have similarly discounted the importance of Tangier as more than imaginative construct, even while sensing the importance of thinking about the materiality of Tangier. Despite the important contributions to understanding *Naked Lunch*'s relationship to questions of modernism and sexuality, such critics have been variously perplexed when trying to make sense of the relationship of Burroughs's masterwork and the idiosyncratic and historically anomalous place where the writer discovered himself.[8] For students of this criticism, this has led to confusion about Burroughs's political position and the Moroccan and geopolitical context of his work. As a result, Mary McCarthy's startling 1962 statement about *Naked Lunch*—that "the national novel, like the nation-state, was dying and that a new kind of novel, based on statelessness, was beginning to be written"—loses its immediacy and power.[9]

Rereading *Naked Lunch* in its Tangier context demonstrates the ways in which Burroughs's piercing indictment of a culture of control and a society of hypocrisy emerges from an especially rich global imagination that helps provide the energy and terms of his disruption. *Naked Lunch* sees the expanding U.S. global presence as an extension of a culture addicted to consumption, its foreign policy based on the language manipulation of false advertising, and understands the geopolitical system of the early cold war as a network grown to support the so-called algebra of need on a grand scale, making docile subjects out of citizen-subjects. Burroughs's critique of American domestic relations—most pointedly his vehement indictments of capital punishment, of the structural violence of racism, of science after the Manhattan Project, and of the homophobia of McCarthyist America—are inseparable from his sense of the United States as imperial power and his prophetic sense of globalization. Not only do we understand better some of the local referents of *Naked Lunch* when we consider Burroughs's response to the particular context in which the work took shape, but we understand better the work's structural and aesthetic innovation (its disembodied "routines," its antinarrative, its deconstruction of the authorial subject) as a sophisticated response to Tangier, a location that was already understood as discordant within the American national narrative. Further, to recognize that *Naked Lunch* took shape within an anticolonial revolutionary context gives its sense of immediacy and political potentiality an explicit referent and helps us be more specific about its oppositional relationship to the nation form in all its manifestations.

The text's invocation of the possessed narrator and its disavowal of that narrator—both of which Burroughs's early self-mythologizing claim not to recall the writing of the book supported, even if that claim lead unwittingly to Burroughs's deification by his fans—is thus engaged in a project more grounded in its political moment and geopolitical context than recent readers have understood. Burroughs's proposal of a larval network and diasporic confederation emerging from the Interzone, the disintegration of the "I," and the rupture of the narrative mark *Naked Lunch* as a work that engages the dynamic of the early cold war on a powerful set of terms and unravels them. The disorienting and interruptive temporality that emerges from the work can be seen in contrast to the conservative temporality of Luce's "American Century." Burroughs's aversion to the nation form itself—richly a part of his experience of Tangier—is echoed and staged in the refusal to adopt the Lucean temporality, one associated with a "global racial time." Burroughs's subsequent work, such as *The Ticket That Exploded* (1962) and *The Wild Boys* (1968), with its invocation of Marrakech as Wild West, will build on the concerns and lessons first expressed in *Naked Lunch*, particularly the eventual proposal of a diasporic network of gun-toting, jock strap–clad homosexual outlaws. Fueled by conversation and collaboration with Brion Gysin, Burroughs's work of the 1960s will delve more deeply into Sufism and Arab mysticism. After further breaking down narrative with his fold-in and cut-up techniques, he will return to narrative (roughly coincident with his definitive return to the United States in 1974). Yet not only does *Naked Lunch* lay much of the groundwork for the rest of his literary career, the larval connections made here are especially potent because they stage the appropriate response to a global system in the form of *potentiality*, as larval possibility, as undeveloped code.

Burroughs's letters from his time in Tangier offer evidence of the complexity of his thinking regarding Tangier, cold war geopolitics, and the work in progress, and they must be read in concert with *Naked Lunch*.[10] In these letters, Burroughs worked through the material, the collapse of the space between fiction and nonfiction, the routine form, and the means by which he would figure an intellectual collaboration with Allen Ginsberg in his book (initially as receiver of the letters, later as editor and collaborator in Tangier in 1957, finally as an effaced and elusive "you" that *Naked Lunch* puts into question). The letters reveal a Burroughs who was paying attention to current politics, aware of his local surroundings, reading newspapers; they also provide evidence of friendships with David Woolman and Charles Gallagher, both Americans with special interest and expertise in contemporary Moroccan politics.[11] Woolman lived in the same medina hotel (called Dutch Tony's, just off the Petit Socco) as Burroughs in 1954 and joined Burroughs in moving to the Hotel Muniria, outside the medina, in 1956. On Burroughs's request, he administered an unsuccessful morphine cure for Burroughs at the Muniria, removing the latter's clothing and doling out small quantities of a derivative. Beyond these tidbits, known from the standard biographies, Woolman was also a journalist writing two columns for the Casablanca-based weekly *Moroccan Courier* (one on Tangier, called "Soco Chico," and another on Gibraltar, "Chips off the Old Rock"),[12] and a historian, whose study of Abd el

William Burroughs with Peter Orlovsky and Paul Lund at "Dutch Tony's," Tangier, 1957. *Photo by Allen Ginsberg, courtesy of the Allen Ginsberg Trust.*

Krim and the Riffi resistance to Spanish occupation was later published by Stanford University Press. He was a companion with more than passing knowledge of and interest in his surroundings. Charles Gallagher, whom Burroughs relied on for conversation, was back and forth between Tangier and Rabat ("to be with the Archives" as Burroughs put it),[13] where he was actively researching and writing about contemporary Maghrebi politics and history on a Ford Foundation grant. In a letter to Ginsberg not included in Oliver Harris's 1993 collection, Burroughs relates more about Gallagher, the "interesting Harvard man": "he says Arab literature and notably the Koran is very great. They have a special mood-tense to express intense religious experience. I have been studying a spot of Arabic but despair of learning to read it. Just figure to pick up a few words for conversation purposes."[14] That Woolman, Gallagher, Paul Bowles, and Brion Gysin were a part of Burroughs's world in Tangier surrounded him with individuals who had a deep sense of Moroccan history, culture, and politics.[15] For a writer for whom conversation and collaboration was central, and who formed deep attachments with individuals with whom he could connect intellectually, these relationships are not incidental. Woolman would in the 1970s publish under a pseudonym the most comprehensive social history of Tangier, discussing the 1950s (as well as previous periods) in great detail and with impressive range.[16] In this book, Woolman recalls Burroughs sitting in the Hotel Muniria, receiving individuals at any time, writing, talking politics; these three activities must be rejoined in thinking about the fiction that emerged from Tangier.

Tangier Tonic: Race, Revolution, and the Orientalist Trap

> I have a strange feeling here of being outside any social context.
> I have never known any place so relaxing. The possibility of an all-out
> riot is like a tonic, like ozone in air: "Here surely is a song for men
> like wind in an iron tree."—*Anabasis* more or less. I have no nostalgia
> for the old days in Morocco, which I never saw. Right now is for me.
> —William Burroughs, letter to Allen Ginsberg, October 29, 1956

There are many points of entry into a rereading of *Naked Lunch* that considers its Tangier context seriously. Jumping a bit between the final text and the letters, journals, and essays that Burroughs wrote from Tangier is not meant to disregard the distinction between these texts nor an awareness that Burroughs rejected some of this material from the final version of *Naked Lunch*, including long passages and a formal structure that he had considered. Harris is surely correct when he describes the "trauma" of *Naked Lunch* as falling between Burroughs's 1954 statement to Ginsberg that "the real novel is letters to you" and a late 1959 letter that disavowed both that Burroughs-the-author was "myself" or that the text was written for Ginsberg (243). Passages that Burroughs did not include in the 1959 draft of *Naked Lunch* were rejected from a work that had evolved. Bearing this in mind, we may locate a series of responses to Tangier that appear and develop in Burroughs's letters and journals and as they enter (and exit) *Naked Lunch*. To sketch it out linearly, after Burroughs's initial disappointment that Tangier was not what he had expected, neither as writer's colony nor as haven, he for a while sees it as a place of noninterference: "There is an end-of-the-world feeling in Tangiers. . . . something sinister in complete *laissez faire*." He sees the city as a trap that will some day close: "We will see it closing, but there will be no escape, no place to go."[17] After an unpleasant trip to the United States in the fall of 1954, however—punctuated by surgery in New York, a bad visit with his parents in Florida, and the receipt of a letter from Ginsberg rejecting him as a romantic partner and calling off their planned reunion in San Francisco— his return to Tangier was welcome. "I am counting my blessings in Tangiers."[18] Burroughs soon moved to a new house in the upper medina, close to Bowles's at the Place Amrah (just below the casbah).

Rather than complete lawlessness and laissez-faire, Burroughs in early 1955 understands Tangier as ruled by a libertarian order. In January, he compares the Tangier police who do "their legit function of maintaining order" to U.S. police who are presumptuous and "out of hand": "One of my reasons for preferring to live outside the US is so I won't be wasting time reacting against cops and the interfering society they represent."[19] Burroughs now begins to see Tangier as interesting in its own right and composes an essay on the city (dated January 12, 1955). His portrait of Tangier, imagined as a "Letter from Tangier" for the *New Yorker* (but not published for thirty years), is of a vast market with sellers far surpassing buyers, where everything has a price: "There is quite simply too much of everything, too much merchandise, housing, labor, too many guides, pimps, prostitutes and smugglers. A classic, archetypical depression."[20] Though written in a tone that immediately distinguishes the essay from others published in the United States during the 1950s, in a general sense his portrait conformed with the sense described in chapter 3 that Tangier was a location of excess, to which Burroughs adds the further disparagement of "stasis." Yet Burroughs himself began to associate this overflowing excess—to recuperate it, as it were—with what must be called an anal economy, one he would bring profitably into his ever-changing work-in-progress. Within the month he would write the draft of the talking-asshole routine, the most famous passage in *Naked Lunch*, and one that connects artistic performance (including that of the writer of routines) with a self-sustaining anality.[21] The anal economy—the radical incorporation of all waste—was a modern counterpoint to the corrupt and corrupting economy of Tangier and the global system, which fed off each other and which relied on the rejection of detritus (commodity as well as human), rather than its reincorporation or representation. This anal economy would also provide the aesthetic form and the textual economy of his work. From the detritus of his letters and journals he would form a text named as a meal, an "enema of my word hoard, been dissolving all the shit up there man and boy forty-three years and who ever held an enema longer?"[22] Burroughs's vision of a zone of potential, of larval possibility, would crystallize in that Tangier space—imagined before arrival during his *yagé* expeditions in South America (and maintaining his prophetic descriptions of a Composite City from Peru in 1953) but developed and finding its form after Burroughs's experience with the Zoco Chico, a place to which all was drawn by the "inexorable process of suction" and which existed as "the meeting place, the nerve center, the switchboard of Tangier."[23]

As the momentum for Moroccan independence gained ground, Burroughs would enlarge his understanding of Tangier further. The stakes for Burroughs of his own presence in Tangier were made clear on August 1, 1955, when Abdelkrim Ben Abdeslam, a Moroccan vendor whom Burroughs called a "local 'eccentric,'" went on a spree with a butcher's knife, killing four or five people and wounding several others. For Burroughs, what was "ominous" about the occurrence was not merely that he himself barely missed the scene of the attack—"I wonder if he would have attacked me?"—but that he shared a secret intimacy with Ben Abdeslam. After rejecting Ben Abdeslam's request for small change some weeks earlier, an appeal accompanied by the Moroccan's expression of friendship, Burroughs became aware of the man's presence:

> His communications are progressively more cryptic; obviously he has built up an elaborate delusional system in which the U.S. Embassy is the root of all evil. I am an agent, a creature of the Embassy. I decide he is insane, probably dangerous. (An uninhibited paranoid is always a bad deal.) I cut the interviews as short as possible, holding myself always on the alert, ready to kick him in the stomach, arm myself with a bottle or a chair, at the first hostile move. But he makes no hostile moves in my direction. In fact there is something curiously sweet about him, a strange, sinister jocularity, as if we knew each other from somewhere, and his words referred to private jokes from this period of intimacy.[24]

Ben Abdeslam's cryptic communications that signal a forgotten period of intimacy double Burroughs's own "elaborate delusional system" regarding the world around him and presage the secret communications and "invisible currents" between Mugwumps and Reptiles, in Burroughs's developing mythology.[25] Is it this shared "sinister jocularity" that Ginsberg, the recipient of this letter, recalls a couple of months later when referring to Burroughs's self-imposed exile as symptom of national crisis in his poem "America": "Burroughs is in Tangiers I don't think he'll come back it's

William Burroughs in the Grand Socco, Tangier, 1957. *Photo by Allen Ginsberg, courtesy of the Allen Ginsberg Trust.*

sinister"? More to the point, does Burroughs think that the Moroccan errs when he suggests that Burroughs is an agent of the U.S. Embassy? As an American, Burroughs was entitled to the same extraterritorial rights as an American subject in Tangier, the same exemption from the International Zone's court system, which kept Arab Moroccans in the lowest rung of the juridical and political order; Burroughs makes a point of this in his 1955 "Letter from Tangier." Burroughs doesn't reject Ben Abdeslam's accusation that he is an agent of the United States, an assertion implicitly made by many less extreme Moroccan subjects at the same time. During the mid-1950s, many Moroccans felt betrayed by U.S. material support for the French. Bowles's 1955 novel *The Spider's House*—which Burroughs read on its release and complimented[26]—points out the phenomenon, and the *Nation* reported it in 1959.[27] Burroughs had been in this situation before. While in Colombia searching for the hallucinogen *yagé*, Burroughs had been assumed to be a worker for the Texas Oil Company and, based on evidence of his *Yagé Letters*, had felt uncomfortable in the role of Yanqui colonialist. Ben Abdeslam's naming him an agent apparently resonated with Burroughs; recoiling from that role made Ben Abdeslam his secret sharer (Burroughs's deep love of Conrad runs through his work). A year later, Burroughs will recall this allegiance exuberantly as he composes the "Jihad Jitters."

If Burroughs imagines a forgotten period of intimacy with the murderous Abdelkrim Ben Abdeslam, he does not generally identify with Moroccan Arabs, whose perceived hostility toward him he confronts directly, batting his cane at persistent beggars, staring threateningly at those with hostile expressions: "I hate these people and their cowardly, snivelling, stupid, hostility" he writes in late 1955.[28] Nonetheless, after a drug cure in the Jewish Hospital in Tangier, arranged with the help of the local Office of Social Assistance, he becomes increasingly exuberant about Tangier in a state of revolution: "I used to complain I lacked material to write about. Mother of God! Now I'm swamped with material. I could write 50 pages on that walk, which was a mystical vision comparable to your East Harlem Revelations—That letter where I come on sorta whiny like: 'Tanger has nothing for me and it's all your fault I'm here anyhoo.' Well, Al, 'tain't necessarily so. Beginning to dig Arab kicks. It takes time. You must let them seep into you."[29] A week later in a local café catering to Tanjawis more than Tangerinos, Burroughs smokes some especially strong kif. He looks at a table of Moroccans and imagines himself the subject of their gaze. Burroughs feels menace, then remembers the position he enjoys as an American ("it is unthinkable they should molest me"). But the menace returns, and he takes recourse to the form of his work in progress for his escape:

> The meaning of Interzone, its space-time location is at a point where three-dimensional fact merges into dream, and dreams erupt into the real world . . . The very exaggeration of routines is intended to create this feeling. In Interzone dreams can kill [. . .] and solid objects and persons can be unreal as dreams. . . . For example Lee could be in Interzone, after killing the two detectives, and for various dream reasons, neither the law nor The Others could touch him directly.[30]

This description of what Burroughs will elsewhere call "shlupping" and one of his formal innovations in the work here reveals itself to emerge from thinking about the American's special status in Tangier: extraterritorial rights. Lee, one of his fictional alter egos, can kill the fictional detectives (Burroughs is imagining what will become the Hauser and O'Brien section of *Naked Lunch*) and yet be untouchable to either "the law" or to "The Others." Given that the passage follows Burroughs's speculation about the glance of the other in the Arab café, and the close relationship he was at this point drawing between his evolving work and the International Zone itself, the "various dream reasons" would seem to apply multiply to the special legal status that protected Burroughs, as all Americans, from the local law and the awkward identification of Americans with colonialism. Burroughs's exaggerated routines and the shlup seem to offer an escape from the awkwardness of that identification.

This passage is also imbued with racial overtones and allows us to begin to see the complex ways in which Burroughs's work in Tangier continually shifts racial registers. With the increase in tensions between Moroccans and the foreign community (Christopher Wanklyn, a Canadian writer who was a close friend of Bowles and Burroughs, was stabbed in the lung),[31] Burroughs taught himself to blend into his surroundings. In Tangier the local boys call him *el hombre invisible*—the invisible man. Burroughs's identification as el hombre invisible was a strategy for survival within a revolutionary context in which he, a pale and lanky Midwesterner who dressed like an actuary, could be visibly identified with the U.S. Consulate, where he indeed sometimes received mail. Burroughs's invisibility is intertwined with his sense that it is "unthinkable" that Moroccans might attack him; it is the invisibility of pertaining to the dominant, powerful race, nation, and class. But invisibility was also an association with racialized occlusion, as suggested by the proximity of Burroughs's moniker to the title of Ralph Ellison's novel *Invisible Man*, published in 1952. Burroughs, a homosexual junkie, had a deep experience of marginality and was also a fierce critic of American racism and its practices. The letters quoted above would seem to yield competing interpretations. On the one hand, Burroughs seems to draw poetic inspiration from Moroccans along the suspect lines Norman Mailer would later depict in his 1957 essay "The White Negro," comparing his own inspiration in Tangier with Ginsberg's revelations in Harlem and suggesting a touristic relationship to racial difference. On the other hand, in his Tangier writing Burroughs associates violence against colonized peoples with the lynching of African Americans and makes a link in writing that was foreshadowed in the Negro press during World War II. While that link was not made explicit during the war, Burroughs is powerful, vivid, and direct. Here in the Tanjawi café, Burroughs imagines that if "seized" he may be "castrate[d]," and his worry sounds much less like the fear of the empowered out of his element than like that of the minority. Burroughs's embrace of his invisibility in Tangier, while a benefit of his extraterritorial status as an American, is also a tactic in his own warfare with the culture of control. Timothy Murphy, who discusses *Naked Lunch* and *Invisible Man* together in terms of their relationship to postmodernism (but not regarding race), makes a suggestion about Ellison's novel that applies equally to Burroughs's embrace of invisibility: the narrator's going under-ground, "a liminal position of internal exile . . . does not necessarily signify resignation or defeat," but rather the deferral of radical desires "into a future that will allow them to be actualized."[32] Without suggesting that Burroughs was free from racialized thinking, I am arguing that in Tan-gier—which followed residence in Mexico and long travels in Central and South America—he continued a reconfiguration of U.S. racial thinking that he recognized ran deeply through cold war domestic and global poli-tics. His "invisibility" in Tangier, as I see it, was a deferral of the immediate context of his own empowerment by U.S. extraterritorial rights as he worked through the code of the future geopolitical arrangements.

In early 1956, when the non-Moroccan community in Tangier was on edge, Burroughs repaired to London for a more extensive drug cure. There, from a distance, he reports to Ginsberg "a series of dreams in which I am a minority in a vast, hostile country." The dreams contain within them a barely disguised political parable:

> Finally comparative security through Public Works, complicated locks and channels and harbors and markets all synchronized with physiological cal-endars. In short, the Natives can't use the Works without us. If they could understand the Works, they would not be hostile. Some day they will maybe. But that's hundreds of years away now. Now they must use the Works and put up with us or die. An extremist party wants to destroy the Works, and kill us, even if they do die. The Natives and The Work Guards (who form a separate power group) keep the extremists in line. Burning them to death when they catch them.[33]

The letter is punctuated by a recounting of withdrawal nightmares in which Burroughs orders a friend to torch approaching Arabs with gas-oline (an image reworked for the penultimate page of *Naked Lunch*), a vicious image of his own recourse to violence in the face of a perceived hostility (several months later, he will report a sequel to the dream).[34] His vivid dream of hostile natives who must rely in spite of themselves on a foreign-built infrastructure for their survival is also a harsh and cynical portrait of the transition to independence in the Maghreb. Burroughs's mind is clearly on this transition and he is thinking of Tangier, of Morocco, and of the rest of the Maghreb. After a trip to Libya and Algeria in 1956, he reports being "definitely anti the Arab Nationalists and pro-French so far as the Algerian setup goes."[35] While it is tempting to read this in racial terms, the sentiment is expressed in relationship to tactics— he has reported to Ginsberg the bombing of a café in Oran, which he strongly disapproves of—and to hostility demonstrated toward himself on the streets. Burroughs's own tactics focus on disruptive codes, on pseudotelepathic communication, on the viruslike infiltration of language. His disapproval of the nation form extends to the Maghrebi nationalists' projected imposition of a new nation and culture of control to substitute for French colonialism.

What is inspiring to Burroughs about the ensuing chaos is not violence per se but the possibility for disrupting the established order that rioting and chaos present. He sees revolution as opportunity, not as the replacement of one control mechanism with another. On October 29, 1956, back in Tangier, he describes a general strike, thousands of Moroccans marching, and the excitement of potential public violence: "The possibility of an all-out riot is like a tonic, like ozone in air. . . . The chaos in Morocco is beautiful." In a masterpiece of a letter that recalls and extends his shared intimacy with Abdelkrim Ben Abdeslam from a year earlier, Burroughs imagines himself running amok, infected by the "jihad jitters": "Perhaps come the *Jihad* I will have to yell, 'Death to the American queers!' and cut off Dave Woolman's head. It's a cheap baboon trick. When a baboon is attacked by a stronger baboon he leads an attack on a weaker baboon, and who am I to deny our glorious Simian heritage?"[36] He is inspired to write uproarious song lyrics, the "Jihad Jitters" (not used in *Naked Lunch*), in which various groups that had thrived in International Tangier (a "fag," a smuggler, a retired colonial officer, a foreign peddler) sing of their responses to an encroaching riot. Burroughs is exuberant, almost manic, as he "declares the all-out massacre of everybody by everybody else.[. . .] I mean we will have J-DAY once a year. All police protection suspended from the world, all frontiers open."[37] The call for an annual purging, an opening of frontiers, is the energetic hope to keep constantly at bay the controlling ideologies of the nation. Despite the satirical call for "all-out massacre," of course, Burroughs's jihad remains on the level of the infiltration of language, of communication that disrupts the system. His jihad is a song.

Three months later, he encourages Ginsberg to come to Morocco in terms that reflect the shift in his thinking. "Morocco is really great and I know you will like it," he writes, "And the Arabs are not to compare with American counterparts for viciousness, and it is sheer Provincialism to be afraid of them as if they was something special, sinister and Eastern and un-American."[38] In January 1957, in another letter to Ginsberg, and responding to Jack Kerouac's nervousness about traveling to Tangier, he went further:

> I will say it again and say it slow: TANGER IS AS SAFE AS ANY TOWN I EVER LIVE IN. *I* feel a chill of fear and horror at the thought of the random drunken violence stalking the streets and bars and parks and subways of America. . . . ARABS ARE NOT VIOLENT. . . . They do *not attack people for kicks or fight for kicks like Americans.* Riots are the accumulated, just resentment of a people subjected to outrageous brutalities by the French cops used to strew blood and teeth over a city block in the Southern Zone.[39]

This passage clarifies the distinction between Burroughs's antinationalist sentiment expressed earlier and his sympathetic attitude toward Maghrebi independence: the problem (as Fanon also sensed within the Algerian revolution) is whether that which will follow revolution will replicate the established order. If Burroughs disapproves of nationalist violence, it is based on a sense of the detachment of the leadership from the "just resentment of [the] people." He also disapproves of various expressions of violence by colonial forces. The same letter goes on to proclaim that Maghrebi Muslims had a superlative peace of mind, something that Burroughs, Ginsberg, and Kerouac had discussed intensely and explored in Buddhism.[40] He also claimed to have made a "connection" with God (*connection* being Burroughs's central term), learned from Moroccan Islam. Burroughs claims that this religious awakening is inscribed in *Naked Lunch*:

> My religious conversion now complete. I am neither a Moslem nor a Christian, but I owe a great debt to Islam and could never have made my connection with God ANYWHERE EXCEPT HERE. And I realize how much of Islam I have absorbed by osmosis without spitting a word of their appalling language. I will get to that when I, ah, have a free moment. . . . I have never even glimpsed peace of mind before I learn the real meaning of "It is As Allah Wills." Relax, you make it or you don't, and since realizing that, whatever I want comes to me. If I want a boy, he knocks on my door,

etc. I can't go into all this, and [it's] all in the M S. What's with Lucien? He need more Islam to him. We all do and Jack especially. As one of the Meknes rioters say when they shot him, "*Skikut*" [*sic*]—"it is written" . . . And remember "God is as close to you as the vein in your neck"—Koran.[41]

More than any other, this letter begs the question: What is the relationship of *Naked Lunch* to Orientalism? "[It's] all in the M S" Burroughs tells Ginsberg, referring to his conversion experience and his inspiration by the local scene; the text of *Naked Lunch* would seem to be fair game for such a critique. Burroughs's Koran—God as close as the "vein in your neck"—associates text, connection, and bodily fluid/artery. Burroughs's own interpretation of Islamic fatalism and his excited subscription to that interpreted philosophy echoes that of the classic Orientalists, for whom a perceived "Oriental" difference at once inspired economies of departure from the home culture via transvestism ("going native") and justified the imposition of modern Western technologies of control. As critics such as Ali Behdad writing about Isabelle Eberhardt and Edward Said writing about Richard Burton have shown, the apparent distance between those responses to the "Orient" is not so far as they might at first seem.[42] The movement I've charted in Burroughs's response to Tangier is ultimately containable within the logic of Orientalism: from disappointment that colonial privilege is not available to him—the writer's colony, the haven not there, a sense of belatedness (Tangier's boom is over, he writes in the "Letter to Tangier")—to an excitement with the beautiful chaos and Islamic fatalism of the environment. In this sense, Burroughs seems to pertain to an Orientalist register and unwittingly supports the very American presence that Abdelkrim Ben Abdeslam accused him of being an agent for. And tantalizingly enough, Burroughs's letters are sometimes marked with the return address c/o U.S. Consulate, an irony that he himself was not beyond appreciating.

Larval Zone: *Naked Lunch*'s Anal Economy

Clem: "We have come to feed on your backwardness."
Jody: "In the words of the Immortal Bard, to batten on these Moors."
    —William Burroughs, *Naked Lunch*

If Burroughs does work within an Orientalist framework, it is also important to see how he may from this position imagine a contestatory position that undoes the more particular U.S. political position in Tangier and within cold war domestic culture. *Naked Lunch*'s elusive final line: "'No glot...C'lom Fliday...'" offers an example. The line is a repeated phrase, what Burroughs calls elsewhere a "space-time juxtaposition...a folding in and back (the universe is curved, feller say) . . . point of intersection between levels of experience where parallel lines meet."[43] In its first appearance, the phrase is the wildly exaggerated rendering of a Chinese junk pusher's refusal to sell his wares to a Western buyer since according to the text Westerners are considered by the Chinese "so unreliable, dishonest and wrong" (144). Here it represents the unbridgeable gap between East and West, rendered as poor translation, with *l*s substituted for *r*s. Since Burroughs adds extra *l*s where no *r*s would be in English ("glot," "c'lom"), the phrase suggests a further linguistic remove between worlds and words: the poor translation produces an excess of meaning, a surplus akin to static. In its repetition as the closing words of *Naked Lunch*, however, "No glot . . . C'lom Fliday" does not merely repeat the meaning it provoked before; it expands on it. In its final occurrence it recalls that gap between East and West (a condition of Orientalism, but detached from the corporate institutional structures of ruling the Orient) and further suggests *Naked Lunch*'s prerequisite for an escape from the algebra of need: a cutting off of junk at the source. The Chinese pusher recalled by but disembodied from the final phrase breaks the junk economy and allows for escape from it on a larger scale.

In its place, *Naked Lunch* offers a different economy. The book's anal economy—the form of the work, its philosophy, its means of production, and its recurring imagery—is at the philosophical center of the novel, and is Burroughs's rich response to the Tangier of the "right now," a Tangier he finally grasps in late October 1956 with the explicit end of Tangier's International Status (extended by royal decree and kept at a legal and cultural remove from the rest of Morocco until late 1959). By staging this economy, Burroughs queers the queer Tangier of the 1950s American imaginary and renders a potentiality that threatens to undo cold war McCarthyist American supremacist logic. At the same time that C. L. R. James was composing his radical rereading of Herman Melville's *Moby-Dick* from Ellis Island detention—foregrounding the diasporic confederation of "mariners, renegades, and castaways"—William Burroughs placed an inversion of a Melvillean economy at the center of his radical anti-McCarthyist work of fiction. James's critical work on Melville intervened in readings of a text that, as Donald Pease has shown, had deep resonances for cold war liberals in the 1950s.[44] Burroughs, unaware of James's work and whose engagement with Melville is less sustained, nonetheless places within his mythography a radical economy that inverts *Moby-Dick*'s sense of the productivity of sperm. In the "Interzone" section of *Naked Lunch*, Burroughs includes a conversation between Marv and Leif the Unlucky regarding the massive import of sexual lubricant made from whale detritus, a deal that Burroughs had imagined for the opening of *Naked Lunch*: "'Yes, nugget, a shipload of K.Y. made of genuine whale dreck in the South Atlantic at present quarantined by the Board of Health in Tierra del Fuego.'"[45] In his letter of December 13, 1954, Burroughs reports to Ginsberg that he has "written 1st chapter of a novel in which I will incorporate all my routines and scattered notes. Scene is Tanger, which I call Interzone. Did I write you anything about novel in progress? Starts with a deal to import and sell 'a load of K.Y. made of genuine whale dreg [*sic*] in the South Atlantic' . . . As you gather, in my most extreme line."[46] Though the scene was ultimately moved to very late in the book, it remains a central image in the novel and arguably the generative idea of *Naked Lunch*, a productive anality. A parenthetical explanation defines the material: "Whale dreck is reject material that accumulates in the process of cutting up a whale and cooking it down. A horrible, fishy mess you can smell for miles. No one has found any use for it." If for Melville, the whale's sperm generated the life force associated with creativity, with desire, and with American abandon, Burroughs chooses a by-product of the whale that is at the other end of the spectrum. Dreck is the final waste of the whale, an otherwise useless substance, absolute detritus. But within his vision of Interzone, the dreck can be for the first time recycled (turning shit into money, an anal economy in which nothing is rejected and waste is recycled) as a product useful for anal sex, thereby doubling that economy. In the "Atrophied Preface," the author will name himself twice in a gesture redolent of Whitman's "Song of Myself," giving further resonance to the narrator's Whitmanesque promise to "unlock my word horde" (230) and underline his inversion of Melville: "I, William Seward, captain of this lushed up hash-head subway, will quell the Lock Ness monster with rotenone and cowboy the white whale" (226). "Cowboying" the white whale, we know from the K.Y.

episode, means at once roping it, boiling it down, and then lubricating it with its own final waste and sodomizing it.

The two principals of Interzone Imports Unlimited, Marvie and Leif The Unlucky (based on Woolman and Eric Gifford, another companion of Burroughs who wrote for local papers),[47] argue about commission on the deal. When Marvie finally makes his commission on the whale-dreck K.Y., months later, it is paid in a currency so obscure and drawn on a bank so anonymous and distant that he must wait nearly a year for it to clear. He carries a dummy of his check around as a trophy—in "photostatic copy" to protect himself—but has already spent the amount on medicine for his Moroccan lover's venereal disease, which has stricken him both "fore and aft." Marv apparently does not cash the check for several reasons: because he has already spent it, because the transformation of it to money is so elaborate and slow, and because it has more value to him as a trophy. And so it is both valueless and laden with value at the same time; removed from circulation, the check is the miser's hoard.

Marv's miserly treatment of his check is anal and queer, within Burroughs's vision, and recalls Burroughs's description of a doctor whom he encountered in late 1955 at the Benchimol Hospital. Burroughs's account to Ginsberg and Kerouac of a Dr. Appfel, an Austrian Nazi collaborator who attempts to pass as a Jewish refugee but is still the "best physician in Tanger," describes the doctor's use of "Arab trick[s]" when billing Burroughs (e.g., billing a large amount, hoping Burroughs would pay it, but accepting half without complaint). The letter cuts to what the local gossip mill has to say about the doctor: " 'Oh *him*,' the gossip chorus says. 'Notorious collaborator, my dear, *and* he's, well, *queer* for money.' " Burroughs ponders the final phrase, asking in what sense Appfel might be "queer." Discounting the possibility that Appfel likes sex with young men, Burroughs outlines two possibilities: that Appfel is a "modern miser" or a gambler (303). Either way, it turns out, Appfel will be participating in an anal economy. Misers are anal because they store their gold and valuables and keep their family on "starvation rations," refusing to produce waste via consumption. Gambling, on the other hand, is "the one vice that does not thrive in Tanger." (Burroughs had noted the local debates over a casino in Tangier, which pervaded the local press and which he discusses in his "Letter from Tangier.") So Appfel, if he gambles in Tangier, would necessarily do so by participating in Tangier's famous currency markets, keeping "charts and tables and graphs and there is a ticker in his room":

"In short, any gambling he did must be thoroughly anal." Having identified him as an anal type, Burroughs places him as "another character for
my Interzone Hospital," against Doctor Benway, whom he calls an oral
type. Whatever the case, holding onto money is generally associated by
Burroughs with waste: in a rejected portion of "Word," Burroughs refers
to a character with "Money all over him like shit you can smell it."[48]

Since the K.Y. deal was to have been the opening scene of *Naked Lunch*
as-novel, its inverted placement near the end of *Naked Lunch* not-as-novel
(i.e., the final book) suggests that the K.Y. routine as it appears is itself
opposed to the logic of the novel form (just as the placement of the
"Atrophied Preface" at the book's end undoes its implicit claim to explain
the writer's method, and the reader should be wary of the alleged "writer's"
claim to be merely a "recording instrument" [221]). In the "Atrophied
Preface," Burroughs describes the midday meal he uses for his title as "the
long lunch thread from mouth to ass all the days of our years" (230), a
phrase that suggests—since the preface is atrophied, since these putatively
explanatory notes are thrown into question, since the book is named for a
different kind of lunch—that the daily repetition of intake and output
(the shared temporal register of humanity) underlying traditional novel
time is not the sense of time/economy or communication that *Naked
Lunch* is finally built on. Communication in this novel is the space-time
travel that shlups from dream to materiality, akin to sound waves ("what I
can pick up without FM on my 1920 crystal set with antennae of jissom"
[229]) and opposed to novel time. Even the fact that whale dreck is
defined for the reader in a parenthetical remark connects the passage to
Burroughs's attempt to break through the various conceptual impasses he
encountered while composing *Naked Lunch* and searching for its form.
The parenthesis was one of Burroughs's preferred forms of punctuation,
one he considered antithetical to the temporal register of the novel form:
"A parenthesis indicates the simultaneity of past, present and emergent
future. . . . This novel is not posthumous. A 'novel' is something finished,
that is, dead."[49] The whale-dreck K.Y. routine thus helps elaborate the
complex relationship between Burroughs's geopolitical response to Tangier, recurring concerns of the work, and what I'm calling the anal economy of *Naked Lunch*. Marv has of course appeared earlier in *Naked Lunch*,
in a passing reference that combines economy and anality, when he takes
the narrator to a place where they "pay two Arab kids sixty cents to watch
them screw each other," which Marv thinks they'll do because "they are

hungry" (59). The narrator comments there that the event "makes me feel sorta like a dirty old man." Considering the high threshold that the narrator may have for such a statement, the relationship of Arab hunger to degradation by foreigners might be noted.

When this hunger appears again, it is in the mouths of Clem and Jody, in a rich exchange in the text that leads us to the final set of remarks I want to make. Clem and Jody, also known as the Ergot Brothers after a fungus that lives on blighted wheat, are former vaudevillians posing as Russian agents who dress as ugly Americans, in order to make the United States look bad. This doubled performance—the performance of a performance—leaves Clem's and Jody's motives ambiguous, though we gather that they have economic motives (their silent partnership in Islam Inc. is based on an interest in increasing the value of their Venezuelan holdings by destruction of Near East oil fields). In the "Ordinary Men and Women" section of *Naked Lunch*, Clem and Jody enter unannounced to stir up more trouble with the local population. Dressed like "The Capitalist in a Communist mural" and addressing a group of "sour nationalists," Clem announces: "We have come to feed on your backwardness." Jody chimes in: "In the words of the Immortal Bard, to batten on these Moors." The play on *Hamlet* (3.4.67) is intriguing. In the original, Hamlet says to his mother Gertrude, within a speech in which he is presenting her a verbal picture of what she has done to the memory of his late father, "Could you on this faire Mountaine leave to feed, / And batten on this Moor?" The *Oxford English Dictionary* defines "moor," using this very quote from *Hamlet* as its illustration, to signify a "tract of unenclosed waste ground."[50] In altering Hamlet's line from "batten on this Moor" to "batten on these Moors," Burroughs brings together his own imagery of hungry Arab bodies with Shakespeare's reference to feeding on a wasteland. When a nationalist charges back, "Don't you realize my people are hungry?" Clem says, "That's the way I like to see them," recalling Marv's earlier line regarding the screwing Arab boys. Burroughs associates the dirty old man aspect of the earlier scene with a trenchant critique of the American presence in Tangier (and the larger machinations of the United States in Morocco), based on profit at the expense of Moroccan population. Clem's and Jody's representation of the worst of the American— worse yet, a Communist parody of the worst of America—critiques the purity of what was called "the American voice" in Tangier via word play, a between-the-lines potentiality. Clem's and Jody's racialized naming of

Arabs as Moors connects this strand with the obsession in *Naked Lunch* with scenes of lynching and its exposure of the racial violence of domestic America. By associating Clem and Jody's "ugly American" racialization of Moroccans with their cold war project, Burroughs makes a connection to the imperial designs of the cold war state (its geopolitical violence) with the domestic violence at its core.

What's crucial here is the manner in which the critique is made: via wordplay, akin to his codes and larval possibilities, those language mechanisms located in the vast market known as the Meet Café. In the context of Burroughs's concerns as I've laid them out here and in the face of public discourse about the American role in Tangier, this language play is especially compelling. This play on Shakespeare is not in context a "pure voice" but code or allusion. In the context of Burroughs's other concerns and recurring imagery, the word play on *Hamlet*, which converts a line about the breakdown of the family unit as crisis of the state into a line about the cynical cannibalism at the heart of U.S. geopolitical interest in Tangier, is a potent example of Burroughs's disruption of American language as political action. In this sense Burroughs creates in *Naked Lunch* what Deleuze calls a "grammar of disequilibrium" within American English, a disruptive force within the major language (the pure American voice) that Mary McCarthy recognized very early as disruptive to the state. It thus locates Burroughs's response to Tangier as one that queers the American media's queering of Tangier by producing an antidote to the "pure voice" of America: a series of broken signals imagined as illegible doodles that suggest a future community that might oppose the global culture of control associated with McCarthyist America as global force. In an Interzone associated with Tangier, Burroughs saw the conjunction of "the unknown past and the emergent future meet in a vibrating soundless hum. . . . Larval entities waiting for a Live One" (109). Like Frantz Fanon, whose writing about the ongoing Algerian revolution in the late 1950s brought him to advocate a broken signal and a clear message emanating from jammed radio signals as the true voice that would break France's hold on the Algerian nation, Burroughs saw a ruptured "voice" in Tangier as a means to disrupt American hypocrisy, both global and domestic.[51]

Burroughs makes frequent reference in *Naked Lunch* to radio signals, whether to the 1920 crystal set I mentioned before, or to the noise of Cairo stations blaring through Tangier cafés. In the context of my claim that

Burroughs had a sharp awareness of his Tangier context, I want to recall that the United States' main economic and diplomatic interest in Tangier during the formative period of Burroughs's writing (in other words, after the 1952 protocol) was protecting the radio transfer stations built in the Tangier Zone (Mackay, RCA, and Voice of America). And on the public side of American attention to Tangier, the lone aspect about Tangier celebrated in the American media was the presence of what was called "the pure American voice" (i.e., democracy) as model for a U.S. role in the developing world. In 1952, for example, Joseph Wechsberg published two long articles on Morocco in the *New Yorker* (where Burroughs hoped to place an essay on Tangier in 1955). In the second article, focusing on Tangier, Wechsberg had used language as something of a cipher in understanding the zone, which he sees as marked by the conflict between democracy and internationalism. Wechsberg argued that while on the surface Tangier looks like a heartening experiment in international government (because of the multiple languages on street signs, multiple religions practiced, and multiple post offices), internationalism turns out to be in practice pervaded by a multiplicity that is corrupt and indeed the source of its problems. Wechsberg points to multiple standards of justice in Tangier and the scandalous state of utilities (because of corruption). The final image of his article is a battle for voices between the three American relay radio stations and the threat of a Russian voice emerging on the scene. This worry leads Wechsberg to comment about the newly formed American School of Tangier (international in membership, but funded by the United States) as the best and indeed only example of true democracy. The "pure American voice" (one not polluted by others) turns out to be true democracy.[52] *Colliers* magazine also published an article—the most sanguine of the 1950s about Tangier—titled "Why They Love Us in Tangier" and celebrated the American School unequivocally.

Whether or not Burroughs read these articles, he was clearly well aware of the connection between Tangier as international radio relay station, as a site where the voices of the world mingled in static, and as a historical crossroads on which imperial and emergent nations encounter one another in proximity (both geographical and historical). In his journals, Burroughs writes: "It is frequently said that the Great Powers will never give up the Interzone because of its value as a listening post. It is in fact the listening post of the world, the slowing pulse of a decayed civilization, that only war can quicken. Here East meets West in a final debacle of misunderstanding, each seeking the Answer, the Secret, from the other and not finding it, because neither has the answer to give."[53] *Naked Lunch's* achievement—as well as a source of its frustration for many readers—is that the work does not render this message in the same coherent narrative on which the nation form relies. Though his earlier works and passages of *Naked Lunch* reveal that he was a consummate entertainer, Burroughs refuses the narrative coherence or the authorial stability that the pure American voice usually delivers. This must be seen as a response to McCarthyism and the hysterical demand for an accurate and coherent accounting of the past, which it is imagined predicts the present and future. In "Word," Burroughs takes on the voice of a subject refusing testimony to McCarthy, while perverting McCarthy's association of "perversion" and subversion: "I stand on the Fifth Amendment, will not answer question of the senator from Wisconsin: 'are you or have you ever been a member of the male sex.'"[54] The line was not used in *Naked Lunch*, but a scene in the "Hospital" section of the final text offers a yet more layered response to the McCarthyist demand for a coherent accounting of national loyalty by forcibly disassembling the pure American voice while exposing its artifice. In the exuberant and multiply ruptured routine, an American diplomat receives and reads a fractured message via ticker tape, a message that seems to consist of a denial that U.S. citizens resident in Interzone have committed un-American activities. Those alleged activities, as we attempt to grasp them amid a wildly orchestrated performance of the U.S. national anthem performed alternatively in falsetto and by a costumed lesbian, seem to be that male citizens have been accused of giving birth to ambiguous "creatures." By breaking apart the reading of the ticker-tape message, and by emphasizing the instability of national identification as performance (here exaggerated through repeated images of falseness: a falsetto, falsie baskets), the scene powerfully activates the antinational power of static.

Steven Shaviro has suggested that one of the "lessons" Burroughs teaches his readers is that language is a virus. As Shaviro elaborates: "Interiority means intrusion and colonization. Self-identity is ultimately a symptom of parasitic invasion, the expression within me of forces originating from outside. And so it is with language."[55] Language's function in this frame is not to communicate but to replicate itself. From this Shaviro derives the observation that individuals/authors do not try to express a "self" but rather speak in tongues, channel messages as a radio does.

Shaviro refers to Derrida's comment that the author is a sphincter, which he connects to Burroughs's talking-asshole routine: "Everything in Burroughs's fiction is resolved into and out of a spinning asshole, which is also finally a cosmic black hole" (45). The unexpurgated "Word," we might add, eventually resolves into "A vast Moslem muttering ris[ing] from the stone square," an association that further links the anal economy with the language-virus mechanism as minor language.[56] There is thus as much promise in Shaviro's lesson as warning. *Naked Lunch*'s description of the Meet Café links this sense of latent potentiality—a larval zone—with a rupturing of language and tongues and shorthands illegible and powerful in their lurking possibility: "Followers of obsolete, unthinkable trades doodling in Etruscan . . . servers of fragmentary warrants taken down in hebephrenic shorthand charging unspeakable mutilations of the spirit . . . officials of unconstituted police states . . . doctors skilled in the treatment of diseases dormant in the black dust of ruined cities, gathering virulence in the white blood of eyeless worms feeling slowly to the surface and the human host" (108–9). Deleuze's essay "He Stuttered" and his and Félix Guattari's essay on Kafka learn from Burroughs and suggest a potential within the activation of a minor use of English.[57] Thus when Burroughs writes to Ginsberg that he wants to learn Arabic but ultimately won't, it doesn't especially matter to what he does to English, since he brings the impulse back into an English made minor. Morgan's statement in the biography that Burroughs's failure to learn Arabic reveals his dissociation from the place is thus incorrect on a deeper level.

Translation is deeply imbued with questions of economy. Languages that are "unfungible," in Ronald Judy's term borrowed from economics, are those that do not move easily into a register—identified in the present with globalization—that would reduce them to pure difference and thereby occlude them. The breakdown of smooth rendering of speech is connected with Burroughs's antinational project and thus resists globalization, which relies on coherent difference and on the maintenance of nation-states, and which requires smooth translation. In that perpetually intriguing final line of *Naked Lunch*, referencing the global trade of opiates, Burroughs renders the Chinese pusher's resistance to complete legibility: "No glot . . . C'lom Fliday." (Indeed, in one of Ginsberg's own journal entries composed after reading *Naked Lunch*, Ginsberg understands "No glot" as both "No God" and "No Got," demonstrating both its flexibility and its opacity as a phrase.)[58]

Burroughs's preferred Tangier is the Tangier of the "right now," as he puts it in his "Jihad Jitters" letter, the Tangier that was post-Moroccan independence and prior to the end of the International Zone—a literally "preposterous" moment, filled with potentiality. On the very day the letter is dated, October 29, 1956, several months after Moroccan independence, Tangier's status was being decided at a conference at Fedala, Morocco, attended by representatives of several of the interested nations, as Burroughs well knew. It was already clear that Tangier was a Moroccan city, no longer colonial, but also apparent that it would maintain some special status. At this point, U.S. extraterritorial rights in Morocco had finally been renounced, yet the Moroccan nationalists had not yet fully taken over the Tangier Zone and an international impulse still pervaded the city. The potentiality here in this three- to four-year period is for Burroughs arguably more powerful than the 1945–52 moment of international administration that I discussed in chapter 3. The Western powers—the Committee of Control, a name seemingly drawn from Burroughs's fiction—were now checked by the independent Moroccan government. *Naked Lunch*, whatever else it is, learns from this "preposterous" Tangier an alternative. Though it is much more than a response to American media responses to the challenges posed by Tangier, to the abjection of International Tangier, Burroughs's work disassembles the Hoover/McCarthyist straight story, and is allied with what Mary McCarthy called the book's "statelessness." When Burroughs expresses his sense that social context is finally gone in Tangier, he sees something different there, a potential for a space beyond the nation. If, as Etienne Balibar has argued, the precondition for the nation form is the production of foreignness, Burroughs's Tangier may indeed suggest a different formation.[59] With the foreignness displaced and internal and external both put into flux, Burroughs imagines a tantalizing potentiality that emerges. In *Naked Lunch*, he is the poet of the future arrangements.

Hitchcock's Marrakech Expressions

In 1955, when Alfred Hitchcock remade his own film *The Man Who Knew Too Much*, originally produced in England two decades earlier, perhaps the most remarkable change was the relocation of the opening half of the film. In the 1934 version, the vacationing couple who lose their child to international criminals, thus setting the plot in motion, do so at a Swiss ski resort. But in 1955, Hitchcock and his collaborators Angus MacPhail and John Michael Hayes moved the family vacation to Marrakech, layering on the suspense of "mysterious Morocco" and the "dark continent," two phrases that the film itself applies to its setting. Because this is Hitchcock's only remake of his own work, critics have been especially interested in comparing the two films. The critical debate has revolved around the relationship of the remake to social and historical context. Hitchcock became an American citizen in April 1955, during the film's production. Some critics have seen the film as Hitchcock's layered response to cold war America and the national security state. Since the two versions take starkly different positions on the social question of the professional woman's relationship to family and career, the film has provided critics with an opportunity to investigate Hitchcock's thinking about the maternal, a contested category after World War II. As much as such readings have illuminated, however, the implications of the choice of opening location have been left uninterrogated. The setting spills outside the framework of the film's domestic narrative and in turn reflects back on the portrait of Americanness that Hitchcock's purportedly average family represents.

Marrakech, which Alfred and Alma Hitchcock themselves scouted for two days in December 1954 and to which the production traveled to film on location in May 1955, is a major character in the film, one that allows Hitchcock and writer Hayes to explore the limits upon which the national security state relies. The presence Marrakech exerts on the narrative is figured as a disruption of legibility, exceeding the limits of the domestic frame. The original trailer described the fictional family vacation as the "trip abroad that started out as a holiday and ended up as a nightmare." The vacation to Morocco is the encounter of a family traveling to a place they think they know ("Daddy liberated Africa," the boy tells a Frenchman, referencing World War II's North African campaign). Instead they are confronted with an unknowable place, with only the messy spectacle of French colonialism and unreliable British allies as anchors. *The Man Who Knew Too Much*, as released in 1956, ponders the question of surplus knowledge and surplus meaning; in so doing, it suggests the limits of American global power as an index of the domestic. Thus while critics have labored to bring to light and clarify the meanings of the female lead's utterances, there remains an entire strain in the film that insists on unintelligibility—and that calls into question the possibility of its translation. In deciding to reuse the title of the 1934 film for the remake, instead of the working title "Into Thin Air," Hitchcock and his collaborators named again the dangers of excess knowledge and placed that concern as central.[60] Knowing "too much" in the remade film will signify not only knowing state secrets, but also knowing multiple linguistic and national registers, a kind of forced cosmopolitanism dangerous for citizens to possess within the logic of the early cold war U.S. security state. While the carefully plotted film narrative is at a great remove from *Naked Lunch*'s rejection of linear development, and while Hitchcock's understanding of Americanness is apparently far from Burroughs's (for starters, the former apparently upholds the heteronormative family unit as appropriate building block for the nation), there is a shared lesson that the two texts draw from the experience of revolutionary Morocco. Both works explore the possibility that language—as virus, as noise—may cross the borders of the domestic space and is thus a threat to its integrity or to its survival. Like Burroughs, Hitchcock associates that lesson with the structural violence of race.

Although it is an idiosyncratic juxtaposition, I want to read Hitchcock's film alongside Burroughs's *Naked Lunch* as two texts that emerge from and challenge cold war ways of thinking in related ways. Hitchcock, compared to Burroughs, operates intellectually within the national episteme; his powerful imagination of excess knowledge is thus a critique and warning of a potent threat rather than the explosion of the national form, as is Burroughs's. But in turning to Marrakech in the midst of revolution, Hitchcock gathered a mode of critique that may be associated with Burroughs's project. Hitchcock's film about an American family traveling in Morocco helps examine the limits of U.S. cold war logic—as the projection of domestic American ideas about nation, race, and gender onto the foreign space—and in flashes offers the possibility of an interruptive critique.

The Man Who Knew Too Much is obsessed with the ambiguities of language—with homonyms, with slang expressions, with translation, with foreign language beyond translation, with dialects—and more generally with sound and noise as they relate to knowledge. The "crash of Cymbals" that changes the lives of an American family (a phrase projected in the film's opening title) is Hitchcock's own figure for the way in which sound and noise operate symbolically; fittingly Hitchcock offers a homonym or pun to open the film (the cymbals are also symbols).[61] Thus we are alerted to the centrality of sound to the logic of the film. In an agile comparison of the two versions of the film, Robert Corber argues compellingly that the remade film reverses the original's relation between auditory and visual; in the later film the auditory demonstrates itself to be dominant. The voice of the female protagonist Jo McKenna (Doris Day) is a central element of her character (like the actress playing her, Jo is an internationally famous singer). Further, the sound editing permits Jo's/Day's voice to "appear" separate from her image, something that the earlier version forbids its female lead. A sequence late in the film at the unnamed embassy where the McKennas' son Hank (Christopher Olsen) has been hidden represents Jo's voice traveling through physical architecture, up a staircase, down a hallway, through a door, suggesting the autonomy of sound within the realm of visual meaning. And Jo's voice is well known to several characters in the film (such as the villainous Draytons) because of sound recordings that have apparently circulated. The central assumption behind the assassination plot around which the narrative revolves is that a crash of cymbals within a double fortissimo passage in a choral symphony will cover over the sound of gunshots and thereby occlude "knowledge" of the crime. When Edward Drayton (Bernard Miles) reviews the plan for a political assassination with the assassin Rien (Reggie Nalder), he plays a recording of the climatic moment in the symphony that will be playing at the time of the shooting. Drayton says: "No one will know." Rien replies: "No one but one." Not only does this exchange play again on the film's title—which leaves ambiguous just which male character knows too much—here suggesting that knowledge is death, it further suggests that knowledge may be blockable by sensory deprivation; a crash of cymbals can prevent knowledge. The ambassador won't know he's being shot because he won't hear, but he will know because he'll feel. Thus he'll know too much. And no one else in the audience will know what's happening because they won't hear or feel it. The fictional audience at Albert Hall (where the final scene was shot on location) will know too little, but Hitchcock's audience *will* know: the musical passage is played several times to rehearse us.

The film plays on the ambiguities of language as sound, and indeed a substantial portion of the England portion of the plot revolves around the problems of the homonym. When Louis Bernard, a French agent killed in Marrakech (played by Daniel Gelin), reveals the dangerous secret he has discovered to McKenna (Jimmy Stewart), Bernard utters: "A man . . . a statesman . . . is to be killed . . . assassinated . . . in London . . . soon . . . very soon . . . tell them . . . in London . . . to try Ambrose Chap(p)el(l)." I transcribe the last word thus because Bernard speaks the line to McKenna, who makes a point of quickly writing it down on a scrap of paper. McKenna's transcription—he writes "Ambrose Chappell" instead of "Ambrose Chapel"—confuses a place with a person and allows for a narrative detour. McKenna's note-taking brings the audience into the error: when the audience sees him write what he and they have both heard, the writing fixes the sounds for us as marks, lessening the possibility that the audience knows "too much" by steering it into error. At this moment, as the audience will discover retroactively, McKenna in fact knows too little because he thinks Chapel is Chappell. (Or perhaps he knows too much because he knows a secondary meaning of the morpheme combination *cha-pel*: not only a small church but also a British surname.) But he is treated by the authorities and the criminals alike as if he knows too much, because he has had contact with a dead man. Louis Bernard of course has known too much, both on the level of the plot (he has discovered the criminals' secret) and within the film's equation of knowledge and death (no one will know but one). As we will see, he also knows too much by speaking three languages with fluency.

The early scene on the bus to Marrakech is a key scene for making sense of the relationship between sound, language, and the global referents of Hitchcock's interruptive imagination. In the first scene after the images of the London Symphony Orchestra performing behind the title credits, we are introduced to an apparently model American family from Indiana on vacation in Morocco: Ben McKenna, a general practitioner; Jo Conway McKenna, a retired singer; and their son Hank. The opening dialogue establishes a banter about language, naming, and terminology that will run through the film. The film's opening line is given to the boy: "Daddy, you sure I've never been to Africa before? It looks familiar." His mother answers the question: "We saw the same scenery last summer driving to Las Vegas," a line somewhat counterindicated by the scenery visible through the windows of Arabs in djellabas, earthen buildings, and the occasional camel. Hitchcock, who knew that most Hollywood films set in Morocco and the Sahara were filmed in California, gets in a dig at both his Hollywood predecessors and American audiences who think they know what Morocco looks like. *This* film, it's suggested, will actually bring the audience to the place and show Americans that they don't know "too much" at all (the original trailer highlighted the fact that the film was shot on location in Marrakech and London). The knowledge the film promises is quickly framed in geopolitical terms: "Course this isn't really Africa," Jo says, "It's the French Morocco." Jo's comment introduces the importance of the French frame on Morocco, and the triangulation of American, French, and Moroccan characters and concerns. When her husband disagrees, "Well, it's *northern* Africa," he announces his own refusal to acknowledge geopolitical realities and his attempt to assert an individualist relationship to the landscape, which will return later. Hank, to complete the trio of responses, returns to his own child fascination with the hypocrisies of language: "I don't know: in school they call it the Dark Continent. This is twice as bright as Indianapolis." When his father tells him where they are headed, Hank continues along the same lines: "Marrakech, it sounds like a drink." Rather than leaving it as incomprehensible, Hank *translates* the word. His translations maintain the mark of foreignness, of difference. Unlike his father's habit of projecting domestic referents onto Morocco, Hank sees the foreign mark as marketable. He later responds to the sight of a line of veiled women using sewing machines under tents: "Looks like a television commercial." In Hayes's April 25 draft, in which Hank is rude (later toned down), the boy's interest in language is further evident: the McKennas hire a Moroccan babysitter, and Ben suggests that she might teach Hank the language. Hank replies: "Oh boy. How do you say 'drop dead' in Arabic?' "[62]

This seven-year-old boy will shift the scene from a playful exploration of the insufficiency of American idioms for Morocco to the more serious problem of lack of American international knowledge. Exploring his surroundings like a young adventurer, Hank wanders up the aisle of the bus. When the bus jerks, Hank inadvertently pulls off the *litham* (face covering) of a Moroccan woman. This causes a small scene, with the woman's male companion scolding the boy and demanding the return of the litham, all in Arabic. While no subtitles are provided, the basic contours of the man's speech are clear to the viewer, who has witnessed the event, though not to Hank's parents who have been otherwise absorbed—Jo in a magazine, Ben dozing off. Jo wakes Ben, who stands to face the barrage of Arabic.[63] The conflict is resolved, however, by the intercession of a Frenchman who translates between the Moroccan man and Ben.[64] The family thanks the Frenchman, named Louis Bernard. Hank focuses again

on language: "You talk Arab talk," he says admiringly. "A few words,"
Bernard replies. Despite Hank's odd grammar, it is he who first notices
and comments on the language gap. His parents' refusal to acknowledge
foreign languages continues through the film; when the maître d' at a
restaurant later instructs the McKennas to wash their hands while a
waiter stands over them with a kettle of water and a basin ("On se lave
toujours les mains avant de manger"), they look at each other and chuckle
in incomprehension: "Yeah," says Stewart. But when the maître d' translates, "We always wash the hands before eating," they snap to attention.
Later, when Rien mistakenly knocks on the door to their room by mistake, the man excuses himself in French: "Je m'excuse, mais je cherche
la chambre de Monsieur Montgomery." The camera cuts back to the
McKennas to reveal a blank, unmoving stare. And a conversation in
which Jo and Ben discuss Ben's patients irreverently as they stroll through
the Djemaa el-Fna (Marrakech's famous square) is premised on being in a
place outside of comprehension: "One of the reasons I came to a place like
Marrakech is so we could say things like that without everybody hearing
us." Back on the bus, faced with their own incomprehension, they look to
Louis Bernard, who provides Orientalist knowledge to explain the Moroccan man's anger with their son. "The Muslim religion allows for few
accidents," Bernard explains. Ben invites Louis to sit in front of Jo. Louis
is confused: "Oh, I thought his name was Hank." "Oh, no, it's my wife's
name, you see J-O, no E. Short for Josephine. I've called her that for so
long nobody knows her by any other name." Hank trumps his father with
another comment about language: "*I* do: 'Mommy.'" The conversation
that follows has further banter about language in which Hank's pre-
cociousness is countered by his father's down-home linguistic simplicity.

In the context of Henry Luce's American century, and the corresponding imperative to translate the world, the important question in this scene
is that of comprehensible speech. We can draw additional evidence from
Hayes's draft screenplay. The writer initially had the Moroccan woman
cry out when Hank rips off her litham. In his notes, Hitchcock instructed
Hayes to remove references to her cry and Hank's reaction and add a
medium shot of Hank and the woman instead of close shot of the woman
alone. Hitchcock explains to Hayes that this is to emphasize her husband's "outburst."[65] Hitchcock wants emphasis on the outburst of Arabic.
In contrast to the "pure American voice of democracy," heard by reporters
in Tangier when they listened at the American School of Tangier, the

"outburst" is interruptive or oppositional not only because it scolds, but also because it is unintelligible to non-Arabic speaking American audiences of the 1950s. Audiences who did speak Arabic would recognize that the dialogue itself is both accurate Arabic and a nearly impossible conversation, since the Moroccan's outburst is in a dialect of Arabic not spoken for a thousand miles from Marrakech. This scene was filmed and cast back in Hollywood. The role is uncredited, though Abdelhaq Chraibi, who plays the Moroccan, appears in the credits as a "technical advisor."

Elsie Mitchie and Robert Corber have argued that the scene represents a portrait of desires repressed under cold war ideas of the maternal. It is also a revealing site for the ways in which sophisticated thought about domestic crises is intertwined with thought about the foreign. Here the foreign represents the limit case for the domestic, the place beyond which the domestic does not know how to travel but which puts the domestic into such relief that it reveals its impossibility as a discrete space. Given Corber's emphasis on the auditory in the film, it is surprising that he ignores the challenging voices of the Moroccan man and Louis Bernard, both speaking Arabic in a tense scene on the bus. Corber does refer to this scene, but as evidence that Hitchcock wants to demonstrate the effects of Jo's poor mothering and that Hank is growing to be maladjusted. Hank, Corber writes, "almost causes an international incident when he accidentally removes the veil from an Arab woman's face. . . . [a] violation of patriarchal law."[66] To accept that Hank has upset a universal "patriarchal law" on the bus is to overlook, as the film does not, the historical presence of the French in Morocco and to accept the fiction that Moroccans veil themselves with no relation to the history of colonialism. That this is not the case may be gleaned from Frantz Fanon's chapter "Algeria Unveiled," in *L'An V de la révolution algerienne*, in which he notes that before the revolution the "veil was worn because tradition demanded a rigid separation of the sexes, but also because the occupier *was bent upon unveiling Algeria*." That the Algerian woman "sees without being seen frustrates the colonizer. There is no reciprocity."[67] Hitchcock comes back to images of veiled women several times in the film, both individuals—such as a fully covered woman wearing dark sunglasses who attracts Hitchcock's eye for a close-up—and in groups. He films veiled women during the location shooting in Marrakech, and dresses women actors in haiks, lithams, and djellabas back on the Hollywood soundstage. Rather than exhibiting a prurient and colonizing desire to make visible that which cannot be known—as Malek Alloula shows about French colonial postcards from the early twentieth century in his powerful psychoanalytic reading of the obsession with unveiling Algerian women[68]—Hitchcock represents the process of colonial unveiling itself. Thus Hank's unveiling of the Moroccan woman identifies him with the French obsession with unveiling, one ineluctably linked with colonialism in Algeria and Morocco. Just as Hank's wandering up the bus aisle suggests a belated desire to be an explorer, his unveiling suggests a desire for the American to occupy the place of the French.

The veil itself is not merely a sign of Muslim patriarchy and oppression, as Moroccan feminists such as Fatima Mernissi have argued, but also a symbol of private space, an escape from the national security state, and a division from the European community that sought to unveil and rule Moroccan women. Thus in *Dreams of Trespass*, Mernissi is able to call the French protectorate a French harem and a violation of *huddud* (borders) on both national and domestic levels. In her writing for the Moroccan women's magazine *Femmes du Maroc* during the 1990s, Mernissi noted the hypocrisies of Western injunctions for Muslim women to remove the veil based on the principle of exposure, championed within a media culture that celebrates the emaciated female body and exhibits it via pornography.[69]

By extension, Hitchcock's interest in the image of the veiled Marrakechi woman wearing dark sunglasses in the Djemaa el-Fna can be seen in the context of his own concerns about the national security state and the surveillance of citizen subjects under McCarthyism. He had staged an elaborate critique of McCarthyism as a form of psychopathology in *Rear Window*, an earlier collaboration with screenwriter Hayes and actor Jimmy Stewart.[70] If *Rear Window* engaged the political climate by attempting to reforge the distinction between private and public, *The Man Who Knew Too Much* recognizes an international analogue in French Morocco. Hitchcock's Morocco is not a densely layered ethnographic portrait—for the most part the visual pleasure it takes in Marrakech remains touristic, lingering over the acrobats, observing the storytellers, noting a malnourished-looking child, asking questions about the basic customs—but rather a way of thinking through questions about the U.S. space that obsessed him. Lingering over the veiled woman demonstrates his interest in the withdrawal from visibility and from French colonial surveillance. That fragile colonial state appears multiply in this film via police stations, inspectors, and officers (and with which the production had to negotiate). Among Hollywood films set in Morocco, especially during the 1950s, this one is remarkable for not including a scene of sensuality—there is no belly dancer in the restaurant, for example. Hitchcock's Moroccan woman is unveiled on the bus as an expression of the violation of the private sphere, and the images of veiled Moroccan women that follow seek to reinstate the integrity of the private sphere.

Through its exploration of putatively illegible Arabic as a limit case for American understanding, the bus scene offers French intercession as an uneasy model for American engagement with the international. Recall that the narrative follows a hapless American caught up in an international intrigue he didn't ask for but which he must follow through (the paradigmatic American narrative about international engagement). As Ben attempts to negotiate his rapid insertion into the international scene, he is provided with both British and French models for engaging the foreign. Bernard demonstrates a French intimacy with Morocco while the Draytons, criminals who pose as a British couple working for the United Nations, suggest an almost academic remove from their surroundings (when Mr. Drayton instructs the McKennas how to eat Moroccan-style, he sounds like an anthropologist: "It's more social than religious"). As Ben struggles to decide which model to trust, domestic concerns are displaced onto the foreign. When his own domestic unit is fractured, Ben decides (incorrectly, as it goes) that the French are the wrong group to trust.

The film represents French relations with Morocco as a miscegenational homosocial encounter. As the film's portrayal of French Morocco is a reflection of the filmmakers' thinking about contemporary America, the film's interest in race in Morocco suggests that the domestic crisis of race in the United States is like Americans' inability to speak Arabic or French in the film: a block to a mature international role and a hurdle the cold war state must negotiate. In a film whose theme song asks what a child will grow up to be, Hitchcock's thinking about race in the international frame deflects his own response to race onto thinking about the nation he had just joined as citizen. The identification of Louis Bernard with Moroccans makes Jo McKenna deeply uncomfortable. (Most things about Morocco make Ben physically uncomfortable—as played by Stewart in a masterpiece of physical acting. But Bernard puts Ben at ease.) After the bus stops, Jo notes Bernard greeting the Moroccan who had shouted at Hank: "I just saw Louis Bernard talking to that Arab . . . and they were talking like they were very dear friends." That Bernard should speak with Moroccan strangers as he did with Americans is seen as suspect; the granting of recognition to the colonized implies a reciprocity that Jo cannot imagine. Later, Hitchcock goes further and has Bernard dress as a Moroccan, wearing a djellaba during the famous sequence in which he is chased through the streets of the Marrakech medina and stabbed in the back. As the disguised Bernard falls into McKenna's arms, Stewart's fingers touch his face, rubbing off the makeup he wears to darken his complexion. Bernard is not only visually identified with a Moroccan here, but he becomes a black man. Bernard's excess knowledge moves beyond language; his sympathy with the Moroccan is now racialized.

Invoking the specter of racial mixing in Marrakech allows Hitchcock to evoke the recoil from the foreign named earlier as the nightmare of the Dark Continent. The dark residue left on the hands of Jimmy Stewart from that close encounter, residue he tries to rub off and which leaves him feeling "kind of funny," is a visceral souvenir of American obligation at home and abroad. It has come back to race: the Dark Continent that Daddy "liberated" during the North African campaign in World War II turns out to be reaching out and grabbing the American who thought he could leave it behind. The American abroad who thought he had left the domestic crisis of race at home finds it inescapable. The dark residue on Stewart's hands is a physical sign, too, that the alternative international model (the British) is the wrong choice. Hitchcock later revealed in his interviews with François Truffaut that he had long imagined this scene, though with a British man in dark face chased across a ship manned by South Asian sailors.[71] Here he translates that British colonial imaginary to a French imperial framework, and he has it fall in the lap of the Americans. In transposing his long-held fantasy, Hitchcock tricks the American viewer into a series of errors revolving around the racialized and heteronormative assumption that the Draytons are "safe." The film mobilizes a false recognition between the Draytons and the McKennas, playing on a perception of shared racial, marital, and class status. In contrast, Louis Bernard is associated with the Moroccan man on the bus and another dark French character—the assassin Rien (whose name means "nothing" in French). When Rien mistakenly knocks on the McKennas' door and meets eyes with Bernard, the gaze of the two darker men visually divides the blond Day from the gray Stewart. This is the audience's sudden cue to mistrust Bernard.

10336-75

The Man Who Knew Too Much: the Frenchman gone native, Louis Bernard, staggers toward the McKennas (Jimmy Stewart and Doris Day), while the Draytons look on. *Courtesy of the Wisconsin Center for Film and Theater Research.*

The film thus reveals itself to have a strong racialized unconscious. After his hands have been sullied by too close an engagement with a Frenchman, and after his mistake about the Draytons is revealed, Ben's desire to avoid involvement with either French or British police is more than prudent caution. Such a position also allies McKenna with one of the enabling myths of American national identity: the belief in individual agency without regard to the social networks and ties that are everyday reality. As Michael Rogin has argued powerfully, such a myth is tied deeply to the historical organization of American politics around racial domination, something too painful to remember and thus perpetually forgotten by Americans.[72] Ben's refusal to engage with the French security forces in Marrakech, and his later refusal to cooperate with Scotland Yard in saving his son against all apparent reason and logic, invoke the comforting American mythology of individual agency. In this context, Hitchcock's choice to eliminate a sequence written by Hayes between Ben and the Mamounia Hotel concierge (the concierge wants to call the police, then helps Ben search the Draytons' room) would seem to emphasize Ben's individual agency over his engagement with the Moroccan population.[73] With no official American representatives brought into the plot, Ben and Jo are conflated with the U.S. state and take on its problems.

The beautiful friendship between Rick and Louis Renault in *Casablanca*, which leaves them strolling off arm in arm, has become a dirty encounter between Ben and Louis Bernard in *The Man Who Knew Too Much*, with the latter left dead in the street. Recall the opening shot of Morocco in *The Man Who Knew Too Much*: a close-up of the side of a bus marked "Casablanca-Marrakech." The hyphen suggests both a connection to the earlier film and a handoff. *Casablanca's* racial conservatism brackets off Sam and keeps him and the colonized Moroccans at a remove from the allegiance of Rick and Louis, who remain safe in their knowledge of "fundamental things." But by the time of *The Man Who Knew Too Much*, the French colonial apparatus was falling apart and the "blackness" of North Africa was apparently too close for Hitchcock. He cannot be the collaborator in *Casablanca's* "Vichy gamble." Louis is killed and Ben McKenna will look with disgust at the blackness rubbing off on his hand from the encounter. Despite the rich potentiality for an interruptive discourse that it summons, *The Man Who Knew Too Much* ultimately elides or cancels the collaboration with cosmopolitan Frenchness.

Marrakech, closest to the Sahara and most African of Moroccan cities culturally and architecturally, is the apposite setting for a film about American racial logic, a logic Hitchcock saw in colonial terms and in relation to America's newfound global power. As he prepared to travel to Marrakech in spring 1955, what Hitchcock did not apparently realize was just how unstable Morocco was. As the production rushed to finish filming before the holy month of Ramadan began, after which French officials told producer Herbert Coleman that filming would be impossible, tensions were rising. Unit production manager C. O. Erickson told Steven DeRosa: "We were all very nervous because of the situation in Marrakech at the time with the French and the Arabs. We used to hear the cracking of gunfire at night, and there were mini riots going on where you saw police hammer people over the head."[74] Though he did not represent that political reality—the screenplay was already written and Hayes himself did not travel to Morocco but relied on reports from Hitchcock and Herbert Coleman—the theatrical trailer made for the film's 1956 release invoked the revolution. In the trailer, Jimmy Stewart announces that Hitchcock "took us thousands of miles away from Hollywood, to Marrakech, which is right in the center of a North African trouble area." In so doing, the trailer linked explicitly the political climate of the contemporary Maghreb with the domestic concerns at the center of the picture. Though Marrakech's distance was named, so was its centrality to geopolitical concerns.

If Tangier signified excess to Americans in the 1950s, Marrakech, a very different kind of city, marked the limit of familiar experience, the exotic. In the mid-1950s, when Marrakech's population was approximately 280,000 and Tangier's about 180,000, the contrast between the two cities was perhaps even starker than it is today. Tangier's international administration and the haven it offered for Moroccan nationalists were at a far remove from Marrakech's oppressive government, under the strong control of Thami el Glaoui, the most powerful Moroccan man during the French protectorate. Hitchcock's Marrakech is likewise very different from William Burroughs's Tangier.[75] It is as impossible to imagine Hitchcock's remake of *The Man Who Knew Too Much* being set in Tangier as it is to imagine Burroughs writing *Naked Lunch* in Marrakech. Hitchcock's film does not have the relationship to his career that *Naked Lunch* does to Burroughs's. But I put them into conversation because it seems to me telling that two texts that respond deeply to McCarthyism and the crisis of domestic America emerge from Morocco at a similar moment. Steven

Shaviro argues that one of the primary lessons to be learned from Burroughs's work is that language is like the parasite living on surplus value from the intestine, a relationship that throws into question which is primary: host or parasite. Burroughs questions the notion of interiority before intrusion/colonization and self-identity without invasion from the outside. This is what Burroughs means when he says that "human consciousness . . . is basically a virus mechanism." The connection to Hitchcock is that in *The Man Who Knew Too Much*, Arabic language functions as a limit case to American domestic arrangements, throwing them profoundly into question. If we adopt Burroughs's terms to understand Hitchcock, Arabic signals the virus that the American family has picked up in Morocco, the national(ist) problem with American domestic arrangements. Which is the parasite, which the host?

5

THREE SERIOUS WRITERS

TWO SERIOUS AUTHORS

Jane Bowles, Mohammed Mrabet, and the ~~Erotics~~

~~of Collaboration~~ Politics of Translation

It is He who has let free the two bodies of flowing water: one
palpable and sweet, the other salty and bitter; yet has He made
an interval or isthmus [*barzakh*] between them, a limit [*hijran*]
that is forbidden to be passed. —The Koran, 25:53

Comment rester nomade

Thus far I have discussed comparatively well-known representations of the Maghreb, texts that were celebrated at the time or
since and which in various ways figured French North Africa or International Tangier for Americans. While those texts have in various ways
been misread, with some of the most interesting and radical possibilities
issuing from them deadened, several still exert a significant presence
within American film and fiction. The case in the present chapter is
notably different. The work of Jane Bowles and Mohammed Mrabet fits
uncomfortably within established literary traditions of American literature, African literature, or Maghrebi literature and has been perpetually
marginalized and forgotten. My goal here is to draw attention to these
projects and provide a way to read them without effacing their challenge
to prevailing modes of organizing literature. That they are both deeply
collaborative projects and rethink processes of communication between
or across the American-Maghrebi divide is central to their productive
interruption.

Jane Bowles repeatedly was caught within her own inability to move beyond private communication, a tendency she was well aware of and which she sometimes figured within her finished work—as secrecy, for example, which she imagined as a way to achieve what she sometimes called "salvation." As an intellectual problem, Jane Bowles's private communication led also to her inhabiting within her fiction an in-between space I will liken to the concept of *al-barzakh* (Arabic for interval or isthmus), a space elaborated within her notebooks for an unfinished novel but that also led to an indeterminacy and incompleteness in her late work. By highlighting a reading of her "unfinished" work including alternative drafts and excised material and connecting it with her completed works, I claim that there is more of Jane Bowles's work to engage than usually granted. The plaintive refrain by her admirers that she published so little and the unfinished state of much of her late writing provides Americanists with an implicit excuse for not engaging the difficult work of an elusive author.

Another set of critics has not known what to do with Mrabet as African author, since he is not literate in any of the accepted languages of African literature. The Moroccan *darija* (colloquial Moroccan Arabic) in which he narrates is not accepted as a literary "language" within Morocco, the greater Arab world, or among North Africanists, and has no codified spelling or grammar, no tradition of publication. The works by "Mrabet" exist first in English translation, a translation produced at the scene of composition by his translator Paul Bowles, who was also his collaborator and editor. Without accepting a role that exceeds author for Mrabet, it's hard to place him within existing literary traditions. If Mrabet is the author of these works, in other words, and Bowles the translator into English, then it's impossible to consider the works authored by Mrabet as either anglophone African literature or American literature: the author doesn't write in English nor is he American. Calling Mrabet's work translations, then, means insisting that his work has disappeared (the unpreserved "originals" of those narrated tales, tapes which have not been circulated or cataloged);[1] it also requires an embrace of colloquial Moroccan Arabic as a language of Maghrebi literature, politically problematic in Morocco when Mrabet composed his major works and still difficult or impossible to imagine today in Morocco. Considering Mrabet's works as collaborations poses additional problems if they are to be considered part of Moroccan literature, because of the political implications of an alliance of Moroccan and American and an apparent embrace of the disappearance of the very Moroccan vernacular at the heart of the project. The categories themselves are at stake.

Comment rester nomade? I borrow the title from Moroccan anthropologist Hassan Rachik's fascinating ethnography of the Beni Guil in eastern Morocco—*How to Stay a Nomad*. Faced with the modernization of the desert, the Beni Guil abandon their camels for *camions* (trucks) and thereby maintain the mobility central to their social arrangement. "In the city where I was born," the American woman at the heart of Jane Bowles's story "Everything Is Nice" tells a group of Moroccan women: "there are many, many automobiles and many, many trucks."[2] Jeanie, the American, means it as a justification for why she wants to spend time with the Moroccan women, recalling the flight from mechanization that animates Paul Bowles's *The Sheltering Sky*. "Trucks are nice," one of the Moroccan women replies, undercutting Jeanie. "Trucks are very nice," the others agree (318). *Comment rester nomade?* The question animates Jane Bowles's life and work, especially after her decampment to Tangier in 1948. Her mobile writing may provide clues.

In order to grasp what's most powerful and original about Mrabet's and Jane Bowles's work, it is crucial not to dismember it and necessary not to naturalize it. The goal is not to add Jane Bowles or Mohammed Mrabet to the various canons I've mentioned, but rather to signal their very difference from them and the disruptive potential they have to unseat the presumptions underlying them. Since one of the motivating assumptions of this book is that literary representations of the foreign space have some deep relationship to national narratives, even to the idea of a national narrative, the fact that Mrabet and Jane Bowles have not figured in those canons may say something about the uneasy relationship of their work to the national episteme itself. Regarding Jane Bowles's work, John Ashbery has written: "It is hoped that she will be recognized for what she is: one of the finest modern writers of fiction, in any language"; Tennessee Williams wrote: "I consider her the most important writer of prose fiction in modern American letters."[3] Henry Miller, William Burroughs, and Paul Bowles all gave high public praise to Mrabet's work. Yet neither author appears in the anthologies and pedagogical instruments. Fictions that locate themselves on the edge that separates languages and cultures, rather than reinforcing a polarity or difference, are perhaps antagonistic to the category of national literature. Critics such as Carol Shloss who identify homelessness as both the subject of and the philosophical core of Jane Bowles's work are correct to do so. Homelessness is after all quite different from exile or expatriation, which both rely on the stability (even if in the imagination) of the home and thus reinforce binarisms. Comment rester nomade?

If a disjointed relationship of language to identity connects Jane Bowles to Euro-American modernism and the complicated structure of Mohammed Mrabet's work to postcolonial ambivalence and Creole discourse, neither is an adequate or accurate framework within which to discuss their work. And while critical discourses of borderlands / *fronteras* emerging from Chicana/o studies have been productive for unseating the monolingualism and exceptionalism of American studies, the case of this work emerging from Tangier is notably different. There is something particular about these writers' relationship to Tangier, a place and literary space I've identified with multiplicity, with international and textual collaboration, and which is distinct from the conditions that produced the categories of Creole and Euro-American modernism. My goal in this chapter is to build on possibilities suggested by Bin Buchta's use of the phrase "al-adab at-Tanji," which I discussed in chapter 2, or the crossings of communities in the International Zone of Tangier which I signaled in chapter 3, and to suggest that its most complex formulations emerge from the later work of Jane Bowles and of Mohammed Mrabet. This work and my reading of it is therefore distinct from the category of the postnational, which I invoked in chapter 2; indeed it suggests that Mrabet and Jane Bowles operate outside that very framework, on the edge between something like the postnational and the extranational.

The fictions of Jane Bowles and Mohammed Mrabet repeatedly call into question the overdetermined relationship of language as means for communication and identity within a social order and inhabit the edge that marks the limit of (a) language. In so doing, and they do it differently, they show that edge, or barzakh, as an extranational space itself, different from a border since it is a perpetual limbo and one within which relationships are put in relief. Their work has been elusive because the relationship between language and social identity that they call into question is naturalized in assumptions that circulate around their work (and that are in fact represented within that work). One such assumption is that individuals have an uncomplicated relationship to a "native" language, an assumption that anthropologizes Mrabet and holds Jane Bowles accountable for her own difficulty. Mrabet and Jane Bowles suggest the radical possibilities that emerge from denaturalizing the relationship of language and identity, by which I mean staging foreign relationship to one's native language. As Gilles Deleuze and Félix Guattari describe such a situation, in their discussion of Kafka's "minor" use of German, there is a link between linguistic process and political history: "The breakdown and fall of the [Hapsburg] empire increases the crisis, accentuates everywhere movements of deterritorialization, and invites all sorts of complex reterritorializations."[4] The staging of a foreign relationship to native language in the work of these two authors echoes and enacts thematic concerns of alienation and homelessness that are prominent within their work. So it is not only the literal translation of a work from one language to another—which makes Mrabet's literary output possible at all and which Jane Bowles uses in "Camp Cataract" as a figure for the inability to communicate across the edge that separates individuals in their private languages—that I am interested in here, but something about the edge in between languages, which for both Jane Bowles and Mohammed Mrabet is analogous to the edge in between individuals.

The pairing of the two in this chapter may be controversial, even objectionable. In writing about Jane Bowles in the context of Mohammed Mrabet and about both in the context of Paul Bowles, I do a necessary violence to the idea of the solitary author that has been important to those who would recuperate the reputations of both. The exception to these tendencies has been Millicent Dillon, herself a writer of fiction, who wrote Jane Bowles's biography and edited her letters. More recently Dillon has written a brilliant antibiography of Paul Bowles that is the most sensitive portrait of a much-written-about author. In between, Dillon edited *The Portable Paul and Jane Bowles*, a work that challenges its own impulse toward canonization (by its participation in a prestigious series) by insisting that Paul and Jane's literary work be considered together, "alternating voices" that "seem to resonate, picking up aspects of themes and turns of phrase that double back upon one another."[5] Dillon's edition insists that their sustained literary dialogue is more than a pronounced example of intertextuality or even influence. In her biography of Jane, Dillon remarks on Paul's major editorial work on Jane's fiction (such as the structural changes in *Two Serious Ladies*, which was "Three Serious Ladies" before Paul edited it) and on the deep and sustaining importance of Jane's writing to Paul returning to fiction. It is indeed with the decline of Jane Bowles's health and her inability to continue in this collaboration / marriage, I'll suggest below, that Paul turns away from fiction to a different and sustaining literary project with Mohammed Mrabet.

Though Jane Bowles and Mohammed Mrabet knew each other well, their work operates independently. Jane Bowles had completed her life's writing before Mohammed Mrabet narrated his first fictions, and though he conversed with her, Mrabet could not read Jane Bowles's writings. Yet Mrabet and Jane Bowles are intimately linked by their collaboration with this third. Insisting on the third term, rather than occluding it, helps to structure the reading of Jane Bowles and Mohammed Mrabet around their intimate relationship to collaboration, an erotics that consistently triangulates with Paul Bowles and with the text as alternating third terms. As Carolyn Allen has put it in her discussion of *Two Serious Ladies*, the work, "like Jane Bowles's life, is never just about two women but rather about triangles, jealousies, and sexual fluidity."[6] Though I make reference to literary biography, I am ultimately interested much less in Jane Bowles's life than in attempting to make sense of these challenging and elusive texts. The works that bear the names Jane Bowles and Mohammed Mrabet as author are indeed constantly asking questions about the role of the individual within the couple (imagined as the regard of the other), and are thematically concerned with triangles that vex couples, or shifting patterns of attention. The same holds true about their relationship to the question of authorship; they are works produced in deep collaboration that also attempt to occlude a silenced third partner. At times, they figure the relationship between Americans and Tanjawis in Tangier and attempt to understand the conversation that proceeds from that interaction. Because of the unique way they figure contact itself, they are important, interrupting entries in American Orientalism more largely considered. Moving between collaboration and translation, with "meaning" given secondary importance in the attempt to communicate and the erotics of communication itself—as unbridgable difference, as barzakh or interval— Jane Bowles and the Mrabet-Bowles work demonstrates how within an economy of engagement *al-adab at-Tanji* moves along an edge that a binarism of pure difference seeks to reduce to a border.

Everything is Edgy

I continue loving Tangier—maybe because I have the feeling
of being on the edge of something that I will some day enter. . . . It
is hard for me to separate the place from the romantic possibilities
that I have found in it. I cannot separate the two for the first time in
my life. Perhaps I shall be perpetually on the edge of this civilization
of theirs. When I am in Cherifa's house I am still on the edge of it,
and when I come out I can't believe I was really in it.
—Jane Bowles, letter to Paul Bowles, 1948

In a 1966 profile of Jane Bowles for *Mademoiselle*, Truman Capote remarked: "Jane Bowles is an authoritative linguist; she speaks, with the
greatest precision, French and Spanish and Arabic—perhaps that is why
the dialogue of her stories sounds, or sounds to me, as though it has
been translated into English from some delightful combination of other
tongues." Capote's comment is counterintuitive: why should Bowles's linguistic acumen somehow produce a foreign relationship to her native
language? And yet Capote's sense that Bowles's work sounds as if she is
writing in translation does seem somehow apt, perhaps because it apparently responds to a hard-to-describe mode within Jane Bowles's writing
itself, even borrowing one of Bowles's own figures. In her long story
"Camp Cataract" (arguably a novella in form), the tragic Sadie appears to
her sister's friend wearing "not the foxy look that Beryl expected would
betray itself at any moment, but the look of a person who is attentive
though being addressed in a foreign language."[7] Sadie's experience of
being addressed by another in her own English language as the embodied
experience of foreignness is not unlike the reader's experience of Jane
Bowles's remarkable fiction. Bowles's writing is continually marked by a
syntax of surprise and commands a similar attention of its reader, who is
kept at the slightest remove via the foregrounded awareness of the question of comprehension itself. If this description of Sadie's "look" is one of
the author's own figures for her tone or her approach to narrative, here's
another: " 'Not a night fit for man or beast,' [Harriet] shouted across to
Sadie, using a voice that she thought sounded hearty and yet fashionable
at the same time; she did this, not in order to impress her sister, but to

keep her at a safe distance" (384). Bowles consistently figures the distance between individuals within communication; her pessimism regarding the ability for individuals ever to communicate in language is present in that "safe distance." And yet her work is marked by characters who seek "community" ceaselessly in odd locations, at temporary stops, and in queer configurations; the unbridgeable edge that separates individuals is the state in which her fiction resides.

On the level of the sentence, I suggest that her fiction provides a vivid example of Deleuze and Guattari's description of the minor use of a major language. Elsewhere, Deleuze writes: "[A] great writer is always like a foreigner in the language in which [s]he expresses [her]self, even if this is [her] native tongue. At the limit, [s]he draws [her] strength from a mute and unknown minority that belongs only to [her]. [S]he is a foreigner in [her] own language: [s]he does not mix another language with [her] own language, [s]he carves out a nonpreexistent foreign language *within* [her] own language. [S]he makes the language itself scream, stutter, stammer, or murmur."[8] Following Deleuze, Jane Bowles's writing can be seen as political, or with a political effect, not because it seeks to create an alternative sort of community along the lines of that which is created in the various communes and camps and cooperatives in her fiction, but as an accentuation of deterritorialization and an invitation toward reterritorialization, to paraphrase Deleuze and Guattari on Kafka. One would not call this a tactic on her part, however, or a means for living, as "Camp Cataract" demonstrates. Sadie's look "of a person who is attentive though being addressed in a foreign language" is distinguished from a "foxy look," the latter a beautifully ambiguous descriptive term that implies self-control or authority over one's expression. Sadie's mode of attention is not replicable—if the alternative is self-control, you can't actively not control your expression—and is, after all, painful. And when Sadie before her suicide attempts unsuccessfully to communicate with a stranger, an Irishman made-up as an American Indian manning a souvenir booth, that individual hears her impassioned words as "something [he] couldn't understand," and therefore foreign: "It sounded like Polish," he later tells her sister (401). Sadie is, despite her best efforts at communication, like the orangutan in Poe's "Murders in the Rue Morgue," whose excited screams of inhumanity are heard by witnesses as a variety of foreign tongues, a barbarian or beast (Harriet earlier warns her not to look "so much like a gorilla" [395]). But like Poe's orangutan, she is neither completely ani-

Jane Bowles at the Café de Paris, Tangier, 1963,
during a visit with Leonore Gershwin. *Photograph
by Lawrence D. Stewart, courtesy of the Paul Bowles
Papers, University of Delaware Library.*

malistic, nor completely human, but somewhere on the isthmus between: in a place of foreignness, outside the comprehension of the crowd, on the other side of a door. The status of the heightened mode of living within translation is not in Jane Bowles an easy or relaxed location, and it reflects the tragedy that animates her work. Capote's description of the experience of what I'm calling Jane Bowles's minor English as "delightful" is misleading, then. Jane Bowles's ability in her fiction to inhabit and portray, even to stage, the very failure of communication is the means of deterritorialization of American English for something else.

As a means of describing Bowles's representation of communication between individuals, translation, if it is to be useful at all, is to be understood not as the carrying of meaning from one place to another—a successful transport, the movement achieved, both poles in stasis—but as a continuing process, an unfolding movement, a circulation in which meaning alters depending on temporal context. What Truman Capote thinks he hears in Jane Bowles's dialogue, which I think we can generalize to her writing in general, is something of her ceaseless circulation in incommensurate locations, between Moroccan Arabic, French, and English, and between the community of Moroccan women she frequented and the anglophone and francophone communities she participated in in Tangier. Truman Capote himself did not enjoy his time in Tangier, when he visited the Bowleses in the summer of 1949. He stayed for only a couple of months and was later critical of the expatriate community in print: "Among the planet's most pathetic tribes . . . are those Americans who elect, out of vanity, or for supposedly aesthetic reasons, or because of sexual or financial problems, to make a career of expatriation."[9] For Paul Bowles this was because no one recognized Capote, which I take to mean that in Tangier, Capote felt completely out of circulation.[10] (Though only twenty-four years old at the time, Capote's first novel *Other Voices, Other Rooms*, had been a major success and its author a much fêted literary celebrity.) Perhaps his inability to identify the particular configuration of what I call "queer Tangier" as a unique literary moment and his inclination instead to think of it as a "basin" helps to explain Capote's failure to describe Jane Bowles's peculiar syntax.[11]

Dilip Gaonkar and Elizabeth Povinelli have recently argued that we understand translation not merely in terms of the carrying of meaning, but in relation to cultures of circulation. Seeking to address the critical disjuncture between representations of translation as political and eco-

nomic project and representations of translation as "exemplar of theories
of meaning," Gaonkar and Povinelli link translation with the "cultural
logic of the circulatory matrix itself."[12] Thus, they write,

> It is not sufficient to ask what happens to meaning as it is borne across the
> chasm of two language codes, of genre, of one semiotic mode to another, say
> the movement from oral forms of repetition to written forms of iteration.
> We have to query further: What are the generative matrices that demand
> that things—including "meaning" as a captivating orientation and phan-
> tasmatic object—appear in a decisive form in order for them to be recog-
> nized as value-bearing as they traverse the gaps of two or more cultures,
> habitations, imaginaries, and forms of life? (395)

Meaning is there, in Jane Bowles's work, when the work circulates within
a public that recognizes it. Thus the ability, for example, within some
reading publics to claim her as a queer writer, as a feminist writer. But
such recognition is rare within her work itself. Even in the few moments
in her work when characters seem to understand one another—such as
the posthumously published fragment called "The Iron Table," which
presents the dialogue of an unnamed couple who resemble Paul and Jane
Bowles discussing the fate of civilization in a Muslim setting[13]—their
outward expression frustrates and ironizes successful communication;
the female character decides to provoke an argument by agreeing with her
husband. And before her embrace of Tangier itself and her circulation
within and between expatriate and Moroccan communities in that city,
which was also a movement between language environments, Jane Bowles
did address a public with works that figured intensely a queer relationship to the conditions of domestic America in the 1940s, what Michael
Warner has called a counterpublic.[14] But her time in Tangier led her to
detach herself from an address to that counterpublic and the meaning-
making possible within that matrix. Jane Bowles's late writing does not
traverse the gap of two cultures, but instead figures and resides in that gap
itself. After the critical and financial failure of her 1953 play *In the Summer
House*, and on her way back to Tangier, Jane Bowles spoke to a reporter
for *Vogue* magazine: "There's no point in writing a play for your five
hundred goony friends. You have to reach more people."[15] The "more
people" Bowles refers to are not so much the specific people of Tangier,
including the circle of Moroccan women she was involved with, but is
more precisely a response to her sense that her movement between

communities—her inhabiting the edge between them—had destroyed the possibility of addressing a public again. To borrow from Warner's helpful discussion of the way publics are organized and addressed, it as if Jane Bowles now recognized that the social space created by the circulation of a discourse had been exceeded. Of course, no sooner had she uttered this comment than she hoped it would quickly disappear from circulation, a reflection of her ambivalence about the shift and the pain of it. Paul Bowles reassured her that "nobody much read *Vogue*."[16] But *New York Herald Tribune* theater critic Walter Kerr, who apparently did read *Vogue*, embraced Jane Bowles's comment as a heroic pronouncement about the desire not to circulate or produce theater merely for the "gaping audience," correctly grasping the meaning of the quote.[17]

Despite qualified kind words about her play, Kerr had perhaps inadvertently written Jane Bowles's literary obituary. Back in Tangier, Bowles would not publish or complete a work after that point; she had in fact recognized the relationship of her writing, as it had progressed, to a lack of circulation; the edge she had discovered was also one that only her "goony friends" would recognize. She could no longer address a public larger than her intimates and could therefore no longer complete her work, for a public relies on the ability to imagine a personal and impersonal address to strangers.[18] Jane Bowles's late work reduced the range of that address. This provides a way of understanding her failure to complete her late work not merely as career failure, or psychobiographical failure, but as a removal from circulation and a disconnection from a public that she had earlier misidentified. In the context of my larger argument in this book, Jane Bowles's late writing, including that which she could not complete, is an interruption to the postwar American canon, which negotiated what Alan Nadel has called "containment culture" via fragmented or confidently conspiratorial narratives. And it is now possible to regroup Jane Bowles's "edge" within an American literature that does not behave according to the national logic of the late 1940s and 1950s, when she was writing.

The site itself is one of discomfort, of an untransgressable edge. In the work of Jane Bowles, it is something of an in-between space, an edge, akin to what the philosopher Ibn al-'Arabi (1165–1240) called a *barzakh*, literally an isthmus and used by Ibn al-'Arabi to refer to the intermediate realm between the spiritual and the corporeal.[19] In Jane Bowles's later work I see this figured as the edge between languages and also as a surface chalkiness, tangible and solid (as in "Everything Is Nice"), but we also find in her work images of islands, camps, bridges that cannot be abandoned, hotels as refuges. The well-known story that Paul Bowles has told to describe Jane Bowles's difficulty in completing "Camp Cataract" reveals something different from merely an account of severe writer's block, as it has been taken:

> At one point she had a terrible time with a bridge she was trying to build over a gorge. She would call out: 'Bupple! What's a cantilever, exactly?' or 'Can you say a bridge has buttresses?' I, immersed in the writing of my final chapters [of *The Sheltering Sky*], would answer anything that occurred to me, without coming out of my voluntary state of obsession. . . . After three or four mornings I became aware that something was wrong: she was still at the bridge. I got up and went into her room. We talked for a while about the problem, and I confessed my mystification. "Why do you have to *construct* the damned thing?" I demanded. "Why can't you just say it was there and let it go at that?" She shook her head. "If I don't know how it was built, I can't see it."[20]

The quote suggests not that Jane Bowles had an impossible relationship to the production of fiction, that she was somehow inside it too much, as Paul Bowles seems to imply. "This struck me as incredible," he continues. "It never had occurred to me that such considerations could enter into the act of writing. Perhaps for the first time I had an inkling of what Jane meant when she remarked, as she often did, that writing was 'so *hard*.'" Rather, I take the anecdote to suggest that she was caught on that bridge and that that space is both the end of her productivity and the productive space of her work. Kenneth Burke has written of transcendence as the "building of a terministic bridge whereby one realm is transcended by being viewed in terms of a realm 'beyond' it." Burke calls this process "pontification," or making a bridge, building on the French word *pont*.[21] While it is my argument that Jane Bowles is in fact unable to traverse the bridge (though she did eventually complete the work in question, "Camp Cataract") and instead resides on the bridge itself, Burke's description of the escape from delimiting terministic screens by the glimpse of a different terministic realm is suggestive and analogous to what I am describing. Jane Bowles's syntax is a stuttering use of English, but it is also in Burke's sense pontificating. As such, Jane Bowles's work suggests a way beyond the limitations of U.S. representations of North Africa. As we'll see, Jane Bowles's increasing intimacy with Moroccan Arabic was an intellectual development that resonated silently through her later work. Despite her apparent fluency in the Moroccan dialect, as well as some study of Modern Standard Arabic (*fosha*), she never imports Arabic into her writing. But her intimacy with Arabic, and her association of the language with intimacy, produces a new relationship to her own language.[22]

I came across Kenneth Burke's marvelous word "pontification" in Alton Becker's provocative essay "Beyond Translation."[23] In this essay on anthropology and aesthetics, Becker is responding to José Ortega y Gasset's comments on "the difficulty of reading," that to read a text distant in time, space or conceptual world is utopian, which Becker says is also true about the "activity of language": "One can never convey just what one wants to convey, for others will interpret what they hear" with an interpretation both "exuberant and deficient." Utterances are "deficient," according to Ortega, since they say less than they wish to say, but utterances are also "exuberant" because they say more than they plan. This is the double bind on which communication relies.[24] I want to bring this double bind into my reading of Jane Bowles's pontification, her bridge making, her exuberant and deficient use of an English that stutters. As we will see in Jane Bowles's incredible use of the word *nice* in "East Side: North Africa," her work is in a sense beyond translation, activated by it, on that bridge—that barzakh—between languages and cultural formations. Paul Bowles's famous story about Jane's need to construct a bridge in order to write about it is thus a hint at the structuring relationship of her experience of Moroccan language to her late work.

Finally, Bowles's experience of Arabic as erotic, the private tongue that she maintains separate from the more public realm of her work, and of the erotic in Morocco through Arabic becomes a way of thinking through questions about the radical gap that separates individuals, a question that animates Jane Bowles's fiction. "To surrender in translation is more erotic than ethical," Gayatri Spivak writes.[25] What Spivak means is that when one attempts to be ethical, one must turn the other "into something like the self." Translation on the other hand—"the most intimate act of reading," in Spivak's words—requires a surrender to difference, to a recognition of the limits of the text, not its interchangeability. For Jane Bowles, passionately in love with a Tanjawia woman named Cherifa who kept her at a distance and with whom she spoke Moroccan Arabic (laced with Spanish, in Tangier style), the limits of Arabic and the erotics of alterity

were intermingled. Bowles, who had since *Two Serious Ladies* been interested in the awkwardness of touch between bodies (in a vivid scene, the
touch of women's bodies recalls a recurring dream of embracing a lifeless
flesh-mannequin while rolling over a sharp landscape),[26] now transposes
that distance into an erotics of language.

Bowles's fascination with and finally her literary paralysis by what she
called "the edge" separating "civilizations" is profitably seen with reference
to Ibn al-'Arabi's elaboration of barzakh. When the word appears in the
Koran, the sense of space and temporality—a time that is a space, a limbo,
a holding pen—comes out. "Before them is an interval or isthmus [*barzakh*] till the Day they are raised up. Then when the trumpet is blown,
there will be no more relationships between them that day nor will one
ask after another" (23:100–1).[27] Here is Ibn al-'Arabi, the great Sufi philosopher of the imagination:

> A *barzakh* is something that separates two other things while never going to
> one side, as, for example, the line that separates shadow from sunlight. God
> says, 'He let forth the two seas that meet together, between them a *barzakh*
> they do not overpass' (Qur'an 55:19); in other words, the one sea does not
> mix with the other. Though sense perception might be incapable of separat-
> ing the two things, the rational faculty judges that there is a barrier (*hajiz*)
> between them which separates them. The intelligible barrier is the *barzakh*.
> If it is perceived by the senses, it is one of the two things, not the barzakh.
> Any two adjacent things are in need of a barzakh which is neither one nor
> the other but which possesses the power of both.[28]

Ibn al-'Arabi's elaboration demonstrates the peril of living on this edge. In
fact, he claims that if it can be perceived by the senses, it is not the edge
itself, but rather the things the edge separates. (Thus the difficulty in
describing this space.) This does not mean that the edge does not exist as
an entity, as a temporal space. Rather, it is to emphasize the particularity
of this space as intelligible if elusive. Indeed, one thinks of temporal spaces
within popular practice in the Maghreb that fulfill Ibn al-'Arabi's description of *barzakh*, such as the designation of the end of the day (and within
Ramadan the end of the daily fast) as the moment when a black thread
and a white thread held outside (absent artificial illumination) are no
longer distinguishable. It is not that either the black thread has become
white or the white thread black, but both have for that moment separating day from night, without going to one side, become something else. In

my quotation from the Koran, the sense of an edge or partition as temporal holding pen structures relationships between individuals, as if in a third space. Outside the limbo created by the barzakh, on the other end of it, is a situation in which individuals will be fully outside of relationships. That temporal space is thus not so much a space of passage (or border) but the space of life as limbo.[29]

Though she was not apparently a student of Sufism, Jane Bowles was something of a religious writer, and she seems to have interpreted her own relationship to Tangier in terms that are conversant with this understanding of barzakh. In *Two Serious Ladies*, written before her experience of Tangier, Jane Bowles had linked the search for salvation to a poetics of perpetual movement: "'Certainly I am nearer to becoming a saint,'" one of the two serious ladies of the title, the peripatetic Miss Goering, remarks to herself upon the novel's conclusion. "'But is it possible that a part of me hidden from my sight is piling sin upon sin as fast as Mrs. Copperfield?'"[30] But now as Bowles responds deeply to her Moroccan setting, the movement is left behind and she comes to inhabit a temporal edge that focuses not on salvation but on the temporary status of the relationship between individuals, one that happens on that edge but which threatens always to disintegrate.

Jane Bowles as Tangerian Writer

Can we associate this shift in her writing with her experience of Tangier? Capote's brief portrait attributes Bowles's linguistic acumen and by extension the particular sound of her fiction to her "nomadic nature." The phrase seems apt, though Capote follows up by listing Jane Bowles's more literal nomadic movements around the globe, conflating a nomadic nature with a nomadic biography. The relationship of Jane Bowles's writing to her residence in Tangier is complicated and might at first seem incidental to a consideration of her literary output. She did spend a significant part of her adult life in Tangier; arriving in January 1948, at age thirty, it was her base of operations for the next twenty-five years until her death in 1973 (from 1969 on she was confined in a sanatorium in Málaga, Spain, while Paul remained based in Tangier). But that time coincided with her first stroke and the infamous writer's block that followed. Many have associated her time in Tangier with the deterioration of her career, as the antagonist to her writing. Jane Bowles's own self-description for *World Authors*, composed very late in her life, has not helped: "From the first day, Morocco seemed more dreamlike than real. I felt cut off from what I knew. In the twenty years that I have lived here I have written only two short stories, and nothing else. It's good for Paul, but not for me."[31] But this is the tragic self-portrait of an unwell person: Jane was at this point heavily medicated, had had shock treatment earlier in the year, and had been suicidal. It was dictated in late 1967 at Paul's urging and with Paul typing. We can see it as a form of revenge. We may even read the statement as a recognition of having entered an edge outside of circulation: being "cut off from what I knew" as an intellectually productive experience, even if destructive of her career as a publishing author. Without disputing the personal tragedy of Jane Bowles's last years, we may still read her late works (after her stroke in 1957, her writing career may be said to have ended) in terms of her experience of Tangier as edge.

Upon her arrival in Tangier in January 1948, Jane Bowles's initial experience of dislocation was energizing and productive. She was finally able to complete "Camp Cataract," long in the works, which she finished in Fez in May 1948 while Paul completed *The Sheltering Sky*. A major story, "A Stick of Green Candy," was written in 1949 during a trip with Paul to the Algerian Sahara and published in 1957. In 1950, Jane wrote a remarkable nonfiction essay about Tangier. The second act (in its three different versions) of Jane's play *In the Summer House* was completed after her experience in Tangier, written in a variety of settings including Tangier, Paris (where she took a class in Maghrebi Arabic), and back in the United States. These works are all significant achievements in her career. But there is still much more writing, some of it published posthumously, that Jane worked on without completing: the long, unfinished "Balzacian" novel *Out in the World* and other projects.

It is perhaps not surprising that Bowles would associate foreignness within a native language with the uncomfortable edge she inhabited in her late literature. Bowles's first novel *Le phaeton hypocrite* (never published and subsequently lost) was drafted in French, inspired in part by meeting Louis Ferdinand Céline on a ship as a seventeen-year-old girl and spending time with him while traveling back to the United States with her mother.[32] Though she would eventually lessen her admiration for Céline (she commented to Paul about the Beats who had taken up residence in Tangier that they seemed as if they never got beyond Céline), the meeting was at the foundation of her thoughts about literature. When Deleuze invokes Céline's *Journey to the End of the Night* as an example in his essay "He Stuttered," he comments that the French novelist "places the native language in disequilibrium."[33] It's not a question of Céline's influence on Jane Bowles, or her imitation of him, but rather an affinity. And in choosing French as the language in which she might commence a literary career, on her return to the United States from a partial education in French, the young Jane Sidney Auer was surely not seeking equilibrium. Her young life had been disrupted by a fall from a horse that had left her with a severe limp. (She spent two years in a Swiss sanatorium for treatment on her leg and to cure the tuberculosis of her knee that developed after the accident.) Kafka was a yet greater influence on Jane Bowles; she again felt affinity with a writer whose minor use of a major language is notable. Surprise, Kafka's great skill, pervades Jane Bowles's work. And the hysteria, delirium—which Deleuze calls the process of forcing language "outside its customary furrows" (lv)—is in abundance in both.

On the eve of moving to Morocco, Jane Bowles contemplated what she would find there. Language itself became a cipher for her anxiety about departure. In a late 1947 letter to Paul, as she considers joining him in Tangier, Jane discusses where they might live: "I don't of course know about the Arab town of Tangier (I *refuse* to use that Arabic word)."[34] The problem with living in the Arab quarter, she goes on, is that she worries about being conspicuous among other foreign "eccentrics" who she assumes have moved there. But within the sentence itself, there is a linguistic choice not to use the word medina, which Paul has used, a word eccentric itself in the context of English prose. As I argued in chapter 2, Paul himself used untranslated Arabic words in his work as a textual strategy; indeed Jane is apparently responding to his having done so in a letter. (Perhaps her response to the practice encouraged Paul to expand it in *The Sheltering Sky*, which he was then writing.) Here Jane makes explicit what she otherwise occludes in her work—a specific choice not to import Arabic words. This is yet more remarkable in her work after January 1948 because she apparently achieved a high degree of fluency in colloquial Moroccan Arabic. For Jane, the eccentricity is incorporated otherwise: "a nonpreexistent foreign language *within* [her] own," as Deleuze wrote. If Jane were to drop Arabic words into her writing, the foreignness would be located. Instead, she makes her English something uncentered, something eccentric, something foreign to her reader. The eccentricity of her correspondence itself—literally moving within and outside a circular logic, marked by a repetitiveness, multiple signatures, and postscripts—is intimately related to questions that animate her work as a whole. In a letter written to Paul from Tangier in July 1948 (he was then in New York), Jane comments: "Surely the English in this letter has gone to pieces long ago but I just can't worry about it. You can understand with a little effort what I've written."[35] The English of her works after 1948 did go "to pieces," in a sense, not as postmodern fragmentation but rather as the deterritorialization of American English.

Though it does not have a North African setting, "Camp Cataract," her masterpiece, arguably responds to its author's experience of Morocco as personally as does *The Sheltering Sky*. "Camp Cataract" had been begun before arrival in Morocco, and it is thematically the literary expansion of an idea that had animated Jane Bowles's work long before her arrival in Morocco. She had been working on the story, on again, off again, for several years, but had been unable to finish it. Something about the experiences she had among the Tanjawia women she met in the winter of 1948 allowed a particular crystallization of questions of language and identity that had eluded her. The model of Paul's industry in the connecting room at the Belvedere Hotel in Fez, to which they had repaired from Tangier, and the "voluntary state of obsession" he had entered to finish his first novel were also obvious and serious aids to finishing the work that had eluded her for so long. But, if Paul is to be believed (and there is a mysterious rewriting of their personal history at times in his autobiography, *Without Stopping*), Jane was for several days held up on the cantilever bridge she was mentally constructing. I think we must reread "Camp Cataract" in context of the collaboration with her husband (who was simultaneously writing Kit's mental breakdown in North Africa, which Jane took to be portentous of her own fate) and as response to her intense experience of being on "the edge" of the community of Moroccan women she had recently met. This experience finds its way into the novella and even disfigures it, but not merely as a way of structuring the relationships between the women at the camp itself. I am not suggesting that the story is a transposed portrait of the community of Tanjawia women. Rather, the Tanjawia experience manifests itself in the way in which Sadie's movement "out into the world" leads her to a space beyond comprehension, to a foreignness within her native language, across a bridge to an isthmus of embodied in-betweenness. These concerns will animate the work that follows; identifying them here helps us to identify a turn in Bowles's work.

Despite the difficulties in ascertaining just what in "Camp Cataract" was written after Jane Bowles's arrival in Morocco, it is a crucial bridge to the late work in that it identifies the intellectual isthmus where Bowles will thereafter remain. Dillon suggests that "Camp Cataract" is connected not only to Jane's earlier themes, but also to her experiences in Tangier. "Much in 'Camp Cataract' is tied to Jane's own life," Dillon remarks, noting a series of earlier associations with waterfalls, camps, and suicides in Jane's life. Dillon also notes the ways in which waterfalls figured in Paul's recent writing as the release into a new fiction. "Camp Cataract," Dillon implies, is in part a response to the new world opened up for her: "In Tangier, through Cherifa and Tetum, she believed she was being offered the possibility of entering a new and different world."[36] Before finishing "Camp Cataract," Jane had already met Cherifa, been to several Moroccan weddings, and been initiated into the women's community of Tangier. "In the focus on [the Moroccan women's] daily life, in the repetitions, in their bitter humor she found what seemed entirely natural to her," Dillon writes (157). Her relationship with Cherifa (whose family name has never been provided) would be exceptional. After Paul introduced them in early 1948, Jane fell "immediately and passionately in love" (158). Though there is much ambiguity about the relationship, Cherifa would be Jane's companion until Jane's final departure from Tangier. In a letter dated May 10, 1948, Paul describes Jane putting on kohl she's bought in the Tangier market (where she spent much time with Cherifa) and thinking about getting her chin tattooed in the manner of some of her new Moroccan women friends. He also relates a conversation that Jane has had that will apparently inspire her essay "East Side: North Africa."

The other significant change in Jane Bowles's intellectual life that coincides with her completion of "Camp Cataract" was her engagement with Arabic language. Paul comments in his autobiography that by the time of their 1948 sojourn in Fez, Jane had some real intimacy with Arabic: "Immediately after getting here, she had decided to . . . study under a Moroccan tutor. . . . [H]er powers of absorption were so considerable that . . . less than two months after she had arrived in Morocco [i.e. March 1948], she was able to speak [Arabic] as well as I."[37] There is evidence to support the claim. In a notebook containing a late manuscript draft of

Jane Bowles in Tangier market, 1954. *Photograph by Katharine Hamill,
courtesy of the Millicent Dillon Papers, Harry Ransom Humanities
Research Center, University of Texas, Austin.*

"Camp Cataract" there is a page of simple Arabic script in Jane's hand, apparently with the help of a tutor who has shown her how to form basic Arabic words from the letters she has learned. The lesson apparently included some discussion of the unwritten short vowels that "shape" written Arabic words, shapes that can be indicated in writing but normally drop out. Jane's handwriting in Arabic is careful and childlike (not unlike her handwriting in English), as she practices voweling (shaping) seven letters of the Arabic alphabet. There are a few words of French on the page in her handwriting, translations of the words and sounds she has formed. Other notebooks will contain pages and pages of Maghrebi Arabic vocabulary, phrases and even short passages and the beginning of dictated (?) stories, transliterated using the French system and translated into French. These are likely from her formal study of Moroccan Arabic in Paris.[38]

Jane's work in Arabic allowed her a linguistic experience of difference that was both eccentric and transcendent, in Burke's sense, in that it allowed her to glimpse a realm beyond. It allowed her English to go "to pieces." In a letter, Jane was able once to be explicit about the relationship of Moroccan Arabic to her experience of Morocco and in turn its relationship to her work. In February 1950, while spending the winter away from Tangier in Paris, she writes to Paul (who is in Sri Lanka):

> I am going over to the École des Langues Étrangères or whatever the hell it's called, and look into a course in Maghrebin-Arabic. I don't think I can go much further in it alone, or with Cherifa. As for Kouch [Said, her tutor in Tangier], he can do no more for me, I'm sure. I just can't accept having gotten this far in the damn language, and not getting any further. I think too that it makes my being in Morocco seem somehow more connected with my work. With me, as you know, it is always the dialogue that interests me, and not the paysages so much or the atmosphere. In any case, I cannot express these ever in writing.[39]

Bowles's letter suggests the intimate connection of her experience of colloquial Moroccan Arabic and the work that she attempted to do after completing "Camp Cataract." Very little of that late work is set in Morocco, however. Yet it is not for her representations of the Maghreb that Jane Bowles is most interesting. Rather something that she learns there, that is disruptive to her work, makes her a compelling artist.

But how does she figure this "new and different world"? In "Camp

Cataract," Bowles represents communication as transpiring or failing to transpire on the surface of language, the edge behind which meaning may reside. Bowles associates this failure with something like an artificial foreignness—a staged otherness—and what I earlier called the experience of living in translation (where translation is imagined as impossible, or as failure). But of course none of this is explicit; rather it is staged itself in Bowles's peculiar syntax and her idiosyncratic associations, what I've called her stuttering English.

"Camp Cataract" describes the visit of an adult woman, Sadie, to her adult sister, Harriet, who is on an extended visit to a "camp" that is something like a sanatorium, but also a tourist destination for day trippers who come to visit a waterfall, where they lunch at an outdoor restaurant and shop for souvenirs. Though Harriet has allegedly gone to the camp for a cure ("after a bad attack of nerves combined with a return of her pleurisy" [371]), she herself has a different understanding of her trip: to stay "long enough to imitate . . . natural family roots of childhood . . . then from here at some later date I can start making my sallies into the outside world" (363). So when Sadie arrives with a secret and still nascent plan to take Harriet home, or perhaps to escape with her from their home, Harriet is not welcoming. Harriet, of course, is not able to express such a response directly or in words, and instead takes on tones and verbal postures that exaggerate the distance she normally maintains from Sadie, a different sort of distance than that which she maintains toward others at the camp (such as her companion Beryl, a waitress). Harriet and Sadie have a third sister, Evy (most pairings in Bowles's work involve occluded thirds and shifting triangles in which two individuals battle for the attention of a third), who is detestable and antagonistic. Sadie lives with Evy and Evy's offensive husband Bert Hoffer, and it is from them that Sadie imagines "escape." Sadie comes to awareness of her own plans only on arriving at the camp. This aspect of the novella may be associated with Bowles's earlier work (especially the link between movement and salvation) and thus with the portion completed before her arrival in Morocco. In any case, when Sadie does recognize her own desires and plans for escaping with Harriet, she struggles to express herself. Harriet is wary of her own plans for escape being compromised and invents a previously unmentioned canoe trip, which will make all but a brief conversation between the two women impossible. The sisters plan to lunch the following day.

There are two bridges in "Camp Cataract." The first is a covered bridge connecting the upper level of the main lodge to an annex with guest rooms marked by "imperfectly fitted boards" (389). The second is a "fancy bridge" spanning a chasm, providing a view of the great "cataract" or falls that gives the camp its name and leading to a spot behind the falls where tourists may stand and watch the water flow in front of them: "A series of wooden arches, Gothic in conception, succeeded each other all the way across the bridge; bright banners fluttered from their rims, each one stamped with the initials of the camp" (391). An Irishman dressed and made up as an Indian collects a toll from tourists who cross the bridge (residents of the camp are allowed free passage—they reside on the edge rather than visit it) and also sells souvenir cushions from a booth. The sisters have arranged to meet here.

Sadie waits for Harriet anxiously. The reader is presented with a long section that depicts their meeting, an account that will be reversed or canceled by a subsequent section that suggests the meeting never transpired at all. These passages follow one another without comment. (This is much like Bowles's frequent use of the word *ossir* in her letters, a Hungarian word of negation that cancels out the veracity of that which precedes it and thereby suggests an additional possibility.) Details in the concluding passage suggest that Sadie has experienced some sort of reverie or mania within which she eventually commits suicide. Within this reverie, language itself is dissociated from Sadie's body.

In the first version of events, what I'm calling the reverie, Harriet and Sadie repair to some woods, and Sadie—distraught and in pain—blurts out her desire to go away with Harriet. Harriet is angry and departs. Sadie watches in agony. Preparing to leave the camp herself, Sadie purchases some souvenirs from the ersatz Indian. But as Sadie notices his makeup and becomes aware of his costume, she feels great shame at the exposure of his falsity and drags him off to hide from the tourists. Crossing the bridge, she successfully hides the Indian "behind the cascade where he could be neither seen nor heard." He smiles, "and she no longer saw in his face any trace of incongruity that had shocked her so before" (399). Thus satisfied, she plunges into the cataract, her hand extended as if to touch the man. The section that follows this sequence appears to cancel it: the text suggests that Sadie and Harriet never met on Sadie's second day at the camp and that Sadie has disappeared. But it also suggests that some of what we have read in the previous section does transpire, though differently. The faux Indian, whom Harriet questions, tells her that a woman—"such a queer-looking thing"—was indeed waiting at his stand for "more than an hour, without moving," but that she left after buying several souvenirs. Whereas the earlier version shows communication between the Indian and Sadie, in his account he describes Sadie as incomprehensible: "She sounded to me like a Polak" (401). In this version, the unnamed Sadie walks off alone and plunges to her death.

I am less interested in the crisis represented within the narrative—that it contains conflicting versions of its own truth—than that it is figured around the distanced relationship between speech and communication and that both are associated with physical edges (the bridge and the precipice). As Sadie plunges into the cataract, she extends her hand out to the faux Indian in a moment of failed connection, parodying the concluding moment of E. M. Forster's *Passage to India*. And "cataract" itself, which refers both to eyes and cascading water, is a word that signifies at once opacity and flood, blindness and excess. The conversation between Sadie and Harriet in the reverie version of events transpires in a language that is dissociated from Sadie's body itself. She hears "her own words as if they issued not from her mouth but from a pit in the ground" (296). And Harriet tells Sadie to "try not to look so much like a gorilla." If Sadie's language and her posture become animalistic, and the content of her speech itself is incomprehensible to others, the comparison I made earlier to Poe's "Murders in the Rue Morgue" in which the murderous orangutan is understood to be a foreigner (and thus not understood) seems apt. But it's not only that Bowles as woman recognizes the animalistic quality of sisterly speech "out in the world," as her phrase goes. She had the opportunity to engage in dialogue with Moroccan women in a speech incomprehensible to others within her imagined public (even her "goony friends"). Bowles's archived papers provide suggestive evidence. In Jane Bowles's notebook for the late version of "Camp Cataract," the page facing the final page of the draft contains the page of Arabic writing in her hand.

The moment of rupture between the two versions of events happens when Sadie—thinking as she waits for her sister—recognizes that "all desire to convince her sister that she should leave Camp Cataract and return to the apartment had miraculously shriveled away, and with the desire, the words to express it had vanished too" (392). With the departure of words to express that desire, Sadie is incomprehensible to others.

Thus when she attempts to communicate it will be in a language that uses only foreign words: animalistic to Harriet, "like Polish" to the Indian, which are the same thing. But we also know that communication between Sadie and Harriet never occurs directly through words. Sadie keeps things secret. Harriet explains to Beryl: "Everything that goes on between us goes on undercover. It's always been that way" (381). The final sentence of the novella, set off from the rest, offers Beryl's silent stare: "She would not say anything."

Jane Bowles's first experiences of Tangier are figured on the bridge leading to the space behind the cataract, especially the failure of language. In 1948, she is fast on her way to inhabiting that space. In "A Stick of Green Candy," written in the remote Saharan oasis of Taghit, Algeria, in 1949, Bowles moves ahead with the idea of secret communication. A child, Mary, plays alone in a clay pit dug in the side of a long hill, "about a mile beyond the edge of town."[40] Mary's elaborate game—the command of a regiment of imagined soldiers—is kept private and secret. When anything threatens to betray this secret, she must hide from the outside world while remaining responsible to her soldiers: "She did not dare discuss it with her men, or even think about it too precisely herself. She had to avoid coming face to face with an impossibility." Dillon has described this story as the dramatization of the breakdown in Bowles's belief in the imagination.[41] Dillon suggests that Bowles could suspend that imaginative world long enough to write the story—out in the desert—but that on her return to Tangier it came apart again. But if it's tempting to see Bowles's last completed story as a sort of farewell to the writing of fiction, it's also possible to see it as the continuation, even the elaboration of an idea that would necessarily lead to a position of incommunication—in other words, the productive space of the bridge or isthmus between incommensurate locales. Jane Bowles ends up in that interval, that isthmus, that does not circulate, that cannot circulate: the incommensurate locations of the Moroccan women's world.

In a letter to Paul written shortly after she completed "Camp Cataract," Jane comments: "Certainly there are two different worlds here (the men's world and the women's) as you've often said yourself."[42] But Jane's recognition of the difference of her Morocco from Paul's is not merely about gender division. Rather, the double world she lived in Tangier—divided by language and communities—stuck her in the middle. Ibn al-'Arabi remarks about the interval: "There is nothing in existence but *barzakhs*, since a *barzakh* is the arrangement of one thing between two things . . . and existence has no edges."[43] Jane Bowles makes a similar discovery. Outside of circulation, in secret communication, Jane Bowles could successfully represent only the impossibility of the location in which she found herself.

Jane Bowles's only explicit portrait of Tangier is the 1951 essay "East Side: North Africa," which appeared in different form in 1966 as a short story titled "Everything Is Nice."[44] In both versions, the elliptical nature of conversations revolves around a word, *nice*, that encapsulates the barzakh or edge I am attempting to describe. What this work figures is not so much the reality of Moroccan women's life as the space of incommensurability that the author had reached. She does this both through her representation of conversation between herself and Moroccan women—which focuses on the impossibility of depicting either side of the two communities she occupies without recourse to the edge in between—and through her silent translation of that language into the captivating and elusive phrase "everything is nice." Tangier's elusiveness in granting the desired contact between individuals is, in the 1951 *Mademoiselle* version, centered around the inability of language to communicate at all even if it were able to signify. Moroccan Arabic does not function within the story to represent a block or rupture and is not rendered at all in the text (in the *Mademoiselle* version, the author explains that she has a "smattering of Arabic," which serves as the explanation for not including it;[45] in "Everything Is Nice" this line does not appear). Though the story apparently translates conversation that takes place in Arabic, the language itself and any superficial difference it might represent disappears. In its place is what I earlier called Bowles's stuttering English, a conversation that emphasizes Bowles's location on the isthmus between communities, a location that the story itself considers: the Moroccan women are fascinated with Jeanie's split life.

The distinctions between Paul's and Jane Bowles's representation of conversation in the Maghreb is telling. In May 1948, Paul had written to a friend about a conversation that Jane had had resembling that which she represents in "East Side: North Africa." Paul writes: "Jane's conversation with the daughter ran: 'How do you do?' Reply from daughter: 'Merci.' A cat walked through the patio. Jane: 'Do you like cats?' Daughter: 'Not very much. There are many cats.'"[46] Paul emphasizes the ridiculousness of conversation, expanded on in the scene in *The Sheltering Sky* when Port and Kit disagree about the superficiality of Algerian conversation, discussed in chapter 2. Jane responds to the same situation by recognizing that dialogue itself is staged: "Sometimes I played the part of a Nazarene fool being outwitted by two shrewd market women and it seemed to me that they were playing the parts of two shrewd market women outwitting a Nazarene fool."[47]

The text of "East Side: North Africa" (I use the 1951 *Mademoiselle* version) is episodic and depicts a meandering day in Tangier (called "this blue Arab town") during which an American woman passes through the homes of Moroccan women friends. The first-person narrative begins with the American, named Jeanie, looking over a precipice, held in by a "thick protecting wall" that guards against the precipice and also marks it. The narrative will end at this same wall, marking that which transpires within it as "the edge" that Bowles described inhabiting. But ultimately, as her 1950 letter about the "connection" of Morocco to her work indicates, it is the dialogue, not the "paysages," that is of interest within the story. Two conversational strands emerge: the attempt of the Moroccan women to determine what Jeanie does in her other world with her "Nazarene" friends and the narrator's own failed attempt to establish a common ground with the women. "'This Nazarene,'" one of the women says to the others, "'spends half her time in a Moslem house with Moslem friends and the other half in a Nazarene hotel with other Nazarenes.' 'That's nice,' said the women opposite, 'half with Moslem friends and half with Nazarenes.'" A small point: Muslims are differentiated among themselves, while the foreign community is lumped together without distinction as Nazarenes (Christians), which does not even apply to Jane Bowles (who was Jewish). But the binarism, with Jane Bowles in neither space, is what stands out. Only one of the Moroccans, an old woman with tattooed cheeks, questions this division. "'*Why* does she spend half her time with Moslem friends and half with Nazarenes? . . . Is she crazy?'" As the narrator herself attempts to cross the edge of dialogue—to explain herself, as it were—she is met with the wall of language that does not communicate. "'I hate trucks,' I told them with feeling. The old lady lifted the bowl of meat off her lap and set it down on the carpet. 'Trucks are nice,' she said severely." The narrator turns to her more intimate friend for an appeal: "Do *you* like trucks?" The friend responds: "'Yes . . . They are nice. Trucks are very nice.' She seemed lost in meditation but only for a moment. 'Everything is nice,' she announced with a look of triumph" (285).

The way in which *nice* stands as a block to crossing this edge is compel-ling. "Everything is nice" seems at once to translate and not to translate a common Moroccan expression (*kulshi mizzian*) and more generally a Mo-roccan manner of speech in which precision of meaning gives way to a refusal to condemn or to judge God's world.[48] Indeed, whatever the ex-pression Jane Bowles would have heard in the context, it would likely have been followed by *hamdullah* ("praise to God"), a phrase Bowles doesn't render or include. In this sense, the phrase "everything is nice" is not a translation of the Moroccan expression but rather the representation of the failure of communication. So it is not after all about cultural differ-ence, here, but about Bowles's position of difference from either commu-nity. In a fragment removed from the original draft—and posthumously published as a discrete fragment under the title "The Iron Table"— Bowles presents the inability to communicate even with an intimate (her husband). Though the two apparently understand each other on some level, they do not allow themselves to express this in language: "The moment when they might have felt tenderness had passed, and secretly they both rejoiced."[49] Though the form of failure of communication is different—she disagrees with him, but provokes him by agreeing with his statement—the effect is similar. (The "Iron Table" fragment has not here-tofore been associated with the "Everything Is Nice" project, but it is indeed embedded in the draft notebook.)

In the published portion of this project, Bowles figures the edge or space between incommensurate communities via a conversation that both happens and does not happen. Jane Bowles imports *nice*, a powerful word, at once meaningless and loaded with meaning. *Nice*, so important here, is an especially ambiguous word. It derives (via old French) from Latin *nescius*, meaning "stupid." But Bowles is not using the word to mean "stupid," she's using it to signify or even to figure that isthmus that marks the "edge" she had located in Tangier. It is worth lingering over the word, since it carries this burden. In "Everything Is Nice," *nice* signifies the lack of signification, the block of communication, the isthmus between lan-guage structures, the *barzakh* between incommensurate locations.

In another unpublished fragment in the notebook containing the draft for "Everything Is Nice," Jane Bowles addresses her own inability to "write about Morocco." The fragment has a title, "To love," whose referent is un-clear. Though the text refers to an "article" that it pertains to, there is no in-dication of a larger text that this is a part of; we may guess that it was imagined in relation to the "Iron Table" fragment and that the article in question is "East Side: North Africa" itself. In any case, this fragment breaks off in midword. I reproduce the passage in its entirety, with crossed-out words indicated, to demonstrate just how difficult it was for Jane Bowles to represent what she elsewhere called the "paysages" of Morocco:

> To love
> . . . And they came to a land—to write about Morocco—or to write about a particular place in Morocco—would be very difficult for me—. I don't think that I can evoke a place—though I may—all of a sudden—in the middle of this article—make a terrible effort to describe—something——It is more likely however that I won't describe anything.
> I do find it necessary—however to say that ~~Tangier—the oldest Arab town—Casbah Tangier—in~~ Tangiers—is built on a hill & that the houses are predominantly blue—. ~~The stone doorsteps are blue too—sometimes & even the street—Sometimes this~~ the blue ~~is as a light sky &~~ varies – ~~It is sometimes~~ from a shade so ~~light~~ deep that it seems white at noon—to a deep ~~color—the blue~~ shade color of a match tip—.
> Tangier—is washed in this blue—~~steeped in it—around any blue door step & the base of a blue house the street is stained with it its same color—~~. All along the base of any house that is washed in blue—the street is stained the same color—Often the small bell-like windows are outlined in blue—a shade darker than the wall——the outline is formless as a cloud—an intimate childlike smudge around dark square hole—that has no pane the ~~window—~~. ~~If you touch the wall—of your~~ By rubbing th[50]

The passage, not included in either of the published versions of "Everything Is Nice," amplifies the haunting ending to the published story and the way concerns that had appeared in her earlier work developed in Tangier. As "Everything Is Nice" closes, Jeanie returns to the protective wall that launched the story and rubs her fingers along it: "The wash was fresh and a little of the powdery stuff came off. And she remembered how once she had reached out to touch the face of a clown because it had awakened some longing. It had happened at a little circus, but not when she was a child."[51] Here in the fragment, the pervading blueness of the town echoes a melancholy that another excised portion of the text attributes to the American woman: "She was leaning ~~through an archway~~ over a wall looking down at the ocean far below. The wall was ~~washed~~ painted with blue-wash ~~like the street~~ as the houses were behind her and even the narrow wavy street skirting the edge of the ~~blu~~ precipice. Whenever she walked along this street she cried."[52] Archways, walls, edges, and precipices are associated with this melancholic blue space, which smudges in the hand and exhibits a soft formlessness associated with childhood. But the childhood is not that of a child, rather evoked by the space. The desire to have contact, to make contact with the other—as Jeanie recalls touching the powdery face of a clown, masked in makeup (recalling also the faux Indian in "Camp Cataract") is the impossibility of bridging the divide. As Millicent Dillon put it recently, discussing the exceedingly rare appearances of Morocco in Bowles's work, "Her imagination was like its own separate country. Yes, she used Panama for *Two Serious Ladies*, and also aspects of her honeymoon with Paul there, but for the most part Jane plunges into the strange territory of her imagination."[53] Dillon further suggests that "when she stays too close to her surroundings, she gets stuck, she just can't go on." But even in the later work that she cannot finish, "she's always striving to get into the strange country of her imagination." As the fragment above suggests, this motif, in all its variants in Jane Bowles's late work, is indeed her own way of "writing about Morocco."

Fixing Morocco: Technologies of Preservation

In a 1956 article for the *Nation*, published in the first year of Moroccan independence, Paul Bowles asserted that with the advent of the new nation, its folk culture was in peril.

> The process of Europeanization which in most other economically "backward" countries of Asia and Africa (however regrettably from an esthetic point of view) is a natural concomitant of awaking nationalism and of the emphasis placed on mechanization, in Morocco is being hastened by a planned "deculturizing" campaign. This project for the destruction of Moroccan culture has been under way for the past three decades, but is only now attaining its full impetus, since the men who have been directing it in more or less clandestine fashion have at last come to power. Why, according to them, must that which is specifically Moroccan be suppressed?[54]

Bowles's answer to his question was that, for the Moroccan nationalists, the products of traditional Moroccan folk culture were "barbarous . . . outward signs of a feudal way of life which must be extinguished in the people's consciousness as well as in objective fact . . . [since] living conditions are a more important consideration than music."[55] Bowles heartily disagreed, not with the proposal that the material conditions in the new Moroccan nation were of grave importance, but with the proposal that the destruction of traditional folk culture was necessary to the improvement of those conditions. In his *Nation* article, Bowles championed Moroccan folk music and lamented its imminent disappearance. The dissolution of the traditional was for Bowles due as much to governmental directives as it was to the new regime's attempt to effect the "urbanization of a pastoral and agricultural people living under conditions which were normal in Europe some fifteen centuries ago" (545). Bowles had no argument against Moroccan independence (he was no supporter of French colonialism, as I discussed earlier). Rather, he worried that the presumption of the Moroccan nationalists was that to be independent from Europe meant to be "like" Europe. Of course, the nationalists did not claim explicitly to want to be like Europe, as Bowles knew: "'nationalism' in Morocco is a misnomer; it does not imply the forging of a political, economic, ethnic or cultural entity in the land, so much as it proclaims Morocco's support of the aims of the Arab League." And for Bowles, Moroccan support of and participation in the Arab League required a suppression of Berber culture, which he suggested was the majority culture of Morocco.[56] Thus, for Bowles, the dissolution of Moroccan folk culture is from the start inherently political, the product of independence, the reflection of a continued Arab domination of the Berbers.

Although he suggests that Moroccan nationalism might forge "a political, economic, ethnic or cultural entity in the land," Bowles is pessimistic that the nationalists would do so. Consequently, he recommends that the varied and manifold folk musical forms to be found in the country be recorded. Since he cannot imagine that the new "pre-democratic" Moroccan government would sanction the endorsement of folk culture, and since he found no Moroccan interest in such a project—"no influential Moroccan has as yet raised his voice against the destruction of one of his country's most precious possessions"—Bowles suggests that some "intrepid field musicologist" work to "capture the music on tape or disc before its disappearance."

Bowles's use of the word *intrepid* to describe the work that he thinks needs to be done reveals the direction such recordings will travel. Despite the political possibilities of "folk" culture—Bowles notes that "no one seems ever to have conceived of the possibility of an independent Berber

Morocco"—he is ultimately more interested in the aesthetic value of Moroccan music for the Western student of music. At this point in his career, Bowles had again returned to musical composition; he was working intermittently on his opera *Yerma*, based on his own translation of Federico García Lorca's play, which premiered in 1958 to high praise (the reviewer for the New York *World-Telegram and Sun* noted that Bowles's score was "strongly flavored with the compelling music of Spain's Arabic background").[57] If the study of Moroccan music could enrich Western composition, Bowles felt that an appreciation of Moroccan folk cultures could benefit the West more generally. In the introduction to a 1956 book of photography, Bowles remarked on the educational potential of a Western knowledge of African cultural forms:

> How greatly the West needs to study the religions, the music, and the dances of the doomed African cultures! How much, if we wished, we could learn from them about man's relationship to the cosmos, about his conscious connection with his own soul. Instead of which, we talk about raising their standard of living! Where we could learn *why*, we try to teach them the all-important *how*, so that they may become as rootless and futile and materialistic as we are.[58]

Bowles's pronouncement connects his concerns in earlier works with his new projects. The goal is stated clearly: that through an awareness of the North African's "connection with his own soul," Westerners can strip away some of their own materialist, rootless tendencies. One is reminded of Port's "existentialist" connection with the blind dancer in *The Sheltering Sky*. But in that novel, Port is denied more than a brief vision of the dancer's "why," as the relationship with the woman does not materialize; in that novel, Bowles does not (or perhaps cannot) interrogate that North African "why" further. With the structural adjustments of independence looming, however, Bowles now calls for a less "superficial" engagement with the North African and his or her cultural forms.

In 1959, Bowles received a grant from the Rockefeller Foundation to record Moroccan music for the Library of Congress.[59] Considering the presumptions of Bowles's recording project—"intrepid" by design, intended for the philosophical enrichment of the West—the "collection" of musical examples he gathered might seem a kind of cultural "theft." And yet, the recording of Moroccan music is only a cultural theft if it in itself eradicates these musical forms from circulation in Morocco; Bowles's recordings are necessarily different from the removal of artifacts from colonized lands to European museums. Bowles's claim that "the destruction of Moroccan culture has been under way for the past three decades" is, however, misleading. Moroccan "culture" cannot be destroyed, it can only alter its meanings. Bowles's worry is that the meanings attached to what he calls "folk culture" will be so altered so as to encourage musical performers and dancers to "forget" how it is (or was) that they conducted their performances. But, as Bowles knows, the recording of musical performances does not preserve them for Moroccans themselves. A repetition of improvised music is not a recreation of it. Indeed, Bowles himself champions the "tension formed by simultaneous improvisatory freedom and strict adherence to traditional form" which he says is lost when the music is "written out in European notation."[60] Bowles's recordings of improvised performances (performances usually arranged and paid for by him)[61] lose the very simultaneity he praises by fixing that tension in tape. (See my discussion in chapter 6 of Brion Gysin and the Master Musicians of Jajouka.) The archiving of performances stands as a testimony to that which is lost; the recording of "folk culture" is the gravestone to a cultural form that has disappeared.

Since Bowles's project required a modern piece of technology—the tape recorder—his archiving of a folk culture that modernization and the globalization of markets were threatening was possible only within the framework of that modernization. The musical recordings, then, stand both as testimony to the death of Moroccan folk music and as resistant act to the eradication itself. In turning to a more extended project of translating Moroccan stories, a similar problematic appears. Yet, as I will argue, the translation of orally recounted stories produced a situation in which Bowles incorporated the texts' own interruption into the very idea of being fixed in a way the musical recordings could not hope to by their very nature.

The translation of Moroccan oral stories is from the start, for Bowles, an attempt to preserve those voices that would take on new accents in postcolonial Morocco. They are, at first blush, the archiving of the necessarily passing strains of narrative that surrounded him. Bowles's first attempt was the translation of tales told him by Ahmed Yacoubi, his friend and companion, in 1952. As Bowles remembered later, Yacoubi's stories had interested him as far back as 1947 (when the two met). But not until 1952 did it occur to him "that I might be instrumental in preserving at least a few of them."[62] These textual collaborations were produced by

Bowles writing out a running translation as Yacoubi narrated. The immediate transcription/translation on Bowles's part was, in his account, necessitated by Yacoubi's style of composition: "These complicated improvisations could not be repeated at will, nor on one hearing could they be remembered" (7). But such a process was difficult to maintain. The very improvisatory quality of the narration that distinguishes Yacoubi's tales—similar to the improvisatory quality of the folk music—is seen as an impediment to their successful preservation. The tension between preservation and elimination is inherent; without Bowles's transcription, the tales cannot be recalled. But the recording of the tales itself becomes a project in their modification if one of their primary attributes is their status as intricate improvisations; since they are "remembered" (when heard) primarily for their complexity, the transcription of the tales alters the experience of them. The reader can both appreciate their improvised complexity and remember their details, while the listener cannot. Yacoubi's tales become something different when they are experienced on the page—the reader directs the pace and can return to reread—than when they are experienced as passing performances.

With the arrival of the tape recorder in Morocco (in 1956, according to Bowles, a date that seems almost overdetermined) a more "accurate" preservation became feasible. In the years following his field recordings of Moroccan music (in 1959), Bowles produced an increasing number of translations—most of them with Mohammed Mrabet, from the Rif Mountains in northern Morocco, with whom he became friends in 1964. The importance of the tape recorder to Bowles's translation projects signals that from the start they are connected to his field recordings of folk music. But the projects share more than a piece of technological equipment. Like the music recordings, Bowles's translations are acts of cultural preservation, the registering (or *enregistrement*, taping) of improvised works of art, the fixing (for an American archive) of the unfixed.

What Happened in Tangier? The Mrabet-Bowles Collaboration

> One of the ways to get around the confines of one's 'identity'
> as one produces expository prose is to work at someone else's title,
> as one works with a language that belongs to many others. This after

all is one of the seductions of translating. It is a simple miming of
the responsibility to the trace of the other in the self.
—Gayatri Spivak, "The Politics of Translation"

There is another component to this project, an erotics of collaboration,
that encourages us to resist too easy an attribution of neocolonialism to
Bowles's project.[63] In 1957, during the month of Ramadan, while Paul was
traveling in Kenya, Jane Bowles suffered a debilitating stroke in Tangier,
an event that precipitated a long mental and physical decline. Her own
ability to write was permanently hampered. According to Paul Bowles's
various comments, during the period of caring for Jane he found himself
less able to maintain a commitment to sustained writing projects. The
turn toward translation was, on the personal level, a response to these
changed conditions. Given the intensity of his literary relationship with
Jane, however, it's difficult not to see his shift toward an extended literary
collaboration with Mohammed Mrabet as a substitute or more precisely a
new and sustaining literary conversation to replace that which was lost.
This is not to equate the two "couplings," since of course they operated
very differently. Mrabet was unable to read what Paul was himself producing as a writer while their collaboration continued. Still, in this context, we may recall Barbara Johnson's comments on translation as a biga-
mous enterprise: "It might . . . seem that the translator ought, despite or
perhaps because of his or her oath to fidelity, to be considered not as a
duteous spouse but as a faithful bigamist, with loyalties split between a
native language and a foreign tongue."[64]

Though their relationship was marked by an intellectual intimacy
rarely achieved by married couples, Paul and Jane Bowles lived in separate
apartments, often traveled for long periods without the other, and pursued amorous affairs with each other's tacit acceptance. Paul's relationship
with Ahmed Yacoubi and Jane's with Cherifa were among the most meaningful of both of their lives, though they seem not to have threatened Paul
and Jane's marriage. Paul and Jane had long since moved to a level of
intimacy that might be considered textual. However, their ideas regarding
dialogue itself—their philosophies of communication—diverge. If Jane's
work puts into radical question the ability of individuals to communicate
with one another on any "serious" level, her characters do not cease to
make the attempt. Paul seems generally more optimistic that communica-

Mohammed Mrabet (right) with Paul Bowles and unidentified
friend, mid-1960s. *Courtesy of the Paul Bowles Papers, University of
Delaware Library.*

tion between individuals may occur, though his characters are less active
in seeking that dialogue. It is telling in this regard that Mohammed
Mrabet, Mohamed Choukri, and Larbi Layachi have all testified to Jane's
superior abilities in speaking Moroccan Arabic (*ad-darija*); the energies
she put into seeking the communication that might never occur were
apparently good language training.[65]

In 1964, before he met Mrabet, Paul Bowles published a startling book
by a young Moroccan from Tangier who called himself Driss ben Hamed
Charhadi in print, but who was otherwise known as Larbi Layachi. That
book, *A Life Full of Holes*, was listed as a novel on its title page but
resembled a life story. It was reviewed in the American and British press
but criticized by Moroccan intellectuals such as Abdallah Laroui. Bowles
may have thought he had grasped Moroccan life at its most authentic,
Laroui wrote in *L'Idéologie arabe contemporaine*, "but what has he grasped
other than his own fantasies?"[66]

It was Jane Bowles who introduced Mohammed Mrabet to Paul
Bowles, according to Mrabet's autobiography. Mohammed Mrabet was
then a young man in his twenties, unmarried though involved with Zohra
bint 'Ali bin Allal, the woman who would soon become his wife. Before

meeting Paul Bowles he had had many interactions with European and American residents in Tangier. One such involvement, with an American couple he met in Tangier, brought him in 1959 to the United States, where he spent time in both New York City (especially Manhattan, shuttling between the two worlds of Spanish Harlem and the Upper West Side) and Iowa, in the heart of the American Midwest. In both locations, despite their stark differences, he quickly identified the hypocrisies and structural violences of race as lived experience in the United States. He was determined not to be silent about North American racism—as *Look and Move On* evidences powerfully—and not to remain in the United States.

When Mrabet met Paul Bowles they quickly connected on the subjects of narrative and of kif: related topics for both men. According to Mrabet's account in *Look and Move On*, when Paul showed him the recently published book by Larbi Layachi, illustrated with a photograph of the young Tanjawi, Mrabet felt an instant sense of rivalry as well as the sense of an opportunity for profit. But the collaboration was to overshadow Bowles's other work with Moroccans. Together Bowles and Mrabet published twelve books, including two novels, Mrabet's autobiography, and collections of novellas, stories, and tales: *Love with a Few Hairs* (1967), *The Lemon* (1969), *M'Hashish* (1969), *The Boy Who Set the Fire* (1974), *Hadidan Aharam* (1975), *Look and Move On* (1976), *Harmless Poisons, Blameless Sins* (1976), *The Big Mirror* (1977), *The Beach Café and the Voice* (1980), *The Chest* (1983), *Marriage with Papers* (1986), *Chocolate Creams and Dollars* (1993), and Mrabet's contribution to the collection *Five Eyes* (1979).

What happened in Tangier? I pose a critical question in the form of a mystery in order to highlight the many unresolved questions and controversies revolving around the Mrabet-Bowles texts. In 1972, on the publication of the French translation of *Love with a Few Hairs*, Tahar Ben Jelloun compared *Love with a Few Hairs* to a police interrogation, an analogy by which he meant to damn the text, a work he called variously "pseudo-literary" and a "bastard literature." Tahar Ben Jelloun argued that Bowles had violated Moroccan reality with his project and suggested that the same might be true about Bowles's relationship to his "autochtone de service."[67] Under a title that implied that Bowles's technique was that of rape, Ben Jelloun's "bastard literature" suggests a deep discomfort with a literary project that relied on two men in intimate conversation. The erotics of collaboration here are inseparable from the politics of translation. In restating what I think is extraordinary about the Bowles-Mrabet collaboration, including the very question of how the work was created, in the form of a mystery, I mean to redirect the energy behind Ben Jelloun's dismissal and embrace the energy of the mystery itself. I adapt the title of Mrabet's intriguing story "What Happened in Granada," collected in *The Boy Who Set the Fire*. "What Happened in Granada" purports to relate an event in the lives of Paul Bowles, Jane Bowles, and Mohammed Mrabet— barely disguised—but it also demonstrates Mrabet's own struggle for authorial control against an anthropologist who asks him questions about the Rif and speaks to him in the Riffian dialect. As Mrabet discovers in that story, there are techniques available to him even within the structure of his collaboration with Bowles to assert authorial primacy (in this particular case that means asserting his untranslatability). In Mrabet's later work, especially *The Big Mirror* and "The Voice," still other strategies are developed to resist and to reformulate a structure in which his tales are simply exotic wares created for export or the objects of Bowles's cultural theft. But of course nothing in this extended collaboration is simple. The critical questions revolving around the Mrabet-Bowles texts are like mysteries to a solution. We must draw on the sometimes perplexing clues that we have to work with within the texts themselves. (If I am emphasizing the mystery of this collaboration, recall too that the major detective stories by Arthur Conan Doyle and by Edgar Allan Poe—Bowles's favorite American writer—are solved by pairs of men in private, even intimate conversation.)

Gayatri Spivak has written that intimacy in the language of the other is a prerequisite for translation ("Politics of Translation"). That Paul Bowles would be drawn to such a project is not surprising considering that his literary work had always been erotic because of the role of intimacy in his textual partnership with Jane. The project was political on external terms as well in that it evaded the linguistic categories that the nationalists were debating; in moving into English, it silently triangulates Moroccan literary production. We should ask, following Spivak, what the translations communicate. Layachi's book was controversial because it communicates something troubling but also predictable about the new Moroccan nation: the oppression of its jails, the corruption, and so on. Mrabet's work is quite different, however, since from the start it engages and foregrounds the disconnect of communication between Moroccan and European expatriate in Tangier. In this sense also it is "Tangerian."

A clue that there is a mystery to be solved is the apparent difficulty in naming Paul Bowles's role on the title pages of the various works that appeared under Mrabet's name. The first British edition of *Love with a Few Hairs*, published by Peter Owen in 1967, states that the work was: "Taped and translated from the Moghrebi by Paul Bowles." The first U.S. edition of the same work, published in 1968 by George Braziller in New York, changes this formulation slightly: "Translated from the tape in Moghrebi by Paul Bowles." Note that the second formulation places the taping in a third space, an action whose authorship is left ambiguous. According to both Mrabet's and Bowles's accounts, the second formulation would seem more accurate. But not because Bowles didn't do the taping; indeed it was Bowles's tape recorder employed at Bowles's home. The second formulation leaves ambiguous an element that some may consider crucial: whether Bowles did or could move directly from Moroccan darija to English. According to Mrabet, whom I interviewed over several days in June 1999 on the subject of his work with Bowles, Paul had too little a command of Moroccan Arabic to complete this translation without Mrabet using a fair amount of Spanish (a language both were comfortable speaking) in order to translate his taped narrative. Such a situation would seem to be covered by the Braziller formulation, even if that formulation is a bit vague or misleading. Mrabet's own role in creating *Love with a Few Hairs* would seem to be more than what is stated (authorship) and include a partial role as translator. Indeed, when *The Lemon* was published a couple of years later, in 1969, by Peter Owen, the formula was altered to: "Translated from the Moghrebi and edited by Paul Bowles in collaboration with Mohammed Mrabet." Mrabet was named twice: as author of the narrative and as collaborator in its translation and editing. If this description is accurate, though cumbersome, it was nonetheless dropped from their later books.

The question of editing is important. The dust jackets for the first British and American editions of *Love with a Few Hairs* both name Bowles's role of editor in addition to translator, suggesting that Bowles's role exceeds that of working with a tape in Moghrebi. (On the American first edition, there is a photo of Mrabet on the inside back flap of the dust jacket, while a photo of Bowles graces the more prominent back cover.) The subsequent books published under Mrabet's name continue to play with the formulation of Bowles's role. Though the task of the translator is theoretically rich, mere "translator" does not seem to have appeared sufficient to Bowles. Does this inability to contain Bowles's role in a simple formulation counterbalance the attribution of authorship to Mrabet, which Mrabet apparently exceeded? If Mrabet helped in the translation of his "tape in Moghrebi" by moving some, part or all of it into Spanish for Bowles, does that modify Bowles's role in relationship to the text? Are these texts properly considered translations at all, or are they literary collaborations that occurred in a variety of tongues with a single product?

These are questions that do not merely revolve around the outside of this and the other Mrabet-Bowles texts. They are inscribed in *Love with a Few Hairs* itself and are developed in the later works, as Mrabet alternatively attempts to evade the trap of translation and refigures it. In *Love with a Few Hairs*, the young protagonist named Mohammed occupies a place in the British and American communities of Tangier as well as one in the Moroccan community (in both cases a marginal place). He demonstrates his mastery of different sets of rules of communication and finesses the moments when those rules will come into contact. Mohammed is able to manipulate David, his British employer and lover, by following David's rules about communication to the letter (being direct when he needs money), on the one hand, and allowing David to translate Mohammed's implied or expressed worries (indirect communication) into occasions for payment, on the other. Mohammed also knows when to invoke difference as an oversimplified translation of a complex act, as when he instructs his European and American friends on customs for presenting gifts to Moroccans; Mrabet's protagonist thereby demonstrates a deep understanding of the economy of "cross-cultural" translation. Mohammed, as translator, is an intermediary. Moments of illegibility across language systems (such as David's inability to read marriage papers prepared for Mohammed by the notary, written in Arabic) are thus not incidental to this work. Such moments are in fact keys to some of the complex thinking at its center. Mrabet's narrative is continually imagining its own relationship to text, to written language.

In the narrative "What Happened in Granada," Mrabet creates a situation that allows him to interrupt the very processes of translation within which he exists as a published author. The story, published in 1974, the year after Jane Bowles died in Málaga, Spain, is layered in that it appears to offer a (auto)biographical account of an incident in the Bowleses' life, though the names of the principals are changed. Told in the first person, the story recounts a trip taken by an American (named Mr. James in the story) and a Rifi (named El Rifi), the narrator, who works as a chauffeur for the American, to Granada, where the American's wife has been staying with British friends. Mr. James has been summoned to retrieve his wife who, El Rifi tells us, has been in and out of "the hospital" in Málaga. The British couple turn out to be an anthropologist and his wife.[68] The anthropologist is portrayed as bookish and hapless. When he first appears, he is "carrying an open book in front of him, looking down at it as he walked."[69] He asks El Rifi where in the Rif he is from and reveals that he has "lived for a long time in the Rif" and "speak[s] a little Riffian." El Rifi is "surprised to hear that." El Rifi and the anthropologist's wife have a tense interaction. When El Rifi senses that she has become too familiar, and effects a threatening demeanor to keep her at bay, she sniffs: "All Riffians are like that."

As antagonisms rise in the household—the British woman accuses Mr. James of "trying to make his wife sicker than she was, because he wanted to get rid of her"—El Rifi intercedes, removing an Arab sword from the wall (apparently a souvenir from the anthropologist's fieldwork days) and threatening her: "I'm going to finish you off, you and your race! . . . You're only an English whore and I'm a Riffian!" (37). The woman challenges El Rifi: "If you're a Riffian, speak Riffian!" The anthropologist enters, again reading a book while walking. His wife looks to her husband to arbitrate:

Here he is! Speak to him in Riffian and see!
He looked over his glasses at me and said: *Mismiuren? Mismiuren* means:
    What's going on? But I did not want to speak Riffian.
I don't understand what you're saying, I told him.
He hung his head, and his wife cried: You see? He's not a Riffian.

El Rifi refuses the anthropologist's authority, feigning lack of comprehension. For El Rifi, the question implies a lack of understanding greater than merely the linguistic: "You think you know something about the Riffians? All you ever saw of them was their teeth when they smiled at you. They never let you find out the important things" (38). His resistance to being named or not named as Riffian then is his maintenance of silence in the Riffian language. If language is the marker of ethnicity, here, El Rifi will not participate in the anthropological translation of him to a cultural example; he pretends not to understand. He will not be a Riffian like "all Riffians."

To be Riffian, however, has already been established as to be irascible, to refuse to conform to the anthropologist's questions. And so El Rifi is put in a double bind: if he speaks Riffian to the anthropologist, then he will be a Riffian. But if he refuses to converse, he will be a Riffian too, since "all Riffians are like that." Of course the reader knows that El Rifi *is* Riffian, since he provides a translation of the anthropologist's question. Bowles in turn translates the translation provided by El Rifi (who himself is variously character, narrator, and—as Mrabet, a Riffian—teller of the story that El Rifi narrates). Bowles renders Mrabet's darija translation of the Riffian word *Mismiuren* into English: "What's going on?" The double translation encourages the reader to side with El Rifi, to understand his refusal to understand. In this sense, El Rifi's "foreignness" is domesticated; the American reader understands El Rifi as "different," in opposition to the American and British couples.

If the reader is allowed in on the game, El Rifi guards the final word. When everything falls apart, El Rifi and the Jameses are forced to leave the house in the middle of the night. El Rifi gets the car and commences honking its horn: "Spaniards leaned out of their windows to watch. I looked at the house and said: *Inaal din d'babakum*" (38). The phrase stands out; no translation is provided. It is clearly a curse on the anthropologist's house, a curse the anthropologist will presumably understand. But now the reader is left unable to comprehend. Like the untranslated phrases in *The Sheltering Sky*, the phrase is a moment of disjuncture in the text, where the official English gives way to unofficial northern Moroccan Arabic. By not translating the phrase, Bowles leaves the tale open to allow Mrabet a primary act of resistance. For if the anthropologist and his wife cannot be sure if El Rifi is Riffian, which the reader knows, the reader cannot know the meaning of El Rifi's curse on the anthropologist. Only Mrabet (with Bowles's sanction) can know both. Finally, Bowles cannot translate the phrase, since Mrabet has constructed the tale in such a way that it relies on an incomplete translation to have its effect. It is after all Mrabet's tale, a tale that both relies on and defies complete translation. The reader is first placed in opposition to the anthropologist, but then placed in company with him. Both want to know more than Mrabet has decided to deliver:

> I'd like to talk to you, [the anthropologist] said. About you and about
>   the Rif.
> Why? I mean, I want to know why you want to know about me.

I just want to ask about some things I don't know, he said.

I see. You're writing a book, and you need to know those things before you
can finish it. Is that right?

No.

I can't tell you anything, I said. You see, I'm writing a book about the Rif
myself. I need to know some things too before I can finish mine. (33)

El Rifi takes control of the tale and reminds both the anthropologist
and the reader of the tale that it is after all *his*. El Rifi's pointed comment,
"I'm writing a book about the Rif myself," alerts the anthropologist to the
motivation for his failure to speak. "I can't tell you anything" does not
mean that El Rifi knows nothing, but rather that he places his own book
before that of the anthropologist. And since El Rifi's "book" *might* be the
collection of Mrabet's tales, within which "What Happened in Granada"
is collected, that which El Rifi still needs to know is how the tale will turn
out. To deliver information to the anthropologist here would be to allow
the tale to go in another direction; it would allow the anthropologist to
direct the course of the story. Instead, El Rifi refuses to translate himself
for the anthropologist. If Bowles in turn translates Mrabet's refusal to be
translated, it is after all Mrabet who directs the tale in ways that defy
translation.

Darija: The Language That Circulates

In early 2004, the Moroccan Cultural Studies Center, based at Sidi
Mohammed Ben Abdallah University in Fez, published the first Moroccan edition of Mohammed Mrabet's work—in the original English of Paul
Bowles's translation.[70] The Moroccan republication of *Love with a Few
Hairs* in English, the language in which it originally appeared, was an
event of much critical interest. The edition continues the circulation of
Mrabet's fascinating text as it survived its thirty-fifth anniversary. Such
movement is both an extension of Mrabet's work in a new direction and
an appropriate response to something inherent within his complex narratives. Translation is after all the survival of literature—its "living on" in
new contexts. As *Love with a Few Hairs* lives on to be published in
Morocco, the place of its composition and the setting of its tale, we should
therefore be wary of saying that the text has returned "home" or at least

qualify the statement. In the novel itself, home is hardly a place to which one wants to return; one sleeps where there is the least danger or the absence of negative passions. And the novel returns to a Morocco that is much changed from the one it left, in particular with regard to Morocco's relationship to the English language and to the collaboration of Moroccans with Americans.

That the interest in and conditions for publishing this book in English exist in Fez today reflects the changed status of English in Morocco and is in part a reflection of the effects of globalization on economic, academic, and cultural realms. In the last decades of the twentieth century, especially with the development and extension of global telecommunications and the Internet, globalization produced a silent imperative for much of the world to translate itself into English or be left behind as a "local" value. Such a situation shifted the dynamic in postcolonial states such as Morocco, otherwise preoccupied with the need to (re)establish national languages and literatures. English as global language, as alternative, as threat, announced an emerging condition that would mark the end of the "postcolonial" as a period of cultural history and signaled the shift into globalization (as episteme), with its own challenges and possibilities.[71]

With the increasing list of Moroccan writers composing fiction, poetry, and criticism in English, it is tempting to speak of an anglophone Moroccan literary tradition. If so, Paul Bowles and Mohammed Mrabet would need to be considered foundational figures. But these are the defunct terms of "postcolonial literary studies" and ones that the Mrabet-Bowles texts themselves confound. The texts that emerged from the collaboration elude the fixed categories professional readers so often like to put on literature. Not surprisingly, then, they have for a long time slipped through the cracks. For those whose business is to categorize or itemize national literatures, it requires a new paradigm. The Mrabet-Bowles collaborations are "Tangerian" works. Tangerian literature emerges from and responds to a particularly rich set of circumstances, as I have discussed in previous chapters: the city's international history, its collapsed communities and the crossing of its social networks, its linguistic multiplicity, and its tension in relation to the rest of Morocco. They are not only set in a Tangier that reflects these geopolitical and social complexities, but its very existence emerges from a situation peculiar to Tangier—a Tangerian condition—frequently inscribed in the texts themselves.

"When a line of communication is established, between a member of

Mohammed Mrabet, at Sidi Mohammed Ben Abdellah University, Fez, surrounded by Moroccan students after his presentation at the first conference on his work, March 2004. *Photo by Brian T. Edwards, copyright 2005.*

subaltern groups and the circuits of citizenship or institutionality," Gaya-tri Spivak writes, "the subaltern has been inserted into the long road to hegemony. Unless we want to be romantic purists or primitivists about 'preserving subalternity'—a contradiction in terms—this is absolutely to be desired."[72] That various systems of communication and translation are represented in *Love with a Few Hairs* is an extraordinary feature of a novel that, whatever the details of its process of creation, issued from the conversation of Mrabet and Bowles. Taking such moments in the texts seriously helps us to begin to answer the questions raised by the historical and critical mystery of the process of creation, questions that I have associated with the role of individual intelligence within a globalizing economy. And perhaps the most promising and exciting lesson of these works of Tangerian literature is the activation of the space of dialogue, from which something different and unforeseen may emerge.

III
Marrakech Express

Overleaf:
Hippies outside walls of Fez medina, 1970.
Photo by Ed Buryn, used with permission.

6

HIPPIE ORIENTALISM

The Interpretation of Countercultures

Marrakech Express

In his guidebook for the love generation, *Vagabonding in Europe and North Africa* (1971), Ed Buryn raved about Morocco: "The in-place, the target for all kinds of tourists, ranging from Hilton Hotel hoppers to dream-dealing druggies."[1] In Morocco, the combination of "history, culture, climate, scenery, inexpensiveness, plus something indefinable (maybe dope)" made the country "the best visit of all." The last two entries in that list get substantially more attention from Buryn than the first two, which suggests much about the vagabond's preferences in international travel. Buryn had practical advice on subjects such as crossing the border—"I advise cutting your hair. It's no big thing, unless you feel your identity depends on your hair style"—where to hitchhike and where to find hashish, other hippies, and postcards of "authentic Moroccan scenes" (197). And he suggested learning some French or even a little Arabic—"if you think you can handle that (!)"—though he provided no vocabulary. His case for picking up some phrases is revealing: "Most of your rides will come from the Arabic rather than the European segment, and the Arabs are a trip. They are soul people who practice brotherhood every day rather than just bullshit about it on Sundays" (199). Buryn gives a few anecdotes that explain what he means by Moroccan soul, all of which revolve around generous rides and easy hitchhiking. *Vagabonding* is all about finding one's place among the many crowds or communities in Morocco. The impulse to connect with Moroccans is present in Buryn's prose, as is the sense that it never quite transpires, blocked by linguistic frames and a failure to get beyond the assumption that Moroccans stood in a premodern world. Like many a traveler to the Maghreb before him, Buryn had a sense of belatedness: "Newly discovered by hippies, travel agents, filmmakers and other exponents of Progress, Morocco is changing rapidly behind the pressure of heavy people and money influx." And then he adds: "Flux you, too!" (196). The desire to occupy a space that might not change, a temporally stagnant place that might resist the incursions of those "exponents of Progress," as Buryn put it ironically, defined the traveling hippies' relationship to Morocco and much of the global South. That this required staying clear of not only the "heavy people" from the outside but also a good deal of the Moroccan youth—the same generation as Buryn's readers—structures the relationship of the hippies to one of the key stops on their global itinerary. The contours of that circumscribed regard and how it organized a wide range of apparently unconnected accounts of Morocco are the subject of this chapter.

Ed Buryn's take on the Maghrebi soul offers an example of the blinders of hippie relativism and the "often silly delight the flower children took in the people who embodied otherness," as Vincent Crapanzano has described attitudes held by many young Americans in the late 1960s, when he too lived in Morocco before turning thirty.[2] Buryn seemed in touch with his generation's relationship to travel and the exotic—and the market for both. His book, copublished in Berkeley and New York, had 50,000 copies in print by 1973, despite Buryn's recommendation not to buy guidebooks, including his own, and rather to take notes from library copies or simply "rip one off" (22). The 1973 revised edition included pages of feedback from readers, including injunctions for him to pay more attention to the needs and experiences of traveling American women, plus a warning from an American based in Essaouira, on the Moroccan coast: "Borders are tighter, girls are turned back from Tangier. Explanation— hippies."[3] This guidebook, so in touch with its moment and its community of readers, emerges from the generation and cultural context that would give rise to scores of American representations of the Maghreb, from popular music to professional anthropology, that together make up what I'll call "hippie Orientalism."

By the early 1970s, large, drifting communities of American hippies in Morocco were testing the limits of Morocco's famous hospitality. While some ventured to Tunisia—fewer to Algeria—Morocco was far and away the most popular location in North Africa. American vagabonds congregated in the cities—especially Tangier and Marrakech—and in smaller towns. A commune had sprung up in the fishing village of Diabet, on the beach just south of Essaouira, where Jimi Hendrix paid an influential visit

in July 1969, a couple of weeks before he played at Woodstock.[4] In the
north, the beach town of Asilah, about an hour down the coast from Tangier; the mountainous town of Chefchaouen, nestled in the kif-growing
region in the Rif Mountains; and Ketama, the epicenter of kif production,
all drew legions of hippies. And these Americans all felt the pressure
of Moroccan authorities, as well as the mounting disdain of regular Moroccans. The *Nation* ran an article in 1973 that described Moroccan
crackdowns on Westerners with long hair. If hippies were transforming
Morocco into a "sort of countercultural watering hole," the Moroccan
government was increasingly "writing off the young tourists as economically expendable," blocking entry at the borders and cracking down on the
hippies already in Morocco.[5] As tourism revenues doubled between 1965
and 1970, the government could afford to harass the hippies, whose potential influence on Moroccan youth worried the regime. The influence
remained superficial, as it turned out, in both directions. The hippies and
Moroccan youth culture never made serious or prolonged contact.

   Underlying the hippie generation's time in Morocco was the war simultaneously raging in Vietnam, which kept a global perspective constantly
at hand. The safety and relative isolation of Morocco allowed young
Americans to have an experience of apparently radical cultural difference
that they could not then have had in Southeast Asia, the place in the back
of every young American's mind. For those Americans in Vietnam at this
time, the significant danger framed and altered their experience. Since
Morocco offered young Americans an apparently unselfconscious opportunity to reflect on cultural difference, then, the ways in which young
Americans did so offers a cipher to a crucial period in American consciousness. Most turned their attention away from points of connection
and contemporary political immediacy and instead saw Morocco in the
temporal lag familiar to Orientalism, suggesting the limits of the counterculture's global imaginary and its inability to counteract the official global
perspective of the U.S. state it so deeply criticized.[6] By extending the
global racial time we have seen operative, the hippie imaginary of Morocco unwittingly supported the official American position toward Morocco during the period. If I note the consistency of official and counterculture perspectives, my goal is neither to indict the generation nor to
collapse the space between the cultural production of young Americans
and the policies of the U.S. state. There were, however, political stakes for
the disengagement of young Americans from Moroccan political reality,

as I'll explore below. Offering a textured account of a wide range of materials, the question I pursue is how, during a moment of geopolitical crisis, the foreign space is (dis)figured as an extension of domestic American concerns. Thus I present in this chapter a group portrait from a moment of cultural and intellectual history in need of interruption.

By the time of the *Nation's* article, Morocco was already associated with youth culture. *Time* ran a long and heavily illustrated travel article in 1969 that called Morocco "one of the newest and chic-est holiday havens," noting the rapid rise in tourism, which had become the country's second-largest industry. *Time* focused especially on the "colony" of American youth in Marrakech. "Morocco is a hashhead's delight," *Time* claims, noting the ease of obtaining kif. *Time* profiled a couple of American women in their twenties: "They deliberately travel around Marrakesh in filthy old market buses rather than tourist coaches, 'to be with the people' as well as to save money."[7] The association of cannabis, escape, and connection with otherness was made in Crosby, Stills, and Nash's (CSN) 1969 song "Marrakesh Express," an anthem of the era:

> Looking at the world through the sunset in your eyes,
> Traveling the train to clear Moroccan skies—
> Ducks and pigs and chickens call, animal carpet wall to wall
> American ladies five foot tall, in blue.
> Sweeping cobwebs from the edges of my mind,
> Had to get away to see what we could find. . . .
> I've been savin' all my money just to take you there,
> I smell the garden in your hair.
> Take the train from Casablanca going south,
> Blowing smoke rings from the corners of my mouth,
> Colored cottons hang in the square, charming cobras in the square, striped
>   djellabas we can wear at home.
> Don't you know we're riding on the Marrakesh Express.

CSN's lyrics painted a picture of Marrakech as a place of escape, a pastoral retreat for contemplation ("the world" seen through telltale "smoke rings"). Their image of Morocco was obviously flat: "ducks and pigs and chickens" are given as distinguishing characteristics of the major city of the Moroccan south, where ducks were rare and pigs unwelcome as swine. CSN's is a tourist Marrakech, cobras and cottons and souvenir

Vagabonds in Marrakech near the Koutoubia mosque, 1970.
Photo by Ed Buryn, used with permission.

djellabas "we can wear at home" written right into the song. Any indica-
tion of the Moroccan police state that ruled the kingdom in the late 1960s
is absent. The music itself bears no mark of the rich and varied Moroccan
musical tradition, even though the Rolling Stones' Brian Jones had recorded *jajouka* music in northern Morocco the previous year. It was not
Moroccan particularity that beckoned the hippies, but the sense of distance from the cultural tensions and moral chaos of domestic America
during the Vietnam crisis. That interval between Morocco and the America left behind was inscribed in CSN's song by the image of a train leading
directly to "clear Moroccan skies." Neither border agents checking the
length of visitors' hair nor customs agents searching rucksacks mar CSN's
image of a land apart.

Such a smooth, borderless transition was belied by other contemporary accounts. James Michener's heavily researched novel *The Drifters* (1971) and the anthropologist Paul Rabinow's memoir of his time in Morocco in the late 1960s both portrayed the Moroccan border as a tight, though manageable squeeze for the young American male, with a mandatory trip to the Casablanca airport barber de rigueur. In his guidebook, Ed Buryn reassured his vagabonds about the haircut: "Once inside, you can grow it back" (196). But Tangier resident David Woolman suggested that it was not only the border where the hippies were monitored: "The [Tangier] police made periodic round-ups, shaved hippy heads and threw many of them out of the country, although they did nothing to stop the kif coming in from Chaouen and the Rif to lure these same hippies and their friends back again."[8] Elizabeth Fernea's account of a year spent in Marrakech with her anthropologist husband and three children during 1971 and 1972 offers similar testimony: American hippies living across the street suddenly disappear in the midst of a major drug bust orchestrated by Moroccan authorities. Given the visibility of the hippies and their lack of a benefit to local economy (they were perceived to have a minor effect on revenues), the enforcement of otherwise loosely followed laws against kif and hashish possession was focused on them. "Tanjawis usually have no time for foreigners unless they spend money, and the hip culture just didn't produce enough of this commodity in Tangier."[9] Americans leaving Morocco took on some notoriety. In 1970, *Life* magazine ran a cover story on American youth busted abroad for drugs and focused especially on hippies in Morocco. A two-page photograph helped illustrate the story: a clean-cut Spanish customs officer sniffs the contents of a young American man's straw basket. The American wears a cape, scarves, and a floral-print bandanna over shoulder-length blond hair. His possessions spread across the table, he looks worriedly at the officer. His female companion, who has scraggly hair and wears a tasseled wool poncho, prepares her own bags for inspection.[10]

Whatever the gaps in representations of Morocco such as those by Crosby, Stills, and Nash or Ed Buryn, the space for flight was nonetheless real and had both a legal component (fleeing the reach of the draft, the enforcement of drug laws) and an epistemological one: the relativism and racialized logic that allowed traveling hippies to perceive Moroccan "soul" even in the actions of a people trying to respond to a highly visible influx of young Americans. Seen as a group, "hippie Orientalism" marks or

Ben Edmonson gets his hair cut in preparation for entry
into Morocco. It was to the middle of his back before the
cut. Algeciras, Spain, 1973. *Courtesy of Ben Edmonson.*

pervades works as disparate as Paula Wolfert's influential cookbook *Couscous and Other Good Food from Morocco*, cultural anthropology and theory
by Clifford Geertz and Paul Rabinow, middlebrow fiction by James
Michener, the recording and marketing of the Master Musicians of Jajouka, and ethnographically rich literary nonfiction by Jane Kramer and
Elizabeth Fernea. There's a significant distance between Buryn's descriptions of hitchhiking, Wolfert's account of the cultural significance of
bisteeya, Kramer's book-length essay on the kidnapping, rape, and subsequent marriage of a young woman in Meknes, Geertz's thick descriptions

of Moroccan cultural forms, Brian Jones's recordings of jajouka (and Robert Palmer's commentary in *Rolling Stone*), Ornette Coleman's collaboration with the Moroccan musicians, and Rabinow's theorization of the comprehension of the self via the detour of comprehension of the other in the isolated marabout of Sidi Lahcen Lyusi. But there are also overlapping meanings that Morocco had for these overlapping communities of Americans living in Morocco during the late 1960s and early 1970s. The hippies who took the "Marrakech Express" and so avoided being drafted and evaded moral and legal restrictions on them in the United States, the group of young anthropologists working in Morocco, and those sympathetic, slightly older American writers who observed and interacted with them shared a sense of the boundaries of the culture being left behind, a sense inscribed subtly and sometimes deeply and self-consciously in their works. The Marrakech and Tangier hippies left their mark on American pop culture through popular music, published recipes for everything from couscous to hashish jam, and Michener's epic depiction of them in his 1971 bestseller *The Drifters*, which concludes with a 112-page chapter set in Morocco. In academia, the work of Geertz's group influenced American anthropology and cultural studies deeply. During their time in Sefrou (1965–71), the group developed a style of fieldwork (the "team study") and a new interpretation of "culture" itself that were resonant with hippie counterculture.

Before hackles are raised against my grouping, I should be clear what I mean by the phrase that purports to contain these various projects. I use "hippie Orientalism" to signal a shared distance between domestic America and its projects (political, intellectual—and Geertz might say moral) and accounts of Moroccan culture that are inscribed in these works. While living independently of each other, both communities' interpretation of Moroccan culture was a direction of energies away from another more troubling Orient, that of Southeast Asia. In some cases, this was explicit, as it was for those who fled the reach of the United States draft. In other cases, Morocco offered an implicit relief from the pressures of domestic America, as for Rabinow, who begins his memoir describing a "wave of revulsion and disgust" with domestic America in spring 1968 and the "sense of giddy release" that departure afforded him.[11] In yet other cases, such as Kramer's, the difference of Morocco might put domestic America *in relief*, a place that itself seemed foreign from a Moroccan vantage. But common to almost all was an underlying cultural relativism that encouraged most to sidestep the question of what Vietnam and the Maghreb might have in common, either with each other as former French colonies or with the United States, and to miss the chance to draw a link between the riots and student strikes in Morocco in 1965–66 (harshly repressed by the Moroccan police state, with several hundreds of students killed) and student and counterculture demonstrations in France and the United States in 1968. For both the hippies and most of the anthropologists, Morocco stood somehow outside of the messy world, allowing Geertz's group to imagine they inhabited a controlled laboratory, and American hippies freedoms unknown back in the United States.

The ethnographic works on this list are sensitive to the question of cultural encounter—Rabinow and Geertz theorize it, Elizabeth Fernea describes it at length—in ways that most hippies in Marrakech were apparently not. The American cultural anthropologists worked to distinguish their own representations from French ethnographies that preceded them, which had been polluted by their colonial context. In this sense, they triangulate their points of reference between the United States, France, and the Maghreb. Geertz and Rabinow are not quite Orientalists in the Saidian sense, then. In *Orientalism*, Said pointedly distinguished Geertz's work from "corrupt" scholarship: "[Geertz's] interest in Islam is discrete and concrete enough to be animated by the specific societies and problems he studies and not by the rituals, preconceptions, and doctrines of Orientalism."[12] Hippie Orientalism does not seek to collapse these differing stances toward dialogue between Moroccans and Americans. Rather, it seeks to address the fact that both professional and popular representations of Morocco in the 1960s tended toward a binarism that separated worlds within differing temporalities. Works such as Rabinow's and Geertz's identified and inscribed an intermediary figure— an American "translator" of the text that was Morocco—but through their emphasis on culture as text and a focus on isolated towns that might serve as laboratories maintained a distance between the world that interpreted the culture and the culture itself.

I use the word *Orientalism* here, despite Said's comment on Geertz and following the impulse behind Said's work, because the distance inscribed between contemporary and "traditional" Morocco and between young Morocco and young America had deep political stakes at the time.[13] As the declassified FRUS papers demonstrate, the Johnson administration's concern was not to extend democracy or rights to Morocco but rather to maintain Moroccan stability. Tensions between Morocco and Algeria and the Algerian alliance with the Soviet Union were worrisome. After the 1967 Arab-Israeli War and the rise in Arab socialism, sustaining Morocco against Algeria was especially crucial, and stabilization was achieved primarily through military aid and financial assistance to the regime. Evidence of mass unrest in Morocco was easily brushed aside by the Moroccan ambassador to the United States with phrases in closed-door meetings such as "the King's authority is at stake," an authority the Johnson administration did not want to jeopardize.[14] The political stakes of hippie Orientalism involved not only specific policies toward the new states, but also more largely the ways in which less philosophically inclined Americans considered, or failed to consider, U.S. relations with the Arab world and with North Africa. Geertz, as we'll see, was indeed concrete in his interest in Islam, but he tended to encourage a slippage between what he discovered in his discrete investigations and the nonregional specialist's sense of the Arab Middle East as a whole. His deeply felt and thickly described sense that the economic asymmetry between U.S. anthropologist and subaltern informant posed a major obstacle to communicative contact was linked to his pessimism about the possibility for "significant social progress in the new states."[15] The "anthropological irony" that structured attempted communication across these cultural and economic barriers could also serve as a justification for dispensing with the idea of commonality that was politically damaging for young Morocco.

As the encounter with Morocco was always and already a racialized encounter, hippie Orientalism is structured as well by domestic racial categories and questions. Buryn's reference to "soul people," Michener's fascination with African American interest in Islam, and Rabinow's comparisons of an Aissawa rite to a John Coltrane performance provide examples. In the 1960s, the domestic context of civil rights and the entry into the United Nations of newly independent African states made international relations a domestic matter and domestic expressions of racism a foreign relations question.[16] As hippies embraced Morocco, then, the question of the political disengagement from young Morocco is interwoven with domestic meaning. The identification of the Black Power movement in the United States with Islam and the Arab world racialized the encounter of hippies with Moroccans and was a screen through which the publics of these texts viewed their accounts. The hippie impulse to gravitate toward the "traditional," the rural, and the fragmented because it was somehow more "real" or "authentic" than urban Morocco must therefore be seen in the knotted context of domestic civil rights and foreign relations. The more that Morocco was placed in the temporal lag of Orientalism, the more the black nationalists' affiliations with the Arab world might be seen as an alliance with a retrograde place. The implicit invocation of racial time that was so disempowering during World War II's North African campaign could thus subtly be recalled as a means by which white liberals and conservatives might turn away from a powerful affiliation.

My claim is limited to a ten-year period (1965–75) that corresponds loosely with the Vietnam War in U.S. foreign relations and the domestic crises it precipitated or exacerbated in the United States, particularly the struggle for civil rights, which on the latter end of the period collided with the further erosion in confidence in American leadership of the Watergate scandal. Vagabonds and doctoral students in anthropology had reason to be happy to leave the United States behind in this period. But the place they went to was in the midst of its own crises, crises that make no ripple in the wave of American representations.[17] These years correspond to the least stable period in postcolonial Moroccan history, marked by riots, strikes, political uprisings, and challenges to the political entity itself, met by brutal repression. Student riots in 1965 and rising domestic tensions precipitated the suspension of the Moroccan parliament under the 1962 constitution, and a declaration of state of emergency during which the king authorized himself to take over all executive and legislative functions. Followed by the strengthening of brutal interior minister Mohammed Oufkir, and the kidnapping and disappearance of opposition leader Mehdi Ben Barka, this period has been called "les années de plomb" (the years of lead) and spans two failed coups d'état on King Hassan II (1971 and 1972, one of which was orchestrated by General Oufkir himself). As Mark Tessler writes, "The years between 1965 and 1973 were a period of serious student unrest in Morocco."[18] After the violent response to the 1965 student uprising in Casablanca, in which more than a thousand students were killed by the army, strikes in late 1971 and early 1972 were met by the closing of much of Mohammed V University in Rabat. The period ends with Hassan's heroic Green March takeover of the contested Western Sahara in 1975, an imperial move on the part of the kingdom that helped solidify and unify Moroccans around the troubled monarch. Though by the mid-1970s, public expression of alienation had subsided in

Morocco, Tessler points out that even after 1973, "students were still strongly opposed to the government and the established political system" (93). Tessler's general point must be kept in mind: that in the Maghreb "young people tend to be well-informed and highly attentive to politics but unlikely to participate in political life . . . the result of a clear recognition that the political system is not responsive to their needs and demands . . . As an alternative, they identify with antiregime movements, either parties of the left or militant Islamic groups, and await an opportunity to tear the regime down violently" (93). The lack of an alliance between young Americans and Moroccan youth, both alienated and anti-regime, is a telling failure.

The Moroccan crackdown on the hippies might seem to have been an impediment to such an alliance. The government's worry, according to Fred Setterberg, who wrote the essay on Morocco for the *Nation* after returning from four months in the Maghreb, was a familiar one: "The extent to which the transients' counter-traditional values and styles may influence Moroccan youth" (686). But what is surprising was not the response of King Hassan II's regime, but that it was echoed by the leftist opposition, who saw "the droves of young invaders" as either counter-reformist or counterrevolutionary" (687). Whatever the hippies' expressed politics, Moroccans on all points of the political spectrum saw them as politically disengaged or reactionary, a threat for the young nation. Ed Buryn's "Flux you!" to the idea of a capital influx to Morocco was apparently heard loud and clear by Moroccans of a variety of political stripes. As Setterberg put it astutely: "Seen from the standpoint of both Moslem traditionalists and economically progressive moderns, a nation of incipient bohemians is anything but an asset" (686). Though the hippies would have some impact on Moroccan youth, particularly in the cities, it seemed to be little more than superficial, such as changing Moroccan hairstyles and the brief and limited popularity of bands like the Rolling Stones or Bob Dylan.[19] A more pronounced alliance did not happen. Setterberg quotes a Moroccan student union member: "The detachment from practical matters evidenced by many of the young, relatively affluent tourists in Morocco negates the promotion of a native spirit for political involvement and reform" (687). Given the hippies' search for Moroccan "soul" and embrace of third world otherness, the Moroccan comment that the hippies might be a force of negation wounded insofar as it was heard at all. Thus it may not be surprising that Setterberg's point that the Moroccan Left kept its distance from the hippies has been forgotten. My point in recalling it is not so much to put the hippies on trial, but to look at the way in which the distance between Moroccan and American communities was structured. The way in which Morocco became associated with distance from contemporary global concerns that *mattered* to Americans—as space for reflection on the problems of the "world," as self-contained laboratory in which to retheorize social theory, as outlet for a connection between white Americans and African "soul"—relied on this structure.

Be-In: On (Not) Being in Morocco

When it came time to write the introduction to her book *Allen Ginsberg in America*, much of which had appeared in the *New Yorker* earlier that year, Jane Kramer was living in Morocco. Several months earlier, she and her husband Vincent Crapanzano, then a doctoral student in anthropology, had moved to Meknes, where he was doing fieldwork. In Kramer's introduction, dated August 13, 1968, she described feeling at a remove from the events described in her text. Morocco had changed her perspective on American youth culture:

> By now, over a year and a half has passed since the Great Human Be-In in Central Park, with which this book ends, and Be-ins seem to have given way to campus sieges as the preferred form of communal enterprise. Whatever changes of heart or tactics may have overtaken the love generation, they are certainly difficult to analyze from a small, imperial city in the middle of Morocco, where all the hippies are tourists and where the last student reckless enough to complain about something is spending several years in jail. The distance here from student activists, hippie lovers, and virtually every other sign of young, revolutionary life is as much spiritual as spatial. It is impossible to imagine a Ginsberg in Morocco, and thinking about him here, I am beginning to understand how very much he belongs in and to the United States.[20]

The poignancy of what has been lost in America, or what Kramer imagines to be lost in the transition from love to militancy, is underlined by her sense of having missed it. This nostalgic tone renders her book more than an act of cultural reporting: it memorializes a passing stage of the history of the American counterculture. However, in the act of separating herself from the context she describes in the book she is able to assert her own authority rather than undercut it, for from afar she can claim to be able to recognize the culture her book describes. Yet this requires the stability of the new place, Morocco, which affords her the scientific distance. The stability she attributes to Morocco, however, is exaggerated and ignores what Morocco did have in common with America. She writes off the idea of youth rebellion in Morocco; the hippies are tourists and "the last student reckless enough to complain about something is spending several years in jail." Without any further explanation, the reference is meaningless to her American audience. If she was aware of the 1965 student riots in Casablanca, Kramer doesn't elaborate on the violence used to stop them or the general climate of political repression in Morocco. Indeed it is impossible to know whether the last reckless student might be Moroccan or one of the hippies on vacation, complaining perhaps about an enforced haircut (which got more press in the United States than did the student riots). As a result, Kramer's Morocco comes off as an exotic and distant empire, with little relation to oppositional politics or the United States. As the introduction goes on, Morocco gets yet more exotic. Kramer juxtaposes Ginsberg's "exceptional tenderness" and the pursuit of the ecstatic life in Morocco, described in horrifying terms: "[In Meknes] expanded consciousness for the other means whacking one's own head open with a doubled-edged axe" (xviii). The example comes from the rather extreme practices of the Hamadsha brotherhood that Kramer's husband was researching at the time, though Kramer leaves out that detail, adding to the mystery. Instead the distance between worlds is emphasized: "Here, where a good part of the population spends its time having visions, there is no appetite at all for Ginsberg's loving universe" (xviii). The lines are drawn. Ginsberg himself had spent time in Morocco, though this is not mentioned, but "a Ginsberg in Morocco" or a Moroccan Ginsberg is impossible to imagine.

Kramer's introduction is not unlike Rick's line in *Casablanca*—"If it's December 1941 in Casablanca, what time is it in New York?"—which I discussed in chapter 1 as an act of temporal displacement with a political effect. Kramer addresses new times but similarly reorganizes her Moroccan subject: If it's August 1968 in Meknes, a place of head-whacking and vision-having, what time is it in America? The new writing she was doing in Meknes, when she paused to write this introduction, would similarly direct American attention away from young, urban Moroccans who might otherwise be in confederation with the young hippies. Kramer's next book, *Honor to the Bride Like the Pigeon That Guards Its Grain under the Clove Tree*, is a brilliant piece of writing that convincingly portrays a way of life and thinking in a particular segment of Moroccan society (uneducated, lower-class, on the urban periphery, living in shantytowns). But given the attention Americans were then paying to Morocco—as a place of flight, as a place of escape—Kramer's tale of Moroccan backwardness and perfidy made more possible, rather than less, the prevailing hippie mantra that Moroccans embodied otherness—the same position that Vincent Crapanzano would later critique. *Honor to the Bride*, then, is an important entry in hippie Orientalism, for it helped underline the cultural binarism that failed to connect the dots between Chicago, Paris, Casablanca, and Hanoi. Because of Kramer's dual role as major journalist and sometime assistant to her professional anthropologist husband, her Moroccan work is central to our topic.

Kramer's book appeared in the *New Yorker* in three installments in 1970 and was published by Farrar, Straus and Giroux that same year under its long and idiosyncratic title, a line borrowed from a Berber wedding song. The power of *Honor to the Bride* to summon a Moroccan world at once illogical (by an assumed American standard) and organized by a recognizable system recalls the work of Paul Bowles, whom Kramer had clearly read. Though the book makes no reference to Bowles or his contemporaneous work with Mohammed Mrabet—by 1969, the third Mrabet-Bowles collaboration had been published in the United States—many American readers in 1970 could draw parallels. Kramer's book appeared with no editorial contextualization, save the author's own abrupt opening: "In Morocco, this story would probably be called a love story. It took place one year when I was living in that country."[21] The narrative's strangeness is due to its decontextualization, emerging from a strange world that itself does not know what meaning to attribute to it.

> [The principal characters] were by no means exceptional Moroccans. Nor was their story really an exceptional one. It was sentimental, complicated, cruel, and a little crazy, but it was a thoroughly Arab story, and it plodded along in time like an awkward arabesque, always elaborating on itself and never appearing to be going anywhere. Its lessons were the familiar lessons of shame, face, favors, and the pocketbook. And its moral was simply that everything in the end depends on Allah's great and inexplicable will. Most Moroccans would say that it was too mundane to bear retelling. By the time I left the country, Omar himself was starting to forget the details. (3–4)

The remarks demarcate the tale as exceptional only in its displacement. Location itself is central to the editorial design of the *New Yorker*, a magazine named as a geographic location, a readerly position at once cosmopolitan and provincial. Kramer's piece appeared under the magazine's occasional heading "Our Far Flung Correspondents," which counterbalances and helps construct the editorial locality at the magazine's center, referred to quaintly as "town" (as in the cultural calendar section "Goings On about Town"). There is also a temporal component. Kramer freezes the tale in a past made present: a temporal displacement that writes the Moroccan past (the time of the story) as the perpetual present. Even as it fades from the memory of the actors, the tale is inscribed as so "mundane" and unexceptional as to be timeless. This is the work of the ethnographer.

A generation ago, Johannes Fabian argued that the work of cultural anthropology was structured around a temporal distancing, written in the present tense in the home country based on field notes taken in the "field" in the past. Such, Fabian argued, explained the peculiar temporality of most ethnography, which doomed the third world to a perpetual pastness explained in the present tense, a displacement that helped justify colonialism as common sense.[22] Vincent Crapanzano has more recently argued that Fabian's point is true of reflection in general (and by extension of representational texts in general, whether they be ethnographies or the "talking cure" at the basis of psychoanalysis) and wonders whether Fabian does not create a "fixity of vantage point that does not do justice to the 'open-ended' nature of the deployment of power."[23] Crapanzano's point is important and his own engagement with questions of dialogue—as well as his critique of Geertz's text metaphor—emerges in part from having shared the experience of living in Morocco in the 1960s and having thought hard on the question of dialogue with Moroccans. But in Kramer's book, and in 1970, the temporal displacement of the Moroccan story has a more immediate effect. In its synchronic focus on a slice of time and by dodging the diachronic question of the conditions that make its own narrative possible (such as the very project that brings her husband to Morocco as an anthropologist, or reflection on what she shares with the hippies of her generation who are in Morocco for reasons other than tourism), she achieves a troubling divorce of representation from politics. That the *New Yorker* could and did publish her book-length piece with no introduction

or editorial apparatus other than to say it came from a "far flung correspondent" blesses, as it were, that divorce.

It is not that Kramer's book did not offer the possibility for cross-
cultural comparison and critique. *Honor to the Bride* tells an elaborate tale
of the kidnapping of Khadija, the thirteen-year-old virgin daughter of a
Meknessi couple, her rescue, and the girl's parents' successful attempt to
marry off the now-deflowered daughter and gain a bride price. The book
exposes Moroccan attitudes toward women as property and the hypocrisies that prevail in societal and legal attitudes. As such, it offers a subtle
feminist critique of traditional Moroccan attitudes. An important scene
in *Honor to the Bride* begins to address a cross-cultural comparison between American and Moroccan ideas about marriage, women, and desire.
That brief scene, very late in the book, takes place between Monsieur
Hugh, a young American scholar (an apparent stand-in for Crapanzano);
Ahmed, the educated, urban Moroccan who is to marry Khadija; and the
American scholar's wife, known as Madame Hugh. Ahmed attributes
Monsieur and Madame Hugh's inability to understand his motives in
marrying the young Khadija to cultural difference (he plans to confine
her): "'But you do not understand . . . Moroccans are different from the
nesraniyyin [Christians]. You *nesraniyyin*, you do not have to lock up your
wives. But here, if I do not lock up my wife, a man will open my door and
she will go with him.'" Ahmed goes on:

> I have heard that in your country even a man who sees a woman dancing
> does not follow her. . . . That would never happen in Morocco. . . . I have
> seen it all at the movies. The men in America think of nothing but business.
> But here no one thinks of business. We think only of stealing women. We
> are very virile, very hot blooded. . . . And the women here are not like the
> *nesrani* women . . . The women here will shame their husbands for a few
> dirhams. (190)

Madame Hugh walks out shocked and annoyed. Her implied feminist
critique is clearly directed at the book's American readers, not Moroccan
women, who are outside the range of her project and excluded from its
circulation.[24] And neither Madame nor Monsieur Hugh says anything to
Ahmed, even though he has invoked American culture and represented
it. Ahmed's references to American films demonstrate the possibility for
communication—for comparison—was available to Moroccans. After

Madame Hugh rejects this conversation by walking out, Hugh restores the facade of cultural difference. The conversation is quickly abandoned, and the book maintains a sense of the distance and lack of mutual comprehension of Moroccan and American. That is, after all, the basis on which the book rests: "Most Moroccans would say that it was too mundane to bear retelling." The presence of the scene and its representation of a crossover moment that challenges the mantra of cultural relativism suggest that possibilities to break the frame within which her "far-flung" narrative is visible presented themselves to Kramer. But left as it is, the scene depicts her turn away from such an interruptive act.

The political effect of Kramer's focus is more clearly seen, and more influential, in an extraordinary essay on Morocco that she jointly authored with Crapanzano in 1969. The long article, titled "A World of Saints and She-Demons" and published in the *New York Times Magazine*, was apparently drawn from Crapanzano's research on spirit possession and curing. The essay was remarkable both for its account of the dramatic activities of the Hamadsha brotherhood and for the fact that it was published in such an influential venue. According to the *Times'* heading, the essay would "shed light on life in a small Arab town," something that in 1969, after the Arab-Israeli War in June 1967, might be presumed to offer its own justification.[25] Otherwise, the article seems out of place in a weekly newsmagazine, recounting a Moroccan family's pilgrimage to a local saint's tomb in the hopes of curing their daughter's sudden paralysis. Inserted somewhat abruptly is further justification: the claim that an understanding of the traditional beliefs of uneducated Moroccan society might in fact be the key to understanding the political reality of the entire Arab world. Whether or not the *Times'* editors inserted the passage, it is explicit about the political implications of its representation of traditional Morocco:

> Morocco, like most other Arab countries, is still divided by the traditions of a vast, uneducated majority and the desires of a comparatively tiny, modern élite. The traditions cut across—and may even override—the incredible political patchwork of the Arab world. Arab governments run a gamut from monarchy to democracy, from tribalism to state socialism, but the diversity can be misleading for anyone trying to puzzle out the quality of life that links the city of Meknes to Damascus, or a small Egyptian village to Beni Rachid [in Morocco].... Westerners, hunting down clues to "the Arab" in the wake of the crisis in the Middle East, too often tend to confuse the various

institutional superstructures of the area for Arab reality, and the official statements of the Arab governments for the perspective of the people themselves. The Arabs never make the same mistake. (15)

Readers after reality, in other words, should attend to traditional society: "The staying power of the Government depends to a great extent on the staying power of the status quo, and the traditional values, styles and superstitions of the Moroccan people are exploited to full advantage by the King and his ministerial élite" (15). Crapanzano and Kramer argue that the Westerner is mistaken if he or she confuses "institutional superstructures" with "reality," or "official statements" with the people's own perspective, something Arabs themselves would never err in doing. It is a stunning turn of argument, for it puts in the disempowered Arabs' own collective mouth an assertion of the way in which power relations work. It's a familiar rhetorical strategy: don't be duped, for the dupes themselves aren't duped, a subtle appeal for the reader to go native. The strategy is an intriguing echo or refraction of Geertz's then-recent writing about Morocco, as newly published in *Islam Observed* and scattered essays.

Even if it is true that official statements and institutional superstructures are elaborate fictions about political reality, there are surely alternative vantage points for understanding the political reality of the Arab world besides a minor Moroccan brotherhood. Would not an examination of political opposition to the kingdom, of urban dissent, of the vibrant intellectual and cultural scene(s) in the Maghreb offer alternatives? In 1970, John Waterbury, an assistant professor of political science at the University of Michigan, would publish a study of political power in Morocco that incisively analyzed the balance of power in Morocco since independence—a work banned in Morocco for years.[26] Despite the professional relationship between Waterbury and Crapanzano (the former named the latter in his book's acknowledgments), this sort of political immediacy is missing from the widely circulating essay in the *New York Times Magazine*. Offering a portrait of the Moroccan king and his ministers as Janus-faced, masquerading at being modern when abroad while keeping traditional at home, Crapanzano's and Kramer's is a synchronic move that suggests the timelessness of power relations. The move writes out the monarchy's political repression (by framing it as traditional), General Oufkir's police state, the disappearance of opposition leader Mehdi Ben Barka in October 1965, and the jails that marked the unstable decade in Morocco. Thus even if they are correct about the role of the traditional in the sustenance of the regime's power, the turn away from a diachronic account is troubling given the reach of the *New York Times Magazine*.

The shift to the synchronic and the emphasis on the detachment of the masses from daily political life could be manipulated by the Moroccan government as it presented its own case to the United States. Washington was focused more on keeping Morocco strong in relation to Soviet-aligned Algeria than on domestic Moroccan complaints. In June 1965, for example, following the riots that provoked King Hassan II to declare a state of emergency, suspend the parliament, and name himself prime minister, the Moroccan ambassador Ali Benjelloun met with the U.S. secretary of state, Dean Rusk, in Washington. According to Rusk's summary, Benjelloun asserted that the opposition was making "unreasonable demands" and that the King's decision to suspend Parliament and assume control "was entirely within constitutional framework and in no way resembled coup d'etat [as] some French papers pictured [it]." That the Moroccan ambassador could safely assume that (foreign) newspaper accounts had some bearing on Washington's understanding and structured Washington's need to respond underlines the significance of the failure of U.S. accounts to challenge the regime. Benjelloun assured Rusk that the "initial reaction [of the] masses [was] favorable" to the king's hard line, a statement that might otherwise seem deeply compromised by its source. Rusk asked him about internal (and "externally-inspired") resistance to the King's action. Despite major party opposition, Benjelloun claimed that the "mass of people want strong and stable government." With that assertion, Secretary Rusk "offered best wishes to [the] King during this trying time as he worked to bring Morocco back to the kind of system of government he had envisaged for his people in promulgating constitution."[27] U.S. emphasis on Moroccan stability carried forward, particularly as a "polarization in the Arab world," as the National Security Council put it in 1967, drew Egypt, Algeria, and Syria toward socialism. Noting Soviet support, the NSC blamed Algerian allegiance with the Soviets for "stir[ring] up instability in Morocco and Tunisia."[28] Thus, the NSC decided, "our immediate problem is to give King Hassan a sense of stability." They recommended a $14 million arms sale and a new food agreement. Eight weeks after the June 1967 war, State Department intelligence reviewed the situation in the Maghreb. It noted Hassan's strengthening the authority of his "tough" interior minister Mohammed Oufkir in order to keep his domestic opposition "in line" and a crackdown on the country's strongest political groups. While the analysis worried that this would prolong the emergency rule still in place and impede the attempt to broaden the political base of his regime, it blamed tensions on a stagnant economy. Given Moroccan struggles to keep up with Algeria in an arms race, the kingdom could not afford to address these conditions without American military assistance.[29]

While we must presume that Crapanzano and Kramer were aware of the political features of les années de plomb (Waterbury included Crapanzano in the "congenial band of doctoral candidates with whom I compared notes frequently" [xvii]), the justification for their article as a means to understand the Arab present led American readers away from questioning the political repression at the heart of a regime that the United States supported financially and politically. It therefore also left unchallenged other popular accounts of contemporary Morocco that more pointedly ignore the political situation. The *Time* essay describing the hippies, for example, was published five months earlier. *Time* described the Moroccan head of state in shockingly benign terms that unwittingly supported the often cruel police state by turning attention away from it: "Under hard-working King Hassan II, Moroccans are still poor, but don't whine about it, and show no complex of inferiority. . . . The nation is Arabic [sic], but it permits full freedom of religion and takes a moderate stand in the Arab-Israeli conflict" (42). By not challenging such startlingly propagandistic misrepresentations of the Moroccan present and by turning American attention away from messy political reality, Crapanzano and Kramer's article effectively rendered invisible the errors of articles like *Time*'s. The essay and Kramer's *Honor to the Bride*, then, were unwittingly instrumental in constructing American understanding of Morocco as place of escape, of cultural and temporal distance. Of course, they didn't invent that position, as previous chapters have shown, and it would have been an uphill battle to have undone it. Crapanzano's writing from this period is, to be sure, terrifically subtle and important in thinking about cross-cultural communication. But my critique here is ultimately on the choice to publish in the *New York Times Magazine* and the ways in which the editing and circulation of the essay makes something different of it.

That my critique of this logic might be linked to Geertz's work might seem at first surprising. Crapanzano was not one of Geertz's students working in Sefrou and would later offer important critiques of Geertz's work on Morocco.[30] But Geertz's newly published book on Moroccan Islam, which was making a major impact on the field, established a basic premise applied here, namely that official statements (about Islam) had little bearing on an understanding of the region (or religion) which is best gleaned via the "perspective of the people," so long as one could glean that. The gesture in the *New York Times Magazine* essay is similar: don't trust the official account, but rather listen to what "the people" are saying. That's reasonable in principle. But in both cases, the turn toward the "traditional" and away from the official is accompanied by a turn away from the urban, from the educated, from those engaged in immediate political struggle, and from those contemporary Moroccan writers and filmmakers involved in the struggle for meaning. Before turning to Geertz's own writing about Morocco during this period, which I'll examine below in detail, I want to return briefly to the larger community of hippie Orientalists in Morocco. The separate strands of discussion of this moment might here profitably be brought together. The influence of Geertz was not as strong on the hippies as it was on Kramer and Crapanzano writing in 1969, though it might be possible to draw a tenuous line between the eminent anthropologist, a doctoral student in anthropology, and the latter's well-read wife who wrote about youth culture for a prominent publication. I begin this quick survey with Paul Rabinow, a young anthropologist who left the United States for Morocco in the late 1960s, not because he was one of Geertz's students (though he was) but because his work helps frame a common generational experience of what I call the turn away. My goal is to associate the shared tendencies in those who would represent Morocco during a certain moment, the final moment this book will consider. The larger problem revolves around the circumscription of the people itself and the occlusion of contemporary political reality from accounts of Morocco. Perhaps the temptations of cultural relativism that pervade accounts by the hippies helped spark the ascent of Geertz's writing more broadly. Perhaps the shared tendency to look at Moroccan culture synchronically and turn away from problems of power relations bespeaks something about the persistence of Orientalism as a way of organizing the world for those pertaining to powerful nations. What is certain is that these texts are part of the recent history of American thinking about the Arab world, have been especially influential, and are part of what Moroccans themselves grapple with and respond to in contemporary cultural and intellectual production.

The Turn Away

> Is our American society so insecure that it cannot tolerate our young
> people taking a year or two off, growing beards, wandering around the
> country, fooling with new forms of consciousness? This is one of the
> oldest traditions in civilized society. Take a voyage! Take the
> adventure! Before you settle down to the tribal game, try out
> self-exile. Your coming back will be much enriched.
> —Timothy Leary, 1966

At the end of his remarkable memoir, *Reflections on Fieldwork in Morocco*, which is part intellectual autobiography, part interrogation of the epistemology of cross-cultural encounter based on the author's experience in a small Moroccan village, Paul Rabinow brings it all back home. Having begun his book with a departure—"I left Chicago two days after the assassination of Robert Kennedy," is the book's stark first sentence—the narrative ends with a return:

> The "revolution" had occurred during my absence (1968–1969). My friends
> from Chicago, many of them now living in New York, were fervently and
> unabashedly "political" when I returned. . . . The whole reverie of future
> *communitas* which had sustained me through months of loneliness refused
> to actualize itself upon my return. . . . Perhaps the most bizarre dimension of
> my return was the fact that my friends were now seemingly preoccupied
> with the Third World; at least the phrase had an obligatory place in their
> discourse. I had just been in the Third World with a vengeance. Yet this
> Third World which they so avidly portrayed bore no obvious relation to my
> experiences. Initially when I pointed this out, I was politely ignored. When I
> persisted it was suggested that I was perhaps a bit reactionary.[31]

The passage suggests an intragenerational gap and confirms the transformative potential of international experience that Rabinow's book sets out to interrogate: the mystique and professional power of the fieldwork trip.

Rabinow ends by focusing on not how different he is from what he once was, but how different he is from his generation. Rabinow senses that the third world serves as an empty signifier for his peers, for whom experience is unwelcome when it doesn't confirm to their own uses. Of course, Rabinow's assumption is that his own particular experience in an isolated minor Moroccan village may discount whatever portrayals of the third world his friends make, an assumption impossible to defend without falling into the same trap he critiques, generalization. Why should the third world (as an entity) bear an "obvious relation" to his particular experiences? One need not defend Rabinow's friends to see the error in Rabinow's logic. When we reintroduce the striking students in Moroccan cities—far from the pastoral world of Sidi Lahcen Lyusi—it's clear that different experiences in Morocco during 1968 and 1969 might have yielded different reports.

Rabinow's peer Vincent Crapanzano makes a similar observation about his experience returning from Morocco in the late 1960s, which he analyzes in slightly different terms:

> When I left to do fieldwork in Morocco in 1967, hippie relativism was in the ascendancy—it was the time of the great be-ins—and when I returned almost two years later, after 1968, revolutionary dogmatism, political protest at least, was at its height. I saw the contradiction between relativism and dogmatism everywhere. Though one dominant stance had replaced another, the values of the former were not abandoned. Both positions shared a deep discontent with the way the world was and a sometimes overenthusiastic appreciation of otherness, be it exotic or utopian. (Often the two were romantically blended.)[32]

For Crapanzano, anthropologists were of especial interest to discontented Americans in the 1960s; they were "bearers of exotic wisdoms [who] described other social and political arrangements: extended families, primitive communisms, the spirit of communitas" (4–5). Given the ascendancy of relativism, it is easy to see the double attraction of writings by anthropologists such as Geertz, who theorized that stance while also delivering "exotic wisdom," and to understand the allure of other bearers of exotic wisdom such as Jane Kramer and cookbook writer Paula Wolfert, who maintained the relativism intact. Crapanzano's comment helps us see what Rabinow and his American friends had in common. Though

Rabinow was neither utopian nor overenthusiastic about Moroccan otherness, the ultimate structure of his project around the "comprehension of self by the detour of the comprehension of the other" (5, quoting Ricouer) allowed him to bypass aspects of contemporary Morocco that might have evaded the double bind. Rabinow claims that his project was attuned to history: "It is the culturally mediated and historically situated self which finds itself in a continuously changing world of meaning" (6). But that claim aside, the "self" Rabinow describes is freed from history while in Morocco, contained only by the historical parentheses of Robert Kennedy's assassination and 1969 New York. That disengagement from Moroccan history allows Rabinow to focus on the "culturally mediated" aspects of the self in Morocco; the historically situated self is situated elsewhere. A final paragraph introduces a Vietnamese character and the promise of another cultural situation in Rabinow's future—suggesting yet more powerfully that the turn to Morocco was a turn away from Southeast Asia.

Rabinow is sophisticated in his attempt to bridge the gap between American and Moroccan. But the failure, as he would call it, to do so is instructive and makes visible the ways in which relativism structures hippie Orientalism more largely considered. The passage quoted above is the coda to a discussion of Rabinow's difficulties forming a friendship with a Moroccan peer. Driss ben Mohammed had refused to work as Rabinow's "informant," thus opening up the possibility of friendship. But Rabinow concludes that different histories and pasts place a "fundamental Otherness" between them. For Rabinow, working within his teacher Clifford Geertz's paradigm of rapport, "dialogue was only possible when we recognized our differences, when we remained critically loyal to the symbols which our traditions had given us" (162). This is, for Rabinow, the beginning of "a process of change"—the final words of his memoir— though the contours of where that process may lead remain as vague as the final line of *Casablanca* it somehow evokes. Rabinow engages ben Mohammed on a sensitive topic: apparently racist comments about American blacks made by another, less educated Moroccan in the town where Rabinow worked, a man named Malik. When Rabinow brings up the topic with ben Mohammed, the latter "straddle[s] the cultural divide rather artfully" (146). The Moroccan criticizes Malik's expressions of racism and attributes them to lack of education. Then, ben Mohammed compares Malik's racist comments to discrimination in the United States: "No Moroccan would ever keep someone out of a hotel or a job because of his skin color." Rabinow interprets: "Cultures were different, ben Mohammed was saying. Even when they say the same thing, an expression can mean something entirely different when it is played out in society" (147).

Ben Mohammed has, in Rabinow's understanding, delivered back the relativism that had sustained Rabinow as anthropologist. In fact, however, ben Mohammed may not be saying what Rabinow interprets. His comparison of Moroccan expressions of racism and U.S. material actions is antirelativist. Still, Rabinow ignores what ben Mohammed has apparently said and himself bridges the relativist divide: he inquires whether ben Mohammed believes that Muslims and non-Muslims are equal. When a flustered ben Mohammed states that no, even the most "unworthy and reprehensible" Muslims are superior to all non-Muslims, Rabinow recoils. For ben Mohammed, according to Rabinow, "the division of the world into Muslim and non-Muslim was *the* fundamental cultural distinction, the Archimedean point from which all else turned. This was ultimately what separated us" (147). Rabinow steps back, quotes Aristotle on friendships of virtue, and recalls the "lessons of tolerance and self-acceptance which ben Mohammed had been teaching me during the past months" (148). In other words, he employs the lessons of ben Mohammed (relativism) in order to respond to ben Mohammed himself. This cannot be sustained, and Rabinow, as if in recognition of this crisis, evokes his "strong sense of being American. I knew it was time to leave Morocco." The passage is striking. By Rabinow's own evidence, ben Mohammed has refused relativist understanding. Yet he can be made to provide the lesson in irreducible difference that underlies Rabinow's project and which he brings back to the United States in 1969 to the dismay of his friends. The man who doesn't work as the American's "informant" is the same who compares Morocco and the United States. The work of the cultural anthropologist cannot be sustained by an informant who is able to make his own cultural comparisons. That work relies on the maintenance of separate spheres, unmediated difference. And thus the bearer of "exotic wisdoms" turns away.

Rabinow is provoked to have the conversation because he is troubled by Malik's expressions of racism. Reminders of the place left behind give him license to depart from the "dutiful" relativism that anthropology requires of him. But when Rabinow explains his "dutiful" refusal to confront Malik, he describes an imagined confrontation in troubling terms: "I am light in complexion with blue eyes and light brown hair," Rabinow begins. "I was tempted many times to ask Malik, who has a dark skin tone, kinky hair, and large lips, if he thought this made me superior to him, but I never did. There was no point in confronting him" (146). The recounting of racial phenotypes has a disturbing overtone, here, and the rhetorical question about racial superiority is, given the power relations that run through the entire book, hard to forget. Despite Rabinow's gesture not to assume that his readers share his racial characteristics (he identifies his own features and provides a photograph of himself surrounded by Moroccan men), the ways in which race and a hesitation to confront Malik are overlaid replaces or confuses cultural relativism with racial relativism.

Rabinow has earlier in the book encouraged readers to see the links between Moroccans and African Americans, which makes this later rhetorical question the more troubling. Earlier, Rabinow describes a ritual "night" held by the Aissawa brotherhood. His friend Ali has brought him to a curing ceremony for a sick boy, which involves hours of chanting, ritual dancing, "writhing," miming, and fire eating, all of which Rabinow watches from the sidelines:

> Perhaps the most surprising thing to me about the night was how totally natural it seemed. Both at the time and in retrospect, it had the same deeply calming and cathartic effect for me as seeing John Coltrane perform. In both cases, polished performers worked in and elaborated a cultural form in which they could explore feelings and troubled states of mind. Through this form they discovered and communicated a measure of release. The sweaty, drained expression Ali wore at the end of the "night" recalled an image of Coltrane leaning against the wall in a cellar club in New York, also dripping in sweat, also inhaling deeply on a cigarette, also looking peaceful, anticipating the storms of passion and confusion brewing within, but with an air of well-earned temporary release. (57)

For Rabinow, the event is easily observable: "The line between observer and participant was perfectly clear, which greatly facilitated the comprehension and enjoyment of the whole evening for me" (57–58). Fundamental difference is intact. But the reference to Coltrane—which might as well be to a photograph as to a memory of a performance—suggests an aestheticized connection between Moroccan and African American, both categories separated by a schism from the young observer. Strong "feelings and troubled states of mind" can thus be appreciated by white audiences viewing across "perfectly clear" lines of separation. It is worth mentioning that Coltrane himself felt much affinity with Islam, as Moustafa Bayoumi has noted in his reading of Coltrane's great song "A Love Supreme," but Rabinow's analogy summons a less particular linkage. Coltrane's wife Naima was a Muslim and he discussed Islam frequently with his friend Hassan Abdullah, the piano player; his sidemen regularly included Muslim musicians from Philadelphia. To be sure, Coltrane was portrayed by mainstream media as "blowing the sounds of black rage," though he denied the charge. According to Bayoumi, Coltrane was "yearning for a new kind of community, one based on a new universalism that has a (but not by necessity the only) base in Islam."[33] The influence of Islam in African American jazz extended far beyond Coltrane, of course. It was such that *Ebony* magazine had, in 1953, published an article on the phenomenon: "Moslem Musicians." In Rabinow's description, however, the aestheticization of the connection between Ali and Coltrane removes an important political or religious linkage and reduces the commonality to Rabinow's own sense of the clear distance separating himself from either.

This is the context within which Rabinow's turn away from the contemporary struggles of his Moroccan peers should be seen. While Rabinow places his trip within the context of the global crisis of 1968, that context is lost in Morocco. We might offer for contrast the young Moroccan who told French journalist Ignace Dalle, while on the streets of Paris in May 1968: "A revolution without deaths is not a revolution! If you had seen the ferocity of the repression that met the young Casablancans in March 1965, you would better understand what I mean."[34] That sense of shared experience does not appear in Rabinow's work. Ben Mohammed himself would have been the likely subject for such a conversation: he is a student and spends time outside the village where Rabinow works. Rabinow is among the most astute and self-aware chroniclers of the late 1960s ethos. So when he returns to the United States in 1969 and his friends accuse him of being reactionary, what have they discovered? Have they and he uncovered something more generally true about the experience from which he had returned and which he describes so well?

Michener's Vagabonds

> In Djemaa snake-charmers tame the serpents
> While the souls of men stay free,
> Inhabiting the edges of my mind
> In smoke-dreams that become reality.
> —James Michener, *The Drifters*

In *The Drifters*, James Michener takes a generation as his subject—Americans in their late teens and twenties in 1969, when he himself was sixty-one—and follows them on an itinerary beginning in Berkeley and New Haven and Cambridge leading to Spain's Costa del Sol, then Mozambique and finally to Marrakech. Michener, or the sixty-one-year-old narrator of *The Drifters* who resembles him, ultimately renders a harsh judgment about the hippies in Morocco:

> Most of the older people who visited Marrakech were surprised to find that among the young Americans, there were practically no old-style American liberals. This was true for obvious reasons. To get as far as Marrakech required real money, so that those who made it had to come from well-to-do families of a conservative bent, and throughout the world children tend to follow the political attitudes of their fathers. A boy of nineteen might rebel against Harvard University, country-club weekends and the dress of his father, and run away to Marrakech to prove it, but his fundamental political and social attitudes would continue to be those his father had taught him at age eleven. In my work I constantly met conservative adult Americans who, when they saw the young people with long hair and beards, expected them to be revolutionaries; they were pleasantly gratified to find that the young people were as reactionary as they were.[35]

There is a reductive quality to Michener's automatic association of presence in Morocco with wealth and of wealth with conservative politics (though the cost of a ticket to Casablanca was more expensive in 1969 dollars than today: "I've been savin' all my money just to take you there," csn sang). But the depth of Michener's research for the Marrakech portion of his novel and his extended interest in youth culture—his heavily researched report *Kent State: What Happened and Why* was published in the same year—encourages us to consider the author's implied question.

Were the hippies in Morocco reactionaries? Were the Marrakech hippies antipathetic to their countercultural brothers and sisters back in the United States? And further, was the lack of interest by the Moroccan left in connecting with American youth based on a correct interpretation of hippie politics?

Michener himself took a crack at understanding the hippies' soul. Michener's narrator in *The Drifters*, an American banker called George Fairbanks, is a sensitive observer of the hippie scene. Fairbanks wonders about the effect of Marrakech on the "soul" of the generation. He estimates that only a fraction of young Americans could survive places like Marrakech, with its temptations and freedoms and the accompanying dangers. So according to this narrator, places like Marrakech are both necessary and perilous. Michener's documentary portrait is remarkably vivid thirty-odd years later. His portrait skips over Moroccans of the same generation, however, which has two likely explanations: he followed the hippies' detachment from young Moroccans themselves accurately or he echoes the others I discuss here by turning his attention away from young Morocco.[36] The two positions are not necessarily isolated from one another, as Michener himself would have known. In the fictional song quoted above, composed by one of the Marrakech hippies in *The Drifters*, the narrator comments on the use of the word *reality*, which in the novel is a cipher for the generation's understanding of the term: "Its philosophical concept was a teasing one: 'Our generation had found reality.' The misty smoke-dreams so often alluded to in the new songs had little to do with reality; they referred specifically to marijuana and hashish, and this constant indoctrination explained in part why so many young people wanted to try the two experiences" (685–86). The comment seems as much a critique of Crosby, Stills, and Nash's "Marrakesh Express," which must have been very much on Michener's mind as he wrote this chapter set in 1969, as it does on the general tendency he calls reactionary. It also jibes with Elizabeth Fernea's account of conversation with American hippies in 1971 and 1972. Fernea saw them on a pathetic search for "the truth," which turns out to be a flight from family (who support them) and blurred by a romantic idea of poverty. They find themselves encountering hostility from Moroccans, a class structure they weren't expecting, the misery of true poverty.[37] For Michener, the hazy attempt to grasp Moroccan reality was a deferral of the political energies of young Americans that might otherwise have been directed toward politics or helping with Moroc-

A young vagabond walks through the Tetouan medina,
1973. *Photograph by Ben Edmonson, used with permission.*

can economic development. Development was Michener's own impulse,
modeled in the novel by Fairbanks and Harvey Holt, an American engi-
neer in his forties. Michener's young antiwar characters and draft dodgers
never engage or even discover the local population, outside the drug
dealers and touts. The poet of the group discovers there the theme or soul
of the generation but not in relation to Moroccan politics or culture: in
her ballad, to which Michener gives much attention, movement of Western youth across landscapes becomes a crusade rather than a cross-
cultural conversation.

The only character that exhibits any connection with young Moroccans is offered as a warning: Cato Jackson, a young black nationalist who has embraced Islam, identifies strongly with Moroccans. According to the novel, this identification exacerbates his worst tendencies. In a tense scene, Cato agrees with Moroccan engineers on the importance of doing away with Israel—the reflection of an anti-Israel attitude prevalent in Arab populations after the 1967 Israeli military victory. The novel sides against this position and offers the connection between Cato and the Moroccans only to unseat it, forebodingly. Fairbanks steers Cato to Meknes to show him the place where Sultan Moulay Ismail had tortured and killed thousands of black slaves. By employing a typical Michener strategy—opposing historical truth and myth, here the "truth" about Islam and black Africans—the narrative offers a warning about contemporary black radicalism's turn to Islam. In the novel, Cato is not convinced, and he leaves the novel wearing a red fez, planning to make his way to Mecca on foot. While Michener sympathizes, he depicts Cato's anger as unproductive and hopeless, employing the narrative techniques and what Edward Said has called the "aesthetics of lost causes."[38]

Michener's implicit association of Moroccans and African Americans is different from Rabinow's. In Michener's case, the association is dictated by contemporary politics. In an excellent discussion, Melani McAlister has shown ways in which African American cultural leaders engaged Middle East politics during this period and made links to Arab peoples based on race and religion, transnational alliances that superseded the nation form. In 1964, for example, when newly crowned boxing champion Cassius Clay announced his conversion to Islam, he garnered additional media attention. Muhammad Ali, as he was renamed by Elijah Mohammed, based his resistance to the Vietnam War on his religion: "I'm a member of the Black Muslims, and we don't go to no wars unless they're declared by Allah himself. I don't have no personal quarrel with those Viet Congs." According to McAlister, that stance "transformed Ali's image: vilified in the mainstream media, he became one of the most visible and influential antiwar figures in the country."[39] If Ali, along with other major converts to Islam such as LeRoi Jones (Amiri Baraka) and, earlier, Malcolm X, employed Islam in the domestic American context of the struggle for rights and against the war, he did so by invoking transnational relations based on race and religion. The Nation of Islam associated itself with the political struggles of the Arab world both as a "'colored' nation oppressed by whites," and on the basis of "cultural and religious identifications with Arab nations, which were understood to be also racial and historical."[40]

Michener's characterization of Cato Jackson responds to contemporary racial politics and delivers for his massive readership an account of a potent alliance. The author's management of this conversation between a young African American and professional Moroccans suggests a conservative recoil from that alliance on the part of white liberals. In *The Drifters*, Cato is romantically involved with Monica, a white woman whom the Moroccan engineers will eventually take away for a sexual weekend that precipitates her own horrible death. Because of the association of Cato with the Moroccans, the depravity of Monica's death suggests a narrative resolution and punishment for Monica's involvement with Cato and Cato's association with Arab nationalism. Thus the narrative fascination with the relationship between a strikingly beautiful young white woman and a black nationalist becomes a horror story. Michener's mediated response to the contemporary alliance of black nationalism with the Arab world mixes and confuses white American anxiety about mixed-race sexual relationships, American misgivings about the sexual liberation of young women in general, contemporary white liberals' anxiety about black radicalism, and a tradition of Orientalism that emphasized Arab sexual depravity.

We should not assume that the deferral of an engagement with Moroccan individuals within hippie Orientalism uniformly follows this racialized logic, but it does provoke further examination of the patterns with which Moroccan "reality" is met. Because domestic and international questions of race were so deeply intertwined, the association of Moroccans with temporal lag wrote the place, region, and religion that black nationalists were affiliating themselves as retrograde and itself racist. This management of the national narrative is a disturbing effect of Michener's commanding narrative.

Paula Wolfert's Philosophy of Abundance

To move among these things, amid a swirl of people buying and selling,
bargaining and bustling, is for me one of the great pleasures of life.
—Paula Wolfert, *Couscous and Other Good Food from Morocco*

Before moving on the most sophisticated writer emerging from this period—Clifford Geertz—I want to look at two last cases of hippie Orientalism from quite different locations: a cookbook and a music phenomenon. These cases were influential enough in their own right to help further consolidate the hippie tendency to disengage from the urban, but they also suggest the power and the persistence of the logic I've identified as it crosses over into apparently independent areas.

Paula Wolfert's extremely popular cookbook, *Couscous and Other Good Food from Morocco*, published in 1973 and continually in print, is an important example of the impulse toward disengagement even among those who would collaborate with Moroccans. On the one hand, Wolfert engaged directly with Moroccan women in the research for her book. In her quest for rare ingredients and regional ways of making the same dish, Wolfert entered markets and kitchens and spoke about her project with Moroccan women, several of whom are thanked in the acknowledgments. On the other hand, in her effort to describe the particularity of Moroccan culture—linked intimately with its cuisine—Wolfert tended to leave behind the comments made by Moroccan women and lean toward an understanding that resonated with hippie Orientalism. In the former case, the emphasis on the "good food" of Morocco meant that the traditional was equated with the best the culture had to offer and the modern or cosmopolitan (e.g., fusion cooking or local interpretations of international dishes) was written out of the picture. In the latter, the "translation" of Moroccan cooking for American kitchens meant leaving behind certain techniques used by Moroccan women; it also came with a certain amount of implicit ridicule of Moroccan women for not being able to acknowledge that there were different ways of cooking the same dish across the country. None of this is surprising for a cookbook—indeed it is common to the genre. But because of the way in which Wolfert consistently "explains" the food by explaining the culture, and vice versa, it bears comment. Wolfert's book did a great deal to popularize couscous in the United States. The ubiquity of instant couscous in U.S. supermarkets today—one contemporary brand available since the early 1990s is called "Marrakesh Express"[41]—contrasts with Wolfert's advice three decades ago on where to order it by mail. Since her book has been so influential and since its genre is different from those I've considered before in *Morocco Bound*, I want to linger briefly.

What's particularly interesting about Wolfert's representation of Morocco is how it mixes formulas familiar from literary Orientalism, an ethnographic impulse, and hippie relativism. Wolfert lived in Morocco for two years beginning in 1959, when she met the Bowleses and experienced the tail end of "queer Tangier." After eight years in Paris and the end of her first marriage, she returned to Morocco at the end of the 1960s.[42] She was accompanied by William Bayer, who would become her second husband and who himself wrote a novel set in Tangier (Bayer's photographs illustrate *Couscous*). Wolfert announces from the start that her project was not encyclopedic in its coverage, but a matter of "finding or developing a good recipe for every dish that I felt tasted good" (xiv). The book is remarkable for its attempt to express through a translation of the cuisine something about the extraordinariness of Moroccan culture. This is, certainly, a formulation common to cookbooks of foreign or ethnic cuisines, which often confuse the colorfulness or flavors of a cuisine with its peoples. And if Wolfert's cookbook is more fully and passionately committed to this idea than most—there are twenty pages of ethnographic prose on Morocco before even the spices are introduced, and the first recipes don't appear until page 51—it is very much a part of the genre to which it belongs. Still, her prose descriptions of Morocco echo the tendency to turn away from young Morocco and toward a relationship structured by Orientalism. Wolfert, who counted Paul Bowles among her friends and whose romantic partner's first novel was a fictionalization of Swiss adventurer and travel writer Isabelle Eberhardt's life, exhibits throughout her cookbook a deep awareness of Orientalist travel literature. The bibliography includes works by Bowles, Walter Harris, Westermarck's 1931 book of anthropology, and nineteenth-century travel accounts. Her description of kitchen equipment turns to Bowles for an esoteric flourish:

> If you are really dedicated, you can go to the Valley of Ammeln in the Anti-Atlas and find a special kind of unglazed earthenware pot that I first heard about from Paul Bowles. It looks like a pumpkin with a handle at the top; if you tap it lightly near a small air hole it cracks around the circumference, making a perforated line. Tapping along this line you end up with a perfectly matched top and bottom that fit together and will seal in the juices when you cook *tagines*. (47)

The object would seem to belie Wolfert's comment that one needs "very little new equipment to cook Moroccan food" (46). But the passage reveals how she authorizes her own knowledge on first-hand experience and privileges the anthropological.

The image of Wolfert that emerges resonates with colonialist literature and underlines the most striking aspect of Wolfert's book: the philosophy of abundance she attributes to Moroccan culture. She returns to this ethnographic point frequently: "At a Moroccan *diffa* (banquet) so much food is served that you can't imagine who is expected to eat it. . . . To puritans like us this may all seem vulgar, ostentatious, showy, and chauvinistic. To Moroccans it is the essential requisite of a feast" (8). Wolfert explains that leftover food is not wasted, but eaten by cooks and servants afterward. But she essentializes too: "Moroccans have large, healthy appetites; perhaps it takes them longer to achieve that state of total satisfaction which they call *shaban*." It's both classic Orientalism—she quotes nineteenth-century travel narratives and makes comparisons of Moroccan banquets to the Chinese, on little apparent evidence—and also tied to a hippie mantra. The Moroccan poor do not challenge the Orientalism, in Wolfert's understanding, because they pertain to a philosophy of abundance. Her theory of Moroccan cuisine issues from this philosophy: "Four things are necessary before a nation can develop a great cuisine." They are: "an abundance of fine ingredients—a rich land"; "a variety of cultural influences"; a "great civilization"; and the existence of a "refined palace life" (3). Having established this theory, the dishes themselves tend to bear out the theory, whether it's couscous, "which Craig Claiborne has called one of the dozen greatest dishes in the world" (2) and for which Wolfert gives seventeen variations, or *bisteeya*, a fantastic pigeon pie: "*Bisteeya* is so intricate and so grand, so lavish and so rich, that its extravagance always reminds me of *The Arabian Nights*. . . . *Bisteeya* is a totally Moroccan delight; it is not found anywhere else in the world. For me everything great in Moroccan culture (the influence of the Arabs and the Spanish Muslims, and the indigenous culture of the Berbers) is represented in this extravagant dish" (97–98). The dish inspires Wolfert to extravagant description.[43] What's striking is that Wolfert asserts an interpretation that, based on her own evidence, Moroccan women would reject: "there are numerous variations, though I have observed that Moroccans are so chauvinistic about the *bisteeyas* of their mothers and home-towns that they are shocked when I tell them the dish is prepared differently elsewhere" (100). Wolfert mocks such provinciality and, despite the early disavowal of an encyclopedic enterprise, describes several variations of the dish, including historical preparations gleaned from travel literature, and attempts to reconstruct the history of the dish back to the seventh century. The pages of history and theorizing signal Wolfert's refusal of "local knowledge" and her need to master the dish beyond that of Moroccan women. Wolfert even names an antagonist, a Tangier woman named Mina, locally famous for her *bisteeya*. Mina has apparently refused to teach Wolfert her technique for the most difficult part of the process (making the *warka* pastry from scratch) and though Wolfert is briefly rebuffed, she decides in the end that one need not be "brought up in a Moroccan home" (102), as is claimed, to master the dish. So, while Wolfert's project is an attempt to translate Moroccan cuisine for Americans, her impulse throughout is to capture the "authentic." These are in tension throughout. When she suggests how to adapt American equipment or ingredients to the foreign cuisine, she is nodding at that which is lost in translation. But when she exuberantly tracks down the esoteric, or offers a philosophy of abundance reflected in her epic recipes, she resists translation. That she puts it all in one encyclopedic location separates this book from the lessons of the Moroccan women she has drawn on, a shift that would not bother her. Her Morocco, after all, is admittedly the Morocco she learned about from reading Paul Bowles, Edward Westermarck, and the travel accounts that she quotes so often. The book that teaches couscous to Berkeley and Cambridge overwrites Moroccan poverty with abundance.

The Four-Thousand-Year-Old Rock Band

Around the time Paula Wolfert was wandering the Tangier souks, a separate cadre of Americans was spending time in a village in the Rif Mountains, an encounter that would affect what would eventually be known as "world music." Like Wolfert's engagement with Moroccan women, those who became fascinated with the music known as jajouka and who made it known to millions outside Morocco were in direct contact with their Moroccan counterparts. But like her, the embrace of the traditional and aversion from the contemporary helped solidify the turn away from young Morocco and buttress the sense of Morocco as a culture apart. The small town named Jajouka would quickly become world-famous and host some of the major figures of the music world.

There were strong links to literary Tangier, as with Wolfert, and a puta-
tive engagement with Moroccans—but also a turn away.

When Rolling Stone Records released the Brian Jones recording *The
Pipes of Pan at Joujouka* and Robert Palmer publicized it in *Rolling Stone*
magazine, both in 1971, the mythology of an otherwise obscure group of
musicians became known to millions of young Westerners. It was not of
course the first that the hip generation had heard of the group, which had
played a part in William Burroughs's 1962 cut-up *The Ticket That Exploded*; indeed a quote from Burroughs graced the advertisement for the
record that appeared in *Rolling Stone* magazine in late 1971. The musicians
themselves were closely allied to Burroughs's friend Brion Gysin (1916–
86), a Canadian American avant-gardist who had been fascinated with
the music since 1950, when Paul Bowles had taken him to the village.
Gysin featured the musicians in his fantastical Tangier restaurant 1001
Nights, which he opened in 1954 and ran until early 1958.[44] His 1969 novel
The Process introduced aspects of their mythology. Palmer's article "Ja-
jouka/Up the Mountain" relies heavily on Gysin, whom he calls "our one-
man crash course, filling our heads with sounds from his own tape library
and telescoping his 20 years of field recordings and speculation into a few
intensive weeks of talking and listening."[45] For Palmer, in fact, "the tragedy" was the lack of wide circulation of Gysin's and Bowles's extensive
knowledge about jajouka and Moroccan music in general, a knowledge
which "sits, for the most part, on shelves or in drawers, wrapped in layers
of plastic to ward off dampness and decay." Though Bowles had completed his massive project in recording Moroccan music several years
earlier, when Palmer wrote these words almost none of it had been made
available to the public. In 1967, an LP containing five tracks of Jilala music
(not to be confused with Jajouka) recorded two years earlier by Bowles
and Gysin was released; in 1972, the Library of Congress issued a two-
volume LP, *Music of Morocco*, that sampled Bowles's recordings of a variety of Moroccan musical forms. But jajouka had not been circulated
widely outside Morocco until Jones's recording was released. Thus the
fact that Jones altered his recordings, separating the tracks and playing some backward simultaneous to the accurate reproduction of other
tracks, is important from an ethnomusicological standpoint. Jones's elec-
tronically enhanced and altered trance music sounds quite different from
what Ornette Coleman would hear a couple of years later when he made
his own trip.

Though Palmer spent weeks researching his article and even played his clarinet with the Jajouka musicians, his essay became in large part a conduit of Gysin's knowledge to *Rolling Stone*'s readers. Via his new acolyte, guru Gysin delivers an account of jajouka's relationship to contemporary politics, an account that might appeal to the counterculture:

> Now the political development of the music in all the countries has been that, as soon as a nationalist revolution is successful, they immediately want to put down their own music; to get out of their old clothes and get into levis. Here, at the moment of Independence in 1956, there were enormous parades with the entire population streaming through the streets for several weeks on end. They were beating up any Moroccan musicians who even dared to make a squeak and started huge samba lines shouting, "The samba and the rhumba are the national music of New Morocco."
>
> All the musicians who were caught were taken away and put in concentration camps . . . ; they were going to be settled down and taught useful handicrafts. (42)

Gysin's account is spurious. But what's interesting about it is the way in which it suggests that the music is allied with a resistance to authority, something Western youth culture could identify with, whether or not it heard it in the whining wails of the *ghaita* (a double-reeded wooden horn) and the complex percussive rhythms. The implication is that jajouka is a countercultural force in Morocco, opposed to the state, an opinion counterindicated by the lack of a larger Moroccan audience for the music at the time and the apolitical activities of the musicians themselves. Thus when the advertising campaign for Brian Jones's recording named the group "The 4000 year old Rock and Roll band," it sought to link that unproven countercultural hypothesis with the establishment of a primitive ancestry for Western rock and roll. In so doing, the contemporary struggle of young Moroccans elsewhere was written out. A full-page ad for the new album solidified this account and linked them to the hippie counterculture's elder statesmen. Under the words "The 4000 year old Rock and Roll band," a large picture of a spectral-looking Brian Jones appears. (Jones had died in 1969, a year after recording the musicians.) Jones had, in fact, according to Palmer, spent only one day in Jajouka; his estate, however, stood to receive all the royalties from the album (43). Blurbs from William Burroughs and Timothy Leary attest to the mixture of "hip" and four-thousand-year-old "wisdom" of the musicians, a formula that is classic hippie Orientalism: the musicians' hipness is based on their temporal lag. They are thus named as the "primitives" of the hippie move-ment, contemporaries who are somehow prehistoric ancestors. This tem-poral double bind would seem to promise confusion for those who actu-ally visited Jajouka. When Palmer arrived at the overinscribed place and was met by the stares of children and attentive adults, he took recourse to a space-age metaphor: "Overwhelmed, we sat on a rock in the middle of the surge and the sunlight, utter strangers utterly at home. 'The Mother Ship,' was all I could say, 'the Mother Ship'" (42). To be an utter stranger utterly at home is, after all, the hippie Orientalist mantra. It organizes Palmer's response to jajouka, and the mythology of jajouka that Palmer helped circulate solidified the hippie response to Morocco.

As Philip Schuyler has shown, such a division was carefully orches-trated by Gysin, the single most important force behind the phenome-non. Schuyler surveys the mythologizing of the Jajouka, as a literary phenomenon that crosses over into "world music" and alters a Moroccan community: "Musicians and listeners alike pretend, and perhaps actually believe, that, despite all the exposure to the West, the music of Jajouka is ancient, authentic, and unique."[46] Even before Gysin introduced Brian Jones to Jajouka or mythologized the annual festival of Bou Jeloud as the "rites of Pan" based on a spurious interpretation linking pagan rites of the goat god with contemporary Moroccan Muslim practice (one that Mo-roccan anthropologist Abdellah Hammoudi disproved in *The Victim and Its Masks*), Gysin's approach to the Jajouka musicians was already orga-nized. At Gysin's Tangier restaurant—frequented by Barbara Hutton, William Burroughs, the Bowleses, and the Tanjawi upper class—the Ja-jouka musicians' "authenticity" was guarded through isolation. Gysin for-bade the performers to listen to the radio, "because I had heard the disastrous influence of that sort of movie music that comes from Cairo that has drowned out all the local musics in practically all the Islamic world."[47] Schuyler calls it "schizophonophobia," "a fear of sounds sepa-rated by the recording process from their original source" (153), and notes that Gysin's phobia did not inhibit him from allowing others to record the jajouka musicians themselves.

Palmer's essay was more than an interview; it also served as an invita-tion to his reader to join in. He mentions a folklore festival in Marrakech and another then planned for Tangier. His own participation, repre-sented in the essay, is especially enticing. Palmer describes himself "weav-ing and bobbing to the music, the flutes floating free over a piledriver 6/8 rhythm straight down from remotest Near Eastern antiquity, and the drummers shouting 'Aiwa'—'Everything's groovy.'" To translate "aiwa"—a punctuating remark in Moroccan Arabic that might be rendered "alas" or "well"—as "everything's groovy" is hippie Orientalism *par excellence*. The chief drummer approaches Palmer and interpellates him: "I know you are a musician," he says through an interpreter. Palmer is thrilled: "I am found out, I am recognized, and I can see that putting away the tape recorder and getting out my horn is the only way I am going to get *this* show on the road" (44). Substituting clarinet for pen, Palmer is at home.

Palmer's essay provoked others to follow, leading to one of the most interesting of American-Moroccan collaborations. After reading Palmer's essay and listening to his tapes back in the United States, Ornette Coleman entreated Palmer to take him to Jajouka. Coleman's January 1973 trip to Jajouka, a small part of which was released years later on *Dancing in Your Head* (1977), was a key collaboration for this major jazz composer. Biographer John Litweiler and musicologist Scott Currie both identify Coleman's experience in Jajouka as integral to his elaboration of the "harmolodic," an important development in his musical philosophy. As Coleman defined the notion, "the rhythms, harmonies, and tempos are all equal in relationship and independent melodies at the same time. To read or write or play without reading or writing; to execute our ideas on an instrument; isn't that the result of us all in making musical sounds that we feel and think for those who love music?"[48] The collaboration with the Jajouka musicians allowed Coleman to experiment with playing in "unison," as he used the term, and thus to experiment with the concept of harmolodics across national boundaries. Litweiler explains that Coleman "does not usually use 'unison' to mean musicians playing the same notes simultaneously, but rather in some of the word's other senses . . . a union or combination of concordant sounds; a united and unanimous declaration or utterance . . . Sounding at once or together."[49] In Coleman's liner notes to *Dancing in Your Head*, the Master Musicians of Jajouka themselves achieve this sense of unison playing: "Even though there is no 'Western' pitch, one hears unison (check it out, student)." By experimenting collaboratively, Coleman built on the idea of unison playing in a transnational frame. In his account, "the music conceives a performance of compositional improvising with the Western and Eastern musical forms resolving into each other's lead."

Before arriving in time for the annual Bou Jeloud festival, Coleman composed themes to play with the musicians; after the first evening playing with them, he quickly devised additional themes.[50] Robert Palmer accompanied on clarinet, and Steve Goldstein recorded several nights of Coleman and Palmer playing with the Master Musicians. According to Litweiler, for the first several days recording was a "meeting of cultures: ancient Berber [*sic*] and America's modern jazz" (152). But then Coleman composed a new piece, "Music from the Cave," inspired by a religious shrine located in a cave. The piece was composed for drummers, strings, *gimbris* (a three-stringed Moroccan instrument), and wooden flutes, with Coleman on trumpet. Palmer called this piece "the perfect bridge from his idiom to theirs. . . . All the musicians on 'Music from the Cave' were playing in one world, and I think that world was equally new to all of us."[51] The piece itself, however, has not been released, and the general listener has only this enticing comment to go on. Enough material was recorded for three albums, and Coleman selected enough for release as a Columbia double album.[52] But budget cuts led Columbia to drop the project. "Music from the Cave" was not released, and only one track from Coleman's collaboration with the Master Musicians, a piece called "Midnight Sunrise," was included on *Dancing in Your Head*. In "Midnight Sunrise," Jajouka musicians—on ghaitas, gimbris, and percussion—play a piece locally known as "Hadra," which was regularly performed at a local shrine.[53] Coleman plays a newly composed improvised line on the alto saxophone, complexly interweaving his line with Hadra's complex and asymmetrical rhythmic cycle. Coleman would later comment: "Sounded as if I had rehearsed it with them. It wasn't true. Not at all."[54] A second take, released only in 2000, lets us hear Coleman play the same line over a different piece by the Jajouka, which Currie says "suggest[s] a Jibli folk tune rather than a sacred call to prayer." Palmer's wild clarinet—playing in "unison" on the "harmolodic" concept—can be heard much more clearly on this take. As Currie comments, this wilder "duo improvisation [has] a spiritual fervor that seems at times to border on ecstatic possession. . . . Unfortunately, the intensity of their mutual interaction leaves little room for the Jajoukans, whose music recedes into the background."

Coleman's relationship with Palmer subjected the former to Gysin's interpretation of the Master Musicians, as well as the mutual (mis)comprehension that marks Brian Jones's briefer project. Philip Schuyler briefly mentions Coleman in his essay and suggests that Coleman's rhetoric evokes Gysin's Orientalist project. Schuyler juxtaposes the Jajoukans' own memory of working with Ornette Coleman: "They were very impressed by Coleman's musicianship but also confused by his performance practice: 'He could write down anything that we played, exactly. But when he played what he had written, it didn't sound like us at all.'"[55] Be that as it may, Coleman's project also suggests an interruption of hippie Orientalism. The contours themselves were structured by the temporal presumptions of hippie Orientalism. But Ornette Coleman's unreleased tracks, particularly the enticing "Music from a Cave," offer a possibility for interruption, based on a communication that emerges from his theory of the harmolodic and unison playing. They are therefore comparable to Jane Bowles's unpublished fragments. Coleman's unheard tracks occupy an isthmus between cultures, and like Jane Bowles's late work, Coleman's tracks have not been circulated. As Coleman performs in the cave, he momentarily inhabits that space.

Thick Intertextuality

> If I feel at the moment slightly more optimistic about the Moroccan
> situation than I do about the Indonesian, I fear it is only because I have
> not been studying it as long. . . . the sort of moral atmosphere in which
> someone occupationally committed to thinking about the new states
> finds himself, often seems to me not entirely incomparable to that of
> the cancer surgeon who can expect to cure only a fraction of his patients
> and who spends most of his effort delicately exposing severe
> pathologies he is not equipped to do anything about.
> —Clifford Geertz, "Thinking as a Moral Act"

When Clifford Geertz arrived in Sefrou, Morocco, in 1963, it was long enough after the dissolution of the French protectorate for him to imagine that "the status quo" in his chosen fieldwork site had been "restored." Thus Sefrou could be for him "a place where nothing very spectacular happened, and which remained agrarian, peripheral, and rather traditional" but also a place where things were getting "steadily, carelessly, . . . instructively out of hand."[56] The sense of imminent change in a classic place (as opposed to a new beginning for a recently independent state) ties Geertz's sense of Sefrou, uneasily, to that with which this chapter began.

During the years that Geertz focused on Sefrou, it maintained for him its antique aspect: "In the sixties and through most of the seventies, Sefrou not only looked like a classic medina, Moroccan style, an enchanted oasis defying the Atlas, 'a little Fez'; for the most part, it behaved like one."[57] To behave like a classic medina meant that Sefrou could still evoke "the same scene that had astonished a whole series of earlier experience seekers— Leo Africanus in the sixteenth century, Père Foucauld in the nineteenth, Edith Wharton during the First World War." Geertz's references are tellingly literary, the classic travel accounts and Orientalist adventure stories of previous epochs: "A French-built fort out of *Beau Geste* looked down on all this from one knoll, a white-domed Muslim shrine out of *En Tribu* looked down on it from another."[58] For Sefrou (and Morocco) to be again "peripheral"—despite what Geertz calls a "short period . . . of guerrilla activity" during the struggle for independence—was particularly important for Geertz as he looked for a place in which to set up anthropological shop. His avoidance of Algeria next door, still tense in 1963 after a long fight for independence (1954–1962), and at odds throughout the 1960s with Morocco, with which it was in a minor arms race, is precisely the point; if a culture is to be interpreted like a text, that text must first be made stable.

Geertz's writing about Morocco during the 1960s and 1970s is complex and varied, and to discuss it in the context of some of the much more casual encounters that American hippies had with Morocco during the same period—a song here, a couple of weeks there—is to risk obscuring the deeper connections that Geertz's work has with what I call hippie Orientalism. Geertz himself was greatly concerned with the moral dimensions of the work that he was doing, and he hardly was blind to the possibility that work such as his own operated within a political universe. That awareness leads him to theorize the relationship of thinking to moral action, in his 1968 essay "Thinking as a Moral Act." His conclusion is that thinking itself, and the knowledge production he was engaged in, might have little ability to ameliorate the problems of the "new states" (his principal examples are Indonesia and Morocco). Geertz's pessimism emerges as he considers the epistemological basis of the production of such knowledge. His awareness of the stark economic differences—what he calls "life chances"—between Moroccan informants and the American anthropologist led Geertz to theorize that the communicative act itself was structured around and ultimately hampered by a prevailing irony.

Geertz calls this irony "anthropological irony," and while he distinguishes it from literary irony, he suggests that both are modes of expressing the gap between "reality" and "human views of it."[59] The conversation itself has entirely different relationships to the actors' futures: for the anthropologist it is the source of professional advancement, whereas for the informant, it is of benefit more secondary (temporary financial gains, temporary interest, etc.), if at all. The greater problem that Geertz indicates, then, comes from the knowledge that might emerge from a science based on data gathered from within ironic conversation. Thinking about the "new states and their problems," Geertz suggests, is "more effective in exposing the problems than it is in uncovering solutions for them" (142). Geertz presents the evidence backward, but they are inextricably linked and lead to a depressing thought: "Knowledge—at least the sort of knowledge I have been able to dig up—does not always come to very much in the way of power" (142). This was, to be sure, not merely a theoretical conclusion of the problems in establishing rapport. Rather it was a condition that afflicted the American anthropologist daily. Such conditions structure, whether consciously or not, the anthropologist's own relationship to affective relationships while in the "field":

> This is an alarming thought; and the initial response to it is the appearance of a passionate wish to become personally valuable to one's informants—i.e. a friend—in order to maintain self-respect. The notion that one has been marvelously successful in doing this is the investigator's side of the touching faith coin: he believes in cross-cultural communion (he calls it "rapport") as his subjects believe in tomorrow. It is no wonder that so many anthropologists leave the field seeing tears in the eyes of their informants that, I feel quite sure, are not really there. (151)

This startling scene is played out in Paul Rabinow's turn away from Driss ben Mohammed at the end of *Reflections*, in Jane Kramer's description of the scene between Ahmed, Hugh, and Madame Hugh in *Honor to the Bride*, and, minus the irony, in a scene I haven't discussed: the departure of Elizabeth Fernea's family in 1972 after a year in the Marrakech medina, as described in *A Street in Marrakech*. Here in 1968, when anthropologists were the supposed bearer of exotic wisdom about *communitas*, it is a powerful disincentive to the idea of nonironic rapport.

I am not suggesting that a reading of Geertz's disavowal of the power of knowledge and his explication of the irony structuring relationships between Moroccans and Americans was somehow the justification for the "turn away" that I located above in hippie Orientalists. However, given the urgency of the political impulses in new states such as Morocco in the sixties—recall the malaise among Moroccan youth that Tessler had identified in Morocco between 1965 and 1975—the "pessimism" that Geertz communicates is hardly a call for arms or an inspiration to younger anthropologists and writers such as Rabinow, Crapanzano, Kramer, or Fernea to imagine alliances at all. Geertz's work of the period is occupied with a series of intertwined projects, all of which influenced the course of much study: the gathering of knowledge about the "new states" for a University of Chicago–based institute, the direction of the work of a small group of graduate students as part of a team study in and around Sefrou, and the theorization of the very knowledge he was gathering alongside and inscribed within his presentation of that material. Thus Geertz's thinking played out multiply. If irony might structure the relationships of Americans trained in cross-cultural encounter with Moroccans, on what basis might American hippies imagine an affiliation with Moroccan youth? Geertz understood this at the time, I believe, but he had no philosophical route out of it, except a refusal to give up "reality" and "science" and to resist the postmodern turn that he inspired. By turning attention to the close encounter with otherness, the more quotidian questions of Moroccan government's repression of dissent could be made to seem otherworldly ("experience distant," in Geertz's phrase).

Rather than offer this as a final word, I want to explore Geertz's own recourse to textuality within his discussions of Morocco. I'm not sure whether his move toward textuality is ultimately a dodge from the pessimism that he expresses in "Thinking as a Moral Act," or a distraction that may help to explain his own inability to move beyond diagnosis, to use his metaphor. But it is also a choice on my part that reflects the influence of Geertz's work on a certain brand of literary and cultural studies, for which Geertz's theory of culture as text came attractively ready-made for use. Geertz has been much discussed and debated in the field of anthropology, though less so in literary studies. In the 1960s and 1970s, his strong influence on the group of anthropologists who worked with him and in his wake in Morocco (including Rabinow, Lawrence Rosen, and Hildred Geertz, in the former case, and Vincent Crapanzano, Dale Eickelman, Daisy Dwyer, Kevin Dwyer, and Henry Munson in the latter) directed many of the concerns of American anthropology in subsequent years and was a key touchstone for the textual turn. When Geertz arrived in Sefrou, anthropology based on fieldwork in North Africa had little influence on the larger field as a whole. Yet, in great part because of Geertz's work, which encouraged others to follow him to Morocco (even if to dispute his claims), Morocco subsequently became a "prestige zone" for American anthropologists.[60]

Though Geertz's work made a significant impact on American literary studies and cultural studies, the relation of his ideas to colonial and postcolonial discourse remains underinvestigated. Since Geertz likens culture to a literary text, we must understand Geertz's conception of culture, as developed in Morocco, in the context of his literary precursors in the region. Despite his assertion that Sefrou was "peripheral," Geertz intervened in a region that had been inscribed and reinscribed by Western writers for generations. Thus his comment that "[Sefrou] was not only made for a monograph; it sorted itself into chapters" is striking since his literary-criticism-like analysis of Sefroui culture does not engage itself in an analysis of the literary portraits of Moroccan society that preceded his own.[61] Geertz, who contributed significantly to the analysis of ethnographic writing as literary text, has not critiqued literary writings in terms of their ethnographic impulses. Despite the temporal and regional overlap of his writing with Paul Bowles's, Geertz has barely even mentioned Bowles in his own writing, which is itself distinguished by a Jamesian style and allusions to many writers of fiction.[62] Indeed, the essay I began with, "Thinking as a Moral Act," is perhaps best remembered for its anecdote about a disagreement between Geertz and a Javanese informant over Geertz's typewriter. The Javanese, a clerk with literary aspirations, borrowed Geertz's typewriter with increasing frequency until Geertz inadvertently insulted him by refusing him access one day. Geertz is aware of the battle over words, and though he maintains an asymmetrical sense of the two men's relationship to authorship—"he was as far from being an inglorious Milton as I was from being a Javanese" (154)—the literary battle is key.

Geertz's understanding of "culture," as delineated in "Thick Description: Toward an Interpretive Theory of Culture" (1973) and as applied and refracted in *Islam Observed: Religious Development in Morocco and Indonesia* (1968) and *Meaning and Order in Moroccan Society* (1979), equates culture to a text, a system of meanings which the anthropologist as literary critic must interpret. "The enterprise," he writes in "Thick Description," is "like that of the literary critic."[63] Geertz engages in the "translation of culture," to borrow a phrase the British anthropologist Edward Evans-Pritchard used to describe the work of cultural anthropology. The goal of such a translation is, in the words of Dale Eickelman, to "mak[e] explicit the underlying logic of these shared patterns of meaning and codes of conduct."[64] Thus the "translation of culture" assumes that there are "patterns of meaning" shared across cultural and national boundaries. In colonial anthropology, that translation of difference tended to reinforce views of the other that maintained the colonial order of things.[65] Geertz explicitly seeks to revise the premises and biases of the anthropology that precedes him, both French anthropology during the protectorate and that done elsewhere by his predecessors in the discipline. "Translation," nonetheless, is one of the central impulses in Geertz's interpretive anthropology, which relies on the idea that culture is a text, and that such a text can be translated.

The narrative impulse in Geertz's theory of culture challenges the assumption that Moroccan "culture" is legible. His need for Sefrou to "behave" like a "classic" Moroccan town elides the ways in which a failure of Sefroui culture to behave would challenge his analysis of Moroccan Islam or the Moroccan marketplace, two of his broader projects. One of the problems of taking "local knowledge" (the title of one of Geertz's essay collections) and telescoping out from Sefroui to Moroccan culture at large is thus the requirement that the "local" behave. Geertz's likening of culture to a literary text encourages him to frame the local in narratives that edit out extraneous (i.e., nonbehaving) material. His adoption of the text metaphor when Morocco was already "morocco bound"—overinscribed by "Orientalist" texts—is a problematic corrective to colonial anthropology.

George Marcus has recently argued that Geertz's work represents the apogee of traditionally organized ethnography and that it should be seen in connection with the historical intertwinedness of anthropology and colonialism. Marcus notes the ways in which Geertz comes up against his own reflexivity and glimpses the possibility of a future hyperreflexivity: "After a complicated treatment . . . he turns away from [this subject] in favor of accepting the fictions of fieldwork relations so that ethnographic interpretation and the historic anthropological project to which he is committed can continue."[66] Marcus is ultimately trying to reimagine complicity as a technique for the changed circumstances of fieldwork in the

1990s. In so doing, he looks back carefully at Geertz, working in a different mise-en-scène for fieldwork—the height of the moment of development, but also the height of the belief in positivism in social sciences. Geertz's move toward reflexivity was, Marcus shows, also a retreat from it, and Geertz held on to his "commitment to the frame of reference in which anthropology could be done" (92). Other recent critics, both sympathetic and not, have levied criticism at Geertz for this detachment.[67]

In a critique of Geertz's now canonical essay "Deep Play: Notes on the Balinese Cockfight," Crapanzano notes the centrality of translation to the problems with ethnography. Alluding to Walter Benjamin's essay "The Task of the Translator," Crapanzano writes, "Like translation, ethnography is also a somewhat provisional way of coming to terms with the foreignness of languages—of cultures and societies. The ethnographer does not, however, translate texts the way the translator does. He must first produce them. Text metaphors for culture and society notwithstanding, the ethnographer has no primary and independent writing that can be read and translated by others. No text survives him other than his own."[68] Crapanzano likens the ethnographer to Hermes: "He clarifies the opaque, renders the foreign familiar, and gives meaning to the meaningless. He decodes the message. He interprets." Noting that Hermes was associated with boundary stones, Crapanzano suggests that the ethnographer "also marks a boundary: his ethnography declares the limits of his and his readers' culture" (44). Thus for Crapanzano, the "translation of culture" itself reveals the boundaries of the culture from which the ethnographer travels, and to which his or her ethnography will return. The decoding of cultural messages can take place only within the boundaries of the ethnographer-translator's cultural frame of reference. But since ethnography relies on the presumption that its material is gathered abroad, the "translation of culture" cannot erase the fact that it is a translation: "[The ethnographer] must also communicate the very foreignness that his interpretations (the translator's translations) deny in their claim to universality. He must render the foreign familiar and preserve its very foreignness at one and the same time" (44).

In "Thick Description," his landmark essay of 1973, which Geertz called "an attempt to state my present position as generally as I can" (ix), Geertz enacts this simultaneous familiarization and preservation of the foreign through a staged cultural translation. Geertz offers an excerpt from his Moroccan field journal, the text upon which the theoretical elaboration of his anthropology revolves. The excerpt is a story, set in 1912 and recounted to Geertz in 1968. It is a story about the early days of the French protectorate in Morocco, a tale about shifting and overlapping realms of authority between a Jewish sheep trader, armed Berber thieves, and anxious French colonial officials. For Geertz, it is a story that revolves around misunderstandings between members of the various social groupings represented in Morocco in the first year of the protectorate: "What tripped Cohen [the sheep trader] up, and with him the whole, ancient pattern of social and economic relationships within which he functioned, was a confusion of tongues" (9). The "confusion of tongues" suggests a linguistic problem, but in Geertz's story, the various characters speak each other's languages. The problem posed to Geertz by the story is how to translate it, how to make its logic understandable to a non-Moroccan audience. Geertz's linguistic metaphor leads, or cedes, to a larger one, the one for which the essay is famous: "Doing ethnography is like trying to read (in the sense of 'construct a reading of') a manuscript—foreign, faded, full of ellipses, incoherencies, suspicious emendations, and tendentious commentaries, but written not in conventionalized graphs of sound but in transient examples of shaped behavior" (10). Whereas "culture"—which Geertz goes on to call "this acted document"—is not written in our traditional understanding of writing, it is for Geertz nonetheless written through behavior. Thus, the anthropologist's explication of the foreign culture is ultimately a literary enterprise: "Analysis," Geertz writes, "is sorting out the structures of signification . . . the enterprise . . . [is] like that of the literary critic" (9).

The appropriation of Morocco as a text to be interpreted requires that that text be made stable enough to permit analysis. Thus it is significant that in Geertz's elaboration of his theory of the interpretive study of culture, he offers a narrative from which to argue his theory. The text is Geertz's own, not in the sense that he has invented it, but in the sense that it is he who delivers it, he who provides the terms from which he makes his claims about Moroccan culture. Without a common body of Moroccan "texts" to analyze, the critic of Geertz's work is forced either to reinterpret his material (a daunting prospect, since the material is presented readymade for Geertz's interpretations) or to go to the "field" to gather new information with which to propose alternative interpretations of Moroccan culture. Alternatively, the critic can launch a critique of Geertz's own text-metaphor. Such critiques have not been lacking, but it remains to be argued how Geertz's very choice of a location from which to propound the text-metaphor is implicated in a longer tradition of American representations of Morocco. Geertz's text-metaphor reveals itself in a culture already overinscribed by Western metaphors; Geertz often parrots them.

In elaborating the tale of the sheep trader, Geertz suggests an encapsulated "translation":

> Cohen might have concluded that between renegade Berbers and Beau Geste soldiers, driving trade in the Atlas highlands was no longer worth the candle and retired to the better-governed confines of the town. This, indeed, is more or less what happened, somewhat further along, as the Protectorate moved toward genuine sovereignty. But the point here is not to describe what did or did not take place in Morocco. (From this simple incident one can widen out into enormous complexities of social experience.) It is to demonstrate what a piece of anthropological interpretation consists in: tracing the curve of a social discourse; fixing it into an inspectable form. (19)

As Geertz fixes his tale into "an inspectable form," widening it out to explain larger social complexities, he tacks on curious adjectives, themselves acting as interpretations. The French colonial officers become "Beau Geste soldiers," the Berbers "renegades," and the sheep trader someone who decides that trade is after all not "worth the candle." The reference to *Beau Geste*, the British novel by P. C. Wren and a 1926 American film made by Paramount (remade in 1939 by Paramount and again in 1966 by Universal), is most striking, because Geertz uses it as an explanatory device, condensing his portrait of officers of the French Protectorate into a more familiar (to Americans, that is, not to Moroccans) shorthand. And the "renegade" Berbers fit nicely into his cinematic image, now suggesting (as does the Hollywood *Beau Geste*) renegade Indians of Hollywood Westerns, a place further suggested by Geertz's phrase "worth the candle," with its evocation of a candle-carrying pioneer. Geertz elsewhere encourages us to read his romantic Morocco as half *Beau Geste*, half American frontier, with another of his sweeping explanatory metaphors: "Morocco, Middle Eastern and dry . . . extrovert, fluid, activist, masculine, informal to a fault, a Wild West sort of place without the barrooms and the cattle drives."[69] These curious metaphors—the latter appears not in a travel article or memoir, but in a theoretical essay, titled ironically enough " 'From the Native's Point of View' "—are, I would like to suggest, a prime example of the simultaneous maintenance of foreignness and familiarization of the different which Crapanzano finds typical of Geertz's work elsewhere. If Morocco is like *Beau Geste*, or like the Wild West, it is still "foreign" to Geertz's late-twentieth-century American readers, but it is foreign in a familiar way, modified by those romantic images of a West and East that never quite were.

The problem, of course, is that these explanatory metaphors are not fully detached from "reality," and that with a bit of literary panache, Morocco can be made to conform to them. Such is the danger of not recognizing the productive power of inherited preconceptions of the space considered "exotic," as Edward Said noted in *Orientalism*. As Said argued in that work, the "scholar who is not vigilant, whose individual consciousness as a scholar is not on guard against *idées recues* all too easily handed down in the profession," falls into the trap of a "corrupt" scholarship.[70] Surely Geertz takes a more active "interest" in Morocco than to leave his analyses of the culture at the level of works such as *Beau Geste*, but since his vision of Moroccan culture is that it is "like" a text, and his own work "like that of the literary critic," the reliance on Orientalist texts as shorthand for his own translation of that already overinscribed Moroccan text compromises his very position. In proposing himself as the anthropologist-cum–literary critic of textbook Morocco, Geertz thus establishes his own authority as arbiter in a curious light.[71] He becomes an "experience seeker" in the Orientalist tradition (he places himself after Leo Africanus, Père Foucauld, and Edith Wharton, in that construction). It is a tradition Geertz imagines has something to recommend to the scientist, because (he implies) it deals with texts. Thus when Geertz portrays Fez in his memoir, taking on a nostalgic tone reminiscent of Bowles ("it seemed to be finally, definitively, losing its looks," Geertz writes), he quotes Edith Wharton's description of the city in *In Morocco* and praises her as the forerunner to the modern ethnographer: "The distant, superior, but marvelously observant Edith Wharton, who saw [Fez] for a few days in 1917."[72] As scientist, Geertz becomes the participant-observer (where his visible participation is removed from sight shortly after it is established) to a *Beau Geste*, Wild West drama of cowboys and Indians, without the barrooms, without the cattle. The mixed allusions to both Orient and Wild West are perhaps the by-product of his richly allusive narrative style, but they cross over from style into substance in the interpretive work Geertz sets out to accomplish.

To consider Morocco a text may distance Geertz's work from the classic anthropology he critiques, but it brings him closer to the literary works he invokes. This is not to say that Geertz was not analyzing Moroccan culture itself, or imagining that he was doing so, but to say something about directing attention toward a certain aspect of Morocco. Geertz frequently remarks on his debt to the work of Kenneth Burke (whose essays on "symbolic action" are clearly Geertz's reference), so it is appropriate to reinvoke Burke's idea that the terminology we adapt to discuss "reality" directs the attention toward certain interpretations of that reality to the exclusion of others. As Burke puts it, "Even if any given terminology is a *reflection* of reality, by its very nature as a terminology it must be a *selection* of reality; and to this extent it must function also as a *deflection* of reality."[73] Geertz's text-metaphor terminology, in Burke's terms, selects a certain reality and deflects another. His readings in Wharton, his repetition of the Wild West idea in regards to Morocco, mingle the native's point of view with the unreliable first-order representations of Morocco that he, as scientist, should critique. Geertz's text metaphor ultimately domesticates the foreignness that his texts propose to deliver. The more challenging strains of foreignness from the native's point of view are translated into metaphors and literary allusions that are understandable to the American audience that Geertz is writing for and are thereby edited out. The simultaneous foreignness and familiarity of Geertz's interpretations keep that which would challenge his "translations" of Moroccan culture outside the boundaries of Geertz's work.

Envoi

If Geertz's text metaphor occludes the diachronic and stabilizes Sefroui temporality, the work's own temporality is reactivated in its movement into Moroccan cultural studies. Geertz's work and his mentorship of the Moroccan anthropologist Abdellah Hammoudi led to the latter's powerful ethnography *The Victim and Its Masks* (published in Paris in 1988), which names its powerful study of masquerade and sacrifice as an exercise in "thick description" (6). Hammoudi's yet more trenchant study of Moroccan authoritarianism, *Master and Disciple* (published in Chicago in 1993), reflects on the difficulties of engaging in the study of cultural patterns of submission to authority in the society in which the author grew up. Hammoudi's theoretically powerful "plea for bounded knowledge" takes Geertz's own reflexivity in mind but extends it powerfully in the direction of politically motivated critique. Hammoudi has worked for years as Geertz's colleague at Princeton, but academics based in Moroccan universities have also engaged Geertz's work in the last few years. The 1992 publication of the French translation of *Islam Observed* allowed a greater number of Moroccans to engage with Geertz's landmark work. In 1996, the independent Moroccan journal *Prologues* dedicated part of an issue to responses to Geertz's work. Even if there was a sense that time had passed since the publication of Geertz's work (a quarter century), the contributors to *Prologues* found ways to reclaim it for its methodological possibilities. Geertz's own temporal lag could even be seen as adding value to his text: "Having appeared in times more propitious for serene reflection, when the present of Muslim societies did not yet veil perspectives on their evolution."[74] Geertz's work might thus be seen to Moroccan academics as that of a "pioneer," as one called him (30). Other Moroccan critics responded to Geertz's sense of continuity within Muslim societies, predicted in 1968 and renewed in Geertz's 1991 introduction to the French edition. That Geertz could argue for this continuity after the Iranian Revolution, fall of the Berlin Wall, First Gulf War, Bosnia crisis, and so on, was comforting.[75] What George Marcus calls the changed mise-en-scène of anthropological fieldwork, then, and the sense that globalization has created different conditions for cross-cultural rapport could be bracketed.

As texts such as Geertz's and Rabinow's and Crapanzano's circulate in contemporary Moroccan public discussion, they are of course remade. They are not ignored, though, and they appear in footnotes and bibliographies in a variety of Maghrebi works of sociology, anthropology, and literary criticism. From Mounia Bennani-Chraïbi's study of Moroccan youth and oppositional politics after the first Gulf War to Taieb Belghazi's and Mohammed Madani's study of new social movements and collective action in the 1990s, even work that engages contemporary society from starkly different approaches from those that Geertz and his students took finds itself referring to, building off of, and remaking the writing that had excused itself from believing in the possibility for effective action based on knowledge production. The encounter has proceeded in direct terms as well: the sociologist Driss Mansouri, of Sidi Mohammed Ben Abdellah University in Fez, recently organized a conference in Sefrou that brought Geertz back into conversation with Moroccan academics working three decades after his own study. One of the conditions of the changed mise-en-scène may be that such engagements move beyond questions of debt or postcolonial agonism and confrontation.

But it is not the intention of this chapter to grapple with that changed mise-en-scène and the ways in which an episteme of globalization reorganizes firsthand responses to the Maghreb or Maghrebi culture. Some of the entries on the list of world events that followed the end of the Vietnam War suggest moments when American ideas about the Arab and Muslim world shifted, moments that themselves require careful attention. As I began by stating in the introduction to this book, this project has been researched and written, then re-researched and rewritten, during an extended moment during which American ideas about the Arab world are in crisis. What this chapter can contribute to that topic is an extended look at the paradoxes of a generation positioned and politically sympathetic with the attempt to make contact with the Moroccan other, but which also turned away from that conversation. Given the ongoing crises of otherness—to say nothing of what would follow with respect to the conversation of Americans and Arabs—that turning away may be regretted. Yet lines of communication were indeed drawn that might later be reopened. The continued circulation and rereading of some of the writing discussed in this chapter—and this book—in the Maghreb, where meanings are remade and new contexts established, is something about which we may be optimistic.

NOTES

Introduction

1 In *Blank Darkness*, Christopher L. Miller argues that Africanist discourse in French produces "an object aberrant to the system that created it," namely an image of Africa as a projected "nullity" (6, 17).

2 See Apter, *Continental Drift*, chap. 11, "Impotent Epic."

3 See Slotkin, *Gunfighter Nation*.

4 Seddon, "Dreams and Disappointments," 198.

5 Ibid., 203. See A. Layachi, *The United States and North Africa*.

6 Bowles, interview, Feb. 8, 1996. I have not seen any published accounts of Bowles's trip to Biskra.

7 *Maroc, Algérie, Tunisie*, 197–98; Geoff Crowther and Hugh Finlay, *Morocco, Algeria and Tunisia*, 314.

8 See Wright, *Politics of Design*, and Rabinow, *French Modern*.

9 See my essay "The Well-Built Wall of Culture."

10 See Kaplan, *The Arabists*.

11 Said, *Culture and Imperialism*, 289.

12 Giles, *Virtual Americas*, 263. Giles's interest in virtualization as a critical process emphasizes "reflection and estrangement" and a comparative angle of vision (in his case, the United States and Great Britain) by which to denaturalize the assumptions framing cultural narratives of the United States and "how its own indigenous representations of the 'natural' tend to revolve tautologously, reinforcing themselves without reference to anything outside their own charmed circle" (2).

13 Young, *Postcolonialism*, 59.

14 Pyle, *Here Is Your War*, 60–61.

15 Melani McAlister has argued that American discourse relating to the Middle East since 1945 is marked by what she calls "post-Orientalism," which marks "the period after World War II when American power worked very hard to fracture the old European logic and to install new frameworks" (*Epic Encounters*, 11). There is much to recommend in McAlister's book. However, she defines

Said's concept of Orientalism rather starkly: "binary, feminizing, and citational" (12) and then proceeds to dismiss it. In so doing, she misses the crucial element of Said's definition that would challenge her own theoretical claim, namely the "corporate" aspect of Orientalism and its relationship to the question of "institutions" (such as the media central to her project). Instead, McAlister gravitates toward a loosely defined concept of discourse, within which, it's implied, her critical interventions too must function. She emphasizes the "continuous relationship" between the cultural field and "other fields in the larger social system"; "Foreign policy is one of the ways in which nations speak for themselves." In "putting Orientalism in its place," McAlister's "post-Orientalist" approach mistakenly collapses the institutional space between cultural production and foreign policy" (276, 7, 5, 12). Elsewhere, she dispenses with Said's own account of U.S. Orientalism, which attends to this space, as "the least nuanced and interesting of the book." For her this is because it is "focused primarily on policymakers' statements or the work of area studies scholars" and is "essentially an ideological critique of US foreign policy" ("Edward Said," 553). Unlike McAlister, Douglas Little accepts the Saidian framework in his political history: "something very like Said's *Orientalism* seems subconsciously to have shaped U.S. popular attitudes and foreign policies toward the Middle East" (10). Yet there is no discussion of the way culture works to shape attitudes; for Little the process remains "subconscious" or via "subliminal messages." For an account of misreadings of Said and an argument about Said's greater interest in institutions over discourse, see Brennan, "Illusion of a Future."

16 Said, *Beginnings*, 357.

17 According to the American Film Institute, the film was in production from February 25 to April 23, 1942 (afi.chadwyck.com). It was released in New York on November 11.

18 Bosley Crowther, "The Screen in Review: *Road to Morocco* with Bing Crosby, Bob Hope, Dorothy Lamour at Paramount – Other Films," *New York Times*, November 12, 1942.

19 Wehr, *Dictionary of Modern Written Arabic*, 668.

20 The difficulty of agreeing on an etymology of *Moor* (unrelated to the word *Moroccan*) is apparent in looking at the new December 2002 edition of the OED entry on Moor. This recalls Miller's discussion of conflicting etymologies of the word *Africa* in *Blank Darkness*.

21 Geertz, "Thinking as a Moral Act," 149.

22 Lee and LiPuma, "Cultures of Circulation," 204. For a fuller elaboration of the "global culture of financial circulation" that has emerged since 1973, see LiPuma and Lee, *Financial Derivatives*.

CHAPTER 1   American Orientalism

1 Patton, *Patton Papers*, 116.

2 Patton, *War as I Knew It*, 9.

3 Patton suggested that his wife "might try to get [the story] published" under a pseudonym (*Patton Papers*, 146).

4 Ibid., 122. I reproduce Patton's misspellings. Patton's conflation of "tails" as "tales" is suggestive. See Miller on French descriptions of Africans with tails (*Blank Darkness*, 3–6).

5 Patton, *War as I Knew It*, 11.

6 See McKay, *A Long Way from Home*, 298; and Lewis, *Filibusters in Barbary*. This Rex Ingram is not to be confused with the actor who played Tambul in *Sahara*.

7 Patton, *War as I Knew It*, 289. For the diplomatic webs Patton encountered in Morocco, see Hoisington, *The Casablanca Connection*.

8 Pittman, "Africa against the Axis," 218.

9 Gardiner, "African Opinion and World Peace," 355, 359.

10 W. E. B. Du Bois, "The American Negro Press: Race Pulse Reflected Accurately in Zooming Newspaper Circulation," *Chicago Defender*, February 20, 1943; "The American Negro Press: Du Bois Finds Race Papers Free from Shackles of Big Business Advertisers," *Chicago Defender*, Februray 27, 1943.

11 See especially Borstelmann, *The Cold War and the Color Line*; Dower, *War without Mercy*; Von Eschen, *Race against Empire*; Plummer, *Window on Freedom*; and Baldwin, *Beyond the Color Line and the Iron Curtain*.

12 Borstelmann, *The Cold War and the Color Line*, 41.

13 See Miriam Hansen's discussion in *Babel and Babylon*.

14 McKay, "Little Sheik," 263, in *Gingertown*.

15 McKay, "Miss Allah," 20.

16 *Chicago Defender*, May 22, 1943.

17 John Robert Badger, "World View," *Chicago Defender*, February 6, 1943.

18 *Chicago Defender*, February 13, 1943.

19 *Chicago Defender*, February 20, 1943.

20 Said, *Orientalism*, 10.

21 Ibid., 4.

22 See Stephens, "Foreword," vii.

23 Hoisington, *The Casablanca Connection*, 242.

24 Feis, *Churchill, Roosevelt, Stalin*, 110.

25 Pennell, *Morocco since 1830*, 263.

26 Hassan II, *La Mémoire d'un roi*, 18; my translation.

27 U.S. Office of Strategic Services, *Morocco*, quoted in Hoisington, *The Casablanca Connection*, 284n73. Hoisington mentions discussions between the Sultan and other Moroccan leaders of "creating some joint protectorate or inter-Allied mandate in which the United States and Britain would share authority with France and Spain."

28 Said, *Culture and Imperialism*, 289.

29 A studio memo suggested that the project might "be easily tailored into a piece along the lines of *Algiers*, with plenty of excitement and suspense"; shortly thereafter, producer Hal Wallis changed the name of the story to *Casablanca* and tried to borrow Hedy Lamarr, who had starred in the 1938 film opposite Charles Boyer, from MGM. See Harmetz, *Round Up the Usual Suspects*, 30.

30 Emphasis original. For a reproduction of the ad, see ibid., 265.

31 Marx, *The Groucho Letters*, 14.

32 Harmetz, *Round Up the Usual Suspects*, 284–86.

33 Beatrice Patton, quoted in Patton, *Patton Papers*, 112.

34 See Blum, *V Was for Victory*, especially chapter 1, "The Selling of the War."

35 Roeder, *The Censored War*, 9.

36 This quote is from Steinbeck's 1958 introduction to the compilation of his 1943 war correspondence for the *New York Herald Tribune*, *Once There Was a War*, vi–viii.

37 The reference here is to Edward Murrow.

38 Blum, *V Was for Victory*, 55.

39 Fictions, from *fingere* (to fashion or to shape), are fashioned things—in this context, fashioned from facts. James Clifford emphasizes that fiction is not "merely opposed to truth" but "suggests the partiality of cultural and historical truths, the ways they are systematic and exclusive" (*The Predicament of Culture*, 5).

40 Sgt. Lehman was quoted in Meyer, *The Stars and Stripes Story of World War II*, 79. Lehman won a prize for this piece.

41 Soldier song, printed in *Stars and Stripes* (London edition), December 7, 1942. Quoted in ibid., 24.

42 Pyle, *Here Is Your War*, 153.

43 Luce, "The American Century," 10.

44 This quote is taken from the third printing of the Pocket Books edition, November 1944.

45 See, for example, the 1943 film *Bataan*, which depicted an unseen Japanese enemy as both "monkeys" and savages. Slotkin discusses *Bataan* in terms of the Western myth (*Gunfighter Nation*, chapter 10).

46 The Internet Movie Database (www.imdb.com) lists nearly fifty films shot in Imperial County, including *The Son of the Sheik* (1926), *Morocco* (1930), *The Lost Patrol* (1934), and *The Garden of Allah* (1936). *The Sheik* (1920) was also shot

57 Cripps, *Making Movies Black*, 69–72.

58 See Slotkin, *Gunfighter Nation*, 319–20.

59 *The Lost Patrol*, directed by John Ford, is the story of a British battalion lost in the Mesopotamian desert during World War I. As Basinger (*The World War II Combat Film*, 70), Slotkin (*Gunfighter Nation*, 321) and the original *New York Times* review (Bowsley Crowther, "*Sahara*, an Exciting Picture of Desert War," *New York Times*, November 12, 1943) have pointed out, it is an uncredited source for both *Bataan* and *Sahara*. Neither Slotkin nor Basinger note the insignificance of Arabs in *Sahara*, whereas the Arabs of *The Lost Patrol* are an ominous foe.

60 In comparing Tambul to the Indian scout character of Hollywood Westerns, I am following Basinger, who mentions *Sahara* in her discussion of *Bataan* (*The World War II Combat Film*, 70). Slotkin follows Basinger in his own discussion of *Bataan* in *Gunfighter Nation*. I am indebted to both analyses.

61 Cripps, *Making Movies Black*, 73, 78; emphasis original.

62 Koppes, "Hollywood and the Politics of Representation," 36.

63 For Harmetz, who also sees the role of Tambul as progressive, this scene demonstrates the trust that the white characters have in the black character: "At a time when Lena Horne says she was never allowed to touch a white person in a movie . . . audiences watched Rex Ingram catch the water in his hands, pour it into cups from which white men would drink, lick his moist palms and cup his hands to catch the next drops" (*Round Up the Usual Suspects*, 309).

64 Westbrook, "'I Want a Girl, Just Like the Girl That Married Harry James.'"

65 In the Koran, Mohammed instructs that Muslims should have *no more than four wives*, without idealizing the number. (Tambul's explication does not appear in the Koran.)

66 This is a somewhat different sense of "time lag" than that propounded by Homi Bhabha in his essay "The Postcolonial and the Postmodern."

67 Koch, *Casablanca*, 99. My use of hypercanonical alludes to Jonathan Arac's study of *Huckleberry Finn* and its fate within cold war literary studies, whereby the more troubling problems of the present were located in the literature of the previous century, celebrated, and thereby imagined resolved ("Criticism between Opposition and Counterpoint").

68 Hanchard, "Afro-Modernity," 253.

69 "As Time Goes By" was not original to *Casablanca*. The song, written by Herman Hupfeld for a 1931 Broadway play, was later recorded by Rudy Vallee.

70 The association of Morocco—and Islam—with stopped clocks resonates with earlier American representations of the Maghreb. Edith Wharton associated stopped clocks she saw in Morocco with national immaturity in *In Morocco*. See my essay "The Well-Built Wall of Culture."

71 Ray, *A Certain Tendency of the Hollywood Film*, 89.

72 Gooding-Williams, "Black Cupids, White Desires," 204.

73 I borrow this analysis of the resolution of erotic triangles into conservative couples from Gooding-Williams.

74 Quoted in Harmetz, *Round Up the Usual Suspects*, 309.

75 Harmetz points out that the *Casablanca* production team borrowed sets from *The Desert Song* (the Warner Brothers remake of the 1929 film), which had just finished shooting (ibid., 9). Warner Brothers' research department did see photographs of French colonial architecture (noted by Otero-Pailos, "Casablanca's Régime").

76 For a compelling ethnography of cinema-going in northern Nigeria that theorizes the cinema house's particularity, see Larkin, "Theaters of the Profane."

77 See Rabinow, *French Modern*, particularly the chapter "Governing Morocco."

78 Considerations of *Casablanca*'s relationship to the city are common in travel guides and the popular press, where a Nexis search turns up many articles by Americans gone searching for *Casablanca* in Casablanca. A repetition of this pattern occurs more subtly in academic work of a postmodern bent. Jorge Otero-Pailos begins an article on French colonial architecture and Hollywood cinema set building with a reference to the Casablanca Hyatt, which he claims "could be anywhere in the world," missing the Moroccan particularity of the Hyatt's quotation. The placelessness of this "postmodern" place is made possible by the critic's aversion of his eye from the Moroccan staff of the bar; the piano player to whom journalists invariably refer is replaced in Otero-Pailos by an "almost impercep-

industry in the late 1980s, see Francis Ghiles, "Desert Kingdom Sells Itself as Tourist Oasis," *Financial Times* (London), February 9, 1989. A less heralded yet significant portion of the tourist economy (not discussed by Ghiles) is that of Gulf Arab men, who bring a different set of stereotypes about Morocco, namely that it is a liberal Muslim country where alcohol and prostitution are tolerated.

80 This differs noticeably from the Tunisian tourism industry, which takes a nationalist approach and satirizes Western stereotypes (through many silly camel souvenirs) while presenting a corrective image of Tunisia in museums. Algeria aggressively discouraged foreign tourism in the 1990s with its "no visas, no visitors" policy. In 1997, Libya began marketing itself for international tourism, emphasizing its Mediterranean beaches.

81 In the early to mid-1980s, Hyatt Regency purchased and remodeled the former Hôtel Casablanca, itself built in the 1970s, on what is now known as Place des Nations Unies, abutting the medina. The *Casablanca*-themed bar was not a part of the earlier hotel. For early press accounts of the bar, see Judith Miller, "From Soup to Stew, A Gastronome's Oasis," *New York Times*, August 31, 1986; and Christopher Walker, "Casablanca's Dream of Humphrey Bogart Fades as Time Goes By," *Times* (London), May 23, 1989.

82 Quoted in Terril Jones, "As Time Goes By, Casablanca Lure Grows," *Chicago Sun-Times*, January 9, 1993.

83 For discussions of French colonial architecture as interpretation of Moroccan culture and means of political control, the major texts are Wright, *The Politics of Design in French Colonial Urbanism*, and Rabinow, *French Modern*.

84 These are my translations from colloquial Moroccan Arabic.

85 Indeed, in panning Laqt'a's 1999 film *Les Casablancais*, Karim al Amali complains that Laqt'a exploits the equation of Casablanca with the romance of *al-nima*, due to its association with *Casablanca* and yet fails to justify locating his own exposition of social problems in the particularity of contemporary Casablanca. Al Amali's formulation is complex; he establishes *Casablanca* as a film thoroughly detached from Moroccan reality, yet one that is "the true performance of specialists in the 'cinematic dream.'" He critiques Laqt'a for leaving behind the realm of cinematic dream and moving "simply to a gratuitous horror" for his subject (al Amali, "De la Romance au Cauchemar," 35).

86 Wehr, *Dictionary of Modern Written Arabic*, 786.

CHAPTER 2   Sheltering Screens

1 See Sutherland, "Distant Episodes," and Prose, "The Coldest Eye."

2 More accurately, in the 1950s Bowles lamented the encounter of Arab nationalism with Western modernity and consumer culture.

3 A brilliant exception is Millicent Dillon's *You Are Not I: A Portrait of Paul Bowles* (1998).

4 Mullins's recent study of gay male writers in Tangier, *Colonial Affairs*, is strong on questions of desire and marginality in Bowles's literary work. But it also exemplifies how the tendency to see Bowles's career as dissociated from geopolitical concerns is reinforced by the lack of a broader archive of Moroccan materials that would allow critics without the language training or opportunity to research in the Maghreb to challenge it. Mullins argues: "American expatriate writers inhabit the legacy of American and Moroccan political history" (14). But for Mullins, the assertion that Bowles was "firmly grounded within modernism" means that his work was detached from the world and geography, a position about modernism that Mullins curiously attributes to Edward Said (25); this conclusion authorizes Mullins to make only loose references to political history. Prose's introduction to the 2003 Ecco edition of *The Spider's House* calls the novel a "textbook" of anti-American attitudes. The metaphor not only signals her fundamental misreading of the novel, but also suggests the pedagogical failure of previous Bowles scholarship to offer an alternative to her view.

5 Jackson, "On the Seamier Side," 6.

6 Mel Gussow, "Paul Bowles, Elusive Composer and Author Known for 'Sheltering Sky,' Dies at 88," *New York Times*, November 19, 1999.

7 Adam Bernstein, "Expatriate Author Paul Bowles Dies at 88; Wrote 'Sheltering Sky.'" *Washington Post*, November 19, 1999, final ed.

8 During Bowles's time in Tangier, the population of the city grew from fifty

thousand to neary one million. The primary source of this population explosion was the migration of rural Moroccans to the cities, not tourism.

9 In Ellingham's *Morocco: The Rough Guide*, Bowles is included both in the "Contexts" section for his writing and translations and in the Tangier chapter as a living site.

10 The emergence of Al-Jazeera as counter-CNN offers a potent example. See el-Nawawy and Iskander, *Al-Jazeera*.

11 Bowles, personal interview, July 10, 1994.

12 In his preface to a 1982 reprint of the novel, Bowles commented on al-Fassi's response. Moroccan obituaries also refer to al-Fassi's appreciation; Muhammad Abu Talib disputes it.

13 See Elghandor, "Bowles's Views of Atavism and Civilization."

14 Paul Bowles, "Bowles et Choukri: Le Temps de la polémique," *Les Nouvelles du Nord* (Tangier), February 28, 1997.

15 Muhammad Abu Talib, "Balagha Buwlz az-zuba au A ras l' Bowles" ("Enough with Bowles"), *Al-'Alam ath-Thaqafi* (Rabat) January 25, 1997.

16 Salah Sbyea, "L'Amant de Tanger," *Libération* (Casablanca), November 19, 1999; Mohamed El Gahs, "Pain Nu," *Libération* (Casablanca), November 19, 1999.

17 Tariq as-Saidi, "Baul Buwlz: Thuqub mali'ah bal-hayat" ("Paul Bowles: Holes Full of Life"), *Al-Ahdath al-Maghribiya* (Casablanca), November 24, 1999.

18 "Décès de l'écrivain américain Paul Bowles." *Maghreb Arabe Press*, November 19, 1999. See also Hussan Bahraoui, *Halga rawaya Tanja*.

19 Bin Bushta, Zubir. "Baul Buwlz: Nihaya ustura" ("Paul Bowles: End of a Myth"), *Al-Ittihad al-Ishtiraki* (Casablanca), November 22, 1999.

20 Bin Bushta, Zubir. "Baul Buwlz: Rahil ra'id «al-adab at-tanji»" ("Paul Bowles: Departure of the leader of 'Tangerian literature'"), *Al-Mithaq al-Watani* (Casablanca), November 21–22, 1999.

21 Abdarrahim Huzal, introduction to "Al-Katib baina maghrebain!" ("The Writer between Two Moroccos!"), by Antoine Poysh, *Al-'Alam ath-Thaqafi* (Rabat), November 27, 1999.

22 See Edwards, "Preposterous Encounters."

23 Luce, "American Century," 35.

24 Gayatri Spivak's argument for a reinvigorated critical practice that would bring together the close reading and what she calls "teleopoiesis" of comparative literature and area studies' attention to regions and comparative political economy inspires the reading practice I am imagining here. See Spivak, *Death of a Discipline*.

25 The story appears in Bowles, *The Delicate Prey*. The man's nationality is not specified, but in a 1971 interview Bowles suggested that he imagined the

professor to be American and loosely associates the professor with Port, in *The Sheltering Sky*, and with himself (Evans, "An Interview with Paul Bowles," 51–52). Sawyer-Lauçanno names the professor as French (*An Invisible Spectator*, 248), but there is no evidence to back up that claim; indeed the professor (who *speaks* French, as do Port and Kit) refers to French colonial soldiers in the novel as "the French military police," a distinction a French citizen would likely not make.

26 The story was originally published in the January 1947 issue of *Partisan Review*. *Moghrebi* is the word Bowles uses to refer to the Moroccan dialect(s) of Arabic.

27 Jackson, "On the Seamier Side," 6.

28 Bowles, *In Touch*, 227.

29 In Moroccan Arabic, as in English and French, the word for *tongue—lsan—*also means "language." Bowles may also have in mind a well-known Moroccan proverb: *lsan tyekemmel l-insan*, the tongue completes the person; that is, the individual who uses language well is superior.

30 Of course, a film made on the verge of the end of the cold war is subject to its own historical moment and concerns. Indeed, the film rights to *The Sheltering Sky* had long been optioned, and only in the late 1980s did it seem appropriate to make the film. The nostalgia for a simpler relationship of Americans to the third world and the accompanying occlusion of the source novel's concern with colonialism would in this sense seem to be responses to the unraveling of the cold war world order and to the epistemological complexities of globalization and newer forms of empire. For the filmmakers' own sense of their cold war context, see the companion volume *The Sheltering Sky: A Film by Bernardo Bertolucci*, especially the interview with Bertolucci (53–60) and contribution by executive producer William Aldrich (86–87).

31 Bowles, *The Sheltering Sky*, 6.

32 See Turner, *The Significance of the Frontier in American History*.

33 We should extend Alan Trachtenberg's well-known critique of this foundational text of American studies: not only did Smith separate myth and symbol too starkly from industrialization, he also failed to account for the ways in which his account and its institutional location were coincident with and indebted to post–World War II global expansion. The stakes of this failure are woven into the Americanist enterprise of the postwar period. See Trachtenberg, "Myth, History, and Literature in Virgin Land."

34 See Arac, "Criticism between Opposition and Counterpoint."

35 See Graebner, *The Age of Doubt*.

36 In Bertolucci's version, there is never any doubt that a European is guilty, which reflects the film's conservative turn away from questions of race. This is underlined by its removal of the sexual encounter between Kit and Belqassim's

older partner and the scopic pleasure the film takes in dark-skinned bodies as sites of abundant sexuality.

37 For a contemporary Arab critique of Point Four, see Hakim, "Point Four and the Middle East." Mustafa El Azzou investigates efforts by U.S. businessmen to influence policy toward Morocco before independence.

38 Toledano, "Young Man, Go to Casablanca," 111.

39 Bowles uses his own translation of the lyrics. He does not attribute the song to Slaoui, but calls it "a popular song in Moghrebi Arabic of the 1950s" (*Points in Time*, 92). Bargach, "Liberatory, Nationalising and Moralising by Ellipsis," offers a different translation.

40 *Foreign Relations of the United States (FRUS)* 1946, 7:52.

41 Wall, *The United States and the Making of Postwar France*, 5.

42 In *Our Vichy Gamble*, Langer argues that the United States dealt with Pétain's regime because of national security concerns, particularly to keep the French fleet and North African possessions out of Nazi control. Wall counters that the United States thought France decadent and expected imminent revolution (*The United States and the Making of Postwar France*, 21).

43 See Hassan II, *La Mémoire d'un roi*, 18; U.S. Office of Strategic Services, *Morocco*; and Hoisington, *The Casablanca Connection*, 284n73. In 1948, the State Department noted the legacy of FDR's comments in North Africa (*FRUS 1948*, 3:684).

44 Pennell, *Morocco since 1830*, 263–64, and see *FRUS 1943*, 4:741.

45 Borstelmann, *The Cold War and the Color Line*, 48.

46 Algeria had drought and dismal crops in 1945 and 1947; in Morocco, 1945 was known as "the year of hunger"; Tunisia was threatened by famine in 1947. See V. McKay, "France's Future in North Africa," 299; and Pennell, *Morocco since 1830*, 268.

47 See V. McKay, "France's Future in North Africa," 300; Wall, *France, the United States, and the Algerian War*, 11; *FRUS 1947*, 5:682n.

48 *FRUS 1947*, 5:676.

49 Bess, "We're Invading North Africa Again," 23.

50 *FRUS 1947*, 5:687. The matter was finally brought to the UN in 1953.

51 *FRUS 1949*, 6:1781–85.

52 Wall, *The United States and the Making of Postwar France*, 143–47; Wall, *France, the United States, and the Algerian War*, 12. Article 6 of the Treaty of Washington (North Atlantic Treaty) states: "An armed attack on one or more of the Parties is deemed to include an armed attack on the territory of any of the Parties in Europe or North America, on the Algerian dependents of France, [etc.]."

53 Between 1949 and 1953, one-third of all money invested by France during the entire period of the protectorate (1912–56) was made. Pennell, *Morocco since 1830*, 272–73.

54 *FRUS 1950*, 5:1769.

55 Wall, *France, the United States, and the Algerian War*, 9.

56 *FRUS 1950*, 5:1737.

57 Spivak, *Critique of Postcolonial Reason*, 112. Spivak admits that this is "an old-fashioned binary opposition."

58 Jackson, "On the Seamier Side," 6.

59 Agamben, *Homo Sacer*, 9.

60 Bowles, "No More Djinns." In a personal interview (July 9, 1994), Bowles discussed such Americans:

> Bowles: Some of [the Americans] spent their time crawling on their hands and knees through the [Tangier] medina, eating garbage, which they found in little piles in front of the doors and so on.
>
> Edwards: Because they couldn't afford food?
>
> Bowles: No it wasn't a matter of money. . . . It was a matter of feeling part of the culture, I suppose.
>
> Edwards: I haven't noticed that to be a particular part of Moroccan culture.
>
> Bowles: No, of course. Their idea was that one should be simple. Apparently the simplest thing they could think of was to crawl on all fours down the streets and "feel free." Because no one bothered them; people didn't look and say, "Why are you doing that?" Well, [the Moroccans said]: "Crazy foreigners, crazy Americans."

61 In a long travel article ("Fez"), Bowles names Driss Yacoubi (father of his lover Ahmed and model for the patriarch in *The Spider's House*) and recounts conversations and exchanges. "No More Djinns" is organized around accounts of dialogue with Moroccans. See also Bowles, "Sad for U.S., Sad for Algeria," a dialogue with Algerians on the revolution.

62 A. Layachi, *The United States and North Africa*, 6, 174.

63 I spent a substantial amount of time researching direct overlaps between Bowles after World War II and those who might have been associated with that elite. There are intriguing possibilities: Charles Gallagher, who lived in Tangier and wrote field reports for the American Universities Field Staff between 1956 and 1967, and who lists one of Bowles's novels in his 1963 monograph *The United States and North Africa*, was a frequent dining partner of Jane Bowles. In 1947, when Paul Bowles stayed at the Farhar pension in Tangier, he followed by a couple of months a major group of physical anthropologists led by Carleton Coon who stayed at the Farhar and were engaged in a search for Atlantis off the Caves of Hercules. As was later revealed, Carleton Coon Sr., the eminent anthropologist, worked for the o.s.s. See Coon, *A North Africa Story*. If there were points of overlap, however, I've concluded that Bowles was ultimately moving

away from the sorts of national affiliation—both in his personal life and politics and in his writing—that would make these overlaps matter.

64 Bowles, *In Touch*, 182.

65 Dupin's motto: "Truth is not always in a well. In fact, as regards the more important knowledge, I do believe that she is invariably superficial" (Poe, *Complete Tales and Poems*, 153).

66 Fanon, *Black Skin, White Masks*, 14.

67 Goldberg, "In / Visibility and Super / Vision," 181.

68 Bowles, *Their Heads*, 128.

69 Here I am following Pease's theorization of the postnational as "the complex site wherein postcolonialism's resistance to global capital *intersects* with the questions the global economy addresses to the state concerning the nation's continued role in its management" ("National Narratives"), 2.

70 "Every written work can be regarded as the prologue (or rather, the broken cast) of a work never penned, and destined to remain so, because later works, which in turn will be the prologues or the moulds for other absent works, represent only sketches or death masks" (Agamben, *Infancy and History*, 1). See also Deladurantaye, "Agamben's Potential."

71 Emily Apter suggests that fin-de-siècle writers such as Théophile Gautier, Pierre Loti, and Isabelle Eberhardt dropped "foreign loan words" into their French-language texts on the Maghreb "to impart local color and induce dépaysment" ("'Untranslatable' Algeria," 54–55).

72 Bowles, "No More Djinns," 258.

73 Hibbard, *Paul Bowles*, 102–3.

74 Tahar Ben Jelloun, "Une technique de viol," *Le Monde*, June 9, 1972.

75 Bowles, *Without Stopping*, 262.

76 The notion of reading through is borrowed from Gayatri Spivak, *Critique of Postcolonial Reason*. See also Bal, "Three-Way Misreading."

CHAPTER 3 Tangier(s)

1 Tangier's status had been extended by Mohammed V, but on October 19, 1959, he gave six months' notice of rescinding his decree. See Vaidon, *Tangier*, 328. In 1962, columnist John Crosby got Paul Bowles to admit Tangier was "dead" and wrote the city's obituary, even while noting the arrival of American "beats" (*New York Herald Tribune*, August 8, 1962). On Hutton, see Heymann, *Poor Little Rich Girl*, 220–26, 314–17. Heymann quotes the Tangier delegate of the Moroccan Tourism Ministry: "With her arrival Tangier became a boom town, one of the 'in' spots for café society" (223).

2 *Fortune*, August 1950, 67; *Fortune*, April 1948, 138; the *New Yorker*, April 12, 1952; *Newsweek*, December 12, 1955; *American Mercury*, December 1952; *Saturday Evening Post*, April 16, 1949; the *Atlantic*, March 1950; *Fortune*, August 1950, 140.

3 The International Settlement of Shanghai (1842–1941) was administered by an elected committee; in the 1930s, up to 90,000 Europeans and Americans lived there, and the city was known for political refugees, financial speculation, freedom from taxes, as the "Florence of the East" and "the Whore of Asia." Japan's occupation in 1941 rapidly ended that period. See Sergeant, *Shanghai*. After 1945, those represented on the Tangier Committee of Control were Spain, Great Britain, France, the United States, Portugal, Italy, the Netherlands and Belgium. The USSR and Sweden were signatories but did not participate.

4 The films were produced by United Artists, Monogram, and Paramount, respectively. Others include *The Woman from Tangier* (Columbia, 1948), *Tangier* (Universal, 1946), and British films distributed in the United States such as *Thunder over Tangier* (1957) and *The Captain's Paradise* (1953).

5 The city allowed free convertability of currency, with no restrictions on gold import, export, buying, and selling.

6 See Dalton, Pearson, and Barrett, "The Urban Morphology of Tangier."

7 Burroughs, *Interzone*, 58.

8 Ginsberg, *Howl and Other Poems*, 43.

9 On Beckett in Tangier, see Rondeau, "Beckett chez Gagarine," in *Tanger*, 71–75.

10 Torres, leader of the Spanish Zone nationalists, was based in Tangier from 1948 to 1952. Laghzaoui, "economic expert and financial wizard of the nationalist movement," escaped to Tangier in 1950; after 'Allal al-Fassi escaped to Cairo in 1951, Laghzaoui became the local leader of the nationalists (Landau, *Portrait of Tangier*, 221–22). See Stuart, *The International City of Tangier*, 156–61.

11 With Moroccan independence the functions of the legation, which had served as the American diplomatic mission to Morocco since 1821, were transferred to the American embassy in Rabat. The legation continued to serve as a consulate, providing visa and American-citizen services until 1962 when a newly built consulate on Boulevard des Amoureux in the new city opened its doors. In 1976 under a rental agreement with the U.S. Department of State, the Tangier American Legation Museum Society (an American nongovernmental organization) reopened the site as a museum and research center. Since 1991, it has been administered by Thor Kuniholm, a retired FSO who had during his State Department career served in Casablanca, as well as in Mali as deputy chief of mission, and in Zanzibar as principal officer at the consulate there, among other locations.

12 *FRUS 1949*, 6:1797.

13 Gallagher, *The United States and North Africa*, 239.

14 *FRUS 1955–57*, 18:88–94.

15 *FRUS 1955–57*, 18:135.

16 Wall, *France, the United States, and the Algerian War*, 85–86.

17 Burroughs, *Interzone*, 49.

18 In a May 7, 1952, memo (see *FRUS 1952–1954*, 11:189–90), Mary Crain of the Office of African Affairs writes that the American school "is looked upon with great favor by native Moroccans, and which is an excellent means of putting across American ideas" (190). Compare to Negley, "Why They Love Us in Tangier," and Wechsberg, "Anything Goes," where identical sentiments are expressed.

19 Stuart, *The International City of Tangier*, 189.

20 Blake served from 1925 to 1940; J. Rives Childs, 1940 to 1945; Paul Alling, 1945 to 1947; Edwin Plitt, 1947 to 1951; John Carter Vincent, 1951 to 1952. According to Stuart, Vincent "was away much of the time and the post remained vacant for a period until Joseph Satterthwaite was named in 1953." Satterthwaite was soon replaced by Julius Holmes. Referring to Holmes, named diplomatic agent and consul general in May 1955, Stuart wrote: "It remains to be seen whether the State Department will give him time to become an expert in this very important post" (ibid., 189–90). Holmes was recalled in July 1956 (*FRUS 1955–57*, 18:xix). Lower-ranking figures, such as legal adviser Edwin Smith, had spent longer terms in Tangier. Smith and Holmes appear in figure 13.

21 See Hahn, "National Security Concerns in U.S. Policy toward Egypt."

22 See Stuart, *The International City of Tangier*, 48–52 and 56–59.

23 Ibid., 161.

24 From 1945 until 1952, the administration was comprised of the Committee of Control, an International Legislative Assembly (which included European representatives, plus six Moroccan Muslims and three Moroccan Jews—both chosen by the *mendoub*, the sultan's representative, and thus under French supervision), the administrator (who, under the 1945 agreement had to be Belgian, Dutch, Portuguese, or Swedish), and a Mixed Court. Under the 1952 protocol, the Mixed Court became the International Jurisdiction, a system of four courts, revised to privilege the French and Spanish.

25 See *Tangier Gazette*, November 2, 1946, for a discussion and analysis.

26 Landau, *Portrait of Tangier*, xi.

27 Spain wanted Spanish appointments to run the police and to direct local intelligence services (*FRUS 1952–54*, 11:139). Landau lamented that the French and the Spanish had sent troops into the Tangier Zone, against the spirit of the statute, to quell the March 30, 1952, disturbances (*Portrait of Tangier*, 69n).

28 Henry Gemmill, "Tangier Turmoil," *Wall Street Journal*, April 12, 1956.

29 *FRUS 1952–54*, 11:195.

30 *FRUS 1952–54*, 11:192–93.

31 The sultan appointed the mendoub, the highest Moroccan official at Tangier; this appointment was approved by the French Protectorate, which limited the sultan's authority. Stuart analyzes the 1923 and 1928 statutes, arguing that "[the sultan's] sovereignty over the Zone was more nominal than real" (*The International City of Tangier*, 110). See Landau, *Portrait of Tangier*, 54ff, on postwar developments on appointments of the mendoub.

32 Stuart, *The International City of Tangier*, 166.

33 The composition of the Legislative Assembly was now to be determined not by a fixed numbers of seats, but on a vaguely defined formula based on population, property, and trade, which presumably would remove the presence of the Soviets, since they had neither community nor commercial interests (Stuart, *The International City of Tangier*, 252).

34 See *FRUS 1955–57*, 18:515.

35 Landau, *Portrait of Tangier*, 138.

36 In "Rights of Nationals of the United States of America in Morocco (France v. United States) (1950–1952)," delivered August 27, 1952, the International Court of Justice at the Hague (ICJ) rejected the U.S. claim that its nationals were immune to Moroccan laws that the United States did not assent to, and rejected that U.S. nationals were fiscally immune within Morocco, whether or not most-favored-nation status under an 1836 treaty with Britain still applied (the U.S. claim), since no other nation had this immunity. Though the ICJ did not address Tangier, in 1953 the U.S. Office of African Affairs (OAA) concluded that U.S. rights in Tangier were based on the same treaties. "In brief, in the light of the ICJ decision, we are without a legal basis on which to maintain our present position in Tangier" (*FRUS 1952–54*, 11:224–25). OAA suggested voluntarily giving up such rights in order to obtain "maximum protection for our own interests and the interests of RCA, Mackay and other commercial companies" (*FRUS 1952–54*, 11:225–26). But on March 9, 1954, a Tangier tribunal decided the case of two Moroccan subjects (Fatma Bent Si Mohamed El Khadar and her son) versus Mackay Radio and invoked the 1952 decision at the Hague to limit U.S. claims. See *FRUS 1952–54*, 11:230–32.

37 From the mid–nineteenth century, there were five postal services in Tangier: British, French, Spanish, German, and (after 1892) Moroccan. After 1942, three remained: Spanish, British, and Moroccan (controlled by French). Schools operating in Tangier included the Deutsche Schule, Spanish Colegio, Lycée Regnault, and American School of Tangier.

38 Landau, *Portrait of Tangier*, 109.

39 The work of a team of geographers recently examining the "urban morphology" of Tangier makes a strong case that the physical space of the city reflects its exceptional political form during the International Zone period: "Any similarities [to other Moroccan cities] seen in the urban morphology of Tangier are

accidents of geography and history and the city stands apart from the Moroccan experience." See Dalton, Pearson, and Barrett, "The Urban Morphology of Tangier," 110. See also "The Diplomatic Geography of Tangier" in Refass, *Tanger*, 113–23.

40 The plight of Tanjawis received frequent attention in the *Tangier Gazette*. Landau described local *bidonvilles* in his 1952 book *Portrait of Tangier*: "These tin-can towns are probably the most ghastly form of habitation known to twentieth century humanity. . . . No British or American farmer would dream of housing his pigs in such hovels" (47).

41 This was Schlamm's impulse; he responded explicitly to the "exuberant" Robert Ruark and the "slightly morose" Leigh White (author of an exaggerated article in *Reader's Digest*). Careful reading of the *Tangier Gazette* demonstrates that the local press did in fact cover murders and violent crimes, contra Ruark.

42 This is akin to Judith Butler's famous description of "queering": "As a term for betraying what ought to remain concealed, 'queering' works as the exposure within language—an exposure that disrupts the repressive surface of language—of both sexuality and race" (*Bodies That Matter*, 176).

43 Balibar and Wallerstein, *Race, Nation, Class*, 96.

44 Lears, "A Matter of Taste," 39.

45 Dryer, *The Image Makers*, 38.

46 Columbia Pictures paid $150,000 for the film rights. Clark Gable was chosen to play the lead, but his sudden death in 1960, followed shortly by the producer's in 1963, apparently killed the project.

47 Nadel, *Containment Culture*, 14.

48 Corber, *In the Name of National Security*, 3. See May, *Homeward Bound*.

49 In a fine essay, "Trafficking in the Void," Jonathan Eburne suggests that William Burroughs and Jack Kerouac were demonized within cold war domestic culture due not "to their fundamental positioning 'outside' US culture, but because of the ability of their essential 'otherness' to be compounded into an 'abject' which could be located as the source of internal differences within the US self" (64). Eburne draws on the work of Julia Kristeva to define the abject as the "fundamental lack" that disturbs identity, system, order. Eburne is concerned with the domestic context of these two writers. I want to extend his suggestion not so much to their tenure in Tangier, but to Tangier itself: namely that accounts of Tangier did not focus on how fully outside America it was, but rather saw it as a threat because of the proximity to America of aspects of Tangier.

50 Potter, *People of Plenty*, 134.

51 My article "Yankee Pashas and Buried Women," from which this paragraph and the preceding paragraph on Potter are drawn, looks more closely at *Yankee Pasha* (1954), set in early nineteenth-century Morocco, *Land of the Pharaohs* (1955), set in ancient Egypt, and *Kismet* (1953), set in Baghdad.

52 Examples include *Song of Scheherazade* (Universal, 1947), *Samson and Delilah* (Paramount, 1949), *Flame of Araby* (Universal, 1951), *The Prince Who Was a Thief* (Universal, 1951), *Son of Ali Baba* (Universal, 1952), *Veils of Bagdad* (Universal, 1953), *Yankee Pasha* (Universal, 1954), *The Egyptian* (Twentieth-Century Fox, 1954), *Bagdad* (Universal, 1949), *The Desert Song* (Warner Brothers, 1953), *Adventures of Hajji Baba* (Twentieth-Century Fox, 1954), *Land of the Pharaohs* (Warner Brothers, 1955), *Kismet* (MGM, 1955), and *Istanbul* (Universal, 1957).

53 Kael, "Film Chronicle: Night People," 112.

54 See Shohat, *Unthinking Eurocentrism*, 164.

55 Heymann, *Poor Little Rich Girl*, 226.

56 Bess, "Uncle Sam Sponsors a Smugglers' Paradise." Bess called Tangier a "plush-lined hide-out for some of the world's oddest characters" (20). He noted that the American Legation offices used what "once was a harem" (122) for American stenographers.

57 Gemmill, "Tangier Turmoil."

58 See Wechsberg, "Anything Goes"; and Negley, "Why They Love Us in Tangier."

59 Simpkins, "Banking in Tangier," 84.

60 See Fanon, *L'An V de la révolution algérienne*, chapter 3.

61 Schlamm, "Tangier," 67.

62 Taberner, "The Phoney Gold Rush," 80.

63 Butler, *Bodies That Matter*, 176.

64 Maugham, *North African Notebook*, 37. Maugham is quoting Alan Brodrick.

65 Michael Warner's brilliant reading of Thoreau's *Walden* has suggested the radical economics behind composting, recycling one's waste. Warner locates Thoreau's erotic economy of waste, learned from nature's economy but also simultaneously an erotics: that one have no waste by enjoying one's waste. See "*Walden*'s Erotic Economy."

66 Twain, *The Innocents Abroad*; *Roughing It*, 63–64.

67 The climax of Bowles's *Let It Come Down* revolves around a currency exchange and the theft of convertible cash, based on an actual case. Bowles later claimed that the real details were "so improbable that I had to modify [them] to give it credibility" ("Thirty Years Later," 9).

68 Warner, "*Walden*'s Erotic Economy," 167.

69 I am sympathetic with Jarrod Hayes's effort, in his study of postcolonial francophone Maghrebi literature, to summon up what he calls "queer nations": heterogenous nations made up of peoples (French speakers, Berbers, homosexuals, women, Jews) who were marginalized within postindependence national cultures that pretended to homogeneity. Hayes's method is different from my own, however. See my review of *Queer Nations*.

CHAPTER 4 Disorienting the National Subject

1 Burroughs, letter dated January 26, 1954, *Letters of William S. Burroughs*, 195.

2 Rolo, "The New Bohemia," 27.

3 Burroughs, letter dated November 2, 1955, *Letters of William S. Burroughs*, 302

4 Finlayson, *Tangier*, 225.

5 Introduction to Burroughs, *Interzone*, xiii.

6 In *Literary Outlaw*, Morgan devotes one chapter to the book, "*Naked Lunch*: 1959–1966," and a different chapter to its place of composition, "Tangier: 1954–1958."

7 Bowles, "Burroughs in Tangier," 43.

8 I am referring especially to recent major readings by Timothy Murphy, Greg Mullins, and Oliver Harris, all of which I find rich in many places and from which I have learned. Murphy is compelling on *Naked Lunch*'s relationship to exile as a category but surprisingly tentative when it comes to the location of Burroughs's exile. Mullins wants to engage Burroughs's "relationship to the international politics attendant upon the ascendancy of postwar American hegemony over former European colonies like Morocco" (*Colonial Affairs*, 51) but turns away from this project, claiming that Burroughs's political struggles were "extremely personal." Mullins's argument for the sexual metaphors in Burroughs's "own private interzone" must be approached carefully, however, especially as he bases his understanding of Tangier's geopolitical and historical context largely on a 1931 edition of Graham Stuart's study (apparently missing the 1955 revision and the major changes after World War II). Oliver Harris's attempt to engage Burroughs's Tangier context is most pronounced and original. But his abandoned project of obsessively photographing the Tangier medina at dawn as a point of entry leads to a claim that the real material base for the novel is not, after all, the city, but Burroughs's correspondence to Ginsberg. We might note that Harris's Tangier at dawn is a city evacuated of people, unlike Burroughs's.

9 McCarthy, "Burroughs's *Naked Lunch*," 42. The essay is an expanded version of her famous review of *Naked Lunch*, "Déjeuner sur l'herbe," which ran in the inaugural issue of the *New York Review of Books*.

10 Harris argues that the mostly occluded epistolary history of *Naked Lunch*'s composition should be recalled.

11 It is important to consult both collections, *Letters to Allen Ginsberg* and *Letters of William S. Burroughs*, which overlap. The latter does not include some letters that refer to Tangier and removes some references within letters that do appear (e.g., references to books he was reading), giving an exaggerated sense of Burroughs's detachment from the world around him.

12 See Vaidon, *Tangier*, 304.

13 Burroughs, letter dated April 20, 1955, *Letters of William S. Burroughs*, 274.

14 Burroughs, letter dated March 31, 1955, *Letters to Allen Ginsberg*, 92.

15 Burroughs met Gysin at Bowles's house in 1955, and apparently made a positive impression (Morgan, *Literary Outlaw*, 254). Burroughs was familiar with Gysin's famous Tangier restaurant, 1001 Nights (see chapter 6). It was not until Paris, 1958, however, that the two became close; they bonded strongly. Gysin helped with the final draft of *Naked Lunch*; Gysin then told Burroughs about Hassan i Sabbah, which figured deeply in his later work.

16 The work is Vaidon, *Tangier*. According to several sources, Woolman allegedly gave names of homosexual foreign residents to the Moroccan authorities in the 1960s, which precipitated Burroughs's final departure from Tangier. (See Finlayson, *Tangier*, for an account.)

17 Burroughs, undated letter [June 16, 1954], *Letters of William S. Burroughs*, 215.

18 Burroughs, letter dated December 13, 1954, *Letters of William S. Burroughs*, 245.

19 Burroughs, letter dated January 9, 1955, *Letters of William S. Burroughs*, 254.

20 Burroughs, *Interzone*, 54.

21 The editors of *Letters to Ginsberg* date the letter, within which the routine was first drafted, as February 7, 1954, as Burroughs dated it, but Harris corrects the date to February 7, 1955.

22 Burroughs, *Interzone*, 144.

23 Ibid., 49.

24 Burroughs, letter dated August 10, 1955, *Letters of William S. Burroughs*, 278.

25 Burroughs, *Naked Lunch*, 54.

26 Burroughs, *Letters of William S. Burroughs*, 337.

27 See Mage, "Little America."

28 Burroughs, undated letter [October 6, 1955], *Letters of William S. Burroughs*, 282.

29 Burroughs, letter dated October 23, 1955, *Letters to Allen Ginsberg*, 119.

30 Burroughs, letter dated November 1, 1955, *Letters of William S. Burroughs*, 300.

31 Ibid., 307.

32 Murphy, *Wising Up the Marks*, 24.

33 Burroughs, letter dated May 15, 1956, *Letters of William S. Burroughs*, 319.

34 Burroughs, letter dated September 13, 1956, *Letters to Allen Ginsberg*, 148.

35 Ibid., 147.

36 Burroughs, letter dated October 29, 1956, *Letters of William S. Burroughs*, 342.

37 Ibid., 342.

38 Burroughs, letter dated December 20, 1956, *Letters of William S. Burroughs*, 345.

39 Burroughs, letter dated January 23, 1957, *Letters of William S. Burroughs*, 349.

40 See Burroughs's letter of July 15, 1954, about his experiences with Tibetan Buddhism, *Letters to Allen Ginsberg*, 47–48.

41 Burroughs, letter dated January 23, 1957, *Letters of William S. Burroughs*, 349–50.

42 See Behdad, *Belated Travelers*, and Said, *Orientalism*.

43 This is Burroughs's excised explanation for why "The Reader will frequently find the same thing said in the same words" in the text. "This is not carelessness nor is it for The Infatuation With Sound Of Own Words Dept." Grauerholz, *Naked Lunch: The Restored Text*, excised passage, 288.

44 Pease, "Doing Justice," 4.

45 Burroughs, *Naked Lunch*, 179.

46 Burroughs, letter dated December 13, 1954, *Letters to Allen Ginsberg*, 77–78.

47 Gifford wrote a gossip column for the *Tangier Gazette*. See Vaidon, *Tangier*, 275.

48 Burroughs, *Interzone*, 156.

49 Ibid., 128.

50 *Oxford English Dictionary* (2nd ed., Oxford: Clarendon Press, 1989, vol. 9), s.v. "moor," def. 1a.

51 See Mowitt, "Breaking up Fanon's Voice." See also my "Fanon's *al-Jaza'ir*, or Algeria Translated."

52 See Wechsberg, "Anything Goes."

53 Burroughs, *Interzone*, 65–66.

54 Ibid., 167.

55 Shaviro, "Two Lessons from Burroughs," 40.

56 Burroughs, *Interzone*, 194. Joseph McNicholas's essay linking Burroughs's sense of betrayal by the manipulation of language by a prominent uncle working in public relations is a helpful analogue.

57 Deleuze, "He Stuttered," in *Essays Critical and Clinical*; and Deleuze and Guattari, *Kafka*.

58 Ginsberg, *Journals: Early Fifties, Early Sixties*, 101.

59 See Balibar, "The Nation Form: History and Ideology," in Balibar and Wallerstein, *Race, Nation, Class*.

60 According to DeRosa, Hitchcock initiated a copyright search on *Into Thin Air*; when it came back as unavailable, he reverted to *The Man Who Knew Too Much* (*Writing with Hitchcock*, 185, 191).

61 I thank Alan Nadel for pointing out this pun to me when I presented an early version of this section at the Narrative Conference, University of California, Berkeley, on March 27, 2003.

62 DeRosa, *Writing with Hitchcock*, 179.

63 I disagree with Corber that the scene suggests that Jo has failed as a mother because she is "absorbed in a fashion magazine" and that Hank's behavior suggests that he is poorly socialized and thus coded as potentially homosexual (*In the Name of National Security*, 145–46). Rather, the scene shows Hank as "properly" curious, as "explorer." Hank's act is the paradigmatic act of male colonialism (see Fanon's "Algeria Unveiled," in *L'An V de la révolution algérienne*).

64 For Elsie Michie, too, this scene "show[s] most vividly the kinds of fantasies that can be articulated around idealized images of the mother and the domestic sphere." Though Michie comments that the "moment of exposure is represented as shocking in terms of Muslim culture," she leaves the Muslim woman behind and employs unveiling as a metaphor for the "veiled desires of the 'typical' American wife and mother [which when] exposed turns out to be equally shocking." Disputing Slavoj Žižek's reading of the film that calls the mother's desire terrifying because it is unknowable, Michie argues that the film "suggest[s] that the mother articulates her desires quite clearly if one can learn to listen carefully enough to what she says" ("Unveiling Maternal Desires," 31, 32).

65 DeRosa, *Writing with Hitchcock*, 181.

66 Corber, *In the Name of National Security*, 145. See also Michie, "Unveiling Maternal Desires," 31–32.

67 Fanon, *A Dying Colonialism*, 44.

68 See Alloula, *The Colonial Harem*.

69 See Mernissi, "Les Bébé-Belles Européennes," in *Etes-vous vacciné contre le «harem»?* and "La Taille 38: le harem des femmes occidentales," in *Le Harem Européen*.

70 Corber has argued that Stewart's character's voyeurism is linked to arrested sexual development, and that the film attempts to reclaim those technologies that the national security state had appropriated for surveillance (e.g., the camera) for a private erotics. See *In the Name of National Security*, chapter 3.

71 Truffaut, *Hitchcock*, 171.

72 See Rogin, "Make My Day!"

73 See DeRosa, *Writing with Hitchcock*, 180.

74 Erickson, quoted in ibid., 190.

75 Marrakech doesn't figure in *Naked Lunch*, but in *The Wild Boys* Burroughs depicts Marrakech as a Wild West kind of place: "Unlighted streets carriages with carbide lamps. It looks like an 1890 print from some explorer's travel book. Wild boys in the streets whole packs of them vicious as famished dogs. There is almost no police force in operation and everyone who can afford it has private

guards." If Burroughs's Tangier was a vast market, his Marrakech is organic and spreading: "Waves of decoration and architecture have left a series of strata-like exposed geologic formations. There isn't a place in the world you can't find a piece of it in Marrakech, a St Louis street, a Mexican cantina, that house straight from England, Alpine huts in the mountains, a vast film set where the props are continually shifting. The city has spread in all directions up into the Atlas mountains to the east, south to the Sahara, westward to the coastal cities, up into the industrial reservations of the north. There are fantastic parties, vast estates and luxury such as we read about in the annals of the Roman Empire" (414–15).

CHAPTER 5 ~~Three Serious Writers~~ Two Serious Authors

1 In June 1999, Mrabet told me that many of the tapes had been destroyed; Bowles professed to be unaware of the whereabouts of the original tapes. After Bowles's death, several unmarked tapes were deposited at the University of Delaware library.

2 Bowles, *My Sister's Hand in Mine*, 318.

3 Ashbery, quoted in Dillon, *The Portable Paul and Jane Bowles*, i; Williams, foreword to *Feminine Wiles*, 7.

4 Deleuze and Guattari, *Kafka*, 24.

5 Dillon, *The Portable Paul and Jane Bowles*, viii.

6 Allen, "The Narrative Erotics of *Two Serious Ladies*," 20.

7 Bowles, *My Sister's Hand in Mine*, 379.

8 Deleuze, *Essays Critical and Clinical*, 109–10.

9 Capote, *Answered Prayers*, 72.

10 Paul Bowles, personal interview, February 13, 1996.

11 In "Tangier," Capote refers to the city as a "basin that holds you, a timeless place" (120). Discussing the summer of 1949, Michelle Green writes: "Each night at dinner, [Jane] regaled Truman and Jack [Dunphey] and Paul with absurd little stories about her pursuit of Cherifa" (*The Dream at the End of the World*, 68). Capote was well aware of her circulation between communities.

12 Gaonkar and Povinelli, "Technologies of Public Forms," 393.

13 Dillon calls this the "most directly autobiographical rendering of a conversation between herself and Paul that she was ever to write" (*A Little Original Sin*, 256).

14 See Warner, "Publics and Counterpublics."

15 J. Bowles, quoted in Dillon, *A Little Original Sin*, 235.

16 Ibid., 243.

17 Ibid., 237.

18 See Warner, "Publics and Counterpublics."

19 Chittick, *The Sufi Path of Knowledge*, 14.

20 P. Bowles, *Without Stopping*, 287.

21 Burke, *Language as Symbolic Action*, 187. Burke is discussing Emerson's *Nature*.

22 The situation is analogous to T. E. Lawrence's relationship to Arabic, which for Deleuze inspires his "stuttering." In "Fanon's *al-Jaza'ir*," I argue that Fanon employs an Arabized French in his writings about revolutionary Algeria, using loan words and French words with Arabic etymologies, dissociates French language from nation, and produces a global French. Fanon had less intimacy with Arabic than Lawrence and Jane Bowles, which changes the effect.

23 Becker's remarkable essay in anthropology, translation, and aesthetics recounts his experiment in translating a line of Emerson's *Nature* into Old Javanese.

24 Becker, *Beyond Translation*, 298.

25 Spivak, "The Politics of Translation," 181.

26 Bowles, *My Sister's Hand in Mine*, 97–98.

27 I have slightly altered the translation. Yusuf 'Ali, translator of the edition I cite, *The Holy Qur'an*, says that a *barzakh* is a partition or bar or barrier, the place or state in which people will be after death before Judgment. Behind them is the barrier of death, and in front of them is the barzakh, a quiescent state until the Judgment comes. In the epigraph to this chapter, the editors of *The Holy Qur'an* give "barrier" and "partition" as translations for *barzakh* and *hijran*. Wehr translates *barzakh* as "interval, gap, break, partition, bar, obstruction; isthmus" (52) and *hijran* from the verb *hajara*, meaning to deny access, to stop, detain, hinder (157).

28 Ibn al-'Arabi, cited in Chittick, *The Sufi Path of Knowledge*, 117–18.

29 Stefania Pandolfo's brilliant ethnography *Impasse of the Angels* discusses the idea of barzakh in relationship to communication with her Moroccan interlocutors. Pandolfo sees the idea as analogous to concepts of the major Maghrebi writers of decolonization, who theorized a literary and linguistic space around the concept of *la différence intraitable* (intractable difference): "A hiatus which destabilizes the assignment of places and parts, which displaces the categories of classical and colonial reason and opens a heterological space of intercultural dialogue—an atopical intermediate region that might be called a *barzakh*. There in that interstitial mode of identity between languages and cultures, between genders and categorizations, a certain listening becomes possible" (5–6). In her book, Pandolfo responds to the idea of *barzakh* as solid edge and attempts to write an ethnography that attends seriously to the voice of the other, one that allows itself to be reoriented or disrupted by the voices of others. See also Qader, "Fictional Testimonies or Testimonial Fictions."

30 Bowles, *My Sister's Hand in Mine*, 201.

31 Dillon, *A Little Original Sin*, 397.

32 Ibid., 27.

33 Deleuze, "He Stuttered," 112.

34 J. Bowles, *Out in the World*, 62.

35 Dillon, *A Little Original Sin*, 160; J. Bowles, *Out in the World*, 78–80.

36 Dillon, *A Little Original Sin*, 170.

37 P. Bowles, *Without Stopping*, 284.

38 In *Without Stopping*, Paul states that prior to her arrival in Tangier in January 1948, Jane spent the previous autumn studying Arabic formally in Paris, "with the result that on her arrival in Tangier she already had a basic understanding of Arabic word formation and grammar" (284). This statement, however, is controverted by Jane's letters from the period, when she vacillated about whether to join Paul in Morocco while living in Vermont and Greenwich, Connecticut. (Millicent Dillon confirms: "I think there is no question that Paul was wrong in saying Jane was in Paris studying Arabic in 1947" (personal communication, December 10, 2003]). *Without Stopping* was written as Jane languished in Málaga, shortly before her death. Whether or not Paul intentionally predated her formal study of Arabic (Jane would do so in Paris in 1950) so as to downplay her ambivalence about joining him in Tangier, his comment about her quick and intense relationship to Moroccan Arabic is relevant. She did study Arabic with a tutor shortly after arrival.

39 J. Bowles, *Out in the World*, 154.

40 Bowles, *My Sister's Hand in Mine*, 420.

41 Dillon, *A Little Original Sin*, 184.

42 J. Bowles, *Out in the World*, 93.

43 Ibn al-'Arabi, quoted in Pandolfo, *Impasse of the Angels*, 1.

44 There is some disagreement among scholars regarding the publication history of this work. Dillon comments that Jane originally wrote the work in New York in 1951 as a travel essay for *Mademoiselle*, in which it appeared under the title "East Side: North Africa." In the mid-1960s, late in Jane Bowles's decline, Paul edited the work in order to bolster a collected edition of his wife's short stories. According to Dillon, he changed its voice from first to third person, shortened it, and republished as fiction under the title "Everything Is Nice" (*A Little Original Sin*, 210). Maier accepts Dillon's version and emphasizes the non-fiction status of the 1966 version, which he reads as ethnographic (*Desert Songs*, 124–34). Gena Caponi, however, who looked at the manuscript notebook, quietly challenges Dillon's version and suggests that Paul simply used a different draft ("The Unfinished Jane Bowles," 144). My own examination of notebook 22 reveals not only that Jane experimented with the third and first persons, as Caponi notes, but also that there are chunks of manuscript not published in either version. Looking through these drafts demonstrates Bowles's concern in

the project with question of walls, chalky surfaces, and the melancholic attempt to touch or reach out to connect with the physical space of Tangier. Differing versions of a deleted conversation between husband and wife—one version later published as the fragment "The Iron Table"—reveal that within the thinking associated with the "Everything Is Nice" project was Jane's meditation on Paul's dismay at Moroccans' embrace of the cultural forms of European modernity. On the challenges of reconstructing Jane Bowles's fragments, see Hibbard, "Out in the World."

45 Bowles, in Dillon, *Portable Paul and Jane Bowles*, 280.

46 P. Bowles, *In Touch*, 197.

47 J. Bowles, "East Side: North Africa," in Dillon, *Portable Paul and Jane Bowles*, 280.

48 Maier suggests that Bowles is translating the word *mlih* (*Desert Songs*, 133) and reads Bowles's use of the word *nice* as her representation of the "characters' inability to make the kind of subtle distinctions that come from genuine familiarity": "Misunderstandings abound, partly because of a language barrier, and partly because certain features of one culture are not understood in the other." But Jeanie is hardly representative of a stable culture, and stability is necessary for Maier's reading of the story as ethnographic. His approach leaves him at a loss to describe the dialogue: "Why the porcupine?" he asks, and then says the conversation "degenerate[s] to an exchange about trucks" (132, 133). To claim the conversation degenerates implies that a meaningful conversation is possible between individuals, with which I think Jane Bowles would have disagreed. (The porcupine, incidentally, is an ingredient in a Moroccan soup and commonly available at the market, where Jane spent much time.) Maier makes an error in suggesting that Jeanie proclaims "Everything is nice." Zodelia makes the comment.

49 Bowles, *My Sister's Hand in Mine*, 467.

50 Bowles, notebook 22, Jane Bowles archive.

51 I refer here to the version as published in 1966. *My Sister's Hand in Mine*, 320. Compare to "East Side: North Africa," in Dillon, ed., *Portable Paul and Jane Bowles*, 287, where these lines appear at the end of the piece.

52 Bowles, notebook 22, Jane Bowles archive.

53 Dillon, personal communication, December 10, 2003.

54 Bowles, "Letter from Morocco," 544.

55 Bowles's use of the word *barbarous* puns on its shared etymology with the word *Berber*, from the Greek onomatopoetic *barbaros*, meaning "foreign, ignorant," and apparently a description of the "nonsense" sounds of people not speaking Greek. The word carried into Latin (*barbarus*) and, in turn, into the Moroccan Arabic word for Berber (*berbri*, plural *braber*).

56 Bowles enters volatile ground. His emphasis on the Berbers as the indigenous population of Morocco (Arabs invaded in the late seventh century) is

associated with a pro-French position because of the protectorate policy of emphasizing Berber particularity as part of a general divide-and-conquer strategy. The French maintenance of Berber "difference" during the protectorate, while not "inventing" a Berber tradition, certainly reorganized it. See Laroui, *History of the Maghrib*, chapter 1.

57 Quoted in Sawyer-Lauçanno, *An Invisible Spectator*, 345.

58 Bowles, *Yallah*, 17.

59 Bowles made four trips through Morocco over five months in 1959, covering 25,000 miles and recording over 250 selections. After three months, the Moroccan government revoked the permission they had granted him. With the consent of the U.S. Embassy, Bowles continued for two more months before stopping. Not until 1972 did the Library of Congress issue a two-volume record set of Bowles's recordings (Sawyer-Lauçanno, *An Invisible Spectator*, 346–51).

60 Bowles, "Letter from Morocco," 545–46.

61 See Sawyer-Lauçanno, *An Invisible Spectator*, 347.

62 Bowles, "Notes on the Work of the Translator," 7.

63 Mullins argues that in his translations, Bowles "attempted to erase his own interests and position as an American writing about an 'Oriental' culture," but the texts themselves "frustrate this attempt" since "they call attention to themselves as 'colonial' texts and foreground the economic and sexual dimensions of their production" (*Colonial Affairs*, 134), confirming what Western anthropology and Orientalist discourse have already told the West about sexuality in Maghreb. As such they repeat a pattern Mullins finds throughout Paul Bowles's, Burroughs's, and Alfred Chester's Tangier work, work he sees as failed because it is "framed by the structures and stereotypes of colonial discourse."

64 Johnson, "Taking Fidelity Philosophically," 143.

65 Personal conversations with Mrabet and Choukri, Tangier, June 1999. See also L. Layachi, *Yesterday and Today*, chapter 6.

66 Laroui, *L'Idéologie arabe contemporaine*, 176. My translation.

67 Much later, Ben Jelloun partially apologized, without withdrawing his critique ("Témoignage d'un 'Arabe de service,'" *Le Monde*, May 20, 1994).

68 In April 1967, Jane Bowles, suffering from depression, "obsessive ideas," and epileptic seizures, was admitted to a psychiatric hospital in Málaga. There she was administered shock treatment. In late June, on the advice of the clinic, Paul brought her to stay at a pension run by an American couple living in Granada. After about a week, the Americans summoned Paul (who had returned to Tangier) to retrieve her. He installed her in a different clinic in Málaga. In 1969, Jane returned to Tangier, but after four months returned to the clinic. She died there in May 1973. Mrabet worked for the Bowleses as a chauffeur (Dillon, *A Little Original Sin*, 391–420). Mrabet's "British couple" is evidently based on David Montgomery Hart (1927–2001), an eminent American anthropologist

who wrote several ethnographies about Morocco and the Rif, including *The Aith Waryaghar of the Moroccan Rif* (1976), and his wife Ursula Kingsmill Hart, author of *Behind the Courtyard Door: The Daily Life of Tribeswomen in Northern Morocco* (1994).

69 Mrabet, *The Boy Who Set the Fire*, 30.

70 Some of what follows is reprinted from my critical introduction to this Moroccan edition.

71 See Judy, "On the Politics of Global Language."

72 Spivak, *A Critique of Postcolonial Reason*, 310.

CHAPTER 6   Hippie Orientalism

1 Buryn, *Vagabonding in Europe and North Africa*, 196.

2 Crapanzano, *Hermes' Dilemma and Hamlet's Desire*, 4.

3 Buryn, *Vagabonding in Europe and North Africa*, rev. ed., 159.

4 Shapiro, *Jimi Hendrix*, 377–79.

5 Setterberg, "Morocco," 685–87.

6 In *All You Need Is Love: The Peace Corps and the Spirit of the 1960s*, Elizabeth Cobbs Hoffman argues that the Peace Corps, founded in 1961, offers a "window onto the spirit of the sixties" and the "contradictory impulses to altruism and self-aggrandizement" (7). Though she does not discuss the program in Morocco, she shows the limits of the encounters: "Emotional social activism sometimes did more for the helpers than for the helped" (9). By the late 1960s, some Peace Corps volunteers felt that the implications of the program were corrupt. The Committee of Returned Volunteers announced in 1969 that the Peace Corps "should be abolished" because it perpetuated underdevelopment and was effectively a "graduate school for imperialism" (Cobbs Hoffman, 218).

7 "Morocco," 42.

8 Vaidon, *Tangier*, 357.

9 Ibid.

10 Chelminski, "Open Season on Drug Smugglers."

11 Rabinow, *Reflections on Fieldwork in Morocco*, 1.

12 Said, *Orientalism*, 326.

13 Said's study was itself engaged in the various social and political crises of the 1970s from which it emerged and did not step back to look at Geertz's still new work. Early critiques made by anthropologists James Clifford and Vincent Crapanzano immediately identified Said's own implication in the project he sets out to critique. Timothy Brennan historicizes Said's early work in relation to the Vietnam War era and calls *Orientalism* a very American book that finds a way to "manage an American critique that fell into none of these categories [powerless

prophetic anarchism of beat poetry and 60s counterculture, plaintive radical liberalism of C. Wright Mills, or reputable, but slandered, traditions of American communism, made toothless by Cold War prejudices] while drawing on all of them" ("The Illusion of a Future," 577).

14 *FRUS 1964–68*, 24:176.

15 Geertz, "Thinking as a Moral Act," 149–51.

16 See Borstelmann, *The Cold War and the Color Line*, and Plummer, *Window on Freedom*.

17 Setterberg's article for the *Nation* is exceptionally rare in linking the hippies, tourism, and Moroccan student activists.

18 Tessler, "Alienation of Urban Youth," 93.

19 See "Folk the Kasbah," Elias Muhanna's interview with Omar Sayyed, leader of the popular Moroccan band Nass el Ghiwane. In *Three Faces of Beauty*, Susan Ossman has shown the implications of changing notions of beauty and hairstyles among women in Casablanca and Cairo. I don't, therefore, want to minimize the relevance of changes in male Moroccan hairstyles in the sixties and seventies.

20 Kramer, *Allen Ginsberg in America*, xvi–xvii.

21 Kramer, *Honor to the Bride*, 3.

22 See Fabian, *Time and the Other*, chapter 3.

23 Crapanzano, *Hermes' Dilemma and Hamlet's Desire*, 317n2.

24 In 2004, female illiteracy in Morocco was estimated at 90 percent for rural women, and about 60 percent for urban women. Kramer's book does not appear to have appeared in French translation, so in English it would be yet further isolated from all but a handful of Moroccan women.

25 Crapanzano and Kramer, "A World of Saints and She-Demons," 14.

26 Waterbury, *The Commander of the Faithful*. Waterbury's work uses a quote from Geertz's 1967 essay on new state politics as an epigraph. His project examines continuities with the past and new formations with relationship to tradition.

27 *FRUS 1964–68*, 24:176.

28 *FRUS 1964–68*, 24:11.

29 See *FRUS 1964–68*, 24:13–14. This crackdown alludes in part to Oufkir's implication in the Ben Barka affair, the details of which long remained obscure. For discussion of State Department responses to reports that the CIA was involved in the October 1965 kidnapping, as well as the meeting between President Johnson and the Moroccan king's representative on the Ben Barka afffair, see *FRUS 1964–68*, 24:179–82. The details of Ben Barka's fate were only disclosed in 2001.

30 See Crapanzano, "Review of *Meaning and Order in Morocco*" and *Hermes' Dilemma*.

31 Rabinow, *Reflections on Fieldwork in Morocco*, 148.

32 Crapanzano, *Hermes' Dilemma and Hamlet's Desire*, 4.

33 Bayoumi, "East of the Sun," 259.

34 Dalle, *Maroc*, 195; my translation.

35 Michener, *The Drifters*, 689–90.

36 The rare exceptions are Jemail, a boy who feeds the drug habits of the hippies and is represented as the incarnation of evil. The only other Moroccans are a trio of engineers who plan to build a major resort with Fairbanks's capital, an ineffectual police inspector, and a doctor. Compare Butwin, "On Tour with Fez and Djellaba."

37 Fernea, *A Street in Marrakech*, 183–86.

38 Said, "On Lost Causes," 542.

39 McAlister, *Epic Encounters*, 92.

40 Ibid., 99–100.

41 The company was founded in 1992 by an American woman named Susan Frankel.

42 Knickerbocker, "Paula Wolfert's Pursuit of Flavor."

43 I have prepared it following Wolfert's elaborate instructions. Despite my emphasis on her ethnographic prose, I have also spent many hours following her recipes (as well as those in four other cookbooks dedicated to Moroccan food, including a Moroccan cookbook from the 1970s by Latifa Bennani Smires, *La Cuisine marocaine*). The copy of Wolfert's book that I refer to is splattered with oils and stained with spices.

44 For a detailed description of the restaurant, which featured Gysin's paintings of the Sahara and wooden menus (with names of dishes burned in), see Vaidon, *Tangier*, 288–90. See also Green, *The Dream at the End of the World*, 123–24.

45 Palmer, "Jajouka/Up the Mountain," 44.

46 Schuyler, "Joujouka/Jajouka/Zahjoukah," 158.

47 Gysin, quoted in ibid., 153.

48 Coleman, liner notes, *Dancing in Your Head*.

49 Litweiler, *Ornette Coleman*, 150.

50 Ibid., 151.

51 Ibid., 152.

52 Ibid., 153.

53 Currie, "Reissuing *Dancing in Your Head*."

54 Litweiler, *Ornette Coleman*, 162.

55 Schuyler, "Joujouka/Jajouka/Zahjoukah," 156.

56 Geertz, *After the Fact*, 13–15.

57 Geertz, *Interpretation of Cultures*, 28n6. Geertz studied Sefrou in 1964, 1965–66, 1968–69, and 1972.

58 Geertz, *After the Fact*, 12.

59   Geertz, "Thinking as a Moral Act," 147.

60   Lila Abu-Lughod attributes the popularity of Morocco among contemporary anthropologists in large part to Geertz's work there ("Anthropology's Orient").

61   Geertz, *After the Fact*, 15.

62   In *Works and Lives*, Geertz takes anthropological writing "seriously as writing" (3) and analyzes the style of Bronislaw Malinowski, Ruth Benedict, Edward E. Evans-Pritchard, Claude Lévi-Strauss, and surveys the reflexive works of Rabinow, Crapanzano, and Kevin Dwyer. He rehearses imagined complaints: "If anthropologists were to stop reporting how things are done in Africa and Polynesia, if they were instead to spend their time trying to find double plots in Alfred Kroeber or unreliable narrators in Max Gluckman, and if they were seriously to argue that Edward Westermarck's stories about Morocco and those of Paul Bowles relate to their subject in the same way, with the same means and the same purposes, matters would indeed be in a parlous state" (2–3). This is the only mention of Bowles I have found in Geertz's work. In pairing Bowles with Westermarck, Geertz's temporal distancing is suspect. Bowles was concerned with some of the same problems as Geertz (see my discussion of "A Distant Episode" in chapter 2).

63   Geertz, "Thick Description," 9.

64   Eickelman, *The Middle East*, 18.

65   On colonial anthropology, see Miller, *Theories of Africans*; Asad, *Anthropology and the Colonial Encounter*.

66   Marcus, "The Uses of Complicity," 90.

67   Peter Gran has argued that Geertz's work from this period was "an attack on the Left" and laments the influence of Geertz's work on American political economy: "The symbolized world of elite communication so marginalizes the role of historical dynamics and so reduces history as a means of understanding culture that there is often no overlap" ("Studies of Anglo-American Political Economy," 238). Gran comments that Geertz's reputation was sustained by the limited nature of the area-studies audience, which did not point out his flaws. William H. Sewell Jr. argues that Geertz's idea of culture is not adequate for social historians or for understanding change. Sewell discusses the materialist critique of Geertz's text metaphor: it produces a synchronic gaze that sidesteps the question of the processes (i.e., the diachronic) that produced the culture ("Geertz, Cultural Systems, and History," 36). Sewall agrees. Sherry Ortner defends Geertz against claims that he is a disengaged scholar, intellectually or ethically, by arguing that his work "offers the intellectual grounding for a position of considerable political importance," namely "the cultural construction of 'agency,' of human intentionality and forms of empowerment to act" (*The Fate of "Culture*," 5). Still, Ortner concedes that "Thick Description" maintains too

great a distance in critiquing the role of power in relations between Cohen and the state. See also Agnew, "History and Anthropology."

68 Crapanzano, *Hermes' Dilemma and Hamlet's Desire*, 43.

69 Geertz, *Local Knowledge*, 64.

70 Said, *Orientalism*, 326.

71 I am indebted to James Clifford's 1983 essay, "On Ethnographic Authority" (*The Predicament of Culture*, 21–54), which argues that Geertz's self-dramatization at the beginning of "Deep Play: Notes on the Balinese Cockfight" represents Geertz's establishment of his own authority to interpret the cockfight.

72 Geertz, *After the Fact*, 84.

73 Burke, *Language as Symbolic Action*, 45.

74 Janjar, "La Foi des hommes à l'épreuve du temps," 27.

75 Sinaceur, "L'Islam et les terroirs," 25.

WORKS CITED

Archival Sources

Unpublished

Claude McKay Collection. Yale Collection of American Literature, Beinecke
  Rare Book and Manuscript Library.
Jane Auer Bowles Collection, Harry Ransom Humanities Research Center, The
  University of Texas at Austin.
Paul Bowles Collection, Harry Ransom Humanities Research Center, The Uni-
  versity of Texas at Austin.
Paul Bowles Papers, University of Delaware Library, Special Collections.

Published

Charles Gallagher, American Universities Field Staff reports, North Africa Se-
  ries, 1956–67.
Chicago Defender. Chicago: Defender, Co., 1942–43. Held at the Northwestern
  University Library.
Foreign Relations of the United States, 1943–1968. 14 vols. U.S. Department of
  State. Washington, D.C.: Government Printing Office, 1964–1999.
The Stars and Stripes. Algiers, Algeria: U.S. Armed Forces, 1943–45. Held at the
  Center for Research Libraries, Chicago.
Tangier Gazette. Held at the Library of the Tangier American Legation Museum,
  Tangier, Morocco.

Books and Articles

Abu-Lughod, Lila. "Anthropology's Orient." In *Theory, Politics and the Arab
  World*, edited by Hisham Sharabi, 81–131. New York: Routledge, 1990.
Abu Talib, Muhammad. "Balagha Buwlz az-zuba au A ras l' Bowles." *Al-'Alam
  ath-Thaqafi* [Rabat], January 25, 1997, 6.
Agamben, Giorgio. *Homo Sacer: Sovereign Power and Bare Life*. Translated by
  Daniel Heller-Roazen. Stanford, Calif.: Stanford University Press, 1998.

——. *Infancy and History: The Destruction of Experience*. Translated by Liz Heron. London: Verso, 1993.

Agnew, Jean-Christophe. "History and Anthropology: Scenes from a Marriage." *Yale Journal of Criticism* 3.2 (1990): 28–50.

al Amali, Karim. "De la romance au Cauchemar." *Maroc Hebdo*, November 12–18, 1999, 35.

Allen, Carolyn J. "The Narrative Erotics of *Two Serious Ladies*." In *A Tawdry Place of Salvation: The Art of Jane Bowles*, edited by Jennie Skerl, 19–36. Carbondale: Southern Illinois University Press, 1997.

Alloula, Malek. *The Colonial Harem*. Translated by Myrna Godzich and Wlad Godzich. Minneapolis: University of Minnesota Press, 1986.

Apter, Emily. *Continental Drift: From National Characters to Virtual Subjects*. Chicago: University of Chicago Press, 1999.

——. "'Untranslatable' Algeria." *Parallax* 4.2 (1998): 47–59.

Arac, Jonathan. "Criticism between Opposition and Counterpoint." *boundary 2* 25.2 (1998): 55–69.

Asad, Talal, ed., *Anthropology and the Colonial Encounter*. New York: Humanities Press, 1973.

Azzou, Mustafa El. "Les Hommes d'affaires américains au Maroc avant 1956." *Guerres Mondiales et Conflits Contemporains* 46 (1995): 131–43.

Bahraoui, Hassan. *Halqa rawaya tanja: Baul Buwlz, Larbi Layachi, Mohammed Mrabet*. Rabat 2002.

Bal, Mieke. "Three-Way Misreading." *Diacritics* 30.1 (2000): 2–24.

Baldwin, Kate A. *Beyond the Color Line and the Iron Curtain: Reading Encounters between Black and Red, 1922–1963*. Durham, N.C.: Duke University Press, 2002.

Balibar, Etienne, and Immanuel Wallerstein. *Race, Nation, Class: Ambiguous Identities*. New York: Verso, 1991.

Bargach, Jamila. "Liberatory, Nationalising and Moralising by Ellipsis: Reading and Listening to Lhussein Slaoui's Song 'Lmirikan.'" *Journal of North African Studies* 4.4 (1999): 61–88.

Basinger, Jeanine. *The World War II Combat Film*. New York: Columbia University Press, 1986.

Bayoumi, Moustafa. "East of the Sun (West of the Moon): Islam, the Ahmadis, and African America." *Journal of Asian American Studies* 4 (2001): 251–63.

Becker, A. L. *Beyond Translation: Essays toward a Modern Philology*. Ann Arbor: University of Michigan Press, 1995.

Behdad, Ali. *Belated Travelers: Orientalism in the Age of Colonial Dissolution*. Durham, N.C.: Duke University Press, 1994.

Belghazi, Taieb, and Mohammed Madani. *L'Action collective au Maroc*. Rabat: Faculté des Lettres, 2001.

Bennani-Chraïbi, Mounia. *Soumis et rebelles, les jeunes au Maroc*. Casablanca: Fennec, 1995.

Bess, Demaree. "Uncle Sam Sponsors a Smugglers' Paradise." *Saturday Evening Post*, April 16, 1949, 20–21, 122, 125–26.

——. "We're Invading North Africa Again." *Saturday Evening Post*, June 1949, 22–23, 132, 134, 136, 138.

Bhabha, Homi. *The Location of Culture*. New York: Routledge, 1994.

Bimberg, Edward L. *The Moroccan Goums: Tribal Warriors in a Modern War*. Westport, Conn.: Greenwood, 1999.

Blum, John Morton. *V Was for Victory: Politics and American Culture During World War II*. New York: Harcourt Brace Jovanovich, 1976.

Borstelmann, Thomas. *The Cold War and the Color Line: American Race Relations in the Global Arena*. Cambridge, Mass.: Harvard University Press, 2001.

Bowles, Jane. *My Sister's Hand in Mine: The Collected Works*. New York: Farrar, Straus and Giroux, 1995.

——. *Out in the World: Selected Letters of Jane Bowles, 1935–1970*. Edited by Millicent Dillon. Santa Barbara, Calif.: Black Sparrow, 1985.

Bowles, Paul. "Bowles et Choukri: Le Temps de la polémique." *Les Nouvelles du Nord* [Tangier] 28 Feb. 1997: 6–7.

——. "Burroughs in Tangier." *Big Table* 1.2 (1959): 42–43.

——. *The Delicate Prey*. 1950. New York: Ecco, 1972.

——. "Fez." *Holiday* 8.1 (1950): 12–22.

——. *In Touch: The Letters of Paul Bowles*. Edited by Jeffrey Miller. New York: Farrar, Straus and Giroux, 1994.

——. *Let It Come Down*. New York: Random House, 1952.

——. "Letter from Morocco." *Nation*, December 22, 1956, 544–46.

——. "No More Djinns." *American Mercury*, June 1951, 650–58.

——. "Notes on the Work of the Translator." In *Five Eyes*. Santa Barbara, Calif.: Black Sparrow, 1979.

——. Personal interviews. July 9–10, 1994; February 8–13, 1996; June 4–5, 1999.

——. *Points in Time*. London: Peter Owen, 1982.

——. "Sad for U.S., Sad for Algeria." *Nation*, May 24, 1958, 475–77.

——. *The Sheltering Sky*. 1949. New York: Vintage Books, 1990.

——. *The Spider's House*. 1955. Santa Barbara, Calif.: Black Sparrow, 1982.

——. *Their Heads Are Green and Their Hands Are Blue*. 1963. New York: Ecco, 1984.

——. "Thirty Years Later." Preface to *Let It Come Down*. Santa Barbara, Calif.: Black Sparrow, 1980.

——. *Without Stopping*. New York: Putnam, 1972.

——. *Yallah*. New York: McDowell, Obolensky, 1957.

Brennan, Timothy. "The Illusion of a Future: *Orientalism* as Traveling Theory." *Critical Inquiry* 26 (2000): 529–57.

Burke, Kenneth. *Language as Symbolic Action*. Berkeley: University of California Press, 1966.

Burroughs, William S. *Interzone*. Edited by James Grauerholz. New York: Viking, 1989.

——. *Letters of William S. Burroughs, 1945–1959*. Edited by Oliver Harris. New York: Viking, 1993.

——. *Letters to Allen Ginsberg, 1953–57*. New York: Full Court, 1982.

——. *Naked Lunch*. New York: Grove, 1992.

——. *Naked Lunch: The Restored Text*. Edited by James Grauerholz and Barry Miles. New York: Grove, 2001.

——. *The Wild Boys*. In *The Soft Machine, Nova Express, The Wild Boys: Three Novels*. New York: Grove Weidenfeld, 1980.

Buryn, Ed. *Vagabonding in Europe and North Africa*. New York and Berkeley, Calif.: Random House and the Bookworks, 1971. Rev. ed. 1973.

Butler, Judith. *Bodies That Matter: On the Discursive Limits of "Sex."* New York: Routledge, 1993.

Butwin, David. "On Tour with Fez and Djellaba." *Saturday Review*, April 27, 1968, 62–64.

Caponi, Gena Dagel. *Paul Bowles: Romantic Savage*. Carbondale: Southern Illinois University Press, 1994.

——. "The Unfinished Jane Bowles." In *A Tawdry Place of Salvation: The Art of Jane Bowles*, edited by Jennie Skerl, 134–52. Carbondale: Southern Illinois University Press, 1997.

Capote, Truman. *Answered Prayers: The Unfinished Novel*. New York: Random House, 1987.

——. "Tangier." *Vogue*, April 1, 1950, 120–21, 166–67.

——. "Truman Capote Introduces Jane Bowles." *Mademoiselle*, December 1966, 114–16.

Chelminski, Rudolph. "Open Season on Drug Smugglers." *Life*, June 26, 1970, 28–35.

Chittick, William C. *The Sufi Path of Knowledge: Ibn al-'Arabi's Metaphysics of Imagination*. Albany: State University of New York Press, 1989.

Choukri, Mohamed. *Paul Bowles wa 'uzla Tanja (Bowles and the solitude of Tangier)*. Tangier: Altopress, 1996.

Clifford, James. *The Predicament of Culture*. Cambridge, Mass.: Harvard University Press, 1988.

Clifford, James, and George E. Marcus, eds. *Writing Culture: The Poetics and Politics of Ethnography*. Berkeley: University of California Press, 1986.

Cobbs Hoffman, Elizabeth. *All You Need Is Love: The Peace Corps and the Spirit of the 1960s* (Cambridge, Mass.: Harvard University Press, 1998).

Coleman, Ornette. *Dancing in Your Head*. A&M Horizon SP 722. 1977. Reissue with previously unissued track, Verve, 2000.

Coon, Carleton. *A North Africa Story: The Anthropologist as OSS Agent, 1941–1943*. Ipswich, Mass.: Gambit, 1980.

Corber, Robert J. *In the Name of National Security: Hitchcock, Homophobia, and the Political Construction of Gender in Postwar America*. Durham, N.C.: Duke University Press, 1993.

Crapanzano, Vincent. *The Hamadsha: A Study in Moroccan Ethnopsychiatry*. Berkeley: University of California Press, 1973.

——. *Hermes' Dilemma and Hamlet's Desire: On the Epistemology of Interpretation*. Cambridge, Mass.: Harvard University Press, 1992.

——. "Review of *Meaning and Order in Morocco*." *Economic Development and Cultural Change* 29 (1981): 849–60.

Crapanzano, Vincent, and Jane Kramer. "A World of Saints and She-Demons." *New York Times Magazine*, June 22, 1969, 14–15, 18, 22–32, 36–38.

Crawford, Kenneth G. *Report on North Africa*. New York: Farrar and Rinehart, 1943.

Cripps, Thomas. *Making Movies Black: The Hollywood Message Movie from World War II to the Civil Rights Era*. New York: Oxford University Press, 1993.

Crosby, David, Stephen Stills, and Graham Nash. *Crosby, Stills and Nash*. Atlantic #19117. 1969.

Crowther, Geoff, and Hugh Finlay. *Morocco, Algeria and Tunisia: A Travel Survival Kit*. 2nd ed. Berkeley, Calif.: Lonely Planet, 1992.

Currie, Scott. "Reissuing *Dancing in Your Head*." In *Dancing in Your Head* by Ornette Coleman (liner notes). Verve, 2000.

Dalle, Ignace. *Maroc, 1961–1999: L'Espérance brisée*. Paris: Maisonneuve et Larose, 2001.

Dalton, R. T., R. E. Pearson, and H. R. Barrett, "The Urban Morphology of Tangier." In *Tanger: Espace, économie et société*, edited by Mohamed Refass, 91–111. Tangier: Université Abdelmalek Es-Saadi, Ecole Supérieure Roi Fahd de Traduction, 1993.

Deladurantaye, Leland. "Agamben's Potential." *Diacritics* 30.2 (2000): 3–24.

Deleuze, Gilles. *Essays Critical and Clinical*. Translated by Daniel W. Smith and Michael A. Greco. Minneapolis: University of Minnesota Press, 1997.

Deleuze, Gilles, and Félix Guattari. *Kafka: Toward a Minor Literature*. Translated by Dana Polan. Minneapolis: University of Minnesota Press, 1986.

DeRosa, Steven. *Writing with Hitchcock: The Collaboration of Alfred Hitchcock and John Michael Hayes*. New York: Faber and Faber, 2001.

Dillon, Millicent. *A Little Original Sin: The Life and Work of Jane Bowles*. 1981. New York: Anchor, 1990.

———. *You Are Not I: A Portrait of Paul Bowles.* Berkeley: University of California Press, 1998.

Dillon, Millicent, ed. *The Portable Paul and Jane Bowles.* New York: Penguin, 1994.

Dower, John W. *War without Mercy: Race and Power in the Pacific War.* New York: Pantheon, 1986.

Dryer, Bernard V. *The Image Makers.* New York: Harper & Brothers, 1958.

Eburne, Jonathan Paul. "Trafficking in the Void: Burroughs, Kerouac, and the Consumption of Otherness." *Modern Fiction Studies* 43.1 (1997): 53–92.

Edwards, Brian T. "Fanon's *al-Jaza'ir*, or Algeria Translated." *parallax* 8.2 (2002): 99–115.

———. "Preposterous Encounters: Interrupting American Studies with the (Post)Colonial, or *Casablanca* in the American Century." *Comparative (Post)colonialisms.* Special issue of *Comparative Studies of South Asia, Africa and the Middle East* 23.1–2 (2003): 70–86.

———. Review of *Queer Nations. Journal of North African Studies* 5.2 (2000): 94–98.

———. "The Well-Built Wall of Culture: Old New York and Its Harems." *The Age of Innocence.* Norton Critical Edition. Ed. Candace Waid. New York: Norton, 2003. 482–506.

———. "What Happened in Tangier?" Introduction to *Love with a Few Hairs* (1967), by Mohammed Mrabet, translated by Paul Bowles. Fez: Moroccan Cultural Studies Center, 2004. i–xiv.

———. "Yankee Pashas and Buried Women: Containing Abundance in 1950s Hollywood Orientalism." *Film and History* 31.2 (2001): 13–24.

Eickelman, Dale F. *The Middle East: An Anthropological Approach.* 2nd ed. Englewood Cliffs, N.J.: Prentice-Hall, 1989.

Elghandor, Abdelhak. "Bowles's Views of Atavism and Civilization." *Journal of Maghrebi Studies* 1.2 (1993): 77–94.

Ellingham, Mark, Shaun McVeigh, and Don Grisbrook. *Morocco: The Rough Guide* 4th ed. London: The Rogue Guides, 1993.

Evans, Oliver. "An Interview with Paul Bowles." 1971. In *Conversations with Paul Bowles,* edited by Gena D. Caponi. Jackson: University of Mississippi Press, 1993.

Fabian, Johannes. *Time and the Other: How Anthropology Makes Its Object.* New York: Columbia University Press, 1983.

Fanon, Frantz. *Black Skin, White Masks.* Translated by Charles Lam Markmann. 1952. New York: Grove, 1967.

———. *A Dying Colonialism.* Translated by Haakon Chevalier. New York: Grove, 1965.

———. *L'An V de la révolution algérienne.* Paris: François Maspero, 1960.

———. *Les Damnés de la terre.* Paris: Maspero, 1961.

Fauset, Jessie. "Dark Algiers the White." *Crisis* 29, no. 6 (1925): 255–58; *Crisis* 29, no. 7 (1925): 16–20.

Feis, Herbert. *Churchill, Roosevelt, Stalin.* Princeton, N.J.: Princeton University Press, 1957.

Fernea, Elizabeth. *A Street in Marrakech.* Garden City, N.Y.: Anchor Doubleday, 1980.

Finlayson, Iain. *Tangier: City of the Dream.* London: HarperCollins, 1993.

Gallagher, Charles. F. *The United States and North Africa: Morocco, Algeria, and Tunisia.* Cambridge, Mass.: Harvard University Press, 1963.

Gaonkar, Dilip Parameshwar, and Elizabeth A. Povinelli. "Technologies of Public Forms: Circulation, Transfiguration, Recognition." *Public Culture* 15 (2003): 385–97.

Gardiner, Kweku Attah. "African Opinion and World Peace." *Negro Quarterly* 1 (1943): 355, 359.

Geertz, Clifford. *After the Fact: Two Countries, Four Decades, One Anthropologist.* Cambridge, Mass.: Harvard University Press, 1995.

——. "Deep Play: Notes on the Balinese Cockfight." In *The Interpretation of Cultures,* 412–53.

——. *The Interpretation of Cultures.* New York: Basic Books, 1973.

——. *Islam Observed: Religious Development in Morocco and Indonesia.* New Haven: Yale University Press, 1968.

——. *Local Knowledge: Further Essays in Interpretive Anthropology.* New York: Basic, 1983.

——. "Thick Description: Toward an Interpretive Theory of Culture." In *The Interpretation of Cultures,* 412–53.

——. "Thinking as a Moral Act: Ethical Dimensions of Anthropological Fieldwork in the New States." *Antioch Review* 28.2 (1968): 139–58.

——. *Works and Lives: The Anthropologist as Author.* Stanford, Calif.: Stanford University Press, 1988.

Geertz, Clifford, Hildred Geertz, and Lawrence Rosen. *Meaning and Order in Moroccan Society: Three Essays in Cultural Analysis.* New York: Cambridge University Press, 1979.

Giles, Paul. *Virtual Americas: Transnational Fictions and the Transatlantic Imaginary.* Durham, N.C.: Duke University Press, 2002.

Ginsberg, Allen. *Howl and Other Poems.* San Francisco: City Lights, 1956.

——. *Journals: Early Fifties, Early Sixties.* New York: Grove, 1977.

Goldberg, David Theo. "In/Visibility and Super/Vision: Fanon on Race, Veils, and Discourses of Resistance." In *Fanon: A Critical Reader,* edited by Lewis R. Gordon, T. Denean Sharpley-Whiting, and Renée T. White, 179–200. Cambridge: Blackwell, 1996.

Gooding-Williams, Robert. "Black Cupids, White Desires: Reading the Recoding of Racial Difference in *Casablanca*." In *The Black Columbiad*, edited by Werner Sollors and Maria Diedrich, 201–11. Cambridge, Mass.: Harvard University Press, 1994.

Graebner, William. *The Age of Doubt: American Thought and Culture in the 1940s*. Boston: Twayne, 1990.

Gran, Peter. "Studies of Anglo-American Political Economy." In *Theory, Politics and the Arab World*, edited by Hisham Sharabi, 228–54. New York: Routledge, 1990.

Green, Michelle. *The Dream at the End of the World: Paul Bowles and the Literary Renegades in Tangier*. New York: HarperCollins, 1991.

Gysin, Brion. *The Process*. 1969. New York: Quartet, 1985.

Hahn, Peter. "National Security Concerns in U.S. Policy toward Egypt, 1949–1956." In *The Middle East and the United States: A Historical and Political Reassessment*, edited by David W. Lesch, 2nd ed., 89–99. Boulder, Colo.: Westview, 1999.

Hakim, George. "Point Four and the Middle East: A Middle East View." *Middle East Journal* 4 (1950): 183–95.

Hall, Leland. *Salah and His American*. New York: Knopf, 1935.

Hammoudi, Abdellah. *Master and Disciple: The Cultural Foundations of Moroccan Authoritarianism*. Chicago: University of Chicago Press, 1997.

——. *The Victim and Its Masks: An Essay on Sacrifice and Masquerade in the Maghreb*. Translated by Paula Wissing. Chicago: University of Chicago Press, 1993.

Hanchard, Michael. "Afro-Modernity: Temporality, Politics, and the African Diaspora." *Public Culture* 11 (1999): 245–68.

Hansen, Miriam. *Babel and Babylon: Spectatorship in American Silent Film*. Cambridge, Mass.: Harvard University Press, 1991.

Harmetz, Aljean. *Round Up the Usual Suspects: The Making of* Casablanca—*Bogart, Bergman, and World War II*. New York: Hyperion, 1992.

Harris, Oliver. *William Burroughs and the Secret of Fascination*. Carbondale: Southern Illinois University Press, 2003.

Hassan II. *La Mémoire d'un roi: Entretiens avec Eric Laurent*. Paris: Plon, 1993.

Hayes, Jarrod. *Queer Nations: Marginal Sexualities in the Maghreb*. Chicago: University of Chicago Press, 2000.

Heymann, C. David. *Poor Little Rich Girl: The Life and Legend of Barbara Hutton*. Secaucus, N.J.: Lyle Stuart, 1984.

Hibbard, Allen. "'Out in the World': Reconstructing Jane Bowles's Unfinished Novel." *The Library Chronicle of the University of Texas at Austin* 25.2 (1994): 120–169.

——. *Paul Bowles: A Study of the Short Fiction*. Boston: Twayne, 1993.

Hoisington, William A., Jr. *The Casablanca Connection: French Colonial Policy, 1936–1943*. Chapel Hill: University of North Carolina Press, 1984.

The Holy Qur'an. Translated by and commentary by 'Abdullah Yusuf 'Ali. New rev. ed. Brentwood, Md.: Amana, 1989.

Huzal, Abdarrahim. Introduction. "Al-Katib baina maghrebain! [The Writer between two Moroccos!]" By Antoine Poysh. *Al-'Alam ath-Thaqafi* [Rabat] 27 Nov. 1999: 6.

Jackson, Charles. "On the Seamier Side." *New York Times Book Review*, December 3, 1950, 6.

Janjar, Mohamed Sghir. "La Foi des hommes à l'épreuve du temps." *Prologues* 5 (1996): 27–30.

Johnson, Barbara. "Taking Fidelity Philosophically." In *Difference in Translation*, edited by Joseph F. Graham, 142–48. Ithaca: Cornell University Press, 1980.

Judy, Ronald A. T. "On the Politics of Global Language, or Unfungible Local Value." *boundary 2* 24.2 (1997): 101–43.

Kael, Pauline. "Film Chronicle: Night People." *Partisan Review* 22.1 (1955): 105–13.

Kaplan, Robert D. *The Arabists: Romance of an American Elite*. New York: Free Press, 1995.

Khatibi, Abdelkebir. *Maghreb pluriel*. Paris: Denoël, 1983.

Kilito, Abdelfattah. *La Langue d'Adam et autres essais*. Casablanca: Les Editions Toubkal, 1995.

Knickerbocker, Peggy. "Paula Wolfert's Pursuit of Flavor." In *Morocco: An Inspired Anthology and Travel Resource*, edited by Barrie Kerper, 543–46. New York: Three Rivers Press, 2001.

Koch, Howard. *Casablanca: Script and Legend*. Woodstock, NY: Overlook Press, 1973.

Koppes, Clayton R. "Hollywood and the Politics of Representation: Women, Workers, and African Americans in World War II Movies." In *The Home-Front War*, edited by K. O'Brien and L. Parsons, 25–40. Westport, Conn.: Greenwood, 1995.

Kramer, Jane. *Allen Ginsberg in America*. New York: Random House, 1968.

——. *Honor to the Bride Like the Pigeon That Guards Its Grain under the Clove Tree*. New York: Farrar, Straus and Giroux, 1970.

Landau, Rom. *Portrait of Tangier*. London: R. Hale, 1952.

Langer, William. *Our Vichy Gamble*. New York: Knopf, 1947.

Larkin, Brian. "Theaters of the Profane: Cinema and Colonial Urbanism." *Visual Anthropology Review* 14.2 (1998–99): 46–62.

Laroui, Abdallah. *The History of the Maghrib: An Interpretive Essay*. Translated by Ralph Manheim. Princeton, N.J.: Princeton University Press, 1977.

——. *L'Idéologie arabe contemporaine*. Paris: François Maspero, 1967.

Layachi, Azzedine. *The United States and North Africa: A Cognitive Approach to Foreign Policy*. New York: Praeger, 1990.

Layachi, Larbi. *Yesterday and Today*. Santa Barbara, Calif.: Black Sparrow, 1985.

Lears, Jackson. "A Matter of Taste: Corporate Cultural Hegemony in a Mass-Consumption Society." In *Recasting America: Culture and Politics in the Age of Cold War*, edited by Lary May, 38–57. Chicago: University of Chicago Press, 1989.

Leary, Timothy. *Flashbacks*. Los Angeles: J. P. Tarcher, 1983.

Lee, Benjamin, and Edward LiPuma. "Cultures of Circulation: The Imaginations of Modernity." *Public Culture* 14.1 (2002): 191–213.

Lewis, Wyndham. *Filibusters in Barbary* (1932). In *Journey into Barbary: Morocco Writings and Drawings*, edited by C. J. Fox, 19–186. Santa Barbara, Calif.: Black Sparrow, 1985.

Liebling, A. J. *Mollie and Other War Pieces*. 1964. New York: Schocken, 1989.

——. *The Road Back to Paris*. Garden City, N.Y.: Doubleday, Doran, 1944.

LiPuma, Edward, and Benjamin Lee. *Financial Derivatives and the Globalization of Risk*. Durham, N.C.: Duke University Press, 2004.

Little, Douglas. *American Orientalism: The United States and the Middle East since 1945*. Chapel Hill: University of North Carolina Press, 2002.

Litweiler, John. *Ornette Coleman: A Harmolodic Life*. New York: Morrow, 1992.

Luce, Henry. *The American Century*. New York: Farrar and Rinehart, 1941.

Mage, Shane, and Judith Mage. "'Little America' in Morocco." *The Nation*, June 6, 1959, 515–16, 523–24.

Maier, John. *Desert Songs: Western Images of Morocco and Moroccan Images of the West*. Albany: State University of New York Press, 1996.

Maugham, Robin. *North African Notebook*. New York: Harcourt Brace, 1949.

Marcus, George E. "The Uses of Complicity in the Changing Mise-en-Scène of Anthropological Fieldwork." In *The Fate of "Culture": Geertz and Beyond*, edited by Sherry B. Ortner, 86–109. Berkeley: University of California Press, 1999.

Maroc, Algérie, Tunisie. 2nd ed. Paris: Guide Michelin, n.d. [1929].

Marx, Groucho. *The Groucho Letters*. New York: Simon and Schuster, 1967.

May, Elaine Tyler. *Homeward Bound: American Families in the Cold War Era*. New York: Basic Books, 1988.

Mbembe, Achille. "At the Edge of the World: Boundaries, Territoriality, and Sovereignty in Africa." *Public Culture* 12.1 (2000): 259–84.

McAlister, Melani. "Edward Said, *Orientalism* (1978)." In *A Companion to Post-1945 America*, edited by Jean-Christophe Agnew and Roy Rosenzweig, 550–56. Malden, Mass: Blackwell, 2002.

——. *Epic Encounters: Culture, Media, and U.S. Interests in the Middle East, 1945–2000*. Berkeley: University of California Press, 2001.

McCarthy, Mary. "Burroughs's *Naked Lunch*." In *The Writing on the Wall and Other Literary Essays*. New York: Harcourt, Brace and World, 1970.

——. "Déjeuner sur l'herbe." *New York Review of Books*, February 1, 1963.

McKay, Claude. *Gingertown*. New York: Harper & Brothers, 1932.

——. *A Long Way from Home*. 1937. New York: Harcourt Brace Jovanovich, 1970.

McKay, Vernon. "France's Future in North Africa." *Middle East Journal* 2 (1948): 293–305.

McNicholas, Joseph. "William S. Burroughs and Corporate Public Relations." *Arizona Quarterly* 57.4 (2001): 121–49.

Mernissi, Fatima. *Dreams of Trespass: Tales of a Harem Girlhood*. Reading, Mass.: Addison-Wesley, 1994.

——. *Etes-vous vacciné contre le «harem»?* Casablanca: Editions Le Fennec, 1998.

——. *Le Harem Européen*. Casablanca: Editions Le Fennec, 2003.

Meyer, Robert, Jr., ed. *The* Stars and Stripes *Story of World War II*. New York: David McKay Company, 1960.

Michie, Elsie B. "Unveiling Maternal Desires: Hitchcock and American Domesticity." In *Hitchcock's America*, edited by Jonathan Freedman and Richard Millington, 29–53. New York: Oxford University Press, 1999.

Michener, James A. *The Drifters*. New York: Random House, 1971.

Miller, Christopher L. *Blank Darkness*. Chicago: University of Chicago Press, 1985.

——. *Theories of Africans: Francophone Literature and Anthropology in Africa*. Chicago: University of Chicago Press, 1990.

Morgan, Ted. *Literary Outlaw: The Life and Times of William S. Burroughs*. New York: Holt, 1988.

"Morocco: Sun and Pleasures, *Inshallah*." *Time*, January 31, 1969, 42–49.

Mowitt, John. "Breaking Up Fanon's Voice." In *Frantz Fanon: Critical Perspectives*, edited by Anthony C. Alessandrini, 89–98. New York: Routledge, 1999.

Mrabet, Mohammed. *The Boy Who Set the Fire and Other Stories*. Taped and translated from the Moghrebi by Paul Bowles. Santa Barbara, Calif.: Black Sparrow, 1974.

——. *Love with a Few Hairs*. Translated by Paul Bowles. London: Peter Owen, 1967; New York: Braziller, 1968; San Francisco: City Lights, 1986. Fez: Moroccan Cultural Studies Centre, 2004.

Muhanna, Elias. "Folk the Kasbah." *Transition* 94 (2003): 132–49.

Mullins, Greg. *Colonial Affairs: Bowles, Burroughs, and Chester Write Tangier*. Madison: University of Wisconsin Press, 2002.

Murphy, Timothy S. *Wising Up the Marks: The Amodern William Burroughs*. Berkeley: University of California Press, 1997.

Nadel, Alan. *Containment Culture: American Narrative, Postmodernism, and the Atomic Age*. Durham, N.C.: Duke University Press, 1995.

el-Nawawy, Mohammed, and Adel Iskander. *Al-Jazeera: How the Free Arab News Network Scooped the World and Changed the Middle East*. Cambridge, Mass.: Westview, 2002.

Negley, Harrison. "Why They Love Us in Tangier." *Colliers*, May 16, 1953, 68–73.

Ortner, Sherry B., ed. *The Fate of "Culture": Geertz and Beyond*. Berkeley: University of California Press, 1999.

Ossman, Susan. *Three Faces of Beauty: Casablanca, Paris, Cairo*. Durham: Duke University Press, 2002.

Otero-Pailos, Jorge. "Casablanca's Régime: The Shifting Aesthetics of Political Technologies (1907–1943)." *Postmodern Culture* 8.2 (1998).

Palmer, Bob (Robert). "Jajouka/Up the Mountain." *Rolling Stone* 14 Oct. 1971: 42–44.

Pandolfo, Stefania. *Impasse of the Angels: Scenes from a Moroccan Space of Memory*. Chicago: University of Chicago Press, 1997.

Patton, George S. *The Patton Papers, 1940–1945*. Edited by Martin Blumenson. Boston: Houghton Mifflin, 1974.

———. *War as I Knew It*. 1947. Boston: Houghton Mifflin, 1975.

Pease, Donald E. "National Narratives, Postnational Narration." *Modern Fiction Studies* 43.1 (1997): 1–23.

———. "Doing Justice to C. L. R. James's *Mariners, Renegades, and Castaways*." *boundary 2* 27.2 (2000): 1–19.

Pennell, C. R. *Morocco since 1830: A History*. New York: New York University Press, 2000.

Pittman, John. "Africa against the Axis." *Negro Quarterly* 1 (1942): 218.

Plummer, Brenda Gayle, ed. *Window on Freedom: Race, Civil Rights, and Foreign Affairs, 1945–1988*. Chapel Hill: University of North Carolina Press, 2003.

Poe, Edgar Allan. *Complete Tales and Poems of Edgar Allan Poe*. New York: Vintage, 1975.

Potter, David M. *People of Plenty: Economic Abundance and the American Character*. Chicago: University of Chicago Press, 1954.

Prose, Francine. "The Coldest Eye: Acting Badly among the Arabs." *Harper's*, March 2002, 60–65.

Pyle, Ernie. *Here Is Your War*. New York: Henry Holt, 1943.

Qader, Nasrin. "Fictional Testimonies or Testimonial Fictions: Moussa Ould Ebnou's *Barzakh*." *Research in African Literatures* 33.3 (2002): 14–31.

Rabinow, Paul. *French Modern: Norms and Forms of the Social Environment*. Cambridge, Mass.: MIT Press, 1989.

———. *Reflections on Fieldwork in Morocco*. Berkeley: University of California Press, 1977.

———. *Symbolic Domination: Cultural Form and Historical Change in Morocco*. Chicago: University of Chicago Press, 1975.

Rachik, Hassan. *Comment rester nomade*. Casablanca: Afrique Orient, 2000.

Ray, Robert. *A Certain Tendency of the Hollywood Film: 1930–1980*. Princeton, N.J.: Princeton University Press, 1985.

Refass, Mohamed, ed. *Tanger: Espace, économie et société*. Tangier: Université Abdelmalek Es-Saadi, Ecole Supérieure Roi Fahd de Traduction, 1993.

Roeder, George H., Jr. *The Censored War: American Visual Experience during World War II*. New Haven, Conn.: Yale University Press, 1993.

Rogin, Michael. "Make My Day! Spectacle as Amnesia in Imperial Politics." *Representations* 29 (1990): 99–123.

Rolo, Charles J. "The New Bohemia." *Flair*, February 1950, 27–29, 115–18.

Rondeau, Daniel. *Tanger et autres Marocs*. Paris: Quai Voltaire, 1987.

Said, Edward W. *Beginnings: Intention and Method*. New York: Basic Books, 1975.

——. *Culture and Imperialism*. New York: Vintage, 1994.

——. "On Lost Causes." In *Reflections on Exile and Other Essays*, 527–53. Cambridge, Mass.: Harvard University Press, 2000.

——. *Orientalism*. New York: Vintage, 1978.

Sawyer-Lauçanno, Christopher. *An Invisible Spectator: A Biography of Paul Bowles*. New York: Weidenfeld and Nicolson, 1989.

Schlamm, William. "Tangier." *Fortune*, August 1950, 66–71, 136–40.

Schuyler, Philip. "Joujouka/Jajouka/Zahjoukah: Moroccan Music and Euro-American Imagination." In *Mass Mediations*, edited by Walter Armbrust, 146–60. Berkeley: University of California Press, 2000.

Seddon, David. "Dreams and Disappointments: Postcolonial Constructions of 'The Maghrib.'" In *Beyond Colonialism and Nationalism in the Maghrib: History, Culture, Politics*, ed. Ali Abdullatif Ahmida, 197–231. New York: Palgrove, 2000.

Sergeant, Harriet. *Shanghai: Collision Point of Cultures, 1918–1939*. New York: Crown, 1990.

Setterberg, Fred. "Morocco: In the Toils of Tourism." *Nation*, December 24, 1973, 685–87.

Sewell, William H., Jr. "Geertz, Cultural Systems, and History." In *The Fate of "Culture": Geertz and Beyond*, edited by Sherry B. Ortner, 35–55. Berkeley: University of California Press, 1999.

Shapiro, Harry. *Jimi Hendrix: Electric Gypsy*. New York: St. Martin's Press, 1995.

Shaviro, Steven. "Two Lessons from Burroughs." In *Posthuman Bodies*, edited by Judith Halberstam and Ira Livingston, 38–54. Bloomington: Indiana University Press, 1995.

The Sheltering Sky: A Film by Bernardo Bertolucci. London: Scribners, 1990.

Shloss, Carol. "Jane Bowles in Uninhabitable Places: Writing on Cultural Boundaries." In *A Tawdry Place of Salvation: The Art of Jane Bowles*, ed. Jennie Skerl, 102–18. Carbondale: Southern Illinois University Press, 1997.

Shohat, Ella, and Robert Stam. *Unthinking Eurocentrism: Multiculturalism and the Media*. New York: Routledge, 1994.

Shulman, Irving. *Valentino*. New York: Trident, 1967.

Simpkins, Raoul. "Banking in Tangier." *Atlantic*, March 1950, 84–86.

Sinaceur, Mohammed Allal. "L'Islam et les terroirs." *Prologues* 5 (1996): 24–26.

Slotkin, Richard. *Gunfighter Nation: The Myth of the Frontier in Twentieth-Century America*. New York: Atheneum, 1992.

Smith, Henry Nash. *Virgin Land: The American West as Symbol and Myth*. Cambridge, Mass.: Harvard, 1950.

Spivak, Gayatri Chakravorty. *A Critique of Postcolonial Reason*. Cambridge, Mass.: Harvard University Press, 1999.

——. *Death of a Discipline*. New York: Columbia University Press, 2003.

——. "The Politics of Translation." In *Destabilizing Theory: Contemporary Feminist Debates*, edited by Michèle Barrett and Anne Phillips, 177–200. Cambridge: Polity, 1992.

Steinbeck, John. *Once There Was a War*. New York: Bantam, 1960.

Stephens, Maj. Gen. Richard W. "Foreword." In *Northwest Africa: Seizing the Initiative in the West*, by George F. Howe. Vol. 1 of *United States Army in World War II: The Mediterranean Theater of Operations*. Washington, D.C.: Office of the Chief of Military History, Department of the Army, 1957.

Stuart, Graham H. *The International City of Tangier*. Rev. ed. Stanford, Calif.: Stanford University Press, 1955.

Sutherland, John V. "Distant Episodes." *New York Times Book Review*, October 21, 2001, 9.

Taberner, John. "The Phoney Gold Rush." *American Mercury*, December 1952, 79–84.

Tessler, Mark. "Alienation of Urban Youth." In *Polity and Society in Contemporary North Africa*, edited by I. William Zartman and William Mark Habeeb, 71–101. Boulder, Colo.: Westview, 1993.

Toledano, Edward. "Young Man, Go to Casablanca." *Harper's*, September 1948, 109–14.

Trachtenberg, Alan. "Myth, History, and Literature in Virgin Land." *Prospects* 3 (1977): 125–33.

Treaty of Washington (North Atlantic Treaty). In *The Cold War: A History through Documents*, edited by Edward H. Judge and John W. Langdon, 49–52. Upper Saddle River, N.J.: Prentice Hall, 1999.

Trouillot, Michel-Rolph. *Silencing the Past: Power and the Production of History*. Boston: Beacon, 1995.

Truffaut, François, with Helen G. Scott. *Hitchcock*. New York: Simon and Schuster, 1966.

Turner, Frederick Jackson. *The Significance of the Frontier in American History*. Chicago: University of Chicago Press, 1899.

Twain, Mark. *Roughing It*. New York: Library of America, 1984.

U.S. Office of Strategic Services. *Morocco*. Washington, D.C.: Research and Analysis Branch, 1942.

Vaidon, Lawdom (David Woolman). *Tangier: A Different Way*. Metuchen, N.J.: Scarecrow, 1977.

Von Eschen, Penny M. *Race against Empire: Black Americans and Anticolonialism, 1937–1957*. Ithaca, N.Y.: Cornell University Press, 1997.

Wall, Irwin M. *France, the United States, and the Algerian War*. Berkeley: University of California Press, 2001.

——. *The United States and the Making of Postwar France, 1945–1954*. New York: Cambridge University Press, 1991.

Warner, Michael. "Publics and Counterpublics." *Public Culture* 14.1 (2002): 49–90.

——. "*Walden*'s Erotic Economy." In *Comparative American Identities: Race, Sex, and Nationality in the Modern Text*, edited by Hortense Spillers, 157–74. New York: Routledge, 1991.

Waterbury, John. *The Commander of the Faithful: The Moroccan Political Elite—A Study in Segmented Politics*. New York: Columbia University Press, 1970.

Wechsberg, Joseph. "Anything Goes." *New Yorker*, April 12, 1952, 62–70.

Wehr, Hans. *A Dictionary of Modern Written Arabic*, edited by J. Milton Cowan. Beirut: Librarie du Liban, 1980.

Westbrook, Robert. "'I Want a Girl, Just Like the Girl That Married Harry James': American Women and the Problem of Political Obligation in World War II." *American Quarterly* 42.4 (1990): 587–614.

Wharton, Edith. *In Morocco*. New York: Charles Scribner's Sons, 1920.

Williams, Tennessee. Foreword to *Feminine Wiles* by Jane Bowles. Santa Barbara, Calif.: Black Sparrow, 1976.

Wolfert, Paula. *Couscous and Other Good Food from Morocco* (1973). New York: Harper & Row, 1987.

Wright, Gwendolyn. *The Politics of Design in French Colonial Urbanism*. Chicago: University of Chicago Press, 1991.

Young, Robert J. C. *Postcolonialism*. Malden, Mass.: Blackwell, 2001.

INDEX

Abu Talib, Muhammad, 85, 86

Acheson, Dean, 99

African Americans: alliances with Arabs, 278–79; black radicalism and, 256–57, 278–79; domestic racism and, 46, 58–59, 60, 98, 143; in Hollywood films, 62–70; Islam and, 256, 273–74, 278–79; Maghrebi songs and, 59; in the military, 33, 34, 36, 37, 46, 64; Negro press, 33–35, 36–39, 46, 60, 61; *The Negro Quarterly*, 33, 71; North Africa and, 3, 33–37, 66–70, 73–74. See also *The Chicago Defender*; race and racism

Agamben, Giorgio, 104, 113, 315 n.70

Age of Doubt, 93, 142–43

al adab at-Tanji (Tangerian literature), 80, 86, 116, 130, 138, 201, 203, 242–43

al Amali, Karim, 310 n.85

al-Fassi, 'Allal, 84

Algeria: French colonialism in, 2, 5, 129, 190–91; *The Garden of Allah*, 8, 53, 306 n.46; Morocco and, 7, 256, 267; national identity, 106–9; revolution in, 8, 171, 179, 290; Soviet Union and, 266; tourism in, 248, 310 n.80; unveiling in, 190–91

Algiers (film), 43, 306 n.29

Al-Hubb fi al-Dar al-Baida, 74–76

'Ali, Yusuf, 326 n.27

Allen, Carolyn, 203

Al-Maghrib. See Morocco

"Al Mirikan" (Slaoui), 59, 95

"American Century, The" (Luce), 49–50, 65–66, 87–88, 113–14, 161–62, 189–90, 315 n.71

American Indians imagery, 34, 51–52, 306 n.45

American national identity: abundance and, 146–47, 148–49; Age of Doubt, 93, 142–43

American Orientalism, 2–3, 8, 40–41, 71, 101

American School of Tangier, 131, 132, 139, 149, 180, 317 n.18, 318 n.37

anality, 153–55, 165–66, 174–78

Anthropology: authority of, 239–41; cultural relativism in, 253–55, 257–64, 268–72; informants in, 256, 271–72, 290, 291; as literary critics, 293–94, 295–98, 333 n.62; Morocco represented by, 257; temporal distancing in, 262; translations of culture in, 255–56, 294, 295–96, 333 n.67. *See also* Crapanzano, Vincent; Fernea, Elizabeth; Geertz, Clifford; Kramer, Jane; Rabinow, Paul

Appadurai, Arjun, 15

Apter, Emily, 3, 105, 315 n.71

Arabian Nights, 30, 147, 282

Arabic language, 113–14; American consumerism and, 59, 94, 95, 188; Americans' knowledge of, 11–13, 16, 88–90, 188–89, 192, 197, 207, 211, 217, 247; Paul Bowles's use of, 94–95, 113, 211–12, 215, 217–19, 234, 327 n.38; darija, 16, 21, 88, 113, 116, 199, 226, 234, 237, 240, 241–43; dialects of, 88, 190; eroticism in, 211–12; existentialism and, 106–12, 230; family and, 148, 150, 151, 184, 185, 187, 193; frames of reference for, 88–89, 90–91, 311 n.25; globalization and, 91–93; Hitchcock's use of, 188–90, 192, 193; individual agency and, 195; influenced by English, 85; pioneering and, 92–93, 95, 105; the "pure American voice" and, 179–81, 189–90; in Tangier, 138, 143, 150–51; as textual disruptions, 16, 94, 95, 106, 113–14, 192, 197, 315 n.71. *See also* frontier narratives; Hollywood films; translation
Arab-Israeli War (1967), 264, 267, 278
Arabs: African Americans compared to, 273–74; American Indians compared to, 51–52, 54–55; Black Power movement and, 256–57, 278; William Burroughs and, 166–68, 170–73, 177–79; in Hollywood films, 4–5, 52, 70–71; soldiers' images of, 55–58
Arac, Jonathan, 308 n.67
Ashbery, John, 200
as-Saidi, Tariq, 85
"As Time Goes By," 67, 308 n.69

Badger, John Robert, 37–38
Baker, Josephine, 36
Balibar, Etienne, 142, 183

Baraka, Amiri, 278
Barthes, Roland, 308 n.78
barzakh, 21, 199, 209, 211, 212–13, 223–24, 226, 326 nn.27, 29
Basinger, Jeanine, 307 nn.59, 60
Bayer, William, 281
Bayoumi, Moustafa, 274
Beau Geste, 8, 50, 297–98
Becker, Alton, 211, 326 n.23
Beckett, Samuel, 124
Behdad, Ali, 173
Belghazi, Taieb, 300
Ben Abdeslam, Abdelkrim, 166, 167–68, 171, 173
Ben Barka, Mehdi, 257, 265, 331 n.29
Benedict, Ruth, 333 n.62
Benjamin, Walter, 295
Benjelloun, Ali, 266
Ben Jelloun, Tahar, 84, 116, 235, 236
Bennani-Chraïbi, Mounia, 300
Berbers: Arab nationalism, 84; Paul Bowles on, 88–91, 95, 117, 229–30, 288, 328 n.55; dialects of, 6, 36, 143, 236, 239–41; etymology of, 328 n.55; in Geertz's anthropological studies, 296–97; as indigenous people, 5–6, 229, 328 n.56; music of, 81, 261, 288; in Tangier, 123, 143
Bernstein, Adam, 81–82
Bertolucci, Bernardo, 91–92, 311 n.36
Bess, Demaree, 94, 99, 320 n.56
Bhabha, Homi, 308 nn.66, 78
Bin Bushta, Zubir, 86, 201
black radicalism, 256–57, 278–79
Blum, John, 45, 47
Bogart, Humphrey, 61–62, 66–70
Borstelmann, Thomas, 34, 98
Bou Jeloud festival, 286, 287
Bourguiba, Habib, 126
Bourke-White, Margaret, 46
Bowles, Jane, *206, 218*; Arabic used

by, 207, 211–12, 215, 217–19, 234, 327 n.38; barzakh, 199, 209, 212, 226, 326 nn.27, 29; Paul Bowles and, 202–3, 208, 325 n.13; circulation and, 21, 207–8; distance in writing style of, 204–5; illnesses of, 214, 233, 329 n.68; imagination and, 223, 227–28; language and social identity, 201–2; Moroccan women and, 208, 211, 216–17, 223, 224, 225; Mohammed Mrabet compared to, 203; pontification in work of, 211, 223; secret communication, 223–24; spaces in writing of, 21, 207–10; stuttering English of, 210, 211, 215–16, 220, 224; Tangier and, 213–14, 224; temporal spaces/edges in, 199, 209, 212–13, 225–26, 326 nn.27, 29, 328 n.48; translation in writing style of, 204, 207, 211; works of, 203, 208, 212–14, 224–27, 327 n.44. *See also* "Camp Cataract"

Bowles, Paul, *89, 103*; academic audience for, 84–85; *al adab at-Tanji* (Tangerian literature) and, 80, 86, 87, 116, 201, 203, 242–43; on American consumer culture in Morocco, 94–95; Arabic language used by, 95, 113, 115–16; Jane Bowles and, 202–3, 208, 210, 233, 236, 325 n.13; William Burroughs and, 81, 159, 160; desire in work of, 310 n.4; disruptions in writing of, 102; eroticism in work of, 236; expatriatism of, 79, 81–83, 94, 105, 116, 310 n.4, 314 n.63; on fiction writing, 116–17; Clifford Geertz and, 293, 298, 333 n.62; on language, 103, 112, 127; modernism and, 79, 310 n.4; Moroccan critics on, 84–87, 116; Mo-

roccan music recorded by, 86, 229–32, 284, 329 n.59; Mohammed Mrabet collaborations with, 11, 116–17, 232–38, 242; music composition of, 81, 82, 116, 230; *The Spider's House*, 9, 115, 167, 310 n.4; tape recorder used by, 231, 232, 237; translations by, 85, 87, 95, 113, 116, 235, 237, 241–42; Paula Wolfert and, 281, 283. *See also The Sheltering Sky*

Boy Who Set the Fire, The, 236

Brennan, Timothy, 14, 330 n.13

Burke, Kenneth, 210, 211, 219, 299

Burroughs, William S., *167*; on American culture, 161, 166–67, 168, 170, 179, 180; anality, 165, 174–75, 175, 176; Arabic knowledge of, 182; Arabs and, 166, 167–68, 170–71, 172, 173, 177–79; Abdelkrim Ben Abdeslam, 166, 167–68, 171, 173; Paul Bowles and, 81, 159, 160; in cold war domestic culture, 319 n.49; conversion experience of, 172–73; drug addiction of, 159, 167, 168; flight from United States, 137; friends of, 162–64; Allen Ginsberg and, 121, 124, 159, 166–67; on independence movements, 171, 172, 183; as invisible man (el hombre invisible), 169–70; Islam and, 172–73; on Jajouka music, 284, 285; on Marrakech, 324 n.75; Herman Melville and, 174–76; Moroccans and, 169; Orientalism and, 173, 174; on race, 168–70, 173, 179; on revolution, 171; Tangier and, 123, 158–61, 164–65, 168–69, 174–75, 321 n.8. *See also Naked Lunch*

Burton, Richard, 173

Buryn, Ed, 247–48, 252, 256

Butler, Judith, 152, 319 n.42

"Camp Cataract": Arabic used in, 219; as autobiographical, 217; bridge motifs in, 210, 221; completion of, 214; foreignness within native language, 204–5, 216–17; speech and communication in, 222–23

Camus, Albert, 103, 106

Caponi, Gena, 327 n.44

Capote, Truman, 204, 207, 213, 325 n.11

Casablanca (city): *Al-Hubb fi al-Dar al-Baida,* 74–76; American portrayals of, 44–45; and *Casablanca* (film), 72–75, 308 n.78; student riots, 260, 274; tourism in, 73–74, 309 n.78

Casablanca (film), 68; *Algiers* and, 43, 306 n.29; *Al-Hubb fi al-Dar al-Baida,* 74–76; American-French alliances in, 62, 71; Americanness of, 61, 68; American Orientalism in, 71; and Casablanca (city), 72–75, 308 n.78; frontier mythology in, 68–69; geographic manipulation in, 66–67; homoeroticism in, 69–70; and *The Man Who Knew Too Much,* 195; marketing of, 43–45; Moroccan characters in, 70–71; and *A Night in Casablanca,* 44; opening of, 43–44; race in, 66–67, 69–70, 74; Rick as outlaw hero, 69; temporality in, 66–67, 260, 308 nn.70, 78; tourist sites and, 73–74, 309 n.78, 310 n.81; triangle relationships in, 69–70

Casablanca Conference, 39, 41–42, 44

Céline, Louis Ferdinand, 214–15

Charhadi, Driss ben Hamed (aka Larbi Layachi), 234, 235

Chicago Defender, The: on African American soldiers in the North African campaign, 36–37, 38; Josephine Baker covered in, 36; on French colonialism in North Africa, 37–38, 39; racism discussed in, 33; Warner Brothers studios, 71; wartime reportage and, 46

Choukri, Mohamed, 85, 86

Chraibi, Abdelhaq, 190

Churchill, Winston, 39, 40, 41, 94

circulation, 14–15, 21, 155, 176, 207–9, 223, 224, 241–43

Clay, Cassius, 278

Clifford, James, 306 n.39, 330 n.13

Cobbs Hoffman, Elizabeth, 330 n.6

Coca Cola, 94, 129, 131

cold war era: as Age of Doubt, 93, 142–43; domestic culture and, 319 n.49; family and, 148, 150, 151, 184, 185, 187, 193; hegemonic bloc, 143–46, 148; McCarthyism, 102, 142, 151, 161, 174, 179, 181–82, 191, 196; postcolonialism, 12, 87, 117, 133–34, 255–56. *See also* race and racism

Coleman, Herbert, 196

Coleman, Ornette, 11, 22, 254, 284, 287–89. *See also* Jajouka music collaborations: authorial primacy in, 236; erotics of, 233, 235–36; Jajouka music, 11, 251, 253, 254, 284–89; role of editor in, 237–38; in translations, 233, 235, 237–38, 240–42

Collins, Joan, 148

Coltrane, John, 256, 273–74

commercialism, 44–45, 59, 94–95, 139–40, 188

Committee of Control (Tangier), 134, 135, 137, 138, 183, 317 n.24

Communist Party of the United States of America, 64, 82

Corber, Robert, 142, 145, 186, 190, 324 nn.63, 70

Couscous and Other Good Food from Morocco, 253, 280–83

Crapanzano, Vincent: cultural relativism and, 270; on ethnography, 295; Moroccan critics on, 300–301; on questions of dialogue, 262; on Edward Said, 330 n.13; on the translation of culture, 295; "A World of Saints and She-Demons," 264–67

Crawford, Kenneth, 33, 57–58

Cripps, Thomas, 63–64

Crosby, Bing, 15, 16

Crosby, John, 315 n.1

Crosby, Stills & Nash (CSN), 250–51, 276

Crowe, Smith, 136

Crowther, Bosley, 15, 307 n.59

Culture and Imperialism, 9, 41

Currie, Scott, 287, 288

Dalle, Ignace, 274

Daoudi, Abderrahim, 74

Darija (colloquial Moroccan Arabic), 16, 21, 88, 113, 116, 199, 226, 234, 237, 240, 241–43

"Deep Play: Notes on the Balinese Cockfight," 295

Defender, The. See The Chicago Defender

De Gaulle, Charles, 41, 44, 97

Deleuze, Gilles, 179, 182, 202, 205, 215, 326 n.22

DeRosa, Steven, 196

Derrida, Jacques, 23, 182

Dillon, Millicent: Arabic studies of Jane Bowles, 327 n.38; on "Camp Cataract," 217; "Everything Is Nice," 327 n.44; on imagination in Jane Bowles' writing, 223; on Jane and Paul Bowles' work, 202–3, 325

n.13; on Morocco's absence in Jane Bowles' writings, 228

"A Distant Episode," 88, 90–91, 311 n.25

Dower, John, 34

Doyle, Arthur Conan, 236

Drifters, The, 22, 253, 257–61, 275–78, 332 n.36

Drug culture, 159, 167, 168, 249, 250, 252, 276

Dryer, Bernard, 144–45, 148, 149, 156

Du Bois, W. E. B., 34

Dulles, John Foster, 129

Dwyer, Daisy, 292

Dwyer, Kevin, 292, 333 n.62

"East Side: North Africa," 224–26, 327 n.44

Eberhardt, Isabelle, 173, 281

Eburne, Jonathan, 319 n.49

Edmonson, Ben, 253

Egypt, 40, 137, 147, 148, 266

Eickelman, Dale, 292, 294

Eisenhower, Dwight, President, 129

Ellison, Ralph, 169, 170

English language, 59, 85, 179–81, 210, 211, 215–16, 220, 224

Erikson, C. O., 196

eroticism, 69–70, 211–12, 233, 235–36

Ethiopia, 143

ethnography, 295–96, 333 n.67

Evans-Pritchard, Edward E., 294, 333 n.62

"Everything Is Nice," 224–27, 327 n.44

Fabian, Johannes, 262

family, 148, 150, 151, 184, 185, 187, 193

Fanon, Frantz, 109, 139, 151, 172, 179, 190, 326 n.22

Fauset, Jesse, 50

Fernea, Elizabeth, 252, 253, 255, 276, 291

Finlayson, Iain, 159

Ford, John, 62, 63, 307 n.59

foreign relations, United States: containment motifs in, 145–46; domestic racism, 34–35, 58–59, 98, 143; literary production and, 82–83, 87–88, 93, 95, 101–5, 115, 117, 129–30, 131, 138; relations with France, 96–100, 127, 129, 133, 134, 136, 167; relations with North African nations, 29–32, 42, 78–79, 94–100, 126–29, 133–40, 167, 183, 256, 266–67; Vietnam War, 249, 251, 255, 257, 330 n.13

Four Freedoms, 97, 149, 150

"4000 year old Rock and Roll Band, The," 285

French colonialism: Arab resistance to, 57; Berbers and, 328 n.56; decadence of, 106; as harem, 191; independence movements and, 42, 228–29, 285, 327 n.44; Negro press on, 37–38, 39; Franklin Delano Roosevelt, 39, 41, 42, 97–98, 149, 150; surveillance, 191–92; United States and, 32, 33, 42–44, 96–100, 105, 127–29, 313 n.42; veiling and, 190–92

French North Africa. *See* Maghreb

Freud, Sigmund, 156

frontier narratives: abundance and, 146–47; American West in, 32–33, 47–48, 50–55, 62–63, 307 n.60; deserts in, 4, 15, 53, 60–64, 200, 306 n.46; Clifford Geertz and, 297–98; in Hollywood films, 32, 62–63, 307 n.60; Orientalist images and, 50–51, 105

Gallagher, Charles, 131, 162, 163, 314 n.63

Gaonkar, Dilip, 14–15, 207–8

Garden of Allah, The (Hichens), 8, 53, 306 n.46

Gardiner, Kweku Attah, 33

Geertz, Clifford: on American encounters with Morocco, 22–23, 24; American political economy influenced by, 333 n.67; anthropologist as literary critic, 293–99, 333 n.62; Paul Bowles and, 293, 298, 333 n.62; criticism of, 294–95, 300–301, 333 n.67; cultural relativism and, 253–55, 270; on ethnography, 295–96, 333 n.67; frontier metaphors of, 297–99; Abdellah Hammoudi on, 286, 299–300; influence on young anthropologists, 253–55, 271; on informant-anthropologist relations, 256, 271, 290–91, 293; on Islam, 268, 293, 300; Moroccan responses to, 299–301; on Orientalism, 298; on power of knowledge, 291–92; in Sefrou, Morocco, 289–90, 293; theory of culture as text, 292–94, 295–97; "Thinking as a Moral Act," 290, 292, 293; on translations of culture, 294, 295–96, 333 n.67

Geertz, Hildred, 292

Genet, Jean, 123, 124

Gifford, Eric, 176

Giles, Paul, 12, 79, 303 n.12

Ginsberg, Allen: Burroughs in Tangier and, 121, 124, 159, 166–67, 321 nn.8, 11; Morocco and, 259, 260; *Naked Lunch*, 124, 162

Giraud, Henri, 41

Glaoui, Thami el, 196

globalization, 23–24, 54, 114, 161, 182, 231, 242, 243, 300–301

Gluckman, Max, 333 n.62

gold, 156, 176–77, 320 n.65
Goldberg, David Theo, 109
Goldstein, Steve, 288
Gooding-Williams, Robert, 69, 308 n.73
Goumiers, 58
Gramsci, Antonio, 143–44
Gran, Peter, 333 n.67
Grauerholz, James, 159
Green, Michelle, 325 n.11
Green March, 257
Guattari, Félix, 182, 202, 205
Gussow, Mel, 81, 82
Gysin, Brion, 162, 163, 284–86, 288, 322 n.15. *See also* Jajouka music

Hall, Leland, 36
Hamlet, 178, 179
Hammoudi, Abdellah, 286, 299–300
Hanchard, Michael, 67
Harmetz, Aljean, 307 n.63
Harris, Oliver, 163, 164, 321 n.8
Harris, Walter, 281
Hart, David Montgomery, 329 n.68
Hart, Ursula Kingsmill, 329 n.68
Hassan II, King, 31, 42, 85, 257, 258, 266–67
Hawkes, Howard, 148
Hayes, Jarrod, 320 n.69
Hayes, John Michael, 184, 189
Hegemonic bloc, 143–46, 148
Hendrix, Jimi, 248–49
Herskovits, Melville, 36
Heymann, C. David, 315 n.1
Hibbard, Allen, 116
Hichens, Robert, 7, 8, 53, 306 n.46
hippie Orientalism, 22, 249, 252–56, 261, 271, 285–87
hippies, 251, 253, 277; cultural relativism of, 256–59, 270–71; in *The Drifters*, 22, 253; drug use by, 104, 249, 250, 252; in Marrakech, 250–51, 276; Marrakech Express and, 104, 250–51, 254, 276; Moroccan culture and, 104, 248–50, 253–55; Orientalism, 22, 249, 252–56, 261, 271, 285–87; as reactionaries, 275–76; reality sought by, 276–77; surveillance of, 251–52; Vietnam War, 249, 251, 255, 257, 278, 330 n.13; young Moroccans and, 257–61, 276, 277–78, 332 n.36
Hitchcock, Alfred. See *The Man Who Knew Too Much*
Hoisington, William A., Jr., 43, 306 n.27
Hollywood films: abundance in, 147–48; African American roles in, 30, 62–70, 74, 307 n.63; Arabs in, 4–5, 50, 52, 53, 70–71, 187–90, 191, 306 n.46; black roles in, 62–67, 69–70, 74, 305 n.6, 307 n.63; desert images in, 4, 15, 53, 60–64; frontier narratives in, 32, 48–50, 62–63, 307 n.60; Imperial County, CA as filming location, 15, 53, 187, 306 n.46; North Africa representations by, 40; *Road to Morocco*, 15–17; tourist attractions and, 8, 73–74, 309 n.78, 310 n.81; Westerns, 32, 62–63, 307 n.60; women in, 65, 67, 148, 188–92. See also *The Man Who Knew Too Much*
Homosexuality, 145, 151–52, 153–54
Honor to the Bride Like the Pigeon That Guards Its Grain under the Clove Tree, 261–64, 291, 331 n.24
Hope, Bob, 15, 16
Hughes, Langston, 36
Hull, Edith, 7, 8, 35
Human waste, 156, 165–66, 320 n.65
Hunwick, John, 35

Hutton, Barbara, 121–22, 148–49, 315 n.1
Hyatt Regency, 73, 308 nn.78, 81

Ibn al-'Arabi, 199, 209, 212, 223–24
Image Makers, The, 144–45, 148, 149, 156
independence movements, 42, 228–29, 285, 327 n.44
Ingram, Rex (Sergeant Tambul in *Sahara*), 62–65, 305 n.6, 307 n.63
International Zone, 122, 124, 133, 136, 138–40, 318 n.39
In the Summer House, 208, 214
"Iron Table, The," 226, 227
Islam: African Americans and, 256, 273–74, 278–79; American jazz and, 274; American understanding of, 65; Black Africans and, 278–79; Black Power movement and, 256–57, 278–79; William Burroughs and, 172–73; John Coltrane and, 274; cultural relativism, 272; Clifford Geertz on, 268, 293, 300; Maghreb, 6, 7, 16–17; women in, 58–59, 188, 189, 190–91, 324 n.64
Islam Observed: Religious Development in Morocco and Indonesia (Geertz), 293, 300
Italy, 37, 39

Jackson, Charles, 81–82, 83, 90
Jajouka music, 11, 251, 253, 254, 284, 287–89
James, C. L. R., 174, 175
Japanese Americans, internment of, 33, 60
Jilala music, 284
Johnson, Barbara, 233
Johnson, James W., 36
Johnson, Lyndon, 22, 255–56, 331 n.29

Jones, Brian, 251, 254, 284, 285, 286, 288. See also *The Pipes of Pan at Joujouka*
Jones, LeRoi, 278
Judy, Ronald, 24, 182

Kael, Pauline, 147
Kafka, Franz, 202, 205, 215
Kennan, George, 135
Kennedy, John F., 8, 129
Kerouac, Jack, 121, 159, 172, 319 n.49
Kerr, Walter, 209
Khatibi, Abdelkebir, 84
kif, 81, 104, 168, 235, 249, 250, 252, 276
Koppes, Clayton, 64
Korda, Zoltan, 62, 64. See also *Sahara*
Kramer, Jane, 259–63; on American youth culture, 259–60; *Honor to the Bride Like the Pigeon That Guards Its Grain under the Clove Tree,* 261–64, 291, 331 n.24; on Moroccan exoticism, 260; "A World of Saints and She-Demons," 264–67
Kristeva, Julia, 319 n.49
Kroeber, Alfred, 333 n.62

Labonne, Eric, 126
Laghzaoui, Mohammed, 126, 316 n.10
Landau, Rom, 135, 137, 138, 319 n.40
Langer, William, 44, 97, 313 n.42
language: al-barzakh in, 199, 209, 212–13, 223–24, 326 nn.27, 29; Burroughs on, 180–82; of domestic space, 185; edges of, 199, 209–13, 225–26, 326 nn.27, 29, 328 n.48; English, 59, 179–81, 210, 211, 215–16, 220, 224; French, 105–6; homonyms, 186–87; interruptions and,

16–17, 103, 171, 185–86, 240–41; Kafka's minor use of a major language, 202, 205, 215; national identity and, 50, 88, 90, 112; noise and, 185–86; "pure American voice," 179, 180–81; queering of, 152, 319 n.42; Riffian dialect, 6, 36, 143, 236, 239–41; social identity, 201–2; superficiality of, 103, 106, 112; as virus, 181, 182, 185. *See also* Arabic language

Laqt'a, 'Abd al-Qader, 74–76, 310 n.85

Larkin, Brian, 308 n.76

Laroui, Abdallah, 84, 234

Lawrence, T. E., 326 n.22

Lawson, John Howard, 64

Layachi, Azzedine, 104–5

Layachi, Larbi (Driss ben Hamed Charhadi), 234, 235, 236

Lears, Jackson, 143, 144, 146, 148

Leary, Timothy, 159, 269, 285

Lederman, D. Ross, 52

Lee, Benjamin, 23–24

Lemon, The, 237

Let It Come Down, 115, 124, 158

Lévi-Strauss, Claude, 333 n.62

Lewis, Wyndham, 30

Libya, 7, 37, 39, 62–63, 137, 171, 309 n.80

Liebling, A. J., 32, 40, 53–56

LiPuma, Ed, 23–24

literary criticism: Moroccan voice in, 84–86

Little, Douglas, 303 n.15

"Little Sheik, The,", 35–36

Litweiler, John, 287

Look and Move On, 235

Lost Patrol, The, 62, 63, 307 n.59

Love with a Few Hairs, 235, 237–38

Luce, Henry, 3, 40, 49–50, 65–66,

87–88, 94, 113–14, 161–62, 189–90, 315 n.71

Lund, Paul, *163*

Lyautey, Hubert, 8–9

Lyotard, Jean-François, 146

Madani, Mohammed, 300

Maghreb: Goumiers, 58; history of, 5–7; Libya, 7, 37, 39, 62–63, 137, 171, 309 n.80; opposition to Americans, 58; Orientalism and, 31; racial diversity in, 35–36; State Department interest in, 12; Tunisia, 2, 5, 47–48, 54, 248, 266, 309 n.80. *See also* Algeria; American national identity; French colonialism; Morocco; Sahara; State Department

Maghreb Arabe Presse (MAP), 85–86, 87

Maier, John, 327 n.44, 328 n.48

Mailer, Norman, 169

Malcolm X, 278

Malinowski, Bronislaw, 333 n.62

Mansouri, Driss, 300–301

Man Who Knew Too Much, The: Arabic language in, 11, 12, 188–89, 192, 197; British colonial imagery in, 193; *Casablanca* compared to, 195; commercialism in, 188; cymbal crash in, 185–86; excess knowledge and, 184, 185, 188–89; extraterritorial rights in, 137; filming of, 20, 187, 190, 196; McCarthyism and, 191, 196; race in, 192–95; translations as signs of foreignness, 188; veiled women in, 190–91

Marcus, George, 24, 294–95, 300

Marrakech, 251; atmosphere of, 184, 195–96, 324 n.75; foreignness of, 189; hippies in, 250–51, 276; racial

Marrakech (*continued*)
mixing in, 193; significance of
name, 16, 17. See also *The Man
Who Knew Too Much*
Marrakech express, 104, 250–51, 254,
276
"Marrakech Express" (Crosby, Stills
& Nash), 250–51, 276
Marshall, Edison, 148
Marshall, George, 99
Marshall Plan, 12, 99, 100
Marx Brothers, 44
Master Musicians of Jajouka, 11, 253,
254, 284, 287–89
Maugham, Robin, 153
May, Elaine Tyler, 142, 145
Mbembe, Achille, 35
McAlister, Melani, 278, 303 n.15
McCarthy, Mary, 160–61, 179, 183
McCarthyism, 102, 142, 151, 161, 174,
179, 181–82, 191, 196
McKay, Claude, 30, 35–36, 50
McNicholas, Joseph, 323 n.56
McPhail, Angus, 184
*Meaning and Order in Moroccan
Society*, 293
Mernissi, Fatima, 58–59, 191
Michener, James, 22, 252–53, 256–61,
275–78, 332 n.36
Michie, Elsie, 190, 324 n.64
military, United States: African Amer-
icans in, 33, 34, 36, 37, 46, 64; North
African campaign, 15, 36–42, *38*;
Operation Torch, 29, 46, 71, 97. See
also Patton, George S.; soldiers
Miller, Christopher L., 152, 303 n.1
Miller, Henry, 200
Mills, C. Wright, 330 n.13
Mohammed V, 42, 97, 99, 100, 126,
136, 150, 306 n.27, 315 n.1, 318 n.31
Morgan, Ted, 159–60, 182

Morocco: Algeria and, 7, 256, 267; as
al-Maghrib, 16–17; Arab-Israeli
War (1967) and, 264, 267, 278; in
Casablanca, 67–68; commercialism
in, 44–45, 59, 94–95, 139–40, 188;
cooking in, 253, 270, 280–83;
French-American relations and,
96–100, 105, 127–29, 313 n.42; in
*Honor to the Bride Like the Pigeon
That Guards Its Grain under the
Clove Tree*, 261–64, 291, 331 n.24;
independence movements, 42,
228–29, 285, 327 n.44; Marrakech,
16, 17, 184, 189, 195–96, 250–51,
276, 324 n.75; monarchy in, 42, 85,
257, 258, 265, 266–67; music of, 11,
229–32, 251, 253, 254, 284–89;
origin of name, 16–17; political
unrest in, 22, 135, 255, 257–58, 260,
266–67, 274; *Road to Morocco*, 15–
17; Southeast Asia compared with,
249, 251, 255; tourism in, 8, 73–74,
247, 249–50, 309 nn.78, 79, 310
n.81; western youth culture associated with, 249–50. See also
Anthropology; Arabs; Berbers;
frontier narratives; hippies; Hollywood films; Islam; *and names of
individual anthropologists*
Moulay Slimane, 127
Mrabet, Mohammed, 234, 243;
authorial control by, 236; Jane
Bowles compared to, 203; collaborations with Paul Bowles, 11, 116–
17, 232–38, 242; darija, 199; on
individuals within the couple, 203;
intermediate languages in translations, 237; language and social
identity, 201–2; praise for, 200;
translations of, 11, 21, 199, 232;
"What Happened in Granada," 236

Muhammed Ali, 278

Muhanna, Elias, 331 n.19

Mullins, Greg, 310 n.4, 321 n.8, 329 n.63

Munson, Henry, 292

Murphy, Timothy, 170, 321 n.8

"Music from the Cave," 288

Nadel, Alan, 142, 145–46, 209, 324 n.61

Naked Lunch: anality in, 165, 174–78; critics on, 160–61, 321 n.8; Allen Ginsberg as editor of, 124; K.Y. routine in, 175–76, 177; language in, 161, 197; McCarthyism and, 181, 196; race in, 179; radio signals, 179–80; Tangier's influence on, 159, 160–61, 168–69, 173, 174, 177, 321 n.8

Nasser, Gamal, 134

Nation of Islam, 278–79

native informants, 20, 102, 256, 271–72, 290, 291

Nazi Germany, 33, 34, 37, 60, 62, 63, 69, 98

Negro Quarterly, The, 33, 71

New Yorker, The, 31, 53–54, 149, 180

Night in Casablanca, A, 44

Nixon, Richard, President, 24

Noguès, Charles, 43

Norgaard, "Boots," 54

North Africa: African Americans and, 3, 33–37, 67–68, 73–74; American Orientalism, 8, 41; Arabian Nights compared to, 29, 30; Biblical images, North Africans portrayed in, 29, 30, 34; campaign in, 15, 36–42, 38; censorship, 45–46; commercialism in, 44–45, 59, 94–95, 139–40, 188; French-American alliance in, 44; indepen-

dence movements, 42, 97–100, 138–39; Libya, 7, 37, 39, 62–63, 137, 171, 309 n.80; literary images of, 7–8, 35–36; Marrakech, 16, 184, 189, 193, 196, 250–51, 276, 324 n.75; sub-Saharan Africa and, 35–36; Tunisia, 2, 5, 47–48, 54, 248, 266, 309 n.80; as Western frontier landscape, 50–52, 53–55, 92–93, 94, 101. See also *Casablanca* (film); Maghreb; Morocco; Tangier

North Atlantic Treaty, 99, 313 n.52

Operation Torch, 29, 46, 71, 97

Orientalism: American Orientalism, 2–3, 8, 40–41, 71, 83, 101; anthropologists, 255; William Burroughs and, 173, 174; French representations of Maghreb, 2; hippies and, 22, 249, 252–56, 261, 271, 285–87; Morocco and, 16–17; travel writing, 281, 282; Western models of, 40, 41; Wild West metaphors and, 297–99

Orientalism (Said), 40, 41, 255, 330 n.13

Orlovsky, Peter, 163

Ortega y Gasset, José, 211

Ortner, Sherry, 333 n.67

Ossman, Susan, 331 n.19

Otero-Pailos, Jorge, 308 n.78

Oufkir, Mohammed, 257, 265, 267, 331 n.29

Out in the World, 214

Palmer, Robert, 254, 284, 285–87, 288. See also Jajouka music

Pandolfo, Stefania, 326 n.29

Patton, Beatrice, 29, 45

Patton, George S., 27, 29–32, 40–41, 43, 45, 48, 71

Peace Corps, 330 n.6

Pearl Harbor, 49, 66
Pease, Donald, 142, 175, 315 n.69
Phaeton hypocrite, Le, 214
Pipes of Pan at Joujouka, The, 284
Pittman, John, 33
Poe, Edgar Allan, 93, 103, 106, 205, 222, 236, 315 n.65
Point Four program, 45, 94
Points in Time, 95
Pontification, 210–11
Potter, David, 146, 147
Povinelli, Elizabeth, 14–15, 207–8
Princesse Tam-Tam, 36
Prose, Francine, 310 n.4
Pyle, Ernie, 49, 52; on American ignorance of Arabic, 12–13; American soldiers and, 5, 51; on the Maghreb, 4–5, 40; Western frontier images of North Africa, 13, 47, 48, 50–52, 53

Queerness, 141–42, 145, 146, 150–56, 174, 319 nn.41, 42, 320 n.69
Queuille, Henri, 99

Rabinow, Paul: on border crossings in Morocco, 252; on cultural encounter, 255; cultural relativism and, 270–72; on leaving America, 254; Moroccan critics on, 300–301; *Reflections on Fieldwork in Morocco*, 269–70, 291
Race and racism: African American writers on, 35–36; anthropological research and, 271–73; Arabs and, 55–58; black roles in Hollywood films, 62–67, 69–70, 74, 305 n.6, 307 n.63; William Burroughs on, 169; diversity in Maghreb, 35–36; domestic racism, 34–35, 46, 60, 98, 114, 143, 150, 192–93, 256; hippie Orientalism, 256–57; internment

of Japanese-Americans, 33, 60; Maghrebis on U.S. segregation, 58–59; in *The Man Who Knew Too Much*, 192–95; in Morocco, 271–73; Nazi Germany and, 33, 34, 37, 60, 62, 63, 69, 98; Pacific War and, 34; racial time, 40, 42, 56–58, 66–67, 71, 74, 97, 98, 162, 249, 257, 285–86; segregation of African American troops, 33, 34, 46, 58–59, 63; sexuality and, 150, 169; sexual relationships and, 95, 114, 279; skin color, 35–36, 59, 63–65, 109–10, 192–93, 195, 273, 312 n.36; in Tangier, 142–43; temporality and, 66–67, 97, 308 nn.70, 78; tourism, 169; in the United States, 33, 34, 37, 39, 46, 58–59, 98, 143, 192–93, 256; visibility, 57, 107–11, 169–70, 190–92; in "What Happened in Granada," 239
Rachik, Hassan, 200
Raiders of the Lost Ark, 52
Rains, Claude, 62, 68
Ray, Robert, 67, 68–69, 70
Rear Window, 191
Reflections on Fieldwork in Morocco, 269–70, 291
Road to Morocco, 15–17, 40
Rogin, Michael, 1950
Rolling Stone magazine, 284, 285
Rolo, Charles, 158
Roosevelt, Eleanor, 46
Roosevelt, Franklin Delano, 39, 41, 42, 97–98, 149, 150
Rosen, Lawrence, 292
Ruark, Robert, 121, 141, 319 n.41
Rusk, Dean, 266

Sahara, 40, 61–64, 83, 307 nn.59, 60
Said, Edward: on Richard Burton,

173; on the exotic, 298; on Geertz's
scholarship, 255, 330 n.13; on lost
causes, 278; modernism and, 310
n.4; on representations of the
Maghreb, 2–3; on U.S. foreign
policy, 9, 43, 101; on Giambatista
Vico's concept of beginnings, 14;
on Western models of Orientalism,
2–3, 40, 41, 83, 101, 298
Sartre, Jean-Paul, 81, 108
Sawyer-Lauçanno, Christopher, 311
n.25
Sayyed, Omar, 331 n.19
Sbihi, Abdellatif, 126
Schlamm, William, 151–52, 156–57,
319 n.41
Schuyler, Philip, 286, 288–89
Seddon, David, 6
Sefrou, Morocco, 254, 289–90, 292,
293
Setterberg, Fred, 258–59
Sewell, William H., Jr., 333 n.67
sexuality: 'Abd al-Qader Laqt'a's
films, 76; in *Casablanca*, 69–70; in
Hollywood film, 148; homosexuality, 145, 151–52, 153–54; race
and, 95, 150, 169, 279; triangle relationships, 61, 69–70, 91, 203
Shanghai, 316 n.3
Shaviro, Steven, 181–82, 196–97
Sheik, The, 4, 35, 50, 53, 306 n.46
Sheltering Sky, The: Algerians in,
106–9; "The American Century"
and, 87–88, 113–14; Arabic used in,
95, 112, 113, 215; blindness/visiblity,
107–11; distancing of American
reading subjects, 103–4; existentialism, 106–12, 230; film adaptation of, 91–92, 312 nn.30, 36; flight
from mechanization in, 200;
French colonialism in, 91–92, 101;

105; national identity in, 92–93, 95,
105–7, 111, 113; triangle relationships in, 91
Shloss, Carol, 201
Shohat, Ella, 148
Sidi Lahcen, 254
Sidi Mohammed Ben Abdallah University, 241, 300–301
Simpkins, Raoul, 122, 150
skin color, 35–36, 59, 63–64, 109–10,
192–93, 195, 312 n.36
Slaoui, Houcine, 59, 95, 313 n.39
Slotkin, Richard, 48, 306 n.45, 307
nn.59, 60
Smith, Harry Nash, 92–93, 312 n.33
soldiers: African Americans as, 33, 34,
36, 37; American West mythology
and, 47–48; Arabs and, 55–58;
Blue Book, 45, 47; Goumiers, 58;
heroic images of, 47, 51; media portrayals of war, 47; in Moroccan
folk songs, 59; North Africa portrayed by, 47–48; Ernie Pyle and,
5, 51; transmission of American
values by, 94, 95
songs: Americans in Moroccan folk
songs, 59
Soviet Union, 99, 134, 135–36, 137,
147, 256, 266
Spain, 134, 135, 139, 317 n.27
Spider's House, The, 9, 115, 167, 310 n.4
Spivak, Gayatri, 102, 211, 232–33, 236,
243, 311 n.24, 314 n.57, 315 n.76
State Department: diplomatic service, 8, 95–96, 97, 99–100, 127, 128,
130, 131, 133–34, 137–38, 316 n.11,
317 n.20, 318 n.36; North African
nationalism and, 12, 96, 266–67;
presence in Tangier, 99, 127, 128,
130, 131, 133–34, 316 n.11, 317 n.20;
regional expertise in, 9, 104–5,

State Department (*continued*)
133–34, 266–67; special legal status of American nationals in Morocco, 137–38, 167, 168–69, 170, 183, 318 n.36
Steinbeck, John, 40, 46
"Stick of Green Candy, A" 214, 223
Street in Marrakech, A, 291
Stuart, Graham, 133–34, 317 n.20, 321 n.8
Syria, 266

Taberner, John, 150–51, 152–53
Tangier: abundance in, 148–49, 150, 165; American culture in, 131; American School of Tangier, 131, 132, 149, 180, 317 n.18, 318 n.37; Capote on, 207, 325 n.11; commercial activity in, 131, 139–40, 151–53, 155–56; Committee of Control, 134, 135, 137, 138, 183, 317 n.24; ethnicity in, 142–43; hippies in, 252; homosexuality, 153–54; independence movement and, 125–26, 136, 138–39, 183, 316 n.11; International Zone, 122, 124, 133, 136, 138–40, 318 n.39; literary community in, 124–25; Marrakech and, 196; Claude McKay in, 35; money changers in, 153, 155; Moroccan community in, 139–40, 319 n.40; name of, 123–24; physical layout of, 130–31, 318 n.39; queerness of, 141–42, 145, 146, 150–56, 174, 319 nn.41, 42; radio stations in, 135, 137, 180–81, 318 n.36; reputation of, 121–23, 149–50, 151, 315 n.1, 320 n.56; riots in, 135; schools in, 131, 132, 317 n.18, 318 n.37; Soviet Union and, 134, 135–36, 137; Spain and, 134, 135, 317 n.27; State Department diplomatic mission in, 127, 128, 133–34, 316 n.11, 317 n.20; Mark Twain on, 154–55. *See also* Bowles, Jane; Bowles, Paul; Burroughs, William S.
Tangier Gazette, 125, 126, 141, 319 n.41
temporality: in the "American Century," 65–66; in anthropology, 262; in *Casablanca* (film), 66–67, 71, 260, 308 nn.70, 78; distance and, 68, 103–7, 262, 314 n.60; edges of, 199, 209, 212–13, 326 nn.27, 29; racial time, 40, 42, 56–58, 66–67, 71, 74, 97, 285–86
Tessler, Mark, 257, 258, 292
"Thick Description: Toward an Interpretive Theory of Culture," 293–94, 295–96, 333 n.67
Ticket That Exploded, The, 284
Toledano, Edward, 94–95, 105
Torres, Abdelkhalek, 126, 316 n.10
tourism: in Algeria, 309 n.80; Arabic language and, 247; Gulf Arabs in Maghreb, 309 n.79; hippies and, 249; Hollywood films and, 8, 73–74, 309 n.78, 310 n.81; in Libya, 309 n.80; in Morocco, 8, 73–74, 83, 247, 249–50, 309 nn.78, 79, 81; in Tunisia, 309 n.80
Trachtenberg, Alan, 312 n.33
translation: American West mythology as means of, 47–48, 92–93; anthropologists and, 239–41, 271–72; of Arabic, 21, 95, 113, 315 n.71; Jane Bowles and, 226; Paul Bowles and, 95, 113, 116, 235–37, 241–42; circulation and, 207–8; collaborations in, 116, 233, 235, 237–38, 242; of culture, 207–8, 255–56, 287, 294, 295–96, 333 n.67; eroticism, 211–12; ethnography and, 295–96;

"Everything Is Nice," 224–27; globalization and, 114, 182, 241–43; intermediate languages in, 237, 238; intimacy and, 236; of *Islam Observed: Religious Development in Morocco and Indonesia*, 300; misunderstandings of, 287, 328 n.48; of Moroccan cuisine in American cookbooks, 280–83; national identity, 88–93; recording of Moroccan music as, 230–31, 288–89; role of editor in, 237–38; as signs of foreignness, 188–89; tape recorders in, 231, 232, 237; in writing style of Jane Bowles, 204, 207, 211
triangle relationships, 61, 69–70, 91, 203
Trouillot, Michel-Rolph, 84
Truffaut, François, 193
Truman, Harry S., President, 45, 99, 127
Tunisia, 2, 5, 47–48, 54, 248, 266, 309 n.80
Turner, Frederick Jackson, 92–93, 146–47
Twain, Mark, 154–56
Two Serious Ladies, 203, 212, 213
Tyler, Royall, 7

United States: Age of Doubt, 93, 142–43; "The American Century," 49–50, 65–66, 87–88, 113–14, 161–62, 189–90, 315 n.71; American Orientalism, 2–3, 8, 40–41, 71, 101; Committee of Control (Tangier), 134, 135, 137, 138, 183, 317 n.24; family, 148, 150, 151, 184, 185, 187, 193; French relations with, 32, 33, 42–44, 96–100, 105, 127–29, 313 n.42; McCarthyism, 142, 151, 161, 174, 179, 181–82, 191, 196; Morocco and,

255–56, 259–60, 266; Franklin Delano Roosevelt, 39, 41, 42, 97–98, 149, 150; Vietnam War, 249, 251, 255, 257, 278, 330 n.13. *See also* American national identity; frontier narratives; hippies; race and racism

Vagabonding in Europe and North Africa, 247–48, 252, 256
Van Vechten, Carl, 36
Vico, Giambatista, 14
Vietnam War, 249, 251, 255, 257, 278, 330 n.13
visibility, 57, 107–11, 169–70, 190–92
Von Eschen, Penny, 98

Wall, Irwin, 97, 313 n.42
Wanklyn, Christopher, 169
Warner, Michael, 15, 156, 208, 209, 320 n.65
Warner Brothers studio. See *Casablanca*
Waterbury, John, 265, 267
Wechsberg, Joseph, 180
Wehr, Hans, 326 n.27
West, American. *See* frontier narratives; Hollywood films
Westermarck, Edward, 281, 283, 333 n.62
Wharton, Edith, 3, 9, 30, 298, 308 n.70
"What Happened in Granada," 236, 238–40
White, Walter, 36, 63
Wilson, Dooley (Sam in *Casablanca*), 66–67, 69–70, 74
Wolfert, Paula: Paul Bowles and, 281, 283; *Couscous and Other Good Food from Morocco*, 253, 280–83; relativism and, 270; in Tangier, 281; translations of Moroccan cuisine by, 280–81

Women: on the American occupation, 58–59; Jane Bowles and Moroccan women, 208, 211, 216–17, 223, 224, 225; containment motifs and, 145, 148; cooking and, 280, 282–83; harems and, 59, 191; in Hollywood films, 65, 67, 148; in *Honor to the Bride Like the Pigeon That Guards Its Grain under the Clove Tree*, 263–64, 331 n.24; mixed race sexual relationships, 95, 114, 279; Moroccan attitudes towards, 263–64; as mothers, 190, 324 nn.63, 64; national identity and, 95; veiling of, 188, 189, 190–91, 324 n.64

Woolman, David, 131, 162–64, 171, 176, 252
Works and Lives: The Anthropologist as Author, 333 n.62
"A World of Saints and She-Demons," 264–67
Wren, P. C., 7, 8, 297
Wright, Gwendolyn, 74

Yacoubi, Ahmed, 84, 231–32
Young, Robert, 12
young Moroccans: hippie encounters with, 22, 256–61, 276, 277–78, 332 n.36; Jajouka music and, 285; riots and, 22, 135, 257–58, 260, 274

Žižek, Slavoj, 324 n.64

BRIAN T. EDWARDS

is an assistant professor of English

and comparative literary studies at

Northwestern University.

Library of Congress Cataloging-in-Publication Data
Edwards, Brian T.
Morocco bound : disorienting America's Maghreb, from
Casablanca to the Marrakech Express / Brian T. Edwards.
p. cm. — (New Americanists)
Includes bibliographical references and index.
ISBN 0-8223-3609-x (cloth : alk. paper)
ISBN 0-8223-3644-8 (pbk. : alk. paper)
1. Historiography—Morocco. 2. Orientalism—United States.
3. Orientalists—United States. I. Title. II. Series.
DT313.8.E38 2005
303.48'273064'0904—dc22
2005011389